Macintosh Desktop Presentations

Steven Anzovin

COMPUTE! Books
Radnor, Pennsylvania

To Janet, Raf, Miriam, and Hannah.

Other Books by Steven Anzovin

Exploring HyperCard (A COMPUTE! Book)
COMPUTE!'s Quick and Easy Guide to HyperCard
Amiga Desktop Video (A COMPUTE! Book)
Using Deluxe Paint (A COMPUTE! Book)
The United States: A Handbook
Facts About the States
Speeches of the American Presidents
It Hurts: A Parent's Guide to Children's Needs

Editor: Pam Plaut
Cover design: Anthony Jacobson

Printed in the United States of America

10 9 8 7 6 5 4 3 2 1

Library of Congress Cataloging in Publication Data
Anzovin, Steven.
Macintosh desktop presentation.
1. Lectures and lecturing—Audio-visual aids.
2. Lectures and lecturing—Data processing.
3. Macintosh (Computer)—Programming. 4. Computer graphics—Computer programs. 5. HyperCard (Computer program) 6. Business communication—Data processing.
7. Business communications—Audio-visual aids.
I. Title.
PN4193.L4A59 1990 808.5'1'028566 89-43127
ISBN 0-87455-200-1

Contents

Preface

The hottest new application for the Apple Macintosh today is *desktop presentations,* the process of using a computer to present graphic information to business, educational, and technical audiences. Apple CEO John Sculley has targeted desktop presentations as the next big vertical market application for the Mac, and expects it to match desktop publishing in impact on the way personal computers are used. And Apple is determined to make the Macintosh the standard platform for presentations.

Research has shown that more information is retained by an audience if it is presented graphically. Many managers and teachers already know this, and use the Mac to quickly produce cost-effective presentations. For example, every week there are thousands of business meetings and college seminars in which color slides made by computer are shown. But the trend in desktop presentations goes beyond slides and slideshows, toward multimedia programs that incorporate sound, animation, video, and more.

The problem with creating successful presentations using these more complex elements is that you may need to master not only graphic design, but also the new presentation hardware, video techniques, character animation, scoring, scriptwriting, and more—areas in which most computer users, even graphic designers, have relatively little experience. The explosion of new products aimed at making the Macintosh the standard platform for the display of audiovisual information includes new paint programs, drawing programs, graph-creation programs, animation software, slideshow programs, slidemaking hardware, LCD projection panels, scanners, video digitizers, genlocks, video frame-capture boards, CD-ROMs, and more. Venturers into this new realm are often confused by the lack of solid information about what can and can't be achieved with desktop presentations, especially in the desktop video realm.

Macintosh Desktop Presentations addresses the need for current and accurate information about desktop presenting. Within, you'll find detailed coverage of:

- the basics of desktop presentations and Mac graphics
- desktop presentation hardware and software
- graphic design for graphs, charts, and other practical graphics
- creating slides and slideshows
- techniques for successful presentations on stage
- desktop video production basics
- animation for presentations
- mixing sound and pictures
- interactive presentations
- *HyperCard* as a desktop presentation tool
- a glossary and list of desktop presentation resources

This book is aimed primarily at any Macintosh user who is now preparing presentations on paper—standing up in front of the VPs or the grad seminar with a bunch of cardboard charts—or who is already using the Mac for presentations and wants to create more sophisticated, effective programs. *Macintosh Desktop Presentations* includes discussions of specific products and programs and includes tutorials using the most popular program in each software category, but the emphasis is on basic technical information and presentation techniques that would apply no matter what brand of peripheral or software used. Special attention is given to video applications and using *HyperCard* as a presentation tool.

Chapter 1 is an introduction to what desktop presentations are all about. It covers the theory behind presentations and describes the available types of hardware and software. Graphic design for presentations is the subject of Chapter 2, followed by a chapter on creating charts and graphs, the backbone of most presentation graphics. Chapter 4 takes you step by step through the creation of a Mac-generated slideshow, the most common form of presentation. Chapters 5, 6, and 7 cover the fast-growing world of Macintosh desktop video. Chapter 8 discusses Mac animation, and how to use animation in presentations. Finally, Chapter 9 gives some general guidelines for the creation of sophisticated interactive presentations, in which the audience finds its own way through integrated presentations with sound, graphics, and movement. Appendices include a complete glossary of terms and an up-to-date list of manufacturers and products.

Graphic Wizard Not Required

One thing that's *not* taken for granted in *Macintosh Desktop Presentations* is that you are a skilled computer artist or public performer. The point of desktop presentations, after all, is that just about anyone can get useful results with a minimum of knowhow. Of course, that doesn't mean you can fly completely blind, either. If you are a new Macintosh owner, be sure you are familiar with your computer's basic operations before you read further in this book. You should know your way around the Macintosh's graphic interface and understand disk and file handling. Carefully read the Macintosh operations manual that comes with your computer. Likewise, you should be comfortable with using consumer and business-level audiovisual equipment—slide projectors, overhead projectors, VCRs and camcorders, microphones and audiocassette recorders, and the like.

In this book, you'll find the basic information you need to hone your skills with the new presentation tools. As with all explorations into new territory, you'll have to adopt an adventurous outlook to get the most from the experience. This book will guide you through the world of desktop presentations, but don't hesitate to experiment for yourself—your presentation will be most successful if you put your own imagination into it. If you do, there's nothing to stop you from making your mark as one of the new breed of multimedia magicians.

Acknowledgments

One of the pleasures of writing a book is thanking those who have helped in its conception. I owe my interest in computer graphics and video to Dorene Hyman Schott, one of NBC's great editors, who taught me the basics and showed me where computer and videographics were going. Video producer Sian Evans provided many tips on how the pros make presentations and video productions succeed despite the odds. At Electronic Arts, Diane Flynn and Nicole Noland gave generously of their time and resources. John Pratt at Digital Vision and Aegis Development's David Hopkins and John Sievers were also enthusiastic about this project and supplied needed materials on short notice. Others who contributed to this project include Elaine Rickman at Aldus; Renee Matthews at Claris; Wendy Keough at Farallon; Corinne Smith at Informix; Lee Johnson for MacroMind; Marty Taucher at Microsoft; Maura Brady at Paracomp; and Stewart Henigson at Silicon Beach. At COMPUTE!, Heidi Aycock's suggestions and contact information jumpstarted the book when it had stalled, while Stephen Levy supplied his usual expert editorial guidance and advice on roof repair. Of course, any errors or omissions in this book are mine alone.

Illustrations for this book were created using a Macintosh IIcx; Studio/1 and Studio/8 from Electronic Arts; Aldus *Persuasion*; Informix's *Wingz*; *Showcase F/X* from Aegis Development; *ImageStudio* from Letraset; Claris's *MacDraw II*; ThunderScan from ThunderWare; Digital Vision's *Computereyes*; an Apple ImageWriter II; and an Apple LaserWriter IINTX.

Steven Anzovin
January 1990

CHAPTER 1

What Are Desktop Presentations?

Jane walks up to the podium and turns to face an audience of skeptical medical administrators. "Many of you want to know just what my company's RxScan magnetic resonance imaging scanner can do for your patients—and for the bottom line of your institutions. Let me show you."

Behind her, the wall lights up with a video clip showing a man in a hospital room. The audience hears that his speech is slurred and sees that he has trouble moving his right arm. The video freezes as Jane says: "This patient had no obvious trauma or psychiatric problem. A stroke was suspected, but a CAT scan of the cerebrum and cerebellum was negative." The video changes to a slide of a CAT scan. "As you can see, the CAT scan looks normal."

Jane pauses to let this sink in, and then continues. "Valley Hospital referred this patient to us for a trial MRI scan." Another video clip shows the patient entering the RxScan. A glowing purple picture of a skull scan then fills the wall behind her. "Here's the damage site," Jane says, using a light pointer to indicate the area she means. "Note the clarity and high resolution of the structural imaging. But that's not all. The RxScan provides noninvasive internal chemical analysis, which a CAT scan cannot. Note the blue color—that's low iron, indicating a pattern of decreased arterial flow. Analysis also showed abnormal levels of potassium at sites here and here." Sections of the scan zoom out to reveal greater detail. "Reduced potassium in this pattern is indicative of a rather unusual brain infection; the exact signature is of a T1 or T2 *neurophagia,* one of the marine retroviruses recently discovered by Sonderberg." A new view shows an animation of the suspected virus entering a brain cell. "It turned out that the patient was a seafood connoisseur, and had eaten a rare tropical species infected with the virus." The audience laughs. "Without x-rays, injections of dangerous, radio-contrast media, or exploratory surgery, we found the infection sites, identified the infectious agent, and knew what treatment to prescribe." A video clip shows the patient receiving drug therapy, eating with his right hand and talking normally.

"Since there were no actual structural changes in the brain of the patient, a normal CAT scan would not reveal this information. The CAT scanner, which did not lead to a diagnosis, cost Valley Hospital $1.2 million to install, and $200,000 yearly to operate. A typical CAT scan costs the patient, or the patient's insurer, $800. An RxScan costs $150,000, complete with installation, and yearly operating costs run about $45,000. In other words, you can have a complete RxScan setup and a year's operation for less than the yearly support cost of a CAT scanner. And an RxScan could cost the patient as little as $75." On the wall, a colorful chart shows this information in graphic form. A buzz of excited discussion from the audience accompanies the slide. Jane takes a sip of water while a series of slides recaps the main points of her talk. She gets ready to field questions.

One grizzled veteran of the hospital administration wars comes up to her after the question and answer period. "You know, I started out as a GP, not a nuclear physicist," he said. "When your magnetic scanner came along, it looked like just another fancy box, and the hospital already had a million-dollar CAT machine. I threw out all your brochures. But your show opened my eyes. A real professional job. I see how we can do better medicine and save money, too." He thrusts his card into her hand. "We're reviewing the capital expenditures plan this month. Have your rep come see me in my office on Thursday or Friday."

Everything in Jane's complex presentation was conceived and integrated on her own desktop. She shot and edited the video with her own camcorder and VCR, designed and arranged the slides herself, and even did the animation, all using her Macintosh computer. Jane is a pioneer in the new field of *desktop presentations,* the practice of using a computer to prepare and present graphic information to business, educational, and technical audiences.

The Impact of Images

In any form of group endeavor, communication is the key to effective group action. Anyone who has experienced a well-designed and delivered presentation like Jane's knows that pictures can drive home a point with more force and precision than words alone. Several studies have shown that live presentations augmented by color charts, graphs, and other data graphics are far more effective than verbal presentations without pictures. A 1981 study by the Wharton School of Business found that the use of good presentation graphics shortened the average business meeting by 28 percent—communication was more efficient, increasing productivity and saving valuable time. In a 1986 study by the University of Minnesota, test audiences rated presenters using visual aids as 43 percent more persuasive, as well as more professional, more interesting, and more effective, than presenters who didn't use visual material.

Businesses and institutions have taken these results to heart. According to the *1988 Desktop Presentations Yearbook* (Desktop Presentations, Inc., see Appendix A), more than 17 million computer-displayed presentation graphic images were used worldwide in 1987. In the same year, presenters used computers to create 138 million transparencies and 111 million slides. All told, that's more than a quarter of a billion images. And presentation graphic usage is expected to double or triple in frequency in the early 1990s, fueled by the increasing use of graphically capable computers like the Mac.

Specifically, presentations offer these benefits:

- Faster and more thorough retention of information. Your audience will remember up to 50 percent of what it sees in presentation graphics, as opposed to about 10 percent of what it hears you say. And people will grasp it much more quickly, meaning you can get your point across in less time.
- Greater understanding. Visuals reinforce your words and forge alternate paths to understanding in the minds of your audience. The more your audience understands, the more likely your recommendations will pay off in successful results.
- Increased productivity. Faster input of information and greater understanding mean more productive use of the information you are providing, saving everyone's time.

But why take the time and make the effort to create presentations yourself on your desktop, when there are hundreds of design and presentation firms that will do the job for you? The answers are money and control. Once you've invested in desktop presentation technology, each individual presentation costs little to create. With outside firms, just one presentation could cost as much as an entire Macintosh system—a cost that few businesses, schools, or institutions can afford. A Macintosh can be adapted to all kinds of other uses as well, such as word processing and database management, that help to defray the initial expense of equipment and software.

The control that working on your own desktop gives you is even more valuable. There are no outside contracts, no negotiations with accounting over partial payments, no time-consuming meetings where you try to explain your ideas. You can oversee the presentation through every stage of development without fear that outside people will misinterpret or mangle your message. The schedule you set up is your own.

Last-minute changes are no problem. A basic presentation can be packaged in several different ways—slides, overheads, and video, for instance—at your option. Maybe the most important advantage is that you can take full credit for your presentation's success.

The Mac as a Presentation Platform

Once upon a time it was a laborious task to carve good-looking graphics out of massive blocks of numerical data, or stitch together a coherent slideshow from a patchwork of pictures, but the Macintosh makes it easy. Designed from the ground up as a graphically sophisticated, easy-to-use machine, the Mac also has the power to run the complex applications that desktop presentations demand. With a 68020 or 68030 processor, the Mac can chew through huge spreadsheets, display a data-rich graphic in stunning color, and then print it out as part of a typeset-quality report. The wealth of Mac presentation hardware gives you access to every presentation format—slides, overheads, video, and big-screen displays. And the Mac's *graphic user interface*—the appearance and tools presented to you on the Mac screen—is consistent across Macintosh applications, meaning once you've learned the basic operations of any Mac program, you'll have a good grasp of all of them. This translates into a short, gentle learning curve for each new program you need to learn, and faster operation once you get up to speed. Most programs use visual metaphors for operations, instead of typed-in commands; for example, to arrange a slideshow, you might simply drag reduced images of the slides around on the screen until they are in the proper order. Thus, you don't have to be a computer whiz to get useful work done.

One of the best reasons to use the Mac for desktop presentations is that Apple is pushing strongly into the field. A recent Apple advertising campaign focused exclusively on what the company calls "desktop media," an all-inclusive term for just about any integration of audio, visual, and printed communication with a desktop computer, including desktop presentations. Judging from the statements of Apple executives such as John Sculley and Jean-Louis Gassée, Apple is positioning the Mac in the forefront of the desktop presentation market, and encouraging third-party developers to provide the innovative Mac products necessary to keep it there.

Presentation Media

There's no one right way to give a presentation, just as there's no one way to write a report or give a lecture. In fact, you have several desktop presentation media to choose from, each with its own strengths and weaknesses. Choose the one (or a combination of them) that best suits the presentation environment.

Presentations on the Mac. Many informal presentations are given right on the Mac screen. People crowd around, peering at the captivating words, numbers, and pictures, which you control from the keyboard and mouse. This method of giving presentations has the virtues of simplicity and spontaneity—no expensive peripherals are required, and you can change the presentation with a few keystrokes or mouse movements. Onscreen presentations can be more convincing, too. Your audience knows you did the work on the Mac, and sees the final presentation there as well; this lends an intangible air of authenticity to the material, and a computer-generated aura of authority to you. The Mac is an engaging machine, and can make your presentation engaging, too.

The downside of onscreen Mac presentations is that you are limited to the size of the Mac screen—a squint-inducing nine-inch diagonal screen in the Mac Plus or SE. Presentations on the small screen are only suited to an audience of about two or three other people; to reach a larger group, you'll need to hook up your Mac to a larger display, perhaps even a projection TV. Another, less obvious problem is that you are tied to the Mac during the presentation; you have to be near the machine to change pictures or point to what's going on. (A remote control can solve this problem; see Chapter 4.)

Slideshows. Business and education make and show literally millions of slides every year. Slides have the great advantages of sharp, colorful images, easy portability, and relatively low-cost reproduction. Nearly all businesses and schools own a slide projector, and even presenters with little experience probably have used one. Executives and students are comfortable with the conventions of the typical slideshow—large, static images projected in sequence on a wall in a dark room, with the presenter describing each slide from a podium or corner of the room. No longer limited to a linear, one-slide-at-a-time narrative, slideshows can become true multimedia events, with complex sequences of multiple images projected from many remote-controlled slide projectors, and integrated music and sound effects.

It follows that the most popular use for the Mac as a presentation tool is to design slides for slideshows. Mac presentation programs (see below) are oriented to slide production—but converting Mac graphics to slides on the desktop is still in its infancy. See more on creating slides and slideshows in Chapter 4.

Overhead Presentations. A low-cost alternative to slideshows is overhead projection of transparencies, also called *acetates*. The method is simple; a picture printed on transparent plastic (acetate or mylar) is placed on an overhead projector, which shines light through the acetate and projects it onto a screen or wall. The transparencies are cheap and easy to make; original graphics can be created with any Mac paint program, printed on a laser, inkjet, or dot-matrix printer, then copied onto transparent stock with an office photocopier.

The atmosphere of an overhead presentation is more intimate and spontaneous than that of a slideshow; the technique works best with small groups (30 persons or less), which encourages audience participation rather than passivity. Unlike slideshows, overhead presentations can evolve and grow on the spot; you can add audience comments to your graphics as you go by simply scribbling notes on the transparencies with a wax pencil.

Video. The marriage of television production and personal computers is called *DeskTop Video* (DTV), and the Mac is riding the crest of the wave. Presentations created with desktop video combine color, movement, photographic realism, animated graphics, sound, and music, making it possible to show material, such as the exact methods used in a new manufacturing process, or the interaction of test subjects in a psychological study, that could not be shown in any other way. Dense with easily assimilated information, video presentations reach deep into the minds of your audience, which are already conditioned to accept and believe what is seen on the small screen. A further advantage of DTV presentations is their portability. They can be shown on any VCR—meaning there are tens of millions of potential presentation sites—and distributed on inexpensive video cassettes.

The Mac is an excellent platform for desktop video. It's relatively simple to record directly to video a slideshow created with a Mac presentation program, and then add narration or music. And, with the right hardware and applications, Mac DTV can reproduce many of the snazzy effects seen in high-priced television programming, including titles, 3-D animation, digital special effects, and more. But full-fledged video production can be a major undertaking. Chapters 5, 6, and 7 will guide you through the intricacies of Mac video.

Multimedia, Hypermedia, and Interactive Presentations. *Multimedia* integrates text, graphics, photographic imagery, sound, music, speech, and video to create new ways to access, present, and understand information. The premise behind multimedia is that much useful information exists in nontraditional forms (such as video or sound recordings) that only the computer can combine into one presentation. *Hypermedia* is a form of multimedia presentation in which all areas of the presentation are cross-referenced to each other and are instantly accessible from any part of the presentation. Both multimedia and hypermedia assume some level of viewer *interactivity*—interactivity being the process of establishing a dialog between audience and information so viewers can steer the presentation in whatever direction they desire. For example, a multimedia "lecture" on the life and work of the Irish writer James Joyce might include selected text of Joyce's books, recordings of the author and well-known actors reading from his works; video clips from Joyce-derived films and plays; scanned photographs of the author, his family, and literary associates; and an animated map of the path that Leopold Bloom takes through Dublin in *Ulysses.* Add hypermedia capabilities, and you can roam at will through the presentation. Click on an unfamiliar word in the text of *Finnegans Wake,* and the presentation will show you its Joycean etymology; select the first paragraph of that book, and you'll be taken to a photographic album of Howth Castle and the River Liffey; click on one of the photos, and you'll hear explanatory narration by a noted Joyce scholar. Another click returns you to where you began, while the computer keeps a log of all your excursions. Advocates of the hypermedia approach claim that nonlinear, multidimensional, associative, and intuitional hypermedia presentations are better suited to the way the mind learns.

Interactive hypermedia is one presentation format that, by its nature, demands to be displayed directly on the computer. And constructing this kind of complex presentation demands more imagination and resourcefulness from you. Luckily, the Mac offers a rich field for development of hypermedia. Apple itself gives away one of the best hypermedia applications, *HyperCard,* with every new machine. If you're fascinated by the possibilities in this field, the last chapter in this book will help you get started.

Presentation Hardware

Effective presentations can be created on any Macintosh, including the entry-level Mac Plus. On a two-disk-drive, one-megabyte Plus, for example, you can craft onscreen slideshows with *MacDraw II* (see Chapter 2), 3-D rotating graphs with *Wingz* (as shown in Chapter 3), or interactive presentations with *HyperCard* (covered in Chapter 9). But if you want speed, color, or complex animation, if you'll be producing desktop videos, or if you will be creating presentations as a business, the optimum hardware configuration is a Mac II, IIx, IIcx, or IIci with a color video card, a color monitor, at least four megabytes of memory, and a 80-plus megabyte hard disk drive. (A 68030 Mac like the IIcx is recommended, since Apple will be building the Mac's future on that microchip.) You'll use all that power and storage, and probably want more, especially if eating presentations is the hub of your Macintosh activities. Working with video requires the internal NuBus slots in the Mac II series; there are few video peripherals available for the Mac Plus, which has no internal expansion slot, or the SE or SE/30, which only has one. The IIci has color video built in, opening an extra slot for display cards.

Presentation Peripherals

To the basic Macintosh setup you'll need to add one or more peripherals—extra memory, removable mass storage, a large-screen display, a scanner, a drawing tablet, a printer, a slidemaker, an overhead projection adapter, a remote control, and a modem.

Memory. As noted above, nearly all presentation software, especially animation software, works better with extra RAM. While the cost of memory has risen sharply in recent years, it's still a good idea to buy as much memory as your budget will allow, since software memory requirements are on the increase as well. (Memory is generally cheaper to buy when you buy your Mac, rather than as a later add-on.) Consider one megabyte of RAM as the minimum requirement for black-and-white work only, two megabytes as the minimum for professional applications, four megabytes the minimum for serious color work.

Mass Storage. To supplement the hard disk in your machine—and you must have a hard disk to run most presentation software—you may want to invest in some form of removable mass storage, both for backing up your hard disk and storing the large data files created by color paint, animation, multimedia programs, and color scanners. With removable mass storage, there is no practical limit to the amount of information you can have available to your Mac, as there is with conventional hard disks; just pop in a new disk or tape and keep on stashing away the data. Mass storage options include removable hard disks; "megafloppy" drives that store 10, 20, or 45 megabytes on a special floppy disk; tape drives; and writeable optical disks. Megafloppy drives currently offer the best price/performance ratio—they are relatively fast and cheap per megabyte of storage—but they may soon be overtaken by optical media.

One disadvantage to removable mass storage devices is that there is no current standard for media type, size, storage capacity, and so on. One manufacturer's megafloppy or optical disk may not work in another's drive. If you want to use your disk at another machine, you have to make sure there is a drive there that can read it. For complete flexibility in transporting data, you may have to stick with standard 3½-inch floppy disks. Apple, which sells a CD player, is pushing CDs as the mass data distribution method of the future. Problem is, you can only read CDs, not write to them, and relatively few people have Mac-compatible CD players yet (but even fewer own writeable optical disks). It may make sense, however, to record huge multimedia presentations on CD, since no other digital storage method can handle the hundreds of megabytes required for digital storage of color video, 3-D animation, orchestral scores, and so on.

Displays. A large-screen monitor (13-inch diagonal or bigger) is really a necessity for making presentations right on the Mac screen. You can imagine what it does to your visionary concepts to be shown on the tiny screen of the Mac Plus or SE. A wide variety of Mac-compatible displays are available, ranging from portrait-sized black-and-white monitors to huge color displays weighing 200 pounds and requiring an equivalent weight of cash to purchase. Among color monitors, displays based on Sony's Trinitron picture tube—including Apple's own RGB monitor—

dominate the market due to their superior color and low distortion, but Zenith's totally flat screen FTM monitors yield the best picture overall.

All external monitors for the Mac II and SE series need video cards to drive them, except on the new 25 MHz Mac IIci, which has video driver chips right on the main circuit board, so no separate color video card is required. Large displays for the Plus, such as those produced by Radius, must be driven from a special boards clipped to the Plus's internal video hardware. Color monitors, of course, require color video circuitry, and aren't available for the Plus, SE, and the Mac Portable. (There are one- or two-color displays for the SE, but these provide much more limited color capabilities than are available in the Mac II series and the SE/30.) Color video cards come in two varieties—cards that generate up to 256 colors onscreen (8-bit cards), and "32-bit" cards that can display what Apple calls "true color," a number of onscreen colors limited only by the number of pixels the monitor can display. Chapters 2 and 5 cover display technology in more detail.

Scanners. Scanners, devices for transforming line art or photographs into Mac graphics, are useful for creating presentation graphics, but only essential when your presentations depend on real-world images—for example, when you must incorporate photographs or technical drawings into educational presentations, or when you want to use a graphically enhanced picture of your CEO to kick off your company's annual meeting slideshow. Scanners come in black-and-white, grayscale, and color versions, with the least expensive grayscale scanner (the ThunderScan, see Appendix A) costing about $200, and color scanners starting at about $6,000. (New color scanner models are priced as low as $2,000, but have reduced capabilities.) Some tips on scanning and using scans are provided in Chapter 2; coverage of digitizers, the video equivalent of scanners, can be found in Chapters 5 and 7.

Drawing Tablets. Drawing tablets (also called graphic or digitizer tablets) are supplementary data entry devices designed for freehand drawing. The tablet is a large rectangle with embedded sensors that register the position of a stylus or puck (a kind of mouse) moved over it. Software running on the Macintosh reads the signal from the tablet and moves the screen pointer accordingly. If you are an artist or animator, you may prefer a tablet over the mouse for drawing because you can make the same kind of sketching motions you'd use with a conventional pencil, pen, or brush. You can also trace over existing drawings, such as technical diagrams, something that's impossible with a mouse. A tablet can be very handy when you're giving a presentation with an overhead projection adapter (see below); it's easier and quicker to draw right on the graphics with a stylus.

Printers. A printer is an integral part of most presentation setups, for printing outlines, speaker notes, leave-behinds, reports, storyboards, scripts, budgets, and so on. At the low end of the scale, there are few cheap printers compatible with the Mac, which is why most Mac owners start out with Apple's dot-matrix Imagewriter. If you have to hand a lot of professional-looking paper documentation to clients and audiences, however, a laser printer, which produces far higher-quality type and graphics, is worth the investment; Apple's own laser printers, the IISC, IINT, and IINTX, are excellent printers, but equivalent or better printers can be had for somewhat less money. A laser printer that contains Adobe System's PostScript page description language can also be used for desktop publishing of reports and newsletters. A good compromise between price and performance is Hewlett Packard's DeskWriter, an ink-jet printer that gives laser-sharp results at less than half the cost; it is not PostScript-compatible, however.

Mac color printers are currently quite expensive and have limited use for presentations, except to produce color transparencies. There's more on color printing in Chapter 4.

Slidemakers. Slidemakers, desktop photographic devices to produce slides directly from Mac graphics, are among the newest genre of Mac peripherals. Basically, a slidemaker consists of a CRT and a camera looking at each other inside a box; the CRT shows the Mac picture, and the camera takes a picture of it. If you need to produce lots of slides for regular presentations, these machines are worth their high cost ($6,000–$7,000 for a mid-range unit), troublesome operation, and medium image quality. Sending slides to be developed at a service bureau costs much more per slide. Chapter 4 has more on using slidemakers.

Projection Panels. These see-through LCD displays allow Mac graphics to be projected with any standard overhead projector, a common presentation tool found in every school's A/V department. The panel, which is about the size of a large hardcover book, reproduces the Mac screen in LCD form as it sits on the overhead projector's light screen; light shines through the panel and is projected on the wall.

Projection panels are a practical, relatively low-cost alternative for presenters who use transparencies often, a group that includes most high school and college instructors. Another advantage of projection panels is that they can show animations well as still images—in fact, anything that can be displayed on the Mac screen can be shown to your viewers.

Remote Controls. One thing that will add considerably to your spontaneity on stage is a remote control for the Mac. These little hand-held gadgets, which look and work much like typical infrared VCR remotes, will let you emulate most actions on the mouse and keyboard, run slideshows on compatible presentation software, and generally free you to roam at will about the classroom or the conference hall. That physical freedom can result in a much stronger presentation.

Remote units that allow macro programming—letting you send a complex string of keystrokes to the Mac simply by pressing one button on the remote—are preferable; you'll also want to make sure you can hook the remote to your Mac (some units are ADB only, meaning they can't be connected to the Mac Plus) and that the remote software is compatible with your presentation software.

Modems. A modem connects your computer to the global information net through your phone line. The main use for modems in presentations is to "upload" graphics files from presentation programs to slide-making service bureaus (see Chapter 4), but there are other possible uses as well. You can, for example, observe and control distant Macs via modem with the right software (such as *Timbuktu/Remote,* from Farallon, see Appendix A), a capability that is invaluable for interactive training. A 2400-baud, Hayes-compatible modem is the standard; 9600-baud modems are much more expensive, but can transmit data four times as fast. You'll need telecommunications software to operate the modem.

Hardware Costs. A bargain-basement presentation system (as in Figure 1-1) can be assembled from a Mac Plus, an ImageWriter, an external hard disk, an overhead projection adapter, and some basic software, at a list price of about $4,500 (street price $3,500). This would give you the capability to run black-and-white presentation programs; print out reports, notes, and acetates; and project Mac graphics to an audience of up to 50 persons in a large classroom or small auditorium. Multimedia applications could be addressed with *HyperCard* stacks (see Chapter 9). You won't get color, in-house slides, video, or 3-D animation, but you may not need any of that.

A fully equipped presentation system (Figure 1-2) will require deeper pockets. A Mac IIcx, 4 megs of RAM, an 80-megabyte hard disk,

Figure 1-1. Mac Plus Presentation System

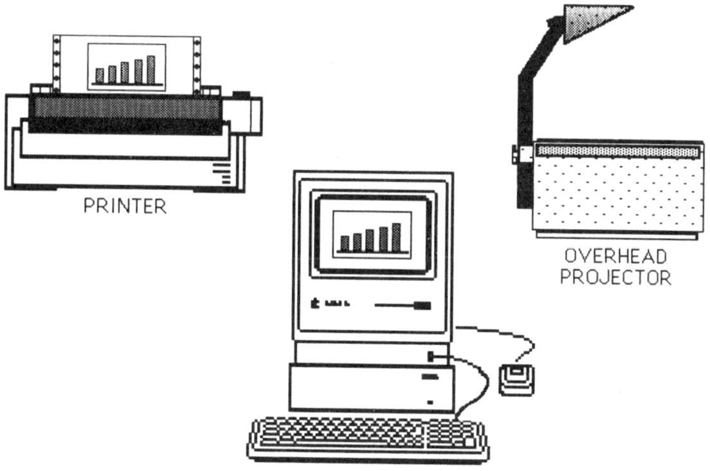

a megafloppy removable media drive, an 8-bit color card and 16-inch monitor, a laser printer, a grayscale scanner, a projection adapter, a mid-range slidemaker, a 2400-baud modem, and an assortment of presentation programs will cost somewhere between $25,000 and $30,000 at list prices. The street price for the same system will be about 25 percent lower. (This doesn't include video capabilities, which add significantly to the cost.) Apple's premium prices for Macintosh hardware make a such a presentation setup comparatively expensive—well out of the reach of individuals and many schools. However, for businesses and larger institutions considering the costly alternative—hiring freelancers to create presentations out of house—purchasing a Mac system seems quite reasonable. The hardware and software could pay for itself with just two or three jobs. Of course, any hardware purchasing decisions should begin with a realistic assessment of your presentation needs.

Figure 1-2. High-End Presentation System

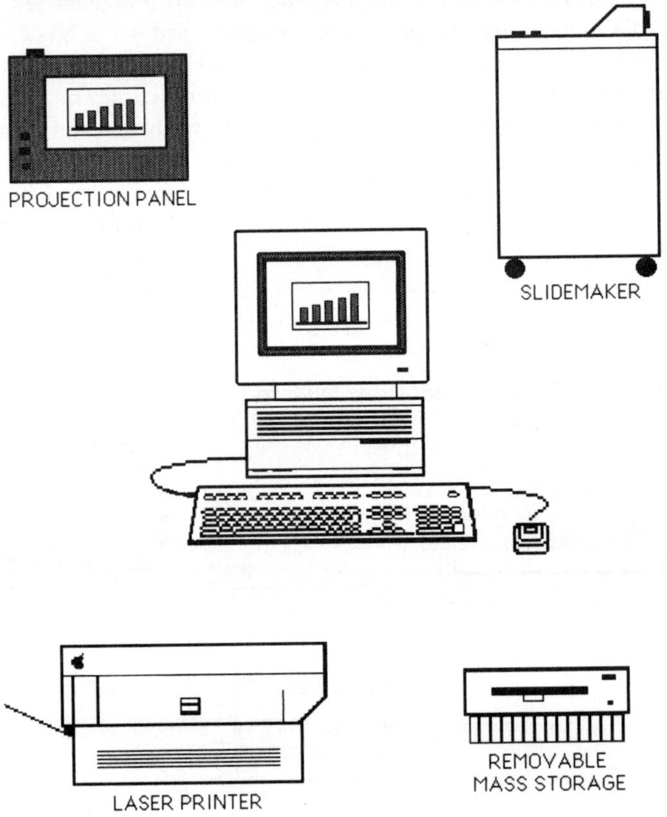

Presentation Software

Your Mac is no more than an expensive sculpture without the right software to run on it. There are several categories of programs that are useful for presentations; you'll probably need to have one or more programs in each.

System Software. System software is like a computer's traffic manager. The Mac's System file takes care of disk operations, peripherals, and other basic matters, while the Finder provides a consistent method of displaying and working with files. The System and Finder programs are located in the System Folder on any startup disk.

Experienced Mac users know there have been many upgrades of the System and the Finder, the Mac's operating system software. Unfortunately, early versions of the System and Finder don't work with many types of hardware and software. Your best bet is to use the latest version, System Update 6.0.2 (System 6.0.3 for 68030-based Macs, and System 6.0.4 for the IIci and portable). If you've just purchased your Mac, that's the version you received with your computer. The most recent System update can also be purchased from your Apple dealer or from many Macintosh user groups.

Apple has announced a major upgrade of the System, dubbed System 7.0, for release in early 1990. System 7.0 will include, among other enhancements, superior color and text handling. Chapter 2 covers these aspects of System 7.0 in more detail. Though System 7.0 will require two megabytes of RAM to run, it should be well worth it.

The Mac System includes MultiFinder, Apple's first multitasking operating system. With MultiFinder, you can run more than one application at a time in separate windows, moving among them at will without having to return to the Finder to close one application and start another. This power and flexibility has a cost; you'll need at least two megabytes of memory to run MultiFinder with most presentation programs, especially those that use color. To run several programs concurrently, you should have four megabytes of memory. While MultiFinder is more costly in terms of memory, the time it will save you in switching from one application to another, something you'll do often in the course of creating presentations and showing them directly on the Mac screen, may make the extra cost worthwhile.

Paint and Draw Programs. These programs are the foundation of Macintosh graphics. Paint programs literally make it possible to create Mac paintings, in black-and-white or color; draw programs are practical drafting kits for diagrams, illustrations, and other structured graphics. As the principle tools for creating custom graphics, a paint or draw program is one of the cornerstones of any Mac presenter's toolkit. Chapter 2 covers Mac painting and drawing in more detail.

Presentation Programs. Presentation programs are the workhorses of Mac presentations. They provide a way of creating and displaying a series of pictures, in effect creating a Macintosh slideshow. Presentation programs are really several applications in one, containing some or all of the following: a draw or paint application for creating pictures from scratch; a charting application for making data graphics; a font manipulator for adding titles to your pictures; a storyboarder or outliner telling the program which pictures you want to display, how long they should be on the screen, and the type of transitions you want between them—dissolves, wipes, and so on; a simple animator for moving text and objects around on the screen; and a collection of printer and slidemaker drivers for creating hard copy of your presentation. The program can display the pictures from disk on the Mac screen according to the script instructions, and may also automatically create speaker notes and outlines, leave-behinds, and reports for you.

Presentation Spreadsheets. All Mac spreadsheets now offer presentation graphics tools. If you spend most of your time crunching numbers, you may get all the presentation capabilities you need with one of these packages. See Chapter 3 for more.

Titling and Font Programs. One of the most common tasks in presentation is putting text over graphics or video, and there is software to help you do this. Most paint and draw programs offer access to the Macintosh fonts (typefaces) in your System file, but dedicated titling software will give you more fonts, as well as distort, resize, and add color to existing fonts. Advanced titling software allows the storage of many pages of text in memory, and will scroll or wipe through the pages according to your instructions. Font design applications provide the tools for creating entirely new fonts from scratch; these are mostly useful for presenters who have to create custom corporate logos.

Animation Programs. Animation, a series of pictures shown quickly in sequence to create the illusion of movement, can add excitement to your presentation productions. Animation programs for the Macintosh, of which there are a growing number, come in two basic categories: two-dimensional (2-D) and three-dimensional. The difference is plain to the eye: 2-D animation deals with images that are resolutely flat, while 3-D animation moves objects that appear to have full height, width, and depth.

Two-dimensional animation programs usually require that art be first drawn with a paint program or fed in through a digitizer before you can begin animation. Some paint programs, such as *Studio/1*, offer animation capabilities of their own. Three-dimensional animation programs include object editors to create the objects you'll move in the animation.

Some Mac animation software tries to do it all—presentation outlining and planning, pictures, animation, titles, and sound. The idea with these full-featured production programs is to provide you with a single source for all (or nearly all) the tools you need to create presentations on the Macintosh. One of the most sophisticated is *MacroMind Director* (from MacroMind; see Chapter 8). Such programs are great for pulling together short sequences in a hurry and with a minimum of resources.

Interactive Multimedia Programs. Among the most complex of Mac applications, interactive multimedia software attempts to mold all varieties of media—text, pictures, sound, and animation—into one program, also providing a way for the viewer to tailor the course of the presentation to his or her needs.

This category of presentation software includes *HyperCard,* Apple's extensible programming toolkit that comes with every new Mac. *HyperCard*'s highly visual approach to portraying information and its point-and-click simplicity make it ideal for training and education. With a little study of *HyperCard*'s scripting language, HyperTalk, it is also possible to construct entire presentations that can run independently of any presenter, that can ask for information from the viewer and then change course accordingly. Several programs have appeared that take *HyperCard*'s basic capabilities and expand on them, adding color, animation, large-screen support, and more. HyperCard and its spinoff programs are described in Chapter 9.

Using Presentations

You now have a general sense of what desktop presentations are all about. But what, specifically, can you do with them? Here are a few suggestions:

Business Presentations. For internal use, desktop presentations can provide information on sales trends and profits, the financial condition of the business, product development, manufacturing techniques, corporate restructuring, marketing efforts, advertising campaigns, and employee programs. Organizational efficiency is much improved when such information is conveyed vividly, accurately, and in a timely way to the right people; that's what desktop presentations excel at.

All organizations have to "sell" themselves to the outside world of investors, stockholders, customers, and vendors. Nothing is more effective than a well-crafted presentation to convince investors to sink venture capital into your new endeavor. Apple itself has taken this idea a step further, providing its annual report on disk in *HyperCard* form. Presentations sell products, too. An interactive point-of-sale presentation can provide information about products to customers, and even allow them to order directly from a computer display.

With the Mac, it's child's play to create the kind of colorful moving presentation that instantly communicates your ideas, and impresses the v.p.'s at the same time. The next time you need to present a complex new project, try using a Mac-generated slideshow—you can incorporate line art you create yourself, charts from charting programs, drawings and photographs digitized with a scanner, and animations designed with other Macintosh programs, as well as fancy graphics, sound, and slick video-style transitions.

Business television is one of the newest corporate buzzwords; it refers to the fast-growing practice of using video as a management communications and presentation tool. Businesses that produce their own video have greater control over the end product, and pay off the higher initial capital costs of setting up a television facility by lower per-program production costs and cheaper distribution. Also, certain kinds of information is more easily digested by CEOs and managers in video presentation than in printed materials or live presentations. The Macintosh makes it possible to add sophisticated effects to business TV programs that might not otherwise be possible for even a well-equipped corporate studio.

Among the advanced uses for business TV presentations are video conferences (also called teleconferences), corporate news reports, special events broadcasts aimed at the press, and *narrowcasting*, the creation and broadcast of programs aimed at selected audiences, including customers and stockholders.

Other business applications for desktop presentations include:

- Animatics (animated storyboards for advertising)
- Design approval
- Directories
- Newsletters and corporate publications
- Interactive training
- Macintosh training
- Online help systems
- Outlining and planning
- Point-of-sale demonstrations
- Product catalogs
- Video promotions

To show how Mac desktop presentations can be used in the real world of business, sprinkled through this book are examples and tutorials using the experiences of an actual company, ScanTech, a manufacturer of advanced medical scanning equipment. (ScanTech is not the company's real name.) Jane, ScanTech's Macintosh graphics and presentation expert, uses her Macintosh to produce everything from the occasional transparency to complete slideshows to video presentations using animation, color graphics, and custom sound.

Education. Teaching can be thought of as the presentation of information, and teachers as professional presenters. As a professional, you have to keep up with what your audience wants. Today's children are used to fast-paced, flashy entertainment; a conventional lesson may not reach them. But a well-designed Mac presentation can offer the qualities they respond to, with real information embedded in the fun. Low-achieving students benefit from the computer's patience—it never tires of waiting for a response, and is always willing to repeat a presentation, while high achievers can pilot the Mac to areas of study beyond the prescribed curriculum.

The graphic power of the Mac makes it possible, even easy to present difficult technical concepts, especially in the sciences, math, engineering, and geography. For instance, a simple animation would be far more effective in showing the evolution of the Earth's land masses over the last billion years than any number of words. Even better, an interactive presentation puts the learner in control, guided by a framework set up by the presentation developer—you.

Since desktop presentations are entirely under your control, the programs you create yourself can exactly match your lesson plan; there's no need to use the ancient filmstrips that are all that many schools can supply. Granted, this will take more of your time and imagination, but your students are worth it, and you'll find much satisfaction in the process. While you are learning desktop presentation skills, your students should be encouraged to create their own presentations, learning computer, graphic, communicative, and cooperative skills at the same time. Most schools already have a good selection of A/V equipment, so only an investment in Macs and software is required. Apple offers a Macintosh school-purchase program, which is pushing Macs rapidly into secondary (Grades 9–12) and higher ed.

Use desktop presentations in education for:

- Art, design, industrial arts, and music instruction
- Flash cards
- Hypermedia tests and term papers
- Interactive training
- Macintosh training
- Preschool education
- Remedial reading and writing
- Science and math instruction
- Special education
- Student reports
- Term paper presentations
- Vocational training

Not all kinds of educational material lends itself to presentation treatment, though; there's no substitute for a student's close encounter with a poem or painting. Unnecessary use of video and other presentation media is just as bad as sticking to a dry workbook, and uses up far more of your resources and time. Good presentation design is everything. For example, a poorly thought-out interactive presentation may encourage aimless rambling rather than concise thinking. Why bother to bring your lesson to a satisfying conclusion when there's always another exciting trail to explore? Interactive lessons shouldn't be completely open environments, but should be carefully structured to allow the student free access to important information without straying too far afield. Every trail should lead back to the main path.

Engineering and Design. Architectural and engineering simulations are increasingly being used to test ideas and concepts. Macintosh three-dimensional modeling and animation programs are perfect for building structures and objects with extreme realism. These can then be mixed with video to create convincing scenes for presentations. For example, an architect can draw up plans with a Macintosh computer-aided design program, such as *MacDraw II* or *VersaCad*, and then load the plans into a compatible modeling program for conversion into three dimensions. The model can then be superimposed onto a digitized photo or video of the building site, and then recorded onto tape to show the client. With this process, three integrated levels of information are available—2-D plans to guide the actual construction, 3-D models to check the "gestalt" of the design, and video for client or management presentations.

Research. Researchers and medical professionals can use the Mac to provide documentation for experiments and examinations, adding titles, explanatory graphics, and digitized images to standard slideshows or onscreen presentations. Desktop video hardware can record time-lapse video images of physical processes and convert them directly to computer graphics for analysis with image processing software and inclusion in training programs. The Mac can be invaluable for putting together technical presentations on short notice and within grant budgets, as well as for creating complex animated simulations that would take weeks to create with conventional techniques.

Presentation Art. In this book, presentations are treated as a species of practical communication, but creative work can fall into the category of presentation, too. The relatively low cost of Mac desktop presentations puts new tools within reach of artists who could never have afforded to work in computers, animation, or video only five years ago. Hundreds of young artists are employing the Mac to stretch the creative boundaries of computer graphics, video and performance art, animation, music videos, and documentaries, using presentation programs for everything from presenting slideshows of their computer paintings to devising complete, interactive multimedia programming that probes thorny social problems.

These are just a few of the many uses for Mac desktop presentations. As you work with your Mac, you'll discover others. Any time you need to communicate complex information, your Mac can be the best vehicle for the job.

At the most basic level, any Mac presentation is a show of pictures in sequence. The next chapter covers the theory and practice behind Mac graphics.

CHAPTER 2

Mac Graphic Design

One important reason for building a desktop presentation system centered on the Macintosh is to take advantage of the computer's graphics power. Most presentations will require you to create some kind of custom graphics—to show your product or illustrate your lesson. Yet the medium of computer graphics has a visual logic of its own that isn't immediately obvious. Some kinds of graphics work well on the computer screen; others don't. This chapter will help you develop an understanding of design principles for presentations; much of the material discussed here applies to other graphic uses of the Mac as well.

How the Mac Makes Pictures

To gain a better understanding of the kinds of images possible with the Mac, let's start by looking at how the computer makes pictures.

All computer screen images are composed of picture elements, called *pixels* for short. The pixel is the smallest possible dot the computer can display—the fundamental particle of computer graphics. The standard Mac display sports square-shaped pixels that are 1/72 of an inch on a side—the same size as the typesetter's "point." In computerese shorthand, the Mac has a screen display resolution of 72 dots per inch (dpi). Don't confuse pixels with the "phosphor dots" painted on the inside of the video tube; those are much smaller than Mac pixels, and many are required to make up one pixel—the *dot-to-pixel* ratio.

On the screen, pixels are arrayed in a grid, usually specified as a number of pixels across by a number of pixels down. Figure 2-1 shows a screen composed of 512 × 342—the size of a standard Mac Plus or Mac SE display. The standard Mac II screen size is 640 × 480 pixels. Large-screen displays from third-party vendors are available that offer up to 1664 × 1200 pixels, and these may also depart from the 72 dpi standard as well, with pixels that are even smaller. The Mac Plus and SE, the "integral-video Macs," as Apple calls them, can make each pixel black or white (except for the SE/30, which has the ability to drive color monitors, even though its built-in display is monochrome), while Mac IIs with a color video display card can make pixels any of thousands or millions of available colors. Computer images, such as the faces in Figure 2-1, are no more than fields of pixels shaded to look like some object. On the most basic level, when you draw on the screen, you're painting with pixels.

Figure 2-1. Pixels

Mac Color

The screen drawing routines embedded in the Mac ROM (Read-Only Memory) are called QuickDraw. As mentioned above, QuickDraw in the Mac Plus and SE doesn't allow onscreen color (although it does have a limited ability to drive color output devices, such as an ImageWriter printer with a color ribbon, allowing only eight colors). The Mac SE/30 and Mac II series contain an advanced version of QuickDraw called Color QuickDraw, which brings color to the previously monochromatic Macintosh world. The range of Mac color is currently the widest in the world of personal computers, and Apple's planned enhancements to Color QuickDraw will keep the Mac ahead. And it's these color capabilities that help make the Mac an exceptional presentation tool. Just keep in mind that Mac color is not the same as color in the real world.

Understanding the workings of Mac color can be a bit confusing, requiring you to be familiar with bit-depths, CLUTs, color words, and other arcana. You can gain some insight into Mac color by thinking about the information the computer requires for each pixel. A standard integral-video Mac screen, like the ones in the Plus and SE, offers but one bit's worth of information for each pixel; another way of saying this is that they display images with one *bit-depth*. A single bit can have only two possible states, 0 or 1. If the pixel bit is 1 (on), then the electron gun in the monitor illuminates it, and the pixel appears white; if the pixel bit is 0 (off), the pixel is unilluminated, and appears black. No additional colors are possible. Monochrome displays make for quick manipulation and thrifty use of memory; the entire screen of a Mac Plus or SE can be stored in a chunk of computer memory (a bitmap) of only 21.7 kilobytes. Even grayscale effects are possible, by logically dividing the screen into small groups of pixels and turning a percentage of the pixels in each group on or off to create a range of grays.

Things get more complicated when color is introduced. One bit won't do for each pixel, since you can only get a monochrome display that way; additional bits of information per pixel are required. Each bit added to the length of the color "word" for any pixel increases the bit-depth of the image, and the number of possible screen colors, by a power of 2. For example, a 2-bit display offers four possible states (2 to the second power), each of which can be assigned a color—00 for black, 01 for white, 10 for red, 11 for blue (or any other combination of four colors). Apple's standard 8-bit color display for the Mac II offers up to 256 possible onscreen colors for each pixel (2 to the eighth power, all the possible on-off combinations of bits in an 8-bit word). It also makes for graphics that eat up computer memory like salted pretzels; a 640 × 480, 8-bit color picture requires 307K of RAM just for the pixel information. Since parts of the System and the current application have to occupy memory also, a one-megabyte Mac is really inadequate for color graphics. Most color paint programs (see below) require at least two megabytes of RAM.

You can see 256 colors onscreen. But the Mac actually has many more colors to choose from—millions more, in fact. Computer color graphics are made by mixing shades of red, green, and blue, the primary colors of video displays. With the Mac, you can mix 256 shades of red, 256 shades of green, and 256 shades of blue in any combination to create a maximum palette of 16.8 million (256 × 256 × 256, or 2 to the twenty-fourth) colors. That's many more colors than the human eye can distinguish. But with only 256 of them on the screen at any one time, there's some artificiality about Mac pictures that attempt to reproduce the subtle shadings of nature. You can see this best in color scans, where bands of Mac color replace the smooth shading transitions in photographs or real life.

Not satisfied with the limitations of current Mac color, Apple recently released a new version of Color QuickDraw that uses 32 bits. The 32-bit color standard (called *full chunky color,* for those of you who follow Apple's obscure display terminology) offers 32 bits per pixel—24 bits of color, with an 8-bit "alpha channel" for video overlays and special effects, such as transparencies. The 24-bit color part lets you show all 16.8 million colors onscreen simultaneously. (That's assuming you have enough pixels on the screen to show that many colors. A 640 × 480 screen only has 307,200 pixels—you'd need a display with around 4,000 × 4,000 pixels to see every possible color, one color per pixel, and none is yet available for the Mac—or any other PC, for that matter.) Sixteen million is more than enough colors to render any scene with excellent fidelity, eliminating banding and making paintings and scans look nearly photographic. Thirty-two-bit Color QuickDraw also has dithering (color blending) routines that convert 24-bit color into 8-bit color with good fidelity.

As of this writing, Apple has not announced a video display card that supports 32-bit color (Apple's current 8-bit cards can't handle 32-bit color), but several cards are available from third-party sources, including RasterOps, SuperMac, and Radius. Some of these cards can drive a standard AppleColor RGB monitor, the kind that most Mac II users own; others work only with the manufacturer's monitors. Unfortunately, there are currently few applications that allow you to manipulate the entire 32-bit megachromatic range of colors.

Before you run out to buy a 24-bit or 32-bit system, keep in mind that a 640 × 480 24-bit image takes up at least 922K, and a 32-bit image of similar size requires at least 1.3MB. Most color image files will be much bigger, since the application that creates them adds additional formatting data to the minimum required for the color information alone. On the other hand, 32-bit Color QuickDraw uses compression routines to squeeze color picture files into a smaller space. All this makes predicting just how big a picture file will be somewhat difficult. You can safely assume, however, that only tiny 24- or 32-bit images will fit on a standard 800K Mac floppy disk, so if you have to transport data you'll want to look into removable mass storage. You may need to buy additional RAM as well; 32-bit paint and image processing programs will probably require at least 4MB of RAM. Expect big phone charges if you need to move 32-bit images to distant locations via modem.

Color Lookup Tables. One more thing you may want to know about Macintosh color is the concept of *Color LookUp Tables,* or CLUTs. In Color QuickDraw, these are places in memory where color information is stored. Each pixel has color index information that sends the Mac looking for the pixel color in the CLUT, rather than reading the color information directly from the bits that specify the pixel. This cumbersome method works well enough, but the Mac's CLUT size is currently limited to 256 colors, the number of onscreen colors in the 8-bit color system. Thirty-two-bit Color QuickDraw uses CLUTs, but can also read color information directly from the screen pixel value—with some cost in speed but the big advantage of avoiding the CLUT color limitations and being able to display millions of onscreen colors. In most cases, CLUTs are things only programmers need worry about, unless you are in the process of switching from 8-bit to 32-bit color, and are puzzled by changes in performance of your system.

A Little Color Theory

Now you know how the Mac makes color, but just what color is and how we perceive it is a matter of continuing scientific debate. It is generally accepted that color is made up of three elements:

- *Hue,* the actual spectral color, such as red, green, blue, or yellow; the spectral wavelength of the color.
- *Saturation,* the purity of the color; how much white is mixed into it.
- *Value,* the lightness or darkness of the color; how much black is mixed into it.

Any color the Macintosh can create can be specified as some combination of hue, saturation, and value. But colors can also be specified by

Figure 2-2. Red-Yellow-Blue Color Wheel

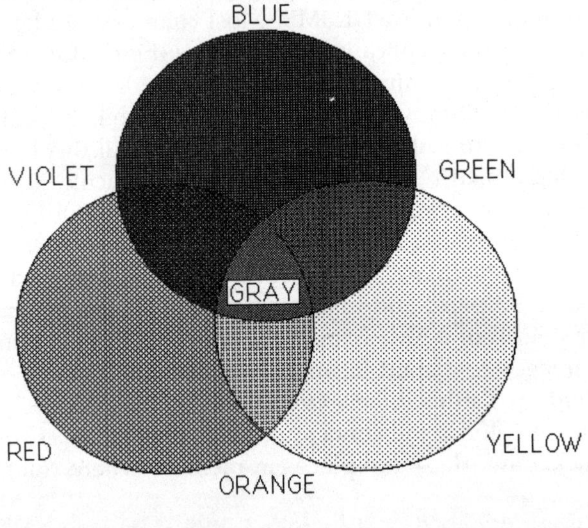

their proportions of red, green, and blue, the primary colors of video and computer graphics.

Figures 2-2 and 2-3 will help you understand how the RGB system of color mixing works. Figure 2-2 shows the color-mixing system everyone learned in grammar school, the one used when mixing paint. In this system, red, yellow, and blue are the primary colors from which all other colors are made. To make medium green, for instance, you mix yellow and blue in equal proportions. But in the RGB color system, mixing green and blue yields yellow. That sounds wrong, but a little experimentation with any color paint program will verify it.

Figure 2-3. Red-Green-Blue Color Wheel

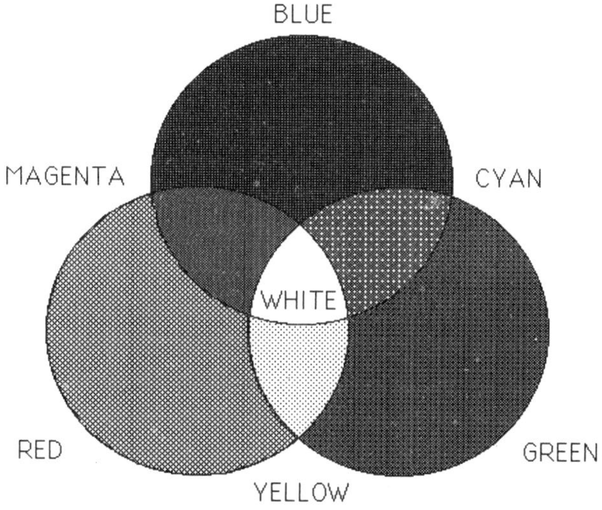

In Figure 2-4, the standard Macintosh Color Picker dialog box, you can see the sliding controls that give you the ability to mix colors either by RGB or by HSV, Hue, Saturation, and Value; value is called "brightness" in the Color Picker. You can also specify colors by number, or by clicking on them in the wheel. (If you haven't played with the Color Picker yet, one is available in the Color part of the Control Panel. Obviously, you need a color Mac for this.) Both HSV and RGB systems work equally well, and most programs that allow color mixing give you the option of using the one you're most comfortable with. There are other color schemes, such as CMYK (Cyan, Magenta, Yellow, and Black) and the Pantone Color Matching System, but these are mainly used in color desktop publishing, rarely in presentations.

Figure 2-4. Mac Color Picker

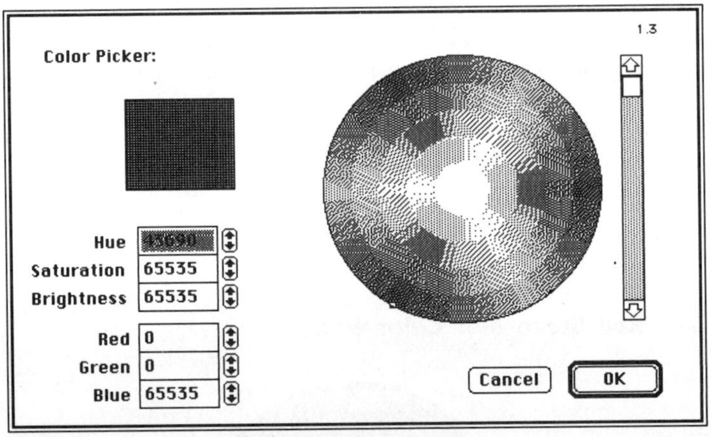

Using Color

So far, we've been talking about color in an abstract way, but no mention has been made of how to *use* color.

Though we rarely think about color analytically, we're profoundly affected by it and depend on the information colors give us to make our way in the world. In our visual memory, color is the key to emotional reactions based on experience and expectation. A ripe red apple, for example, if it were dyed bright blue, would be unpalatable to most people. Colors help us estimate how near or far any object is and whether it will be warm or cool to the touch. The colors of the landscape tell us the season, the climate and weather, the time of day, even the latitude we are in.

As a desktop presentation designer, you can use color to set the psychological tone of your presentation, making it eyecatching or subtle, intimate or aloof, soothing or angry. The adroit use of color can give the appearance of great depth to a flat screen, can make shapes seem to jump, vibrate, and swim; or can create an image that hits the viewer with the force of a blow.

Computer displays look flat and textureless, at least compared to film or print images, but you can use color to give apparent depth to your graphics. Psychologically, we expect deep colors to be nearer, and faded colors to be farther away, because the atmosphere tends to filter and soften distant objects. The illusion is enhanced if the nearer colors are warm—shades of red, orange, yellow—and the farther colors are cool—pale pastels of blue, brown, gray, and green. These color expectations can be also be turned on their heads by making the foreground pale and cool, the background dark and warm; the ultimate use of this scheme is white symbols or letters on a near-black background. This makes the light-colored, information-carrying material snap forward at the viewer, so it has become a popular color scheme for presentation graphics.

Colors have other psychological meanings as well. For example, in most western cultures, red means stop, danger, hot, pain; green means go, safe, cool, soothed (but also jealous or envious). Weather and financial graphics each have their own set of meaningful colors: the colors of maps and clouds, or the red and black of financial performance. The presentation designer should be alert to these color connotations.

Color Caveats. You'll notice quickly enough that the colors in your slides, overheads, and printouts will not correspond exactly to the colors on your screen. Think of the various stages your color art is going through. First, you may be scanning in art with a color scanner. None of these give perfect contrast and color fidelity to the original. Then, you may be using software to adjust colors in the scan, or add titles and graphics. While you're working on the image with your Mac, your eyes don't even see the same color in the same way in each part of the screen; the center of the monitor is brighter than the edges, and this effects the way you see colors. (It helps to let your monitor warm up for 20 minutes and adjust the convergence before starting color-sensitive work.)

Next, the output device (a slidemaker or printer, for instance) interprets the colors yet again. Many slidemakers and printers still can't handle 24-bit or 32-bit color images at all. Finally, colors are affected by the actual presentation environment. In the case of slides, the lighting conditions you show them in and the color of the slide screen all have their effects. So it's not surprising that the colors will look different, sometimes very different, in the final presentation. Should you be using color photocopies of color printouts for paper leave-behinds (see Chapter 4), the printouts will bear even less resemblance to the screen colors; lower-cost color printers and color photocopy machines are notoriously poor in reproducing true hues.

Color fidelity is an endemic problem for computer graphics, one that causes many problems for desktop publishers and videographers, and for which there's no good solution. The underlying problem is that color perception is not absolute; it's partly psychological, partly physiological, and partly at the mercy of the color display technologies you're using. If you need to settle on a standard color scheme for several presentations, trial and error will give you an idea of which colors seem to go through the least distortion through the graphic-creation process—some slide films give better fidelity with reds and blues than other films do, for instance—and you can stick with those colors for your presentations.

Tips for Mac Color Graphics

Here are some additional tips for effective color design on your Mac, or on any video display:

- Colors are seen most clearly when displayed against a neutral field. Gray makes an appropriate background color.
- Small objects should be colored boldly. The low-resolution video screen makes it harder for the eye to resolve small areas.
- Don't use blue for small objects, lines, and text. The human eye has the most trouble focusing on blue, and won't easily be able to see small blue shapes on the screen, which has a blue cast already. For the same reason, it's difficult to see edges between colors that differ only in their proportion of blue. However, blue makes an excellent background color. And blue is perfect for graphic elements that should be unobtrusive, like grid lines.
- Don't use thin vertical lines that contrast against the background, such as black lines on white. Thin, contrasting horizontal lines work well on the Macintosh screen, but jump noticeably on video. Use thick lines, as thin ones tend to disappear when seen from typical presentation viewing distances.
- Fine patterns of contrasting colors blend into one mixed color when seen from presentation distances; this is an effect you can use to mix more than 256 perceived colors on the screen. Fine patterns flicker badly when transferred to video. Patterns to avoid are checkerboards, herringbones, crosshatches, dot patterns, and fine stripes.
- Avoid juxtaposing complementary colors. For example, highly saturated red against highly saturated cyan will create a vibrating border between the colors. This is a distracting irritation, unless a psychedelic effect is what you're after. Other offending combinations are green and magenta and blue and yellow. Try using a line of neutral gray between complementary colors; this will eliminate the vibration.
- Also avoid heavy use of red, magenta, orange, hot pink, and brown. Video displays have the most difficulty rendering these colors with fidelity and clarity (although the Apple RGB monitor does a good job of it overall). Red and magenta are particularly unstable, and red areas almost always exhibit *crawling* (a shimmering border effect) along their edges when transferred from the Mac to video. You can avoid this to some extent by using colors that are less saturated—that have white or black mixed in with them. Black, white, blue, green, and gray are the most stable colors—and, you'll notice, the most used in broadcast video graphics.
- Use the fewest colors that will do the job. People have difficulty keeping track of the meanings of seven or more colors.

Composition

The arrangement of graphic elements on a flat plane is called *composition*. In the Western aesthetic tradition, a wide picture is considered to be appropriate for landscapes, a tall picture for portraits and figures, with the larger dimension often about 1½ times the size of the smaller one. (Other art traditions use different conventions for proportions. Chinese landscapes, for example, are often very tall and narrow.) Though people accustomed to modern and postmodern art may think that the landscape-portrait distinction no longer holds, psychologically we still look for landscape depth in a horizontal picture, and see a figurative or portrait orientation in a vertical one.

Give some thought to the dimensional requirements of your presentation graphics, keeping in mind the ramifications of the composition you choose. By confounding your viewer's expectations, you can add drama to your compositions, or you can adopt a traditional format to give your graphics a classic appearance.

Aspect Ratios. The Mac screen can be small or large but usually has the same ratio of width to height, three by four units, the standard video *aspect ratio*. That makes a bland rectangle that allows for little compositional drama. Wide landscapes or tall figurative compositions don't translate well to video or computer displays, but that three to four aspect ratio is proportioned just right for talking heads. That's one reason why TV imagery is so face obsessed, and also why you'll rarely see great vistas and shots with real depth of field in programming made expressly for TV.

The compositional limitations of the video aspect ratio don't mean much when you're creating presentation graphics that will be translated to other media, like slides, overheads, or print, since most graphics applications let you create pictures in a variety of sizes and rectangular shapes. However, these limitation are binding if your presentation will be shown on the Mac screen or on video. Of course, there are also tall monitors for the Mac, called portrait monitors. Portrait monitors are most often used in desktop publishing, since they are proportioned like an 8½ × 11-inch piece of paper, but they can be used for presentations as well, if there's a good reason for the vertical orientation—if, for example, you're presenting a Macintosh fashion show with lots of tall, skinny models. Keep in mind that no manufacturer has yet come out with a color portrait monitor.

If you're willing to use less than the total available screen area, you can simulate the film aspect ratio (about 1 to 3) by masking off the top and bottom of the screen and placing graphics only in the middle strip. Although this won't look exactly like the Mac graphics most people are familiar with, your audience will ignore it if the presentation is interesting enough. A wider screen allows more flexibility in composing wide-angle shots, landscapes, and any scenes that involve lateral motion. You can use the blank strips above and below to add titles and graphics, without interfering with the main image.

There's no rule, by the way, that says your monitor has to sit on its base. Tip it over on its side, and suddenly your picture is taller than it is wide, good for images of entire bodies. The only tricks are to make sure the Mac imagery is also oriented the same way (that is, tipped over 90 degrees) and to get your audience to accept looking at a tipped-over monitor. (This may not work with monitors that have speakers or controls on the sides.)

Once you've settled on the shape and size of your graphic, you need to arrange the picture elements within. By far the most popular way of arranging picture elements on TV is the two-shot, a composition with two major elements. You see these all the time on news shows, where a talking head may be matched with a second head, block of text, a split-screen graphic, or another video source. These simple compositions work well for the Mac, too, especially if the Mac monitor is the presentation medium. Of course, presentation compositions can get more complex as necessary, with three, four, or more important elements. But, given the confines of the Mac screen and the necessity of getting the visual message across in a relatively short time, it's best to keep presentation compositions as simple as possible. Better to break a complex concept down into several simple graphics and show them in sequence (or change them through animation) than to cram too much into one picture and risk your audience missing something important.

Painting and Drawing

Mac graphics software can be divided into two general categories: paint programs and draw programs. The difference between them is profound, but not obvious; paint programs edit images as *bitmaps,* or matrices of pixel color and shading values, while draw programs manipulate images as *objects,* shapes defined as mathematical formulas. Practically speaking, paint programs give you the advantage of the painterly effects that come from pixel-by-pixel editing control, while draw programs yield pictures with nearly infinite levels of detail and high-quality output.

***MacPaint* 2.0.** Paint programs are among the most adaptable and easiest-to-use presentation software—with any paint program, you can create graphic designs, titles, backgrounds for animation and video, and more. Some paint programs even come bundled with slideshow utilities that let you craft complete, if simple, presentations. Overall, a paint program is a basic and necessary software tool for the desktop presenter.

The grandparent of all paint programs is *MacPaint* (from Claris), the first popular application of its kind for any personal computer. More than anything else, it was *MacPaint*'s sharp black-and-white graphics that sold the Mac in its first struggling year. All modern paint programs now offer some variation on *MacPaint*'s toolset, shown in its current incarnation in Figure 2-5. If you are an experienced Macintosh artist, you undoubtedly got up to speed on the Mac with *MacPaint* or a similar paint program, such as *FullPaint* (Ann Arbor Softworks).

Figure 2-5. *MacPaint*

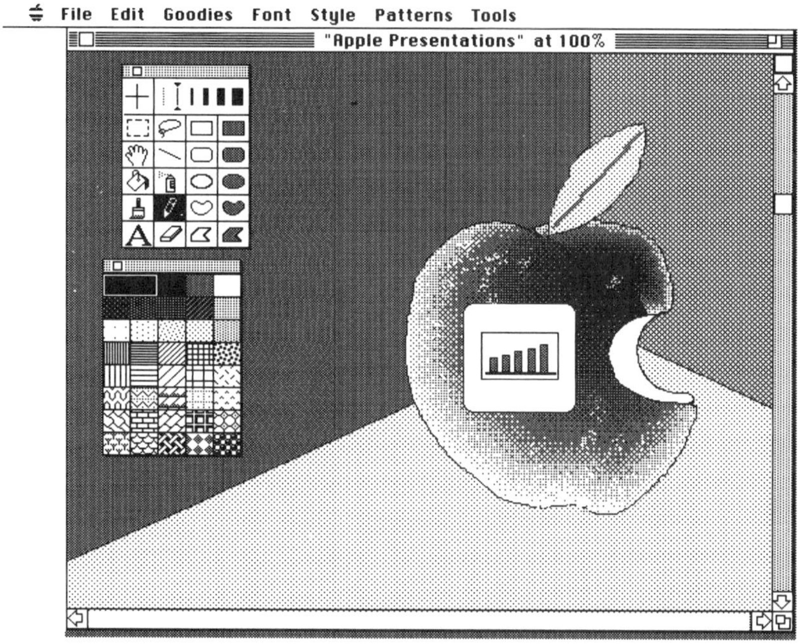

Paint programs, including *MacPaint,* typically offer analogs to the traditional artist's tools—pencils, brushes, erasers, paper, rulers, airbrushes, and so on—as well as new kinds of nontraditional tools—mirrors, custom pattern fills, value inversions, and more—in an iconic toolbox. In *MacPaint 2.0,* the tools can be torn off the menu and positioned anywhere onscreen, as can a palette of readymade patterns. You click on the desired tool icon and pattern, then move to the page—the drawing part of the *MacPaint* window—and start scribbling. Menu options generally modify the actions of tools, or perform some manipulation on a selection. Additional modifiers are available from the keyboard; press the right key while moving the mouse and you can make perfect circles, move objects only along a straight horizontal or vertical path, or make quick copies of the current selection.

MacPaint is a classic, and it still is perfectly useful for creating black-and-white pictures on a standard Mac Plus or SE. However, if you need color, or a more sophisticated toolset, you'll need to look beyond *MacPaint*. Familiarity and simplicity are the program's main virtues now.

Studio/8. Take *MacPaint* to the eighth power, and you have *Studio/8,* a professional-level, second-generation color paint program from Electronic Arts. The *Studio/8* toolset contains many features not available in *MacPaint,* including:

- Multiple pages larger than the screen, up to the limits of RAM
- Full 8-bit color, and multiple methods for mixing and matching colors and color gradients
- The ability to pick up a selection and paint with it like a brush
- Distortions, rotations, and instant perspective of selections and brushes
- An adjustable airbrush
- Smearing, blending, transparency, and watercolor effects
- Directional shading for creating shapes with apparent volume
- Sophisticated text effects, such as neon lettering
- Pattern fills created from brushes of any size

Figure 2-6 shows the *Studio/8* screen and some of the effects you can create with it. One impressive *Studio/8* effect is its gradient shading option. In a few steps, you can create a perfectly shaded sphere, which would be very laborious to make in *MacPaint.*

Figure 2-6. *Studio/8*

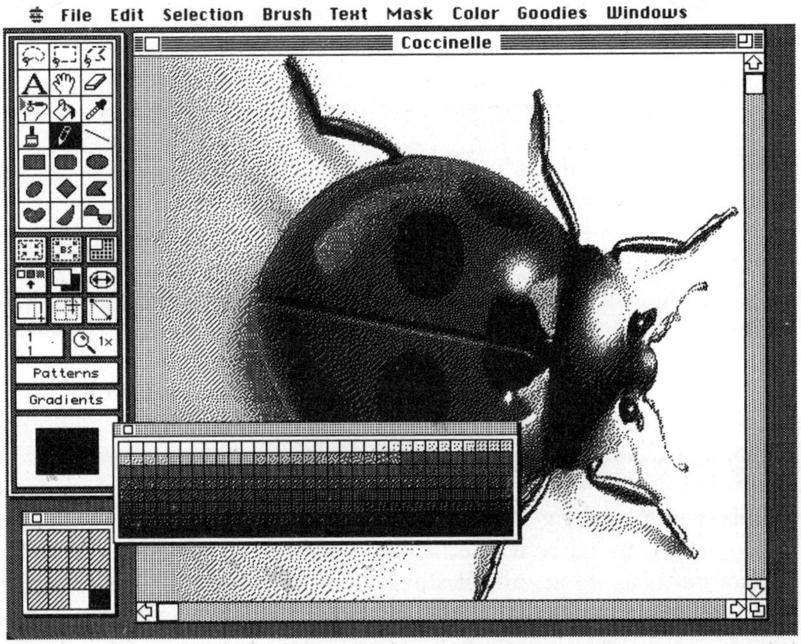

To create a perfectly shaded sphere with *Studio/8:*

1. Select the oval shape tool from the main tool palette.
2. Select a pattern fill—in this case, solid.
3. Select a gradient—a range of graduated shades. *Studio/8* comes with two built-in gradients; choose the grayscale.
4. Draw a circle on the page by dragging from where you want the center of the sphere to be while holding down the Shift key.
5. A gradient line appears, which you can adjust to indicate the direction and distance of shading. Click the mouse and the shading is drawn for you, turning an empty circle into a sphere, as in Figure 2-7.

Figure 2-7. *Studio/8* Gradient Sphere

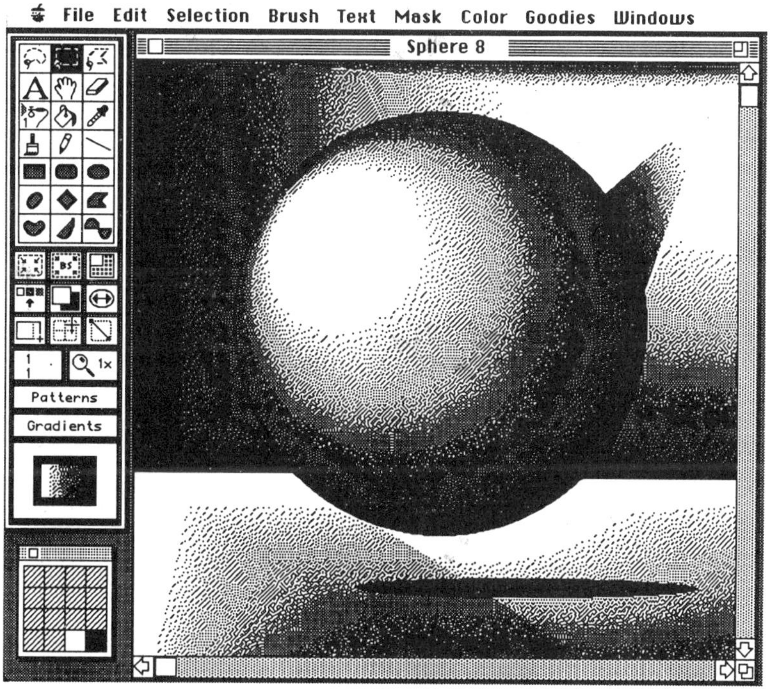

While the *Studio/8* elegant interface and toolset are currently state-of-the-art, its power comes at a price; you can't run the program in less than two megabytes of RAM—more memory is recommended—and you'll need five or six empty megabytes on your hard disk for *Studio/8* and the temporary files it writes during operation. Most of the other high-level paint color paint programs, such as *Pixel Paint* 2.0, make similar demands on your system.

MacDraw II. What *MacPaint* is to the paint programs, *MacDraw II* (Claris) is to draw programs—the illustrious ancestor of the whole genre of object-oriented graphics on the Mac. From Figure 2-8, you can see the difference between a draw program and a paint program; *MacDraw II* offers only a few drawing tools, patterns, and colors, not the wide range of pixel manipulators in *Studio/8*. But the shapes you draw with *MacDraw II* are always "alive." Just click on them at any time, and they can be scaled up and down infinitely without loss of detail; given a new line weight, fill pattern, or color; modified in groups; arranged in layers, each of which can be worked on without affecting the others; and redrawn to a desired level of mathematical precision. In a paint program, it's much harder to change what you've already drawn; often you have to repaint it entirely. Thus, for technical graphics that may have to incorporate many changes, *MacDraw II* or another draw program is the quicker and more precise tool.

Figure 2-8. *MacDraw II*

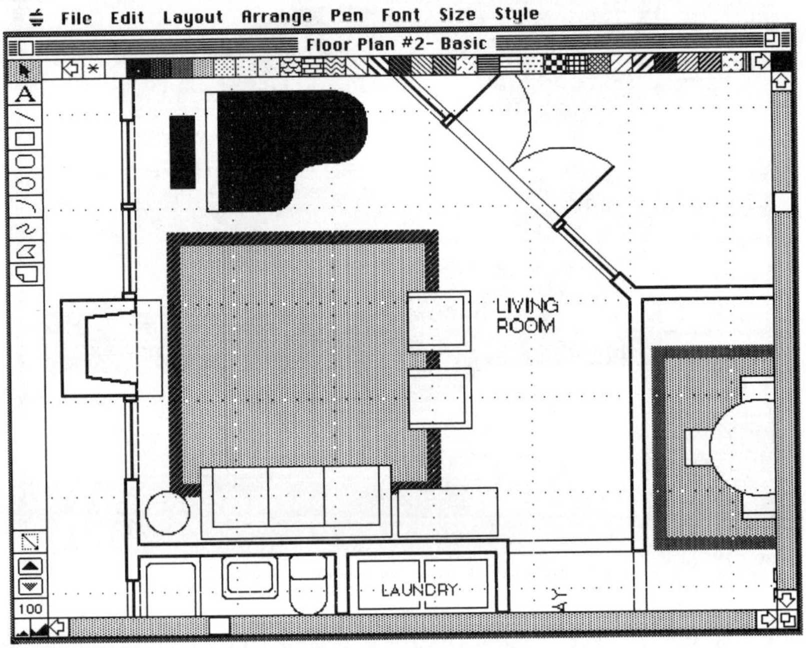

MacDraw II is used widely in the media; *Time* and *USA Today*, among other periodicals, use it for quick news graphics. If you're in media, you'll probably want to stick with *MacDraw II* for compatibility. Version 1.1 even includes a slideshow feature that shows successive picture layers as slides in a screen presentation, as well as the indispensable spelling checker. If *MacDraw II* is your primary graphics program, you may be able to dispense with the need for a dedicated presentation program altogether—although *MacDraw II* doesn't offer the full power of such programs.

If you need to work regularly in both paint and draw environments, you may want to try a program that offers both in one package, such as *SuperPaint*, from Silicon Beach. *SuperPaint* has two layers, one dedicated to paint tools, one to draw tools. A click of the mouse switches back and forth from one to the other, and some simple conversion tools let you import paint pictures to the draw layer, and drawings to the paint layer.

***FreeHand* 2.0.** Another category of draw programs is the professional illustration applications that generate PostScript output (that's Adobe System's page description language, which allows any drawing to be printed at the full resolution of the printing device). The best known are Adobe's *Illustrator* and Aldus's *FreeHand*. The *FreeHand* workscreen is shown in Figure 2-9. The complex set of features in *FreeHand* include draw tools that let you create and edit *Bezier curves*, a type of mathematical curve defined by the placement of external anchors and magnets acting on the curve line. Drawing with Beziers is more difficult than the simple curves available from *MacDraw*, but they are far more precise. One useful feature that *FreeHand* and *Illustrator* offer is an auto-

Figure 2-9. *FreeHand* 2.0

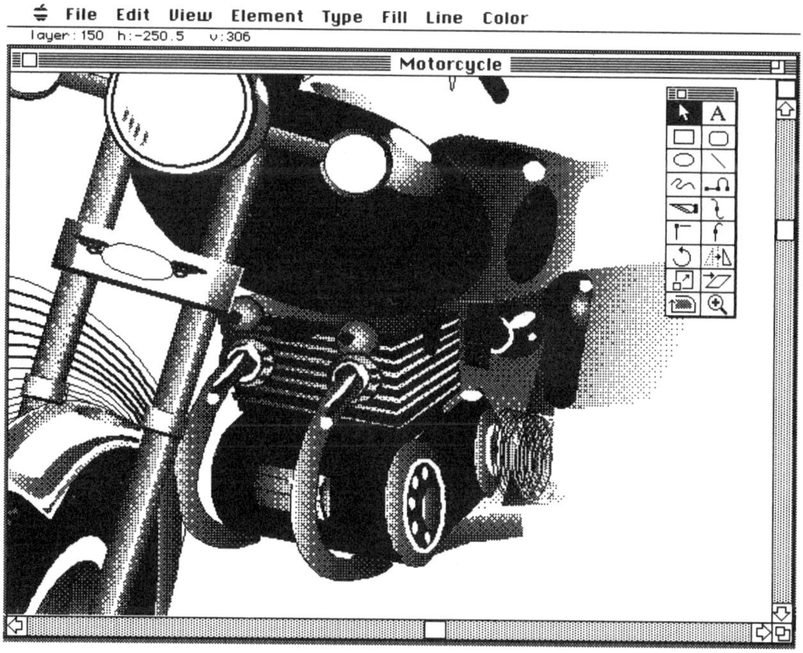

trace tool, which converts any paint or scanned image to a PostScript line drawing; you might find an autotrace tool helpful in creating accurate technical diagrams from scanned photos or line art.

PostScript draw programs fall somewhere between basic design applications like *MacDraw* and high-level Computer-Aided Design (CAD) programs. Complex and nonintuitive in some operations, they are best suited to professional illustrators and presenters who need PostScript output for desktop-published support material. When the next generation of slidemakers supports PostScript, *FreeHand* and *Illustrator* will be a lot more useful to the presenter (see below for a discussion of Mac graphics file formats).

When Jane at ScanTech makes detailed renderings of new products, or comp graphics for presentations and promotional materials, she is likely to need several different programs. One technique she often uses is to draw the outline of her design in *MacDraw,* where it's faster to put together the structure of a graphic, and then import the draw file as a bitmap into *Studio/8,* where she adds subtle color effects, text, and a background. Then the completed picture can be loaded into a presentation or color animation program as part of a complete presentation. She does the same thing with 3-D design programs (see Chapter 7) that can save renderings as bitmaps. If she needs to print the graphic on paper, she'll stay within the PostScript environment of *FreeHand.* A *FreeHand* illustration can be exported as a bitmap to a presentation program with a file conversion or screen capture program (see below).

Graphic Special Effects. There is an infinite number of different pictorial effects possible with paint and draw programs. Here are a few that recall the digital effects often seen on broadcast TV.

- Tiling. In computer graphics, a *tile* is a rectangular image that is repeated in a pattern all over the screen, like tiles on a floor. Figure 2-10 shows a screen covered in tiles.

Figure 2-10. Tiles

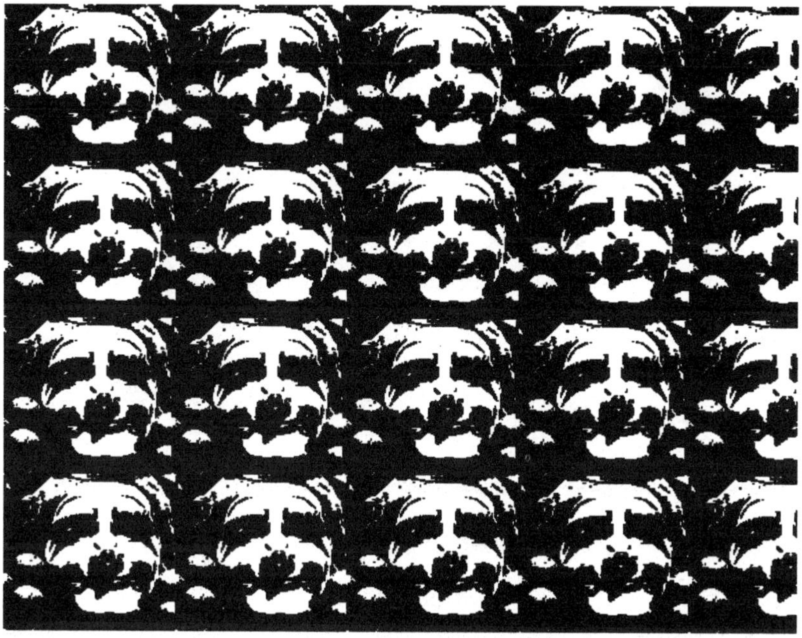

- Image Mapping. Some programs can take any image and warp it to make it look like it's wrapped (*mapped* is the computer graphics term) around a shape, as a drawing on paper could be wrapped around a ball. (This looks like, but is not really the same as, the *surface mapping* used by 3-D object editing programs discussed in Chapter 8). Some examples of image mapping are shown in Figure 2-11.

Figure 2-11. Image Mapping

- Perspective. Programs can take part or all of the flat picture plane and make it appear to recede into the distance, an effect called *perspective.* An example of the use of perspective is illustrated in Figure 2-12, in which the box design was first created as a flat, square image, then tilted to appear three-dimensional. Keep in mind that paint programs only work with flat planes, so your images will always look like tilted flat planes. For real manipulations in computer space, you'll need a 3-D object editor and animation program.

Figure 2-12. Perspective

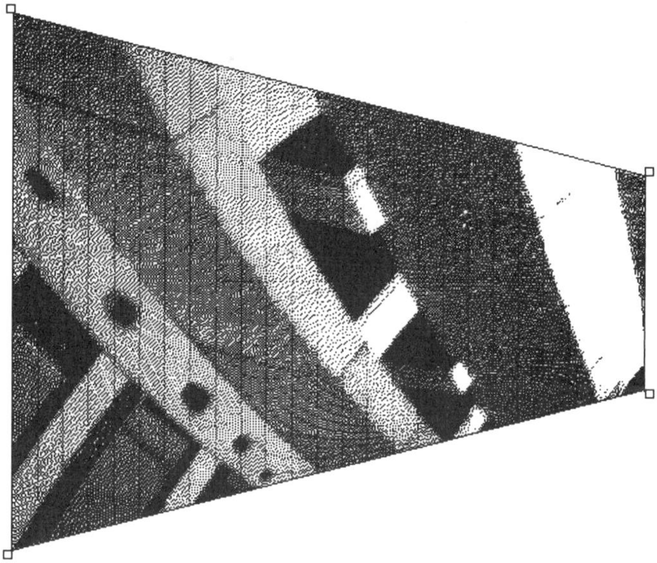

- Zoom Effect. This simple effect (Figure 2-13) looks like the infinite regression created by two mirrors facing each other, or a frozen camera zoom, or video feedback. It's accomplished by repeatedly shrinking an image by increments and pasting it on the screen. Variations can be achieved by making certain colors in the image transparent, or pasting the image down so it appears to be coming from a corner.

Figure 2-13. Zoom Effect

Mac Text

One of the great graphic strengths of the Macintosh is its versatility with text. Even Mac neophytes know the computer is capable of showing an infinite number of different letterforms and typestyles, making it the premiere platform for desktop publishing. Typography and text design on the Mac is an entire area of artistic endeavor all by itself, with thousands of Mac professionals out there basing their careers on mastering the idiosyncrasies of Mac text manipulation.

Fonts and Styles. A *font,* also called a *typeface,* is a complete set of letters and other characters in one typestyle and size. Ten-point Times Roman, for example, is a font often used in newspapers and books. There are many fonts, ranging from the utilitarian to the exclusively decorative. There's a Mac version of nearly every font every designed; Figure 2-14 shows just a few.

Figure 2-14. Macintosh Fonts

Fonts come in various sizes, measured by points (there are 72 points in an inch, the same as pixels per inch on the standard Mac screen). The numbers after the font names in the figure above indicate the font's size in points. As you can see, a smaller point number means a smaller font, and a larger number means a larger font. Currently you have to include in your System file a separate size for every font; note that the larger fonts are not just blown-up copies of smaller versions; the larger letters are actually redrawn with more detail.

In addition to choosing a font type and size, you can specify font styles, whether the letters will be plain, bold, italic, underlined, or any combination of these and other styles, as shown in Figure 2-15.

Figure 2-15. Font Styles

Plain

Bold

Italic

Underline

Outline

Shadow

Condensed

Extended

Most fonts fall into two general categories, *serif* and *sans-serif*. Serif fonts, such as Times Roman, have short bases, caps, and tails on the letters. The little caps and tails add to the legibility of sans-serif fonts on the printed page, but at small sizes tend to get lost in the lower resolution world of Mac graphics. Sans-serif fonts, such as the popular Helvetica, look clean and modern, and many Mac designers prefer them.

Figure 2-16. Serif, Sans-serif, and Display Fonts

Headline is a serif face.

Helvetica is sans-serif.

CAPS IS

FOR

DISPLAY

Fancy type styles, such as Raster and Black Knight, don't really fall into either category. They are *display* fonts, used mainly to catch the eye with a bold typographical statement. Blocks of text should not be in a display font, but in a more sober, traditional style that's easier to read. Figure 2-16 illustrates serif, sans-serif, and display fonts.

Font design programs for the Mac are currently a hot area for third-party software development. Applications like *LetraStudio* and *Fontagrapher* (see Appendix A) let you design your own fonts, if you have the inclination and skill to do it, or work wild distortions on existing type, such as wrapping them around curves for logos. For example, *Showcase F/X*, a presentation titling program from Aegis Development, lets you expand, squeeze, slant, mirror, and flip type (Figure 2-17). You also have the option of importing bitmapped fonts into a paint program like *Studio/8* and adding effects there, such as multiple color outlines, translucent text, perspective distortions, and so on.

Screen and Scalable Fonts. Something that isn't evident to the new Mac user is that the text you see onscreen is different than the text that

Figure 2-17. Type Effects

comes out of a laser printer or slidemaker. The current version of the Mac System uses *screen fonts,* bitmapped letterforms for display on the Mac screen, but many presentation programs and output devices use separate, object-oriented *scalable fonts* (also called *outline fonts,* because the letterforms are stored as mathematical descriptions of each letter's outline), which may or may not correspond to the screen fonts. PostScript fonts are scalable, for example; the Chicago font that comes with your Mac is a screen font only. The reason for having two font types is that screen fonts, being bitmaps, don't resize or rotate without producing the jaggies, while scalable fonts can be manipulated in all kinds of ways and still yield smooth-looking output.

The typical presentation program lets you use any kind of bitmapped fonts for screen graphics (you incorporate them as bitmapped pictures, just like a paint program picture), but will only print a few scalable fonts to slidemakers or laser printers. The drawback is that what you see on the screen is not necessarily what you get as output, a breakdown in the Mac's usual WYSIWYG (What You See Is What You Get) mode of operation. System 7.0, the revised Mac system software planned for release in 1990, should make scalable fonts the standard way of working for all output devices, and all sizes of screen fonts will more closely resemble their scalable partners. Adobe Type Manager (see Appendix A) is one program that can improve the appearance of screen fonts.

Tips for Presentation Text

Most presentation graphics incorporate text as part of the image, but the use of text in presentations is different than the use of text in print media. The place to learn about presentation text is on TV. Here are some basic principles of video text design to keep in mind for presentations:

- Short words and messages work best. It's hard to read text on computer monitors at typical presentation viewing distances and angles. Use your own mouth instead to convey large amounts of verbal information.
- Keep text in the central 80 percent of the screen (the so-called "safe text area"). The curved corners and edges of computer screens distort text and make it hard to read.
- Use large letters (18 points in size or larger). Presentation text has to be large to be readable.
- Don't mix many different styles and sizes of text in one graphic unless you're after a cluttered, eclectic look. One or two fonts and sizes are adequate for most graphics. Your best bet is to use just one typeface—Helvetica, the one font that every presentation program offers.

- Separate text from the background through the use of color, shape, and graphic design tricks like drop shadows and block letters (Figure 2-18).

Figure 2-18. Drop Shadows and Block Letters

Scans and How to Tweak Them

Scanning, the act of capturing photographs or art on paper and converting them to a Mac-compatible picture format, is popular in desktop publishing but just coming into its own in the presentation arena. For scanning, you need a scanner, a device based on photocopier technology, that *digitizes* the art, which you lay down on the bed of the scanner, put underneath the scanning head, or evenly stroke with a handheld unit. One scanner, the ThunderScan (ThunderWare, see Appendix A), substitutes for the ribbon in an ImageWriter, and scans paper and photos run through the printer. Scanners come in two main types, color and grayscale, with grayscale by far the most popular. The better grayscale scanners offer 8-bit grays (256 gray shades) and scanning resolution of 300 dots per inch or more (although the effective resolution is usually less). Apple's scanner, a 4-bit model, captures 16 levels of gray, which is probably enough for most presentation uses, although not really satisfactory for desktop publishing. Color scanners, while producing more true-to-life images, are quite expensive, and few presentation programs can handle the 24-bit image files they produce. Graphics programs such as *Canvas* (Deneba Software) and *Studio/8* let you substitute color palettes for grayscale ones, so it's possible to convert a grayscale scan into a color image. Though the results may not be very close to the original, a scan converted to color may be perfectly adequate for presentation graphics.

There are many uses for scans in presentations. Jane, ScanTech's jack-of-all-Mac-trades, routinely uses a grayscale scanner to pull photos, technical diagrams, and news clippings into her Mac for use with promotional material and leave-behinds (see Chapter 4), and to include in overhead presentations. She finds that scans also make effective backgrounds for animations and data graphics, especially when she overlays brightly colored foreground graphics on a subdued grayscale scan. She uses an image-processing program such as Letraset USA's *ImageStudio* (Figure 2-19) to clean up the scanned image and adjust the range of grays. *ImageStudio* includes Mac analogs of the traditional photo retoucher's tools—pens, brushes, whiteout ink, masks, blending, smearing, and smudging tools—as well as image-processing techniques to increase the definition of edges, globally change gray ranges, and impose patterns on selected areas or shades.

Figure 2-19. *ImageStudio* Screen

On the occasions when Jane needs to work with color scans, she has the art scanned at a desktop-publishing service bureau with a 24-bit color scanner, then retouches the scan back at her office with a color image-processing program, such as *PhotoMac* (Data Translation, see Appendix A). If she knows the scan isn't going to fit on a floppy disk, and most don't, she goes to a service bureau that offers the same type of removable mass storage that she uses in her own office, or has the image sent by modem directly to her Mac from the bureau.

Tips for Grayscale Scanning

Here some suggestions for getting the most from your grayscale scanner:

- Match the number of grays of your scan to the range of tones in your image—more grays for a subtle image with many tones, fewer grays for an image with high contrast. Try scanning in black-and-white (one-bit scanning) for the high-contrast halftones in books and magazines. The aim is to get the best scan the fastest while creating the smallest possible file.
- Match the dpi of your scan to the level of detail in the image—a coarse image doesn't require as much scan resolution as one with fine details. Again, you want a good scan quickly and with not too big a file.
- For scanning color originals, use the contrast and brightness settings to improve the shadings in your scan, or lay a piece of translucent orange or yellow plastic over the original before scanning. Image processing programs like *ImageStudio* can help here, too.
- Align the original squarely on the scanner bed so horizontal and vertical lines look straight and smooth in the scan. Use tape to hold the original in place if necessary; some people use Post-It™ notes for this because the glue doesn't leave a mark on the glass plate.

Graphic File Formats

The issue you'll come up against most often in moving from one presentation application to another is that of file format compatibility. There are now about half a dozen common file formats that Mac graphics programs can use, each tailored to a specific type of image and most with several versions. Unfortunately, not all programs can read and write all file formats, meaning you'll need several different types of graphics programs if you want to be able to handle every possible format (and you probably will). Here are the most popular types:

PAINT—A bitmapped format first developed for *MacPaint*, and still the most widely used for Mac graphics. Strictly black-and-white, and in most cases no bigger than the integral-video Mac screen. Most paint and presentation programs, and some draw programs, can load and save PAINT files.

PICT—The file format approved by Apple. PICT files can be bitmaps or objects, black-and-white, grayscale, or color. Most presentation programs handle PICT images, which can be scaled up and down without loss of detail.

PICT2—A new version of PICT that handles color better than color PICT. Again, there are both bitmap and object versions. Generally acceptable to presentation programs. Apple is also releasing the specifications for a 32-bit color PICT2 version.

TIFF—Tag Image File Format, the bitmap format used for scanned images. TIFF comes in black-and-white (1 bit-depth), grayscale, and color (24-bit) versions. Some presentation programs accept 1-bit and grayscale TIFFs; none accept 24-bit or 32-bit TIFFs as yet.

EPSF—Encapsulated PostScript File, used by PostScript drawing programs such as Aldus *Freehand* and Adobe *Illustrator.* EPSF images can be printed to the limits of the output device's resolution by any PostScript printer, but they are not compatible with many presentation programs or slidemakers. (Aldus *Persuasion* is one presentation program that can import EPSF files, but it does not create them.) *Illustrator* uses a proprietary EPSF format; it can't read *Freehand's* EPSF format, but *Freehand* can read *Illustrator* files.

The trick in handling the various formats is to know which applications can deal with which formats. Do you create lots of graphics with *MacPaint?* Make sure your slidemaking program can load PAINT graphics. Do you use a graphing program for data graphics (see Chapter 3)? Use one of the matched sets of charting and presentation programs, such as *Cricket Graph* and *Cricket Presents.* These, at least, are guaranteed to be compatible. If you have trouble matching format to application, there are several DAs and utility programs that can convert one format to another, with varying degrees of success, and most of the more powerful graphics applications can do some conversions as well. (Don't expect to be able to convert EPSF files to a bitmapped format, though, and get anything like PostScript image quality when you print them out.) You can always try to move a picture "manually" by copying it to the Clipboard from one application, and then pasting it into another application. Many draw programs will accept PAINT or bitmapped PICT images as clips or backgrounds (although you won't be able to edit them with draw-type tools), and can save draw images as bitmaps. No paint program can handle an object-oriented image as anything other than a bitmap, though.

Tips for Capturing the Screen

Sometimes you'll want to use screens directly from your Mac as part of your presentation. Desktop publishers need this capability all the time. You can capture any standard-size (512 × 342 pixel) Mac screen from a Mac Plus or SE to disk by pressing Command-Shift–3. This will create a PAINT picture file named "Screen 0" in the same directory that the System folder is in. You can then rename and load this file via the Clipboard into any program that accepts PAINT images, including nearly all paint, draw, presentation, page layout, and word processing programs. You can save up to ten screens in this way ("Screen 0" to "Screen 9") before you have to delete or rename some of them. Command-Shift–4 sends the screen directly to your printer instead.

Note that this screen capture feature doesn't work if you are pulling down a menu or viewing a dialog box. To include menus and dialog boxes in your picture, you should use a screenshot DA called *Camera* by Keith A. Esau. It's widely available on bulletin boards and from user groups, but only works with integral-video Macs.

Capturing screens on the Mac II is more trouble. Command-Shift–3 won't work for screens bigger than 512 × 342, or for color. Instead, you'll need a utility program like *Capture,* from Mainstay (see Appendix A). Capture allows you to select any portion of a Mac II screen and capture it to the Clipboard or as a PICT file. *Studio/8,* the color paint program from Electronic Arts, comes with a screen capture utility called ColorCam that captures any screen image as a PICT2 file.

Using Clip Art

Even if you're not much of a Macintosh graphic designer yourself, you can take advantage of the skills of top Mac artists and incorporate their work into your presentations. There are scores of Mac clip art collections, readymade pictures of nearly everything under the sun, including every type of business-related image. Most clip art collections are PAINT or PICT object files, but increasingly you can also get EPSF pictures, which look much slicker when output from a laser printer, but which won't load into many presentation programs or slidemakers. The latest wrinkles in clip art are color pictures and collections on CD-ROM.

Clip art collections vary widely in style and quality, from amateurish and whimsical, to slick and professional. Try to get a good look at samples of the art before you buy a collection (especially the ones that are sold on subscription)—not every collection will be appropriate for your use. You'll also find working with clip art a lot easier if you use Scrapbook-enhancing DAs such as *SmartScrap* and the *Clipper,* and an art indexing and cataloging program such as *Curator* (all three from Solutions Intl., see Appendix A).

While every kind of stunning graphic art is possible on the Mac, you rarely see the work of modern Raphaels displayed in presentations. Rather, it's the practical communication of charts and maps that is the meat and potatoes of presentation art. Techniques for the design of data graphics is the subject of the next chapter.

CHAPTER 3

Designing Data Graphics

You step up to give your presentation, clutching a sheaf of papers covered with little numbers. Behind you is a blank white wall. You begin to read: "Sales were down 2.3 percent and 7.6 percent in regions 6 and 8 in the third quarter of 1989, due to a $1.05 drop in thermoplastic shower cap linings and a 77-cent rise in retail prices; 99-percent fat-free wax ink supplies were off 36 percent, 23 percent, 18 percent, 67 percent, and 41 percent in the last five quarters. Profits from divisions A, D, B, C, Q, and H were $12.3 million, $13.5 million, $117 million, $9.97 million, $821 million . . ." As you look out over your audience, you see puzzled faces, glazing eyes, and a stealthy exodus from the rear seats. . . .

Many studies have shown that the ear is an ineffective organ for numerical analysis. The real meaning of large sets of numbers is hard to convey verbally. But bring the eye into play, by converting the naked numbers into *data graphics,* charts, or pictures that display quantitative information in a graphic form, and you give expression and coherence, even elegance, to the relationships among the numbers. The advantages of data graphics are many. They:

- Efficiently display the relationships among sets of data
- Draw comparisons that would be difficult to convey verbally
- Reinforce points made verbally
- Reduce the time needed to present complex information
- Ensure greater retention of information
- Capture the attention of the audience with vivid pictures

You can see one advantage of data graphics in Figures 3-1 and 3-2; the block of numbers in Figure 3-1 tells no obvious story, but lay them out in a graph, and you can see what they really mean.

Figure 3-1. Data Block

	% College Educated	% Families Below Poverty Line
ALASKA	22.4	8.6
CALIFORNIA	19.8	8.7
FLORIDA	14.7	9.9
MICHIGAN	15.2	8.2
MISSISSIPPI	13.0	18.7
NEW YORK	18.7	10.8
TENNESSEE	1.9	13.1
WYOMING	17.2	5.8

Figure 3-2. Data Graphic

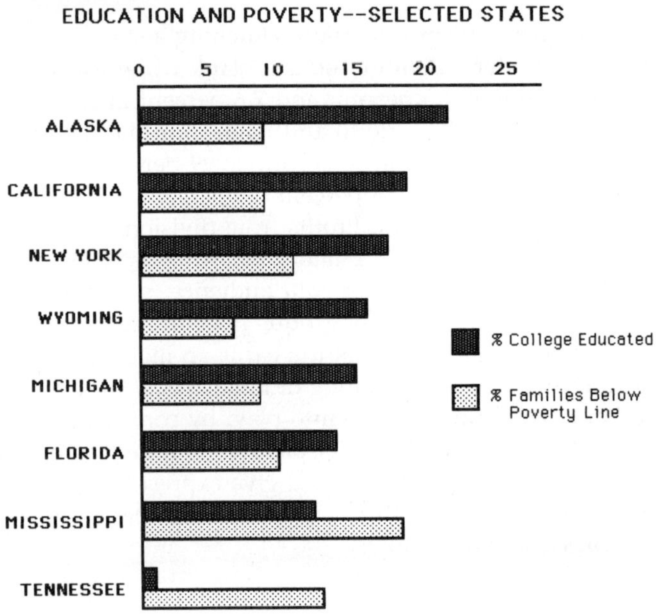

Data graphics can make clear the complex relationships among data—but only if the graphs themselves are clear and well designed. Just as it's possible (and easy) to write bad prose, it's possible to make painfully bad charts. And it is especially easy to make bad data graphics with a computer—the facility with which you can massage numbers and add graphic elements to computer-generated charts is beguiling, distracting from clear thinking about what the chart is really saying. Figure 3-3 is a bad data graphic—ugly, unclear, and unimaginative, the kind you do not want in your presentation. Can you see what's wrong with it? This chapter will review the basics of data graphic design, showing you examples of effective charts and graphs while helping you to avoid the worst mistakes.

Figure 3-3. Bad Data Graphic

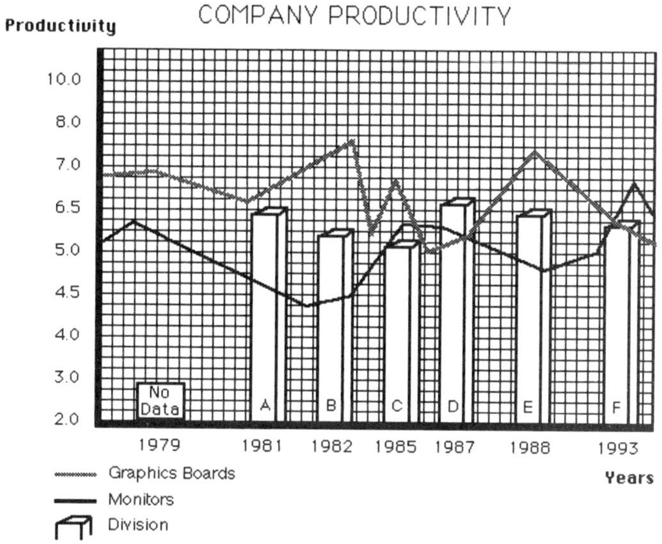

Defining Data

The most general definition of data is the information you want to convey to your audience—anything from a short sentence stating your name to a list of numbers 100 lines long. However, most people think of data as referring specifically to raw numerical or statistical information. These kinds of data form the backbone of many presentations; for example, the latest sales figures for your company's widget, or the current number of televisions per capita in Mozambique, or the resistivities at a given range of microtemperatures of selected superconductors. The purpose of a presentation is to turn the data into *information*, facts made useful, and maybe even into *wisdom*, information applied to deep understanding and effective action.

A *data point* is any single numeric value shown in a data graphic; a *data set* or *data series* is a set of related data points. A *range* is a subset of the entire data set within two limiting values. The type of data set that shows up most often in presentation graphics is the *time series*, which shows the change in a data set over time—for example, the trend of U.S. oil consumption per capita from 1972 to 1990. The time series has one *independent variable* and one or more *dependent variables.* In the example above, oil consumption per capita is the dependent variable, since the amount of consumption depends on the year, while the year is the independent variable, since the date and year progress at a fixed rate regardless of the amount of oil consumption. A data graphic charting many dependent variables is *multivariate,* although for simplicity's sake the typical presentation graphic is likely to show no more than two dependent variables (a *bivariate graphic).*

Another way of talking about multivariate data is in terms of how many dimensions the data has. A simple time series has two dimensions, and can be completely described with a chart on a 2-D grid. A multivariate data set may have three or more dimensions, and may need a 3-D chart or several 2-D charts to fully describe it.

Chart Parts

A data graphic, like the page of a book, is composed of standard elements. Figure 3-4 is a typical, plain-vanilla data graphic, with the main parts labeled.

Figure 3-4. Chart Parts

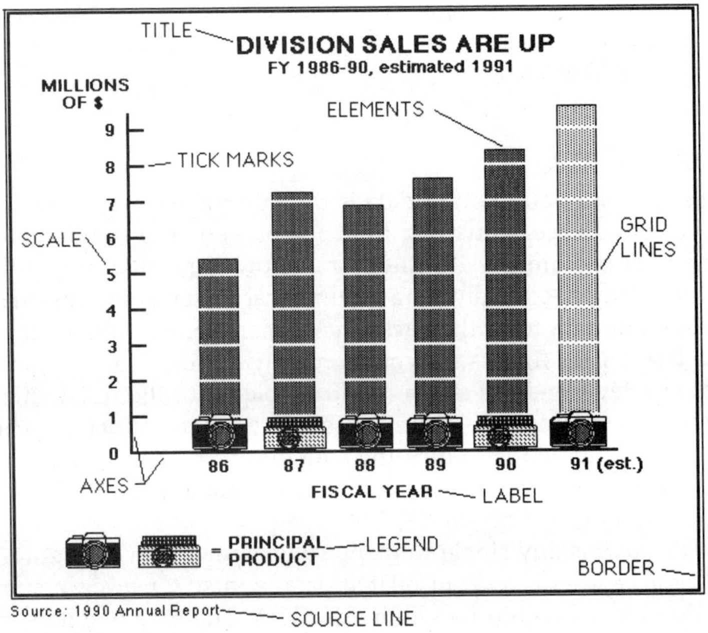

The *title and subtitle* tell your audience what the graph is about, and often summarize the conclusion you want them to draw from the data.

It makes sense to name a chart "Sales Up 34 Percent, FY 190–91" or "Sixty Variable Stars That May Orbit Black Holes."

The *axes* are the main vertical and horizontal frames for the display of data, corresponding to the *x*- and *y*-axes of the Cartesian coordinate system. Axes are usually employed to name the divisions of the data set and show the measurements applied to the data—in Figure 3-4, years along the bottom, and millions of dollars along the left side. The horizontal axis is often reserved for showing the range of values of the independent variable—the month and year in a time series, for example—and the vertical axis for the range of values of the dependent variable. Three-dimensional graphics may have three axes—an *x*-, *y*-, and *z*-axis—for showing multivariate data sets.

The *scales* along each axis show how the data is measured. Scales are usually arithmetical—a simple progression of values, as in the *y*-axis of Figure 3-4—but it's also possible to use logarithmic scales (scales that show a rate of change in the spacing of scale values) when called for, but business graphics rarely call for them. Most scales start with 0 at the lower left corner of the chart, where the *x*- and *y*-axes meet. You can start scales at some other minimum value, but be aware that this may change the look of the chart in ways that may not be desirable—by making changes in values look more volatile than they really are, for example.

A *tick mark* is a small mark on an axis that indicates the division of a the axis into evenly spaced values (10 units, 20 units, and so on). The tick mark may also show the actual position of a data value on the axis.

The field enclosed by the axes is often marked with a *grid* to help your eye read the position of the data elements. Sometimes only the horizontal or vertical lines of the grid are used, and many data graphics are easier to read with no grid lines at all.

Elements are the parts of the chart that actually indicate the data—in this case, bars and lines. Elements can be points, bars, sections of circles, little pictures, or any other pictorial object that efficiently shows the data.

A *trend line* in a graph extrapolates beyond the known data to indicate a trend or anticipated performance—expected profits for the coming year, for example.

Labels identify what variables the graph is measuring. Traditionally, the left and bottom sides of the chart are labeled, and the top and right sides of the chart are not, probably to make it easier for western readers accustomed to text that proceeds from left to right and top to bottom, but you may find good reasons to break this tradition. A *legend* describes any special symbols or colors the graph may employ; these are commonly found in map graphics. A *footnote* adds explanations of measures used or other special information not obvious from the chart itself. The *source line* or *credit line* tells where you got the data. This should include a copyright notice if the format of the data is copyrighted, or if the chart is taken directly from a copyrighted source, such as a book.

A *border* defines the size and limits of the graphics, and sets it off from accompanying material.

Types of Data Graphics

Charts and graphs come in a bewildering number of types and graphic styles, but most belong to one of a few basic families. These include:

- *Bullet or Text Charts.* These are simply bulleted text lists of important points to remember. The majority of slides and transparencies are of this type (Figure 3-5). Creation of these is basically a matter of laying out sentences and headings on a nondistracting background.

Figure 3-5. Bullet Chart

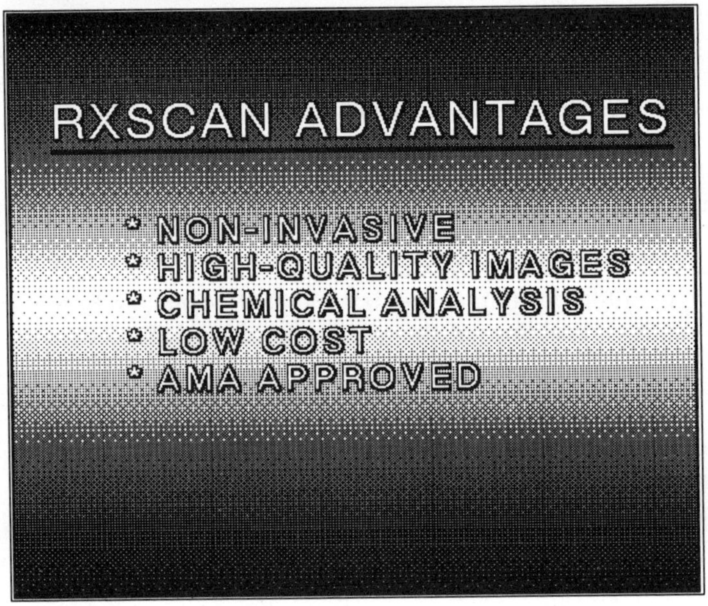

• *Bar and Column Charts.* These are popular chart types that use the length of bars to represent changes in a dependent variable over an independent variable—usually time. For example, a bar chart could show corporate income growth over a five-year period (Figure 3-6). Bars can be shown vertically or horizontally. Bar charts with vertical bars are sometimes called column charts. Charts with horizontal bars provide more room for bar labels, and can be easier to read when there are more than 5 or 6 bars (Figure 3-7). To show the progress of multiple variables, you can stack bars in different colors or patterns.

Figure 3-6. Bar Chart 1

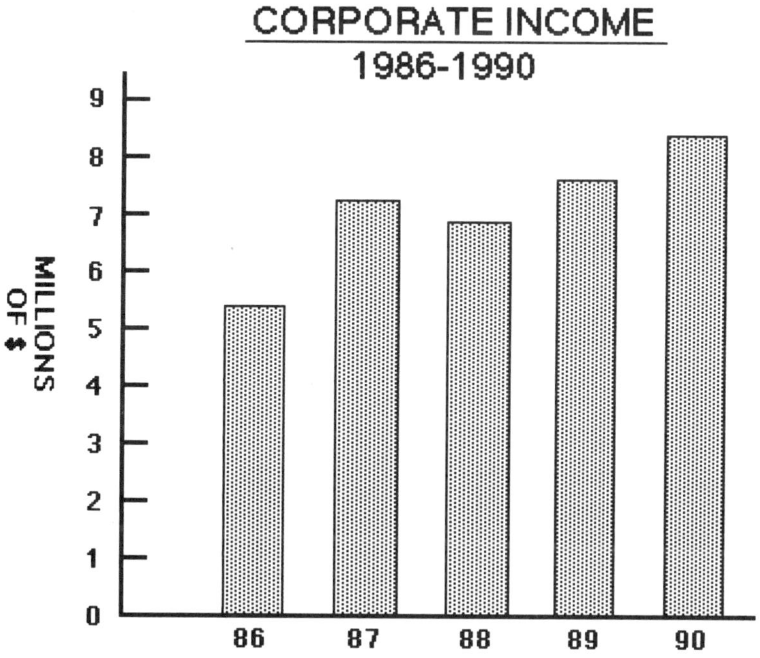

Figure 3-7. Bar Chart 2

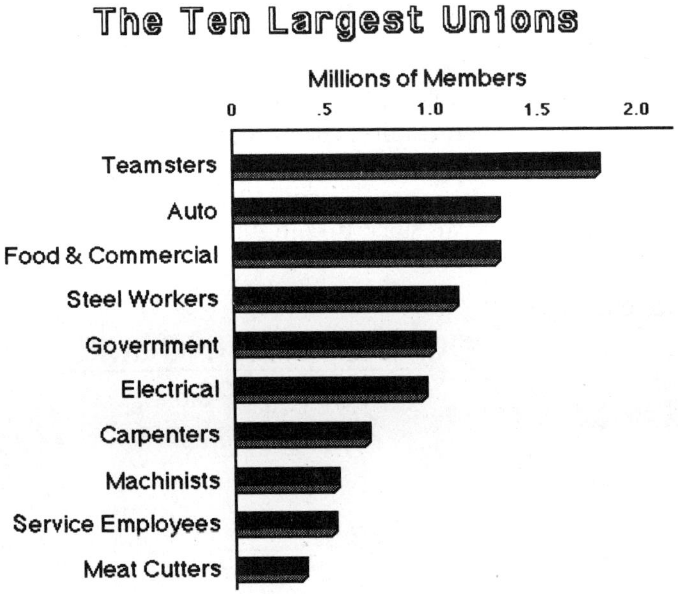

- *Pie Chart.* A pie chart shows the parts of a whole as sections of a circle, or slices of a pie (Figure 3-8). This is a good way to show percentages, for example, of sales by region. Each section should have its own color or pattern and label; one slice can be pulled out for special attention. Pie charts, while easy to make and understand, have a low density of information, and don't work well when you have more than a few parts to the whole. (It's hard to accurately judge the relative sizes of thin slices of pie). And, of course, a pie chart can only show the parts of one whole at a time. Use pie charts in small multiples to show the divisions of several wholes.

Figure 3-8. Pie Chart

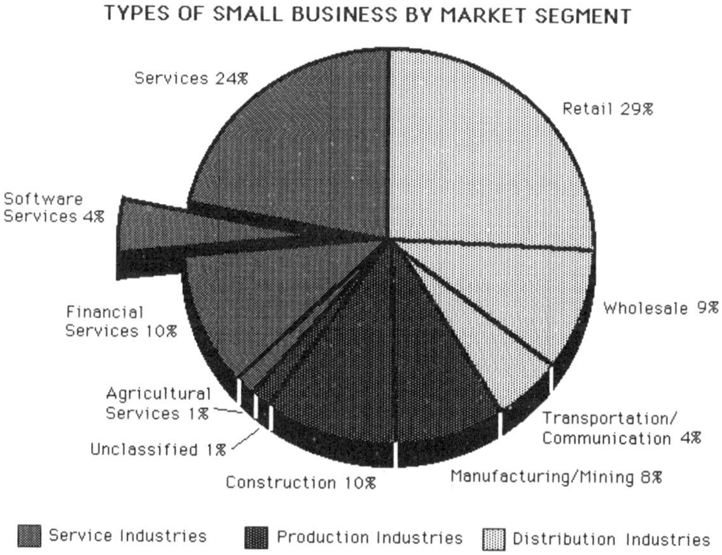

- *Line Graph.* This shows the progress of a dependent variable over an independent variable, usually time, with the rises and dips in the line indicating changes in value. Bar charts can also be used for these types of data sets, but line graphs are better for showing a data set without discrete breaks. As in Figure 3-9, more than one variable can be plotted on a single graph, each with its own line.

Figure 3-9. Line Graph

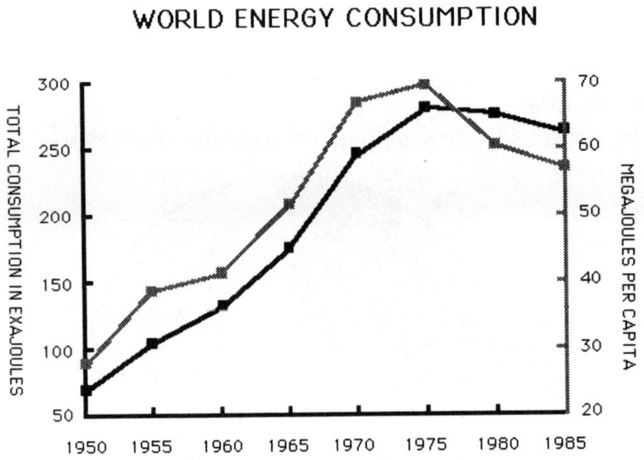

- *Area Graph.* Area graphs express quantity in terms of the area of bars or other elements (Figure 3-10). Most often, a line chart is converted to an area graph by simply filling in the area enclosed by the line; the intention is to make it easier to see the percent of a total area or quantity bounded by the data set that defines the line, or the relative sizes of areas bounded by several data sets.

Figure 3-10. Area Graph

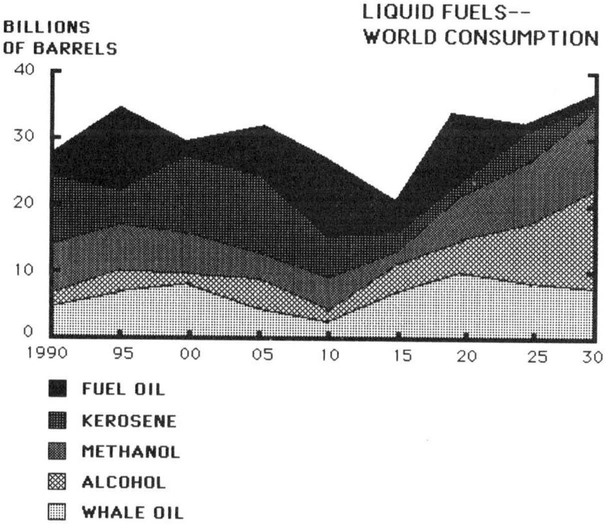

- *Scatter Graph, Scatterplot, Dot Chart, or X-Y Chart*. These display the relationship of two or more dependent variables as measured by values on the *x*- and *y*-axes (Figure 3-11). Values are plotted as sets of unconnected dots, with the positions of the dots telling the story of the data. Randomly scattered dots indicate no strong correlation between the variables measured along each axis; dots that form a pattern or trend indicate a strong correlation between the variables. A line drawn through the dot pattern can clarify the trend. As with other chart types, multiple sets of data can be plotted on one graph; you can use different symbols for each data set; as long as these are clearly identified in a legend or table. Scatter graphs are most often used to present scientific or statistical data.

Figure 3-11. Scatter Graph

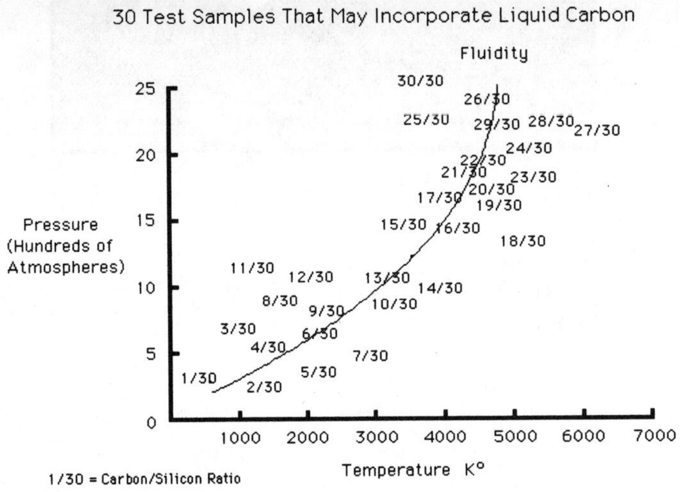

- *High-Low Chart.* This is a variation of the bar chart that shows high and low values of a variable over time (Figure 3-12). High-low charts are most often used in stock market analyses to show the high and low selling prices of a single stock.

Figure 3-12. High-Low Chart

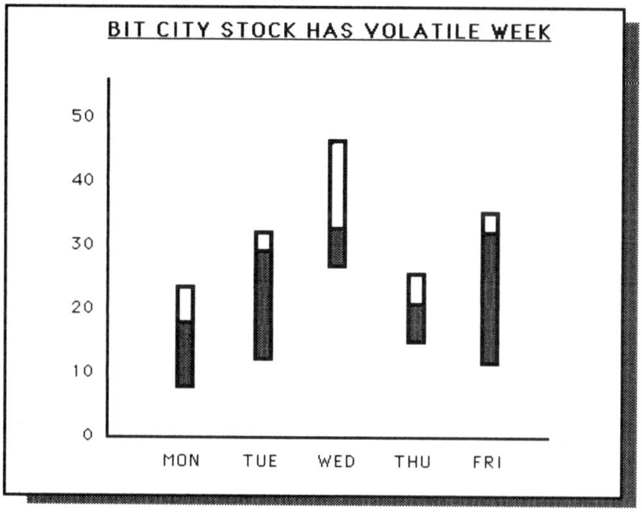

- *Flow Charts and Tree Charts.* These show processes and hierarchies rather than sets of data. A flow chart delineates the stages and structure of a system, such as the movement of emissions, gases, and particles in the atmosphere (Figure 3-13). A tree chart, also called an organization chart, diagrams a branching hierarchy. The classic example is the power structure of a typical corporation (Figure 3-14).

Figure 3-13. Flow Chart

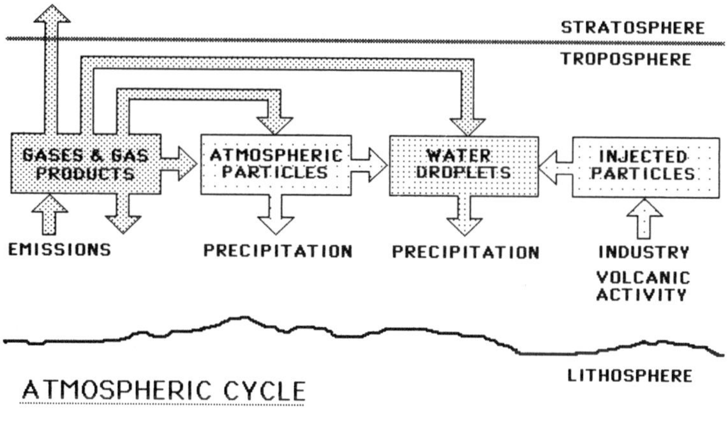

Figure 3-14. Tree Chart

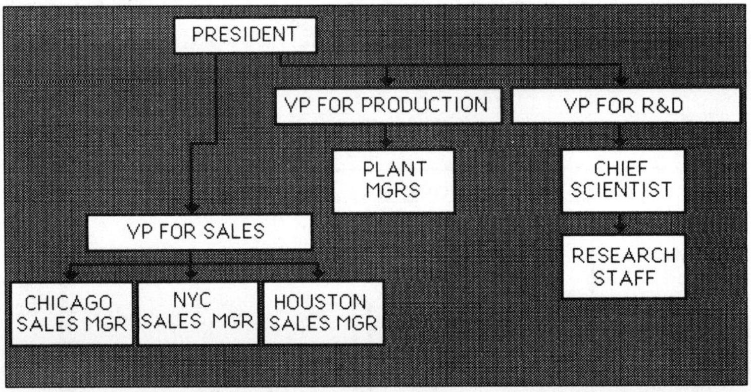

- *Pictographs.* This specialized type of data graphic uses pictograms, visual symbols that identify a theme or idea, to convey quantities or trends. In Figure 3-15, the lines of glowing "bright idea" lightbulbs form bars that graph company sales, as well as symbolize the product being sold.

Figure 3-15. Pictograph

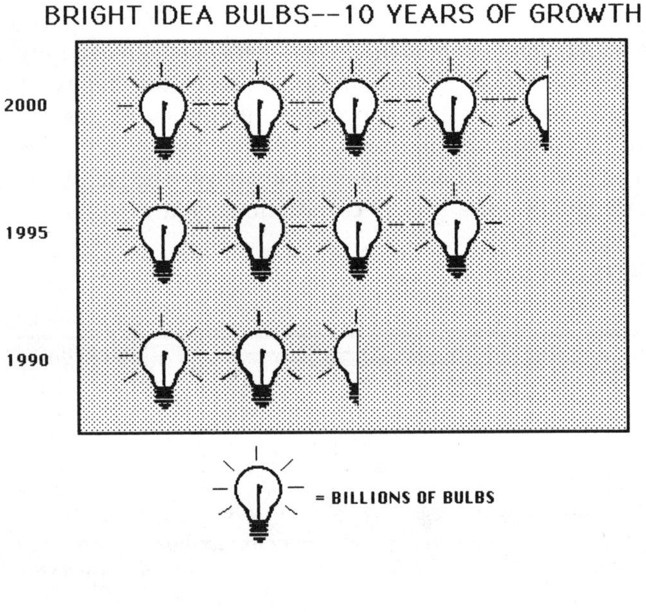

- *Data Maps.* Maps, the oldest form of data graphics, are always multivariate, and on average contain the most data per unit of graphic area of any graphic type. Unless you're a trained cartographer, you'll want to use one of the many collections of map clip art available for the Mac, and overlay your data on them. Applications such as *MapMaker* (Select Micro Systems, see Appendix A) provide the tools to create your own custom maps based on demographic or other geographic information.
- *3-D Charts.* The latest design trend in data graphics is 3-D—drawing a chart to make it look like it exists in three-dimensional space. An increasing number of presentation spreadsheets and number-crunching programs offer some variety of 3-D charting (Figure 3-16). While "3-D-ification" makes for eyecatching graphics, it rarely makes a chart easier to understand. Usually there is less overall room for information in a 3-D chart, and the impact of the data is overwhelmed by the special effects. When you have multivariate data to present, however, a 3-D effect may be the best way to go (see below).

Figure 3-16. 3-D Chart

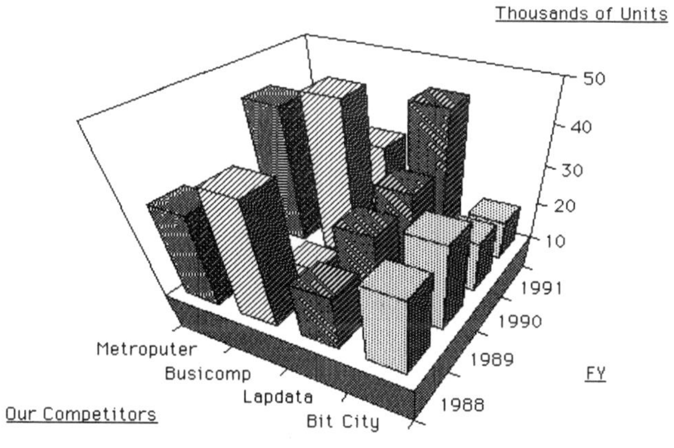

BITBOX SALES--4 YEARS OF COMPETITION

- *Surface Graph.* A surface graph (Figure 3-17) presents multivariate data in a topographical 3-D format. The most common use for surface graphs is to plot geography—the latitude, longitude, and elevation of regularly spaced points on a mountain range, for example. But any multivariate data can be plotted on a surface graph; you could just as effectively plot the color, distance, and absolute magnitude of stars in a star cluster.

Figure 3-17. Surface Graph

- *Small Multiples.* These are not strictly a separate type of graph, but rather a series of similar data graphics that, taken together, describe a larger event or trend (Figure 3-18). Small multiples are useful for showing different aspects of a large data set—each individual chart in the small multiple could be devoted to one or two variables in multivariate data—or efficiently comparing a number of small data sets with related variables.

Figure 3-18. Small Multiple

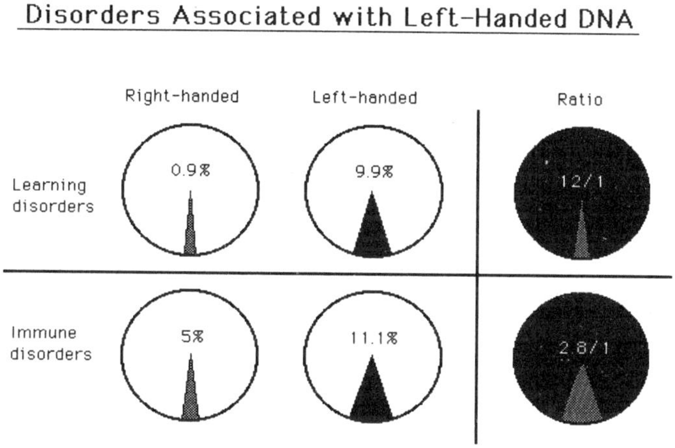

Choosing the Right Graphic

To choose the best chart from the types available, you need to have a good grasp of the message you want to convey to your audience, and an understanding of what kinds of data comparisons your graphic has to make to send that message.

The primary step is to decide what message your data graphics should present. There's always a story in the data, but it's up to you to find it and tell it properly, just as an artist looks at the immense complexities of the visible world and makes a coherent painting from them. Ask yourself:

- What kinds of data should be compared—profits by division, or total profits per quarter, or profits vs. return on investment?
- What trend(s) do the data show?
- What information is your audience most eager to learn?

It helps to write down the message in a short sentence—this can even become the title of the graphic, as in Figure 3-19, "Jupiter Is the

Largest Planet." It's not likely that your audience will miss the message then.

Figure 3-19. Jupiter Is the Largest Planet

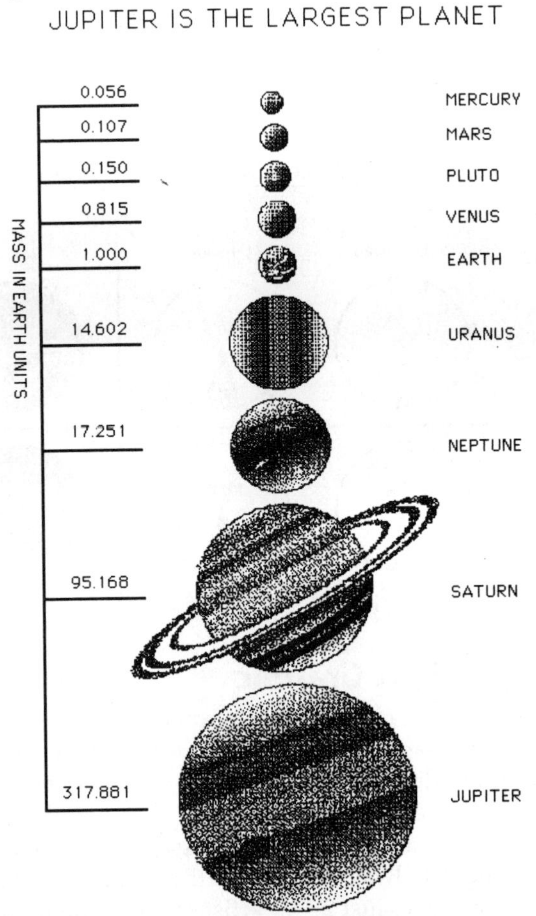

The essential facts supporting your message are the ones that should jump out of your graphic and hit the audience hard. There are a number of ways to achieve this:

- Put the big facts in bigger type
- Prune away unimportant data
- Color the essential chart elements with bright colors
- Add labels that emphasize the important data
- Give the main idea pride of place at the beginning or end of the chart.

Figure 3-19 uses several of these methods. The picture of Jupiter is bigger; it is clearly labeled; and the title tells you what the message is. This is a relatively simple graphic, but most effective presentation graphics are simple; graphic complexities are lost on an audience that may be seeing a slide or overhead for just a minute or two.

The data comparisons you are making will also help determine the chart type. Not every graphic is suited to every kind of data set. A pie chart, for example, can't effectively show lots of small values or multivariate data sets. On the other hand, a pie chart is perfect for comparing a few parts to a whole. If you are comparing changes to time (a time series), a bar or line graphic should be the choice. Column and bar charts also effectively compare ranges, frequencies, and distributions of values. Scatter or dot charts show the correlation between two variables. Table 3-1 lists the appropriate charts for various kinds of data.

Table 3-1. Choosing the Right Graphic

Data Characteristic	Chart Type
Continuous	Line graph
Discontinuous	Bar chart, column chart
Bivariate	Scatter graph
Multivariate	Stacked bar chart, surface graph, small multiple
Small data set	Bar chart, pie chart, pictograph, text or bullet chart
Large data set	Small multiple, data map, scatter graph, surface graph
Percentage	Pie chart, area chart
Ratio	Pie chart, area chart
Correlation	Scatter graph
Distribution	Line graph, bar chart
Frequency	Scatter graph, bar chart
Growth or Decline	Line graph, bar chart
Item list	Text or bullet chart
Process	Flow chart
Ranking	Bar chart, column chart
Structure	Organization chart
Time series	Line graph, bar chart
Upper and lower limited values	Hi-low chart
Demographic	Data map, text table
Geographic	Data map
Statistical	Scatter graph, line graph, surface graph

Before you take your graphic out on the podium, stand back and take a good look at it, or better yet, have someone else criticize it. Does the message stand out? Does the viewer immediately get the point? How could the graphic be simplified? Is there another approach that would work better? Hard questions will result in clearer graphics.

Tips on Using Tables

In some cases, a table will serve to present your data better than a data graphic. Use tables when:

- Dealing with a small data set.
- Emphasizing the numbers themselves rather than the trend they show.
- Titles, labels, and notes are too long to fit in a chart.

Give graphic emphasis to tables by:

- Using different text styles (boldface, underline), fonts, and colors to pull out labels and important data.
- Using horizontal and vertical lines to divide columns and rows, or shading columns or rows in different colors.
- Drawing a frame around the table or superimposing the table over a colored block to separate it from surrounding materials.

Data Graphic Esthetics

The bane of any presentation is graphics that are ugly, confusing, or just plain boring. Most presentation programs and charting spreadsheets (see below) try to make it hard to create ugly charts by offering chart templates, each designed by a professional, and a selection of familiar fonts that work well together. But presenters still seem to be able to make good data look bad, especially when it's necessary to venture beyond the usual chart types and design data graphics from scratch.

The Visual Display of Quantitative Information (Graphics Press, Box 430, Cheshire, CT 06410) by Edward R. Tufte, a professor of political science and statistics at Yale University, is widely recognized as the Strunk and White of data graphic design. Tufte, who has thought long and fruitfully about the presentation of data, identifies several cardinal principles of chart aesthetics:

- *Data Density*. This is the total amount of data per area of the data graphic. Charts with a high data density—lots of information relative to the size and design of the chart—are more communicative than low-data-density graphics with a few small pieces of information lost amid the grids, lines, bars, and tick marks. Tufte recommends the use of tables over graphics for presenting small amounts of data, and the use of small multiples (see above) for high-density presentation of similar data series in a compact space.

- *Data Ink.* Related to data-density, this is the amount of ink (or the number of pixels, in computer displays) devoted to actually carrying the information in a data graphic. The best data graphics have the highest ratio of data ink—they use the least ink to convey the most information. Ink not devoted to telling the story of the data should be minimized or eliminated; that usually means editing out unnecessary tick marks, axis lines, grids, labels, and any other marks that distract from the data. On the other hand, data graphics don't have to be spare and severe, as can be seen from the many beautiful examples in Tufte's book—merely uncluttered and efficient. As Tufte notes, "For non-data-ink, less is more; for data-ink, less is a bore."
- *Chartjunk.* Chartjunk is extraneous, ugly, and deceptive visual material added to data graphics. The decorations favored by chartjunk addicts include multiple types and styles of fonts, fill patterns that vibrate, background grid patterns, confusing pictograms, and random use of color (see Figure 3-20 for an example). On the Mac, data-graphic designers are especially tempted to use chartjunk, because the computer makes it so easy to add one more pattern or typeface. In some cases, the use of chartjunk grows out of lack of confidence in the data itself; the designer tries to make meager or wrongheaded data look more impressive with distracting visual business. But that rarely works with intelligent audiences, and never improves the data.

Figure 3-20. Chartjunk

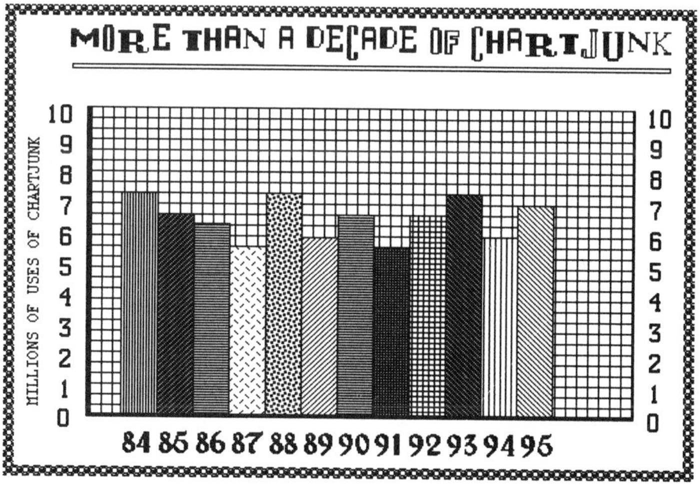

- *Graphical Integrity.* Tufte puts the utmost emphasis on truthful presentation of data. That means, first of all, understanding what the data mean, and then finding an honest way of presenting them. Graphic embellishments, such as showing simple bar charts in three dimensions, or using pictograms without attention to the relative scale of the pictures, are common (and usually unintentional) ways of distorting data (Figure 3-21, for example). The small pictogram is supposed to represent a value half that of the largest one. But the area of the large pictogram is not twice as large, but four times the area of the smallest. In this case, portraying one-dimensional data (the change in a single variable) in two dimensions (the area of a pictogram) results in a chart without graphical integrity. Tufte opposes the arbitrary puffing-up of two-dimensional charts to three-dimensional, a trendy practice in computer-generated graphics; the three-dimensional look adds no information and confuses the data.

Figure 3-21. Deceptive Data Graphic

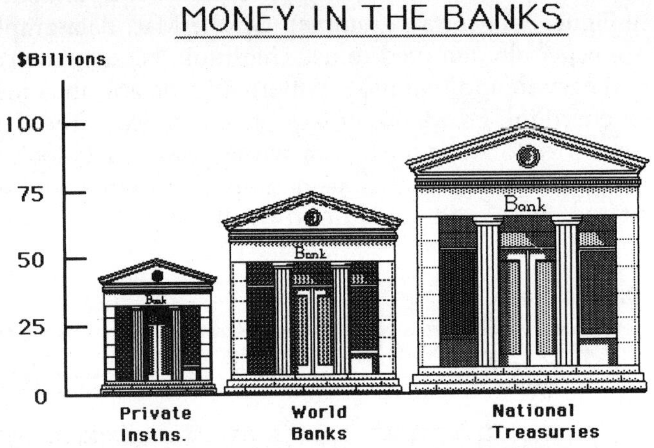

Tips for Data Graphic Design

Here are some additional guidelines to follow when designing data graphics:

- Get the data right, and make sure you understand the relationship between data sets. If you don't, neither will the viewer.
- Give the sources for all your information.
- Include only the data you need; delete extraneous information. But don't hide facts that contradict your point; someone else is bound to bring them up during your presentation and challenge your interpretation.
- For slide or overhead presentation, create charts with roughly half the information you would put into a chart for a printed report.
- Don't mix several chart types in one graphic. A line graph superim-

posed over a bar chart will be too hard for the audience to read. Use two separate graphics instead. Printed charts can be somewhat more complex than graphics for slides or overheads, since they can be studied at leisure and up close.

- Likewise, use the fewest text styles, colors, and symbolic elements that will get your message across.
- Be sure the scales you've chosen for your data reflect the real proportions of the data, and that comparable charts use comparable scales. Start scales at 0 unless there's a very good reason to do otherwise. Avoid using split scales or multiple scales in one data graphic; use separate charts instead.
- Use labels wherever necessary; spell out words and place them near what they describe. But use as few words as possible; avoid graphics that look like tables, and keep footnotes to a minimum.
- Use as few charts as possible. This makes each chart more memorable to your audience, and cuts down on the amount of design work for you.
- Avoid data theatrics. Humor and surprise elements may add zest to your presentation performance, but are likely to detract from the data. Tell the data story plain, and leave the surprises for your opening and closing remarks. Resist the temptation to use cute pictographs.

Using a Presentation Spreadsheet

The computer spreadsheet is the second most useful business software (after word processors). Spreadsheets generate most of the data that will be turned into business data graphics. So, logically, all Mac spreadsheets (and many databases) include basic charting and graphing capabilities. You enter the numbers, and the package automatically creates the type of graphic you've chosen from a menu. Dump the graph to a printer or slidemaker, and you've got presentation graphics untouched by human hands. Usually, however, the spreadsheet chart is bland and uninspiring, and it may not show the data the way you want them to be shown.

The recent crop of Mac number-crunchers, notably Informix's *Wingz* (see Appendix A), are expressly oriented toward data graphic production and presentation. *Wingz,* which bills itself as the first *presentation spreadsheet,* can produce quite sophisticated data graphics, featuring 3-D graphs, multicolor graphics, pictographs, surface graphs, integrated charts and text, and more. Since *Wingz* also creates the basic charts that presenters use most often, you may be able to make all the data graphics you need with it.

The *Wingz* spreadsheet interface (Figure 3-22) sports features that make charting a snap.

Figure 3-22. *Wingz* Interface

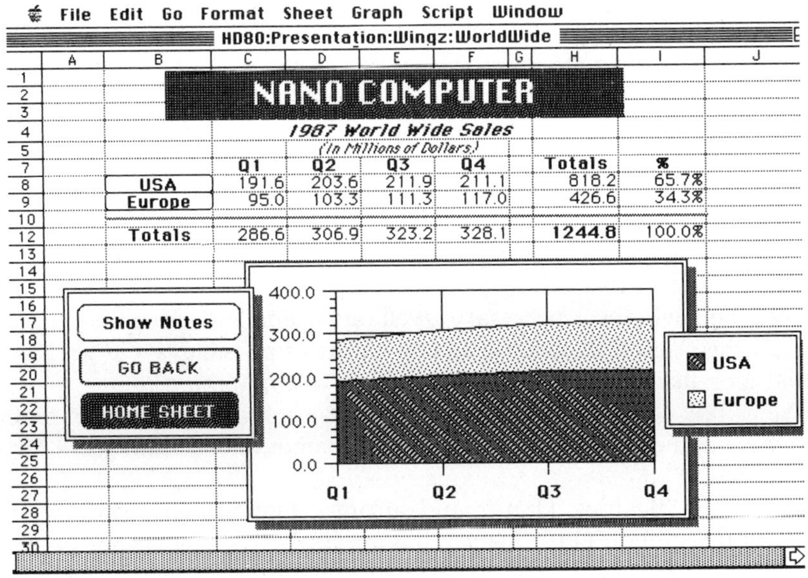

Here's how to make a column chart with several variables (Figure 3-23):

1. Enter the data set for your chart (in this case, the marriage and divorce rates for the New England states) in the spreadsheet. The organization of data in the spreadsheet will determine the look of the chart—which axes show which variables, and so on. You can enter labels for each state at the top of the columns, and labels for the type of data (marriages, divorces) in the first cell of each row. (Or vice versa; *Wingz* lets you plot data horizontally or vertically).
2. Select the cells you want to include in the chart by dragging over them with the worksheet tool (the hollow cross).
3. Choose the chart tool from the toolbox at the left of the screen.
4. Draw a box with the crosshairs over the chart data. A bar chart, complete with legends and labels, is created (a bar chart is the default chart type). Grab a corner of the chart and drag it until it is the right size and proportions.
5. In this case, we want a column chart. From the Graph menu, choose Gallery and then Horizontal Bar. The chart instantly changes to the chosen type (as in Figure 3-23). You can also try 19 other chart types, which include pie, scatter, area, stacked, and 3-D graphs, but most of them don't make sense with the example data set.

Figure 3-23. *Wingz* Column Chart

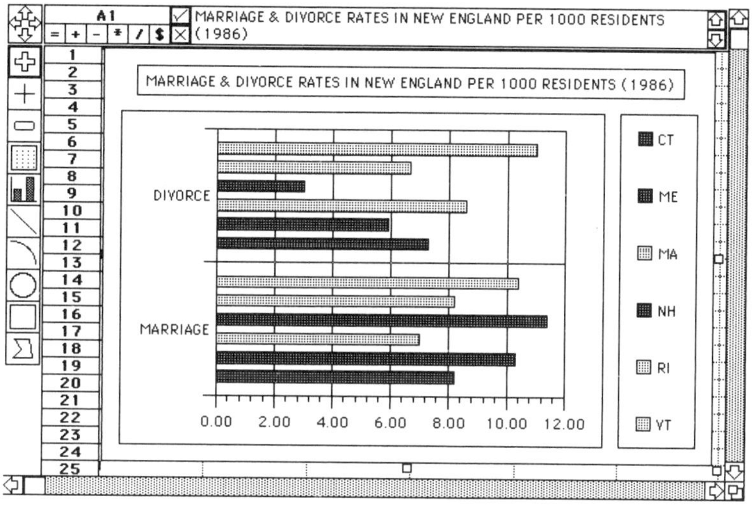

6. Charts can be edited after creation. Turn off Automatic Layout in the General submenu of the Graph menu, and you can select portions of the graph for color and pattern changes, altering labels and titles, moving the legend, modifying the look of axes, grids, and tick marks, deleting unwanted data series, and so on. For example, you might want to emphasize the state with the highest marriage rate by adding a label or changing the state's color.
7. To add a title to the graph, type the title text into any range of cells, and select them. You can alter the font, text style, and text size with menu options. Then choose the Object tool, click on the chart while pressing the Command key, and choose Title Range from the Title submenu in the Graph menu. Add footnotes and axis labels to the chart with a similar technique.

Wingz's printing options allow charts and spreadsheet data to be printed on the same page; you can also add blocks of text, draw graphics, titles, headers, footers, and borders. In short, you can print full-featured slides, overheads, and paper reports without leaving the program. *Wingz*'s programming language, HyperScript (a full description of HyperScript is beyond the scope of this book) gives you *HyperCard*-like powers to create interactive presentations on the Mac screen. The *Wingz* introductory disk provides several good examples. Using HyperScript, it's even possible to create *Wingz* slideshows, although not as easily as with a presentation program.

To export *Wingz* graphics to other programs, your best bet is to copy the chart to the Clipboard or Scrapbook, or grab the screen with

Command-Shift–3 (for Mac Pluses and SEs) or a screen capture utility (see Chapter 2). *Wingz* charts can then be loaded into any program that accepts PICT or PICT2 files, such as *Studio/8* (see Chapter 2) or *Persuasion* (see Chapter 4). Jane at ScanTech uses this technique to create animated 3-D charts of NMR scans, portrayed as surface graphs. She creates the chart, and then uses the 3-D rotation dialog (Figure 3-24) to move the chart incrementally. Sliders allow rotation around the horizontal or vertical axis, while numerical settings permit zooming toward and away from the graphs, as well as adjustments to perspective. Each view of the graph is saved to the Scrapbook as a separate picture, then imported into MacroMind's animation program, *Director* (see Appendix A). With *Director,* she can play back the pictures in sequence quickly enough to create the illusion of smooth motion. (For more on *Director* and Mac animation, see Chapter 7.) Audiences are always impressed by rotating surface graphs and the like, and Jane uses them to good effect in her presentations. (One note: Color animations created this way require large amounts of RAM and hard disk storage.)

Figure 3-24. *Wingz* 3-D Rotation Dialog

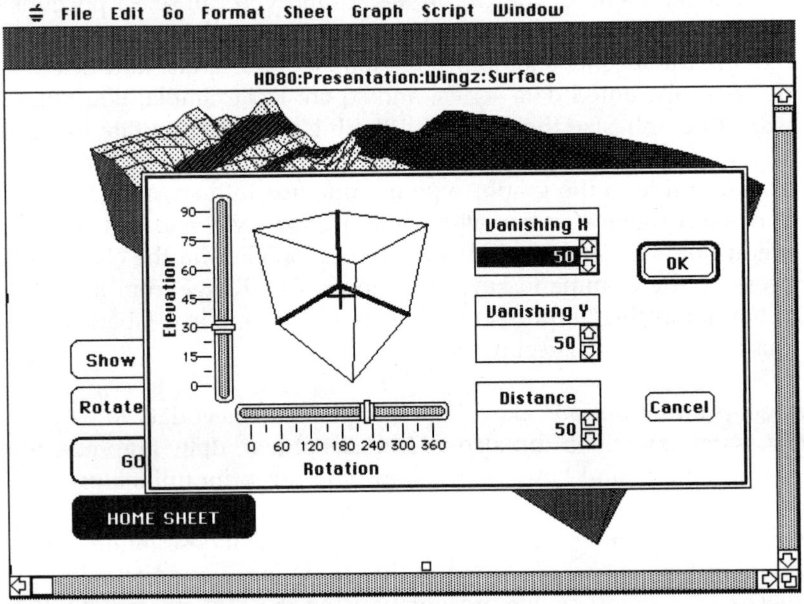

With your hardware, pictures, charts, and graphs in hand, you're ready to actually put on the show. And it is a show, because a live presentation resembles nothing so much as a theatrical performance. While no one expects you to have the stage presence of a trained actor, there are some things you can do to put across your ideas more forcefully when giving a Mac slideshow or overhead presentation. These are discussed in the next chapter.

CHAPTER 4
Slideshow and Overhead Presentations

Slideshows and overhead presentations are the two most popular presentation formats. They are relatively easy to design, don't need to involve expensive hardware, and are very portable. Chances are, you'll be using your Mac more often to make slides and transparencies than to run a show on the Mac screen. The following discussion will demonstrate how to craft effective slides and transparencies, but it also covers the soup-to-nuts detail involved in organizing, designing, and producing the materials for any complete presentation—including what's required of you, the presenter, as a performer on stage. As the manuals of most presentation programs insist, anyone can deliver a dead-on presentation that's lively and compelling—but that's only if

- the presenter is well prepared and self-confident
- the material is well organized
- visual aids are on target

This chapter will show you how to meet those goals.

Planning the Presentation

Without adequate planning, none of above conditions—prepared presenter, organized material, and effective visual aids—are likely to be met. In fact, it's just not possible to put too much effort into planning and preparing your presentation. Start the planning process by asking yourself some basic questions:

What information are you trying to convey? Before you can get your message out to other people, you've got to be sure you know what that message is. And since your message is based in information, you must have the data down cold. Study the numbers; analyze the trends; gather related data; discuss your findings with others, including some people who won't agree with you. Once you've found the real news in the data, discard all information that doesn't apply.

What's the message of your presentation? Try to sum up the point of the show in a short declarative sentence, like "1990 statistics show the scanner market poised for explosive growth," or "Global political trends point to the end of history." That sentence should be able to stand as the title of your presentation. If you can't get the concept down in one sentence, your message needs more refinement.

Who is the audience? A little research here can go a long way—you don't want to deliver the right message to the wrong crowd. What mix of people will likely be in the audience—executives, professionals, students? What do they already know about your topic? How much more background do your need to provide? What do you need to tell them to bring your message home? What kind of presentation style—formal or familiar—will the audience expect? The answers to these questions will determine the level, style, and content of your presentation.

What are the organizational requirements? At the same time you are determining the needs of your audience, you should consider the requirements of your organization. What's your corporate style and culture, and does your presentation design match it? A conservative presentation best suits a conservative organization; a presentation with flair, originality, and even outrageousness may work well for a entrepreneurial company trying to make its mark. Larger organizations may have presentation guidelines already established. Also note if your organization already uses certain design elements in advertising and corporate publishing—a logo, a unique typeface, and so on—and find out if you should use these elements in your presentation, too.

What presentation format best suits audience, organization, information, and budget? At this point you've got to choose what kind of presentation will communicate your ideas to the audience most effectively. A small, tight-knit group responds well to an overhead presentation. A larger group in a more formal setting is best approached with a slideshow. If you've done your audience research, you'll know what kind of presentation to use. Likewise, deciding what presentation format fits your organization is mostly a matter of noting what other presenters use, and doing what the successful ones do. If you want to break the mold by trying a new or different format, just make sure you and your presentation are honed to razor sharpness at show time.

Generally, both overheads and slides can present the same kinds of information. Slides have the advantage of a higher-quality color image, so if you'll be showing detailed color graphics, slides are the best choice. Overhead transparencies can be drawn on as you show them, so they are better for information that will be developed and discussed with the audience—for example, in a classroom.

Finally, slides are quite a bit more expensive to create and duplicate than transparencies, which can be printed on any Mac printer and copied on an office copier. Choose an overhead presentation if your budget's tight and the information will only be valid for a short time. If you plan to show the same presentation many times, though, slides last longer and withstand more abuse, so they may ultimately be less expensive.

Your presentation may need to go beyond slideshows or overhead projection to other approaches—video, animation, interactivity, and so on. See the following chapters for more.

Organizing the Presentation

It may seem like a hopeless task to take your undifferentiated mass of market research and presentation data and distill it into a structure of crystalline beauty and wisdom. But you have to start somewhere. Begin by breaking down your material into smaller chunks, and arrange them in some logical order. You'll find yourself automatically organizing the flow of information so it has a beginning, middle, and end—in other words, a narrative.

- The first part of your presentation should introduce the topic and provide any needed background.
- In the middle part, you develop your own arguments, based on the information you've assembled, and deliver your main message.
- The end of the presentation recaps the main points, reinforces your conclusions, and invites feedback from the audience.

Outlining. Getting the main narrative direction right is relatively easy—it's organizing all the fine details that can be troublesome. At this point you'll need to draw up a detailed outline, and that's where presentation software can be a big help. Most presentation programs have an integrated outliner that not only provides a place for you to develop your presentation's narrative, but also turns the material in the outline into slides or transparencies. (From now on, when talking about both slides and transparencies, we'll call them *frames*).

In this chapter, we'll take a look at the outlining and design capabilities of two capable presentation programs, Aldus's *Persuasion* and Microsoft's *PowerPoint* (see Appendix A). In the *Persuasion* approach, outlining is considered the primary task of presentation development, so you start off in the outlining module. The indention of headings denotes whether a line is the title of a new slide, a subhead, or a series of bulleted phrases. An outline that Jane at ScanTech uses for a slide presentation on the technical features of the RxScan is shown in Figure 4-1. Lines are automatically numbered, and new frames are marked by a little slide icon at left. Parts of the outline can be cut and pasted, copied and shifted around in the usual Macintosh way, at any point in the development of the presentation, so you have the flexibility to change your mind as needed. Outlines can also be imported from stand-alone outliners, such as Acta.

Figure 4-1. Persuasion Outliner

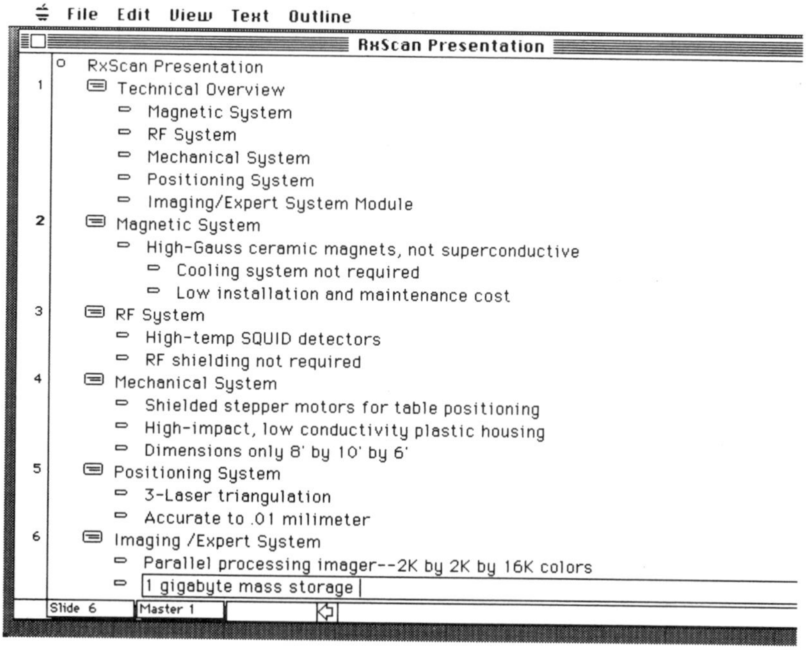

Tips for Outlining

Some guidelines to keep in mind when preparing an outline are:

- Use one concept per frame. Break down complex ideas into several frames.
- Don't overload your audience with too many frames. Pare the outline down to the minimum number of graphics required to reinforce your verbal message. That saves you time, too.
- Restrict yourself to two or three subhead levels—the fewer, the better.
- Use no more than seven bulleted lines per frame, and no more than seven words per line.
- For variety, alternate text-only frames with charts or illustrations.

- Proofread your outline carefully. Cut away unnecessary words—say them directly to your audience instead.
- Read the outline out loud and time the reading to get a sense of how long your presentation will be. At the same time, listen for the logical flow of ideas—sometimes your ears will notice problems that your eyes miss.

Master Frames. Once the outline is established, you've got to do the hard work of presentation design—figuring out the specifications of all the graphic elements, including color scheme, fonts, type placement, background, logos, pictures, and scans, and where they'll go on the frames. To give a consistent, unified look to your presentation, it's best to establish a master design or template that applies to every frame, and then arrange elements unique to each frame "on top" of the master design. For example, frames should all share the same background color, pattern, or border, the same fonts and font size, the same type alignment, and the same placement of titles. Graphics, charts, and text will differ from frame to frame. Figures 4-2 and 4-3 show a master frame and an individual frame created from it.

Figure 4-2. Master Frame

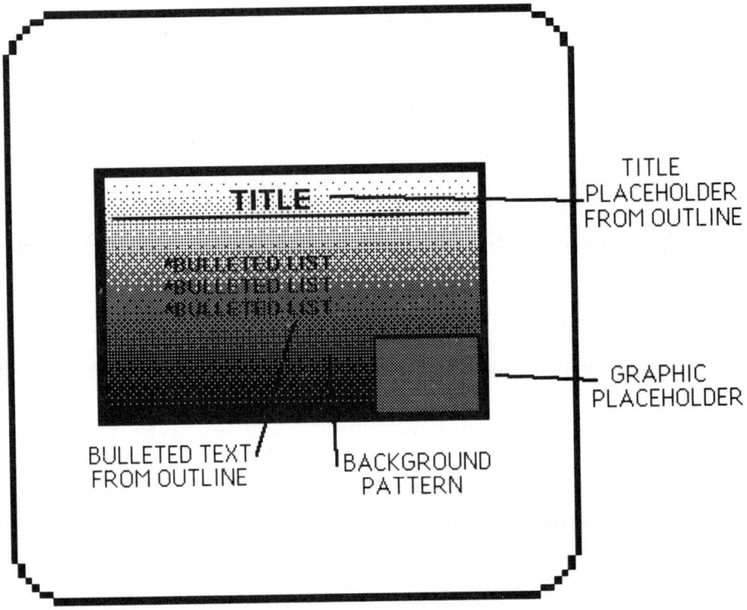

Figure 4-3. Individual Frame from Master

Presentation packages make this process much easier by offering readymade master frames created by professional graphic designers. Master frames make presentation design a snap—all the hard work has been done for you already; you just plug in the text and numbers. *Persuasion,* for example, includes 26 collections of master frames called "auto-templates," each of which specifies a different mix of type, background, and graphic details. Each auto-template includes several master frames for text-only frames, frames with charts, frames with draw graphics, and so on. *PowerPoint,* which starts you off with master frame selection and design rather than outlining, also includes several slickly designed master frames; one is shown in Figure 4-4. (Color samples are shown in the *PowerPoint* documentation, a handy feature.) To use master frames, just select the template that suits your presentation; *PowerPoint* then creates the number of frames specified in your outline and imports text from the outline. The charting module creates charts and graphics specific to the show using data you supply.

Figure 4-4. *PowerPoint* Template

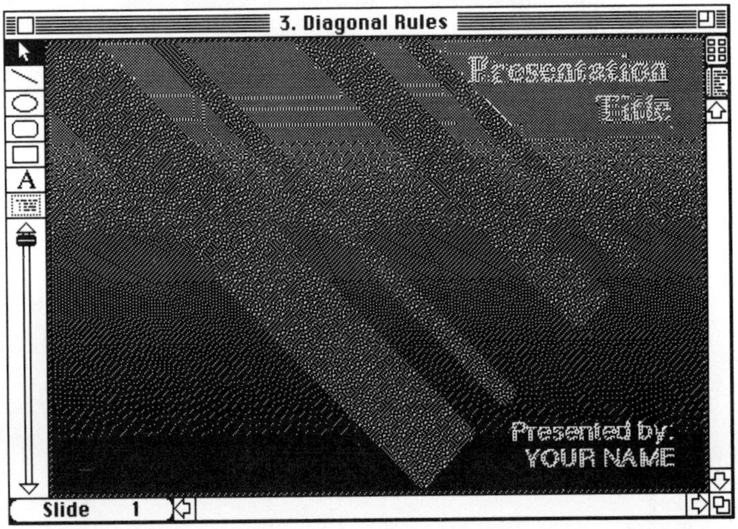

A master frame can be customized with different colors, font characteristics, logos, and so on, and then saved as a new master. (Most presenters find it necessary to customize one or more of the master frames, since as provided they don't have much character.) Different aspect ratios for slides and transparencies are available—slides are more square than transparencies—or you can set a custom size for pasting into a brochure or other printed document.

Sorting Frames. Both programs offer a "slide sorter"—a screen in which you can see all your slides or transparencies laid out storyboard-fashion (see Chapter 6 for more on storyboarding). Rearranging the slide order is as easy as dragging the miniature frame pictures from one position to another. Changes made in the slide sorter are instantly reflected in the outline. Figure 4-5 shows the slide sorter view of Jane's slideshow, based on the outline in Figure 4-5.

Figure 4-5. Slide Sorter

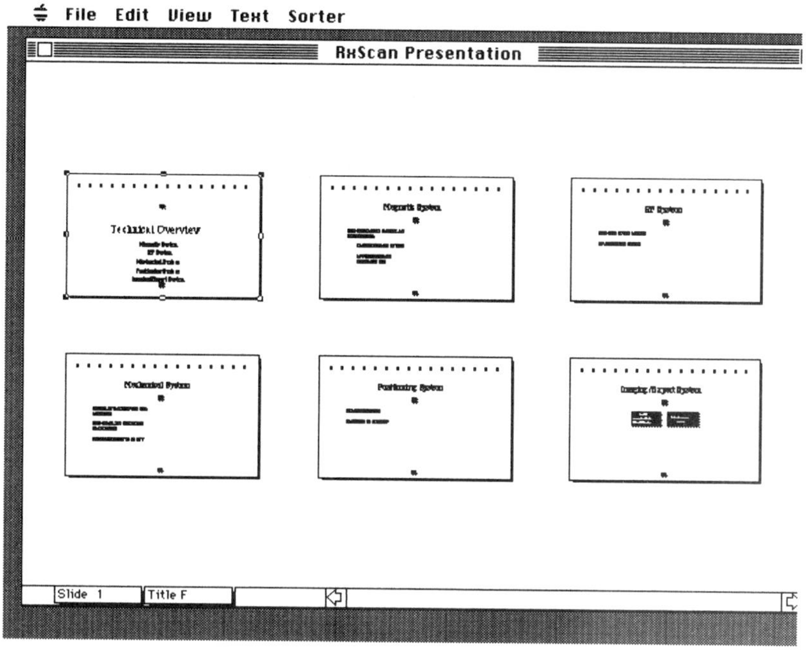

Designing the Presentation

If you just use one of the readymade master frames or templates, you won't need to do much design work—the master designers have taken care of that already. Chances are, though, you'll have to customize one or more masters, or create one from scratch. Below are suggestions for effective slide and transparency design.

Text. The physical appearance of text on slides and transparencies is especially important, since text is the main element in most presentations. Clear, readable text can make the difference between a successful presentation and one that fails.

Generally, presentation programs limit you to scalable versions of Helvetica and Times Roman; these yield good-quality type on a laser printer. Most slidemakers (see below) also substitute their own internal scalable fonts for the presentation program fonts. Other fonts may have to be incorporated as bitmaps, meaning the text will look ragged. If possible, don't use bitmapped fonts for lines of text. All fonts have a bitmapped appearance when viewed on the Mac screen, of course.

The text on frames should be easy to read and easy to remember. Text frames should have:

- No more than seven bulleted lines
- No more than seven words per line
- Display type for the frame title only
- Body copy in large serif type, upper- and lowercase
- Simple, familiar typefaces, such as Helvetica
- A clean background without distractions

Text should be short and to the point, in the active rather than the passive voice. Address your audience directly, as in "You must remember this. . . ." And always doublecheck your spelling. Even if the presentation program includes a spelling checker, don't depend on it, since most won't catch many kinds of simple typos, like the repetition of of "of" in this sentence. But your audience will.

Graphics. Many of your frames will incorporate graphics, such as drawings and charts. Presentation programs include a selection of draw-type tools, much like the ones in *MacDraw II,* for basic illustration. Charts are created from data entered in mini-spreadsheets, like the one offered in *Persuasion* and shown in Figure 4-6. Each application offers several chart types, such as the standard pie, line, and bar charts (see Chapter 3).

Figure 4-6. *Persuasion* Spreadsheet

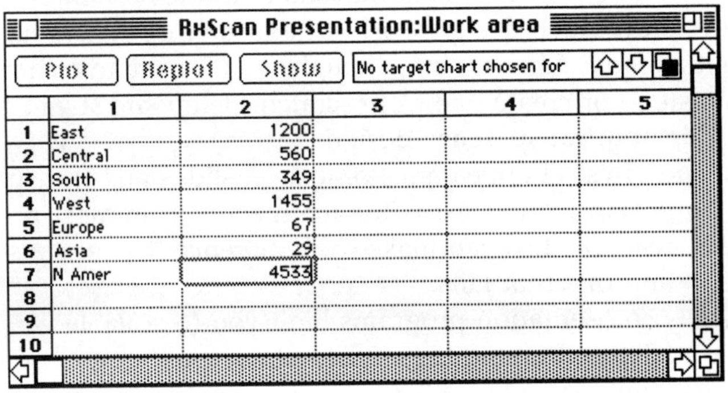

Graphics and charts can also be imported from stand-alone graphics applications. Since these have many more features than the draw modules in presentation programs, you may find it more effective to create graphics outside your presentation program and move them in. If your Mac has enough memory, you can run a presentation program and one or more graphics applications at the same time under MultiFinder.

Your frames will also need background art. Backgrounds can range from a simple solid color and a few borderlines to an elaborate setup with fancy borders, multicolored gradients, and a big corporate logo taking up half the space. A selection of simple and complex backgrounds is provided by *Persuasion* and *PowerPoint*. As a general rule, if you're really concerned about transmitting information to your audience, you'll eschew fancy, distracting backgrounds.

By the way, there's no reason not to include regular slides along with Mac-generated ones. If you have slides of that new production process at the plant, by all means mix them in with the others. It provides visual relief from the computer-graphics style of slides created with presentation programs, and real photos always look better than scans.

Builds. One technique that works well for slides is the *build*. Builds are sequences of related slides that reveal additional information a layer at a time—in essence, a build is a low-powered animation. With a build, you can dramatically reveal the development of an idea, and focus the attention of your audience on that idea as you discuss it in the presentation. For example, instead of just presenting all the lines of text on one

Figure 4-7. Slide Build

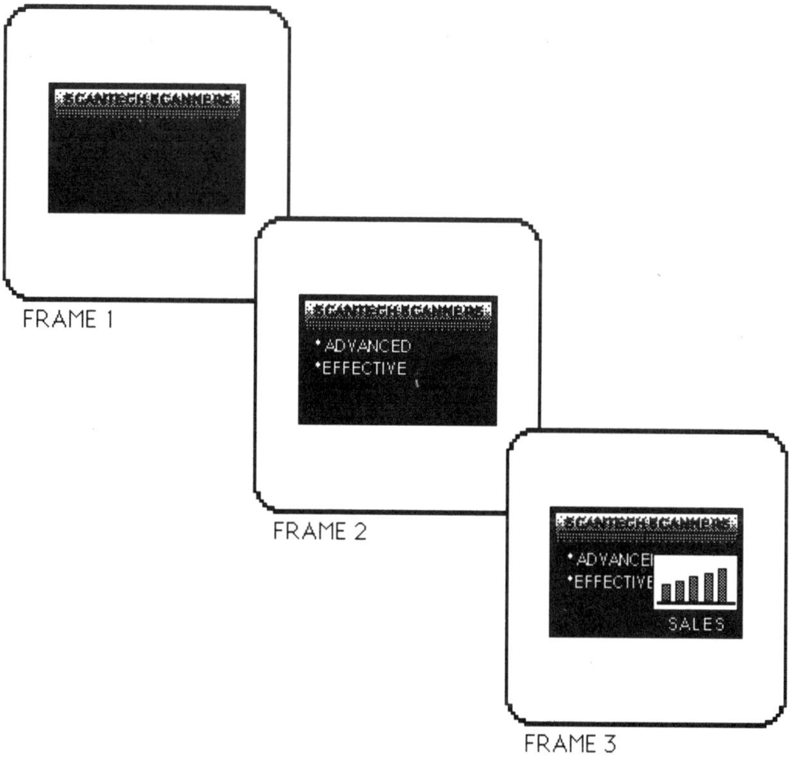

slide, you can show each line one after another in sequence, perhaps dimming the previous line as the new one appears, leading to the final and most important point (as in Figure 4-7, a slide build created by Jane).

Builds involve creating a separate frame for each stage. *Persuasion* can automate the construction of builds for you. The trick is to assign the elements to sequential layers on the master frame, using the Layers option in the lower menu bar. (Think of each layer as a sheet of clear plastic with a text or graphic element; the build is composed of a stack of plastic sheets revealed in sequence. The "backmost" layer is the first layer, and subsequent elements are laid on top of it.) The program prints each layer as a separate slide or transparency; at presentation time, you show them in the proper order.

Onscreen Slideshows. Additional effects are possible if you plan to show your frames onscreen, rather than as slide or transparencies. The automated slideshow utility included with *PowerPoint*, for example, lets you play frames at set intervals, or change frames at a mouse click; play the presentation in a loop; go directly to any slide by typing its number; and show the program screen on one monitor while showing frames on another. If the slideshow utility in your presentation program isn't versatile enough, you can export your frames to a program such as *Gallery*, included with *Studio/8* (see Chapter 2). Gallery includes many of the above capabilities, and adds video-style transitions, such as fades, dissolves, and wipes (see Chapter 7 for more on transitions).

Getting Approval

Organizations usually require that presentations get approval from higher up before you go ahead and spend the money to create slides or transparencies. Both *Persuasion* and *PowerPoint* can generate and print speaker notes that show a reduced image of each frame, along with the words you plan to say at the presentation. These notes also make excellent proofing documentation to submit for approval of your presentation design. Upper-level managers can scribble over your presentation notes to their hearts' content, knowing that you can still make changes with relative ease at this stage. If you can get managers together, preview your presentation for them with your presentation program's slideshow utility.

Making the Frames

With presentation organization and design completed, you've still got to make the actual slides or transparencies.

Slide Service Bureaus. Off-site slidemaking services, such as Magicorp, Genigraphix, and Autographix, can make high-quality slides for you. (Many presentation applications come with an introductory offer from one of the services.) Once you've created the graphics, you express a disk to the service or upload the files via modem, and the developed slides are sent back to you the next day. The charge per slide is typically in the $15 range. That's $375 for a 25-slide presentation (without backup copies), and you also have to pay for any telecom connect time, which can run up to several dollars per slide for color bitmap files. So, while slide services give excellent, consistent, and relatively trouble-free results, they are quite expensive per slide.

If you plan to use a service bureau, it pays to send some sample color slides first. That way, you can see which screen colors come out well on the slides and which don't, and adjust your presentation color scheme accordingly. You might want to try this with several services (some are listed in Appendix A) to see which gives the best results and service. As far as fonts go, most services support all the 35 Apple LaserWriter IINT scalable fonts, so you can use these in your slide designs and get high-quality text back.

Slide service bureaus can help in other ways. Account executives can assist in writing and organizing your presentation; artists can do everything from designing your slides to establishing a complete corporate identity for your business; production support personnel can manage your presentation staging and plan your entire meeting. High-volume slide duplication, brochure printing, and video/animation production may also be available. While convenient, none of these services comes cheap.

Slidemakers. Many presenters who can't afford the quality that a service bureau offers, or who have many slides to make on a regular basis, are turning to desktop slidemakers, also called slide recorders or film recorders, as the most cost-effective way to prepare slides. A slidemaker is basically a 35mm camera in a box that takes a picture of your screen image off a special monitor. The image is piped in either as Mac graphics or as composite video (see Chapter 5). Figure 4-8 illustrates the inner workings of most slidemakers. For color slides, a black-and-white image is displayed on the CRT in the slidemaker. Three exposures are taken through the colored filters in the turning wheel, one each for red, green, and blue.

Slidemakers vary greatly in versatility, price, and performance. Everything from the quality of the CRT, to the operation of the color separation software, to the type of slide film you choose can make a big difference in the final slide. Generally, you want to use the machine that gives the sharpest image (measured in horizontal lines per slide, with the more lines, the sharper the image), the clearest and most accurate color, and the best-looking text, in the least amount of time. The higher-priced units (up to $12,000) give better results, but small increases in resolution or color fidelity may not be worth the extra cost. Good slide-

Figure 4-8. Slidemaker

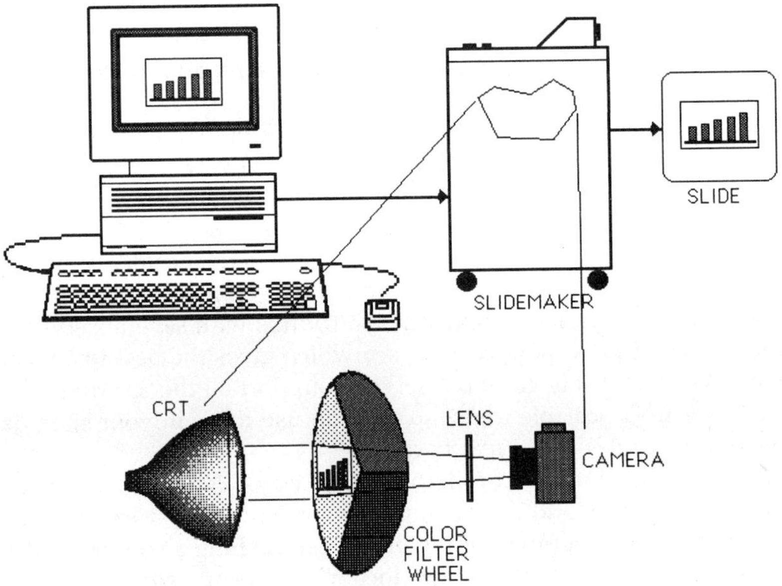

makers can be had in the $5,000–$7,000 range. A $8,000 slidemaker quickly pays for itself if you are making more than 300–400 slides. Add to that the advantage of having more control over the slidemaking process, and the ability to add extra copies of slides at any time—needed for many presentations—and slide recorders look very appealing.

Some Mac slidemakers operate as Chooser-level devices; others are software independent, but all currently work best with Mac IIs. Most of the presentation packages, such as *Persuasion* and *PowerPoint,* claim direct support for one or more of the machines. In either case, you load the image you want to shoot, insert a roll of film (usually 35mm daylight film) into the slidemaker's camera, set the imaging parameters with the controller software that comes with the unit, and press the button. Most slidemakers have detachable cameras so you can insert other backs (for instant film, for example) into the machine. Once you've exposed a roll, you send it off to a film shop for developing; professional labs can usually turn slide film around in less than a day.

Slidemaker Caveats. For all their utility, slidemakers have their problems. Hardware and software setup can be awkward. Most slidemakers take over your Mac completely during the imaging process, leaving you to sit on your hands. (A batch developing option is a selling point for the better machines, since you can set the job to be shot overnight.) Software ranges widely from well designed and flexible to frustrating and nearly useless. Image sharpness also varies among machines, with the sharpest slides produced by the most expensive slidemakers, as you would expect. Few slidemakers yield slides as sharp as those generated by slidemaking services.

Another, more serious problem with the current generation of slidemakers is that you can't depend on seeing every part of the original image reproduced on the slide. Fine graphics details, thin lines, and even text may be lost. With crucial jobs, it pays to check how your image will work out by shooting a test roll of instant slide film; most slidemakers give you that option. Instant film has poor resolution and color fidelity, but it will show you what parts of your image will appear in the final slide, and which won't. Also, the current generation of slidemakers can't handle 24-bit or 32-bit images, and most don't accept EPS (PostScript) files. Nor do most support all 35 LaserWriter fonts. (These capabilities should be widely available by the end of 1990, though.)

Tips for Screen Shots

If you want basic slides of your graphics, you can always photograph the monitor screen. With the right techniques, this works surprisingly well, yielding slides that do the job for an informal presentation. And it's far cheaper than any other slidemaking method. Here are a few tips for taking successful screen shots.

- Use a 35mm single-lens reflex camera with a built-in light meter, manual shutter, and manual aperture: a 70–100mm short telephoto zoom lens with a close-focus feature; fast daylight color print or slide film; and a sturdy tripod.
- Choose the right monitor. The curvature of the monitor faceplate distorts the screen image, especially at the corners. Your eyes ignore this, but the camera doesn't. Flat-screen monitors, like Zenith's FTM series, give the clearest and least-distorted images. Sony Trinitron monitors, including the standard Apple RGB monitor, are the next choice, since they are curved only along the horizontal axis. A good trick is to make your image smaller than the maximum size allowed onscreen, then center the image and zoom in to minimize corner distortion.
- Clean the monitor screen with a glass cleaner; eliminate all smears. Turn off the lights and mask the windows, or shoot at night. Some computer supply companies sell *monitor hoods* that fit over and between the monitor and camera lens, blocking reflections and glare on the screen.
- Position the tripod and adjust the camera so the center of the lens is level with the center of the display. The display should fill the camera's viewfinder; avoid showing the monitor case. Remember to hide the menubar, pointer, and any unwanted windows, unless you want them to show in the shot.
- Use a shutter speed of one or two seconds. This should eliminate any

scanlines. Take a couple of shots of each picture, bracketing the suggested f-stop one-half stop above and below. At least one shot of each picture should be clear and properly exposed. Once you've learned the characteristics of your monitor, it shouldn't be necessary to bracket exposures.

- To offset the bluish cast of some color monitors, including the standard Mac Plus or SE screen, shoot through a yellow filter (81 A, B, or C).

Making Transparencies. Transparencies are much easier to produce than slides, and many presenters prefer them for that reason alone. All you need is a good printer, preferably a 300 dpi laser or inkjet printer, an office copier, and compatible transparency stock (Avery makes a good product; see Appendix A). Either feed the stock into your printer and print out transparencies directly, or print up a copy of each frame on paper and then copy them on an office copier loaded with transparency stock. (Follow the manufacturer's directions for loading and handling the stock.) If you are using a presentation program, make sure you've chosen the transparency aspect ratio in the program's Page Setup or Print dialog.

Viewers looking at transparencies may not be as image-quality-conscious as an audience for a slick slideshow, but the images still have to be sharp and readable. You can help assure this by:

- Avoiding thin lines and small type in your graphic design. These won't show up well. Light colors and fine patterns also may be washed out by the light of the overhead projector.
- Achieving the darkest darks possible on black-and-white acetates. You can print the picture on paper on a laser printer, and then copy it onto acetate in a photocopier. A good office copier can yield an image with more contrast and denser blacks than is possible with a LaserWriter.
- Printing color transparencies directly in a color printer. Most inkjet and thermal color printers can print on one of the brands of transparency plastic. Thermal printers yield the purest colors. Transparency stock also comes in tints.
- Mounting transparencies in cardboard mattes for easier and cleaner handling. (Mattes are available from presentation supply houses.) Label each transparency on the matte.
- Printing two copies of the transparency and layering them in one matte to get the densest blacks and colors.

Projection Panels. Projection panels, also called overhead projection adapters or LCD panels, are flat-panel devices that allow Mac graphics to be projected by a standard overhead projector. You can think of the panel as nothing more than a dynamic transparency, allowing animation, mouse movements, and so on, to be seen by everybody in the room. As in Figure 4-9, the panel, which is connected to the Mac by a cable that hooks into the computer's internal video circuitry (dealer installation is recommended), lays on top of the overhead projector and simply displays on its transparent screen whatever is on the Mac screen—graphics, text, or even animation. Light from the overhead projector shines through the panel and is projected in the usual way.

Figure 4-9. Projection Panel

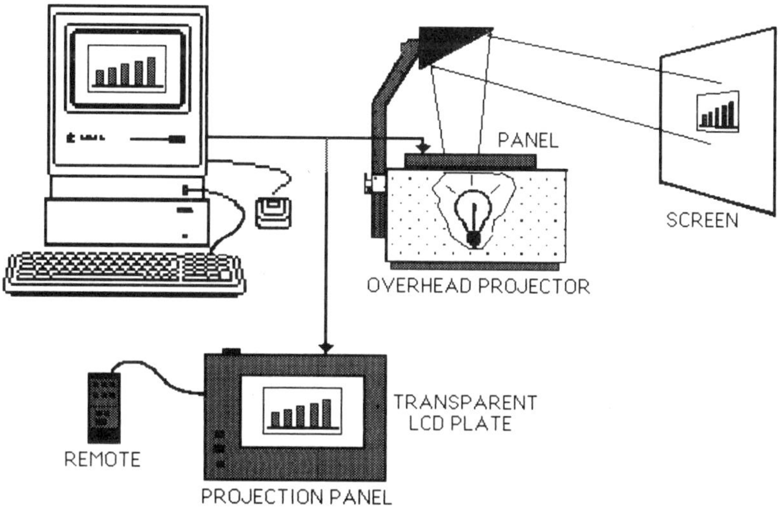

Most projection panels are currently designed for use with the Mac Plus or SE, and thus are restricted to an image size of 512 × 342 pixels. A few Mac II-compatible panels are appearing, with image sizes of up to 640 × 480 pixels. Most units offer either a black-and-white image, or images in various shades of blue, yellow, brown, or purple. The first color projection panels are just appearing. Higher-priced models come with onboard memory and software for storing data right in the panel, so you don't need a computer onsite.

These little gadgets can be very helpful when you don't have time to create transparencies, when animation is crucial to your presentations, or when you want to manipulate data on the Mac as you talk—just sit at the Mac and work, letting the panel take care of the projection. You can try out "what-if" scenarios and change material as you go, making for a much more engaging and dynamic presentation. An added advantage is that most panels offer a remote, so you can move around the room while flipping back and forth randomly among images (assuming you've already created all the graphics you need) without having to bend over a hot projector. Current prices for adapters run $1,500–$2,000, though, so if you don't need animation or interactivity in your presentations, you may be better off using a few dollars worth of transparencies instead.

Choosing Projection Panels. The big issue in projection panel marketing is how good the projected image is. Image quality depends mainly on the type and color of LCD used, and the rate at which the panel redraws the image. Size and shape of the LCD pixels may also determine how clear or distorted the image is when compared to the Mac screen image.

Black-and-white–type LCDs offer good contrast—the ratio between the lightest and darkest parts of the projected image—and a paperlike appearance, but are not as bright as other kinds. They work best in dark rooms. Blue-yellow or purple-brown LCDs offer less contrast, but are generally brighter. These types work better in partially illuminated rooms, but some people in the audience may have difficulty distinguishing shades of purple or blue, especially in patterns. Try to test both types in the kind of presentation conditions you anticipate using them in. Just don't expect the kind of image sharpness and contrast you get on the Mac itself. The new color panels are bright and easy to read, but are more expensive (and, of course, only work with color Macs).

Another factor, important if you plan to show animations or interact with the screen, is how fast the panel *refreshes* (redraws) the image. A fast refresh (12 to 15 times a second) means the cursor will always be visible, and animations will play smoothly. A slow refresh (10 times per second or less) means animations will smear and jerk, and the cursor may disappear when you move it. If possible, play an animated sequence on the panel before you buy it. (See Chapter 8 for more on animation.)

While convenience features don't affect image quality, they certainly make a panel easier to use. A full-featured remote control can make a big difference in the utility of the panel. So do full-featured contrast and brightness controls, onboard memory, and easy-to-use setup software. Newer-model panels are more heat resistant than older ones (incorporating fans and vents to keep the LCDs cool). Make sure your unit will withstand at least a two-hour stint on the projector. It may also be easier to justify the purchase of a panel that connects to PCs as well as Macs.

Tips for Successful Overhead Presentations

- Show the transparencies to small groups sitting close to the projected image.

- Keep the projected image relatively small, so it doesn't get washed out in the light of the room.
- Project on a really white, flat, vertical surface.

If you're using a projection panel, keep these factors in mind:

- Projection panels work only with *transmissive-type* overhead projectors—the kind that shine light up from a bulb below the panel. *Reflective-type* overhead projectors, which shine a light down from above to be reflected back up from a mirror below the image, don't work with projection panels at all.
- Use a lower-wattage bulb in the overhead projector if your projection panel appears to be heat-sensitive; a 200-watt bulb may be bright enough, and is a lot cooler than the standard 350-watt bulb. Older projection panels may need to be removed periodically from the overhead projector to avoid overheating. Switch off the projector when not in use.

Preparing for the Show

Many a presenter with complete mastery of his or her subject has been caught short by poor preparation. Imagine getting to the meeting room a few minutes early with slides and overheads in hand and finding that there's no slide projector available, that all the chairs in the room were removed half an hour ago for use in another meeting room, and that half the people who should attend your presentation are in the other meeting and don't even know about yours. These kinds of problems, and worse, crop up all the time, especially in large organizations.

Since you're the person who cares the most about the success of your presentation, it's your responsibility to make sure that you, your audience, and the presentation site are all prepared for the show. Make yourself a preparation checklist that includes the following items:

Rehearse Your Material. Think about the presentations you've attended. What made the effective ones work? Chances are the main factor was a well-prepared presenter in complete control of material and audience. Rehearsing is one way to improve your onstage performance. At home, try reading your notes in front of a camcorder. Use a stopwatch or the camcorder counter to time your remarks. As you review the tape, listen to your voice. Do you sound nervous? Do you speak too fast or too slow? Work on parts that don't seem to go smoothly. Study your gestures as well, looking for awkward or overexpansive movements. If you have a slide or overhead projector handy, you can also practice integrating the slideshow/overhead presentation with your comments, or you can use the onscreen slideshow utility in your presentation program. Then, ask someone to view to your presentation, if possible, at the site you'll be giving the actual show, and use his or her criticisms to improve your performance.

Check Advertising. Have you made sure everyone who should know about your presentation has been contacted? Getting the word out well in advance is vitally important, so use every avenue at your disposal—call, write, send faxes and electronic mail, post signs on bulletin boards (cork and computer), advertise, distribute brochures, buttonhole potential listeners in the corridor. Don't be shy—speaking to an empty room has never changed the world.

Check the Site Arrangements. Send a schedule and list of requirements well in advance to the management at the presentation site. Call to confirm that everything will be ready. Then, call again the day before the presentation. Get to the meeting room or hall early enough to handle any last-minute problems.

Check Personnel. Someone at the site will be responsible for helping you get set up and providing access to service people—electricians, janitors, and so on. Meet the liaison person in advance, if possible, and tell him or her about her plans (don't assume that the site management has communicated anything about you). Make sure technical help will be available at show time. Line up slide or overhead projector operators and assistants (if you need them) and see that they have transport to the site.

Check the Schedule. Does the site management know your schedule? Are other events scheduled at the same time? Will they be competing for resources (A/V equipment, chairs, and so on) that you need? Have there been any last-minute schedule changes that will affect your presentation?

Check the Power. Are there enough outlets for your equipment, and are they in the right locations? Bring extra extension cords and outlet boxes if needed. Test each outlet to make sure it really delivers juice; a cheap circuit tester should be in your presentation toolkit. Video or multimedia setups, especially if they employ lights, may require additional power and an electrician to route it for you. Consider taking along a surge protector (a power strip that moderates surges or spikes in voltage) for your Mac.

Check the Sound. Test the PA system with the same mike you'll be using for the presentation. Have someone listen in the back row, and then set the audio level a bit louder than the listener indicates (mark the level with a pencil or chalk). Once the hall is full, ambient sound levels will be higher, and your voice won't carry as far. Test your audiotape and stereo setup if you'll be playing music or sound effects. Keep mikes away from speakers to avoid audio feedback.

Check the Equipment. Make a checklist; then set up and operate every piece of equipment you'll be using. Put equipment on carts and tables. Check the bulbs in slide and overhead projectors; wiggle cables to check that they're tight; plug in power cords; make sure remote controls have fresh batteries. Aim, focus, and run a few slides through projectors; hook up and run LCD panels; play a test tape on VCRs; boot your Mac and load the programs you'll be using. In your toolkit, carry a set of screwdrivers and pliers, spare batteries, projector bulbs, audio and video connectors and cables, a small microphone, gaffer's tape, videotapes, and disk copies of applications and data.

Check the Lighting. Display a slide or transparency onscreen and adjust the lighting until the image is bright, but there's still just enough light to read or write by. Light can be at different levels in different parts of the room—dark near the screen, and brighter near the exits. Keep track of which switches control which lights. Mark dimmers for the right light setting.

Check Seating Arrangements. Auditoriums don't offer much in the way of seating flexibility, but you may be able to arrange the seating in a meeting room or classroom. (Make sure there are enough chairs.) The operating principle is, the screen should be off to one side but angled to be visible from all parts of the room, and the podium positioned so you're not between the screen and anyone in the audience. Put the screen on the side you're most comfortable gesturing toward—on the left if you're left-handed, for example. Ideally, viewers should be seated no farther away than about six times the width of the screen image.

Check Your Material. Here's where lapses in preparedness are really embarrassing. Before you leave for the site, count and check the order of your slides, your overheads, your video tapes, or your disks—then do it again. Any slides upside down? Do you have enough handouts? Are they collated, stapled, and so on? Don't forget your notes. The prudent presenter creates spare sets of everything and takes them in a separate box. Make sure all materials are clearly labeled—imagine that a complete stranger is going to give the presentation for you (it could happen).

Seed the Audience. Want your audience to be fully prepared and engaged when you step out on the podium? Make sure there is a copy of your outline on every seat or have someone hand them out as the audience enters. Many presenters go so far as to desktop-publish slick presentation documents, including notes, outline, and other materials (promos, biography, scanned photos and diagrams, and so on), and get the material out well in advance of the presentation. The same materials can be made available to the audience as leave-behinds (see below).

Tips for Presentation Performance

All eyes are on you, and ears are straining to catch your every word. Don't forget that you're the one the audience has come to hear. Slides and transparencies, no matter how well designed, can't do everything for you; in fact, they won't do *anything* for you if the audience is bored or turned off by your performance. If you just read your notes while showing some slides, you'll fail to make that vital emotional connection with your audience, the connection that will put across your ideas and viewpoint. The visual materials are only there to supplement what you, the presenter, have to say.

Following these common-sense stage rules will help you engage your audience's full attention:

- Plan your presentation to last a half-hour or less, and schedule it in the mid-morning or mid-afternoon. Start and end on time.
- Before anything else, make sure everyone can hear you. Introduce yourself and your topic. Tell your audience to hold their questions and remarks until the end, when you'll be glad to answer them.
- Watch your body language. Look relaxed and confident. (The best way to do that is to feel that way.) Don't wave your arms wildly, point your finger at the audience, or play with your keys. Don't stiffen up either. A few stretches before getting up on stage can relax you, or try mediation—anything to project a natural, unworried appearance.
- Maintain eye contact with the audience. Address your remarks somewhere in the middle of the crowd, or look at one or two specific individuals near the center aisle.
- Speak slowly and clearly, and directly to the audience. It's better to be too loud than too soft.
- If you trust your wit, start off with a relevant joke or ad-lib to get the audience on your side. But if you aren't sure you're funny, just give the presentation straight up. You enthusiasm for the material should carry you through.
- Glance at your notes when necessary, but don't use them as a prop. You should know your material well enough to ad-lib or improvise at any point in the presentation.
- Pay attention to audience reaction. If people are getting restless, pick up the pace. If faces look puzzled, ask if you need to clarify any points. If the audience is riveted to your every word, hit your points hard.
- Leave time for questions and answers. If you don't know the answer to a question, say so, and offer to find out the answer for the questioner.

Remember, it's actually possible to have fun while giving a presentation. Imagine you're talking to a few close friends who are really eager to hear what you have to say. In front of a larger crowd, however, that may be hard to do. Stage fright in front of large groups can be a problem for anyone, no matter how experienced (even Lawrence Olivier suffered from it), but once you get on the podium and launch into a well-rehearsed presentation, you'll find that the audience isn't so frightening after all.

WARNING: Do not give a completed canned and memorized performance, as some presenters do. An audience with any sophistication will be turned off by a presentation without spontaneity, or one that insists on some gimmick that distracts from the information itself. Case in point: Apple's own presentation about desktop media, shown at many trade shows in the last couple of years. This show had a live presenter "asking" questions of a video clip. The queries were so well timed that interviewees in the clip appeared to be "answering" the questions. Audiences, rather than accepting the pretense, snickered at the presenter; the otherwise well-done and professional presentation was rendered laughable.

Leave-Behinds

Once the show is over, you want the impact of your message to continue even after you've left the room. One way to keep your presentation fresh in the minds of your audience is to hand out *leave-behinds* or handouts, materials that summarize your main points and direct your listeners to sources of further information. A leave-behind can be a simple photocopied flyer, a slick color brochure, or an entire package of information, with printed materials, slides, disks, questionnaires, bounce-back cards, discount coupons, and anything else you can think of (and afford) to add to your presentation's effectiveness.

For an integrated look, the graphic design of your leave-behinds should coordinate with that of your presentation; use the same fonts, color scheme, and graphics. Presentation programs can generate handouts, incorporating reduced images of your slides or overheads as well as your outline and notes, (see above), but for better-looking materials you'll have to turn to Mac desktop publishing software such as Aldus's *PageMaker* or Quark *Xpress*. Coupled with a laser or LCD printer, these programs can handle most leave-behind publishing tasks. Although you currently can't export text or graphics automatically from any presentation program to any DTP program, you can move material back and forth via the Clipboard. (Under System 7.0, dynamic data links between presentation and DTP programs—for example, between Aldus *Persuasion* and *PageMaker*—should make it possible to prepare high-quality presentations and printed leave-behinds at the same time.) Slides and disks can be duplicated by any professional photo lab and disk-duplication service bureau.

Printing in Color. Color printers are breaking new ground for presentation leave-behinds. With color printouts, you can distribute paper facsimiles of your color slides to everyone in the audience, providing a more accessible visual experience at less cost than handing out copies of the slides themselves. (Slide copies can cost up to $5 each.) Color on the page has real impact, and it is sometimes indispensable, as in technical drawings where each component or layer has its own identifying hue.

The downside of color printing direct from the Mac is that you have to settle for low quality or high cost. You can print color pictures on the ImageWriter II, using special color ribbons and software that supports the process, but the results are not worth looking at. At the high end of the scale, thermal-transfer printers produce gorgeous, dense colors, reasonably close to the screen originals, but currently cost in the neighborhood of $10,000 to $25,000. Unless you're also a desktop-publisher who requires color prepress proofing capability, you don't need one of those (but several are listed in Appendix A, anyway). Rather than purchasing a high-end color printer, consider using one at a desktop publishing service bureau, or make slides with a slide recorder or slide service and take them to your local color photocopy center, which can make color photocopies from slides for about 75 cents each.

At the time of writing, few low-cost color printers for the Mac were on the market; one notable exception is Hewlett-Packard's $1,500 PaintJet color inkjet printer. The PaintJet produces reasonable color fidelity, prints on acetates for making color transparencies, and does a good job with text as well; it is not accurate enough to be used as a proofing device for desktop publishing.

Video. Finally, consider a leave-behind in the form of videotape. With the Mac desktop video tools and techniques described in the next chapters, you can transfer your slideshow presentation to video, add a smashing narration and sound effects, and then copy the tape for your audience so they can review it at their leisure. The more ways your audience can access the presentation, the more likely they'll see your point of view. Video production techniques for the Mac is the subject of the next three chapters.

CHAPTER 5
Getting into Video

There are some times when a slideshow or overhead presentation won't do—when you need to present real-world images that move or require sound for full comprehension. For example, you might want to show your audience an interview with the company director or a demonstration by a world-famous specialist in your field. For this kind of presentation material, video is the medium to use. This chapter and the two following show how you can incorporate video into your presentations, using your Macintosh to custom-tailor them in a way that wouldn't have been possible only two or three years ago.

Imagine two scenes:

- A television studio, New York City, late 1950s. You and your crew are taping and editing the latest episode of "The Dinah Shore Show." Along with a couple of dozen technicians and studio personnel, you're using three massive television cameras; a video switcher; a brand-new Ampex videotape recorder the size of a washer-dryer; and the latest videotape editing system—a marker pen, a splicing knife, a magnifying glass, developing fluid, and sticky tape. The farthest thing from you mind, as you struggle to get your fragile machines to work smoothly together, is that television production technology might ever be available to John Q. Public. And you've never seen a computer—they're for designing bombs, aren't they? Total production time for the show: one week.
- Your desktop, 1990. You have six hours to create a flashy color video presentation for tomorrow's meeting. On hand is the tape you shot earlier at the plant with your camcorder. On your desk is the camcorder, an editing VCR, and, linking them together, a Mac IIcx. You whip up two moving bar charts and a video slideshow showing shop

floor innovations with animation software, then quickly insert them into the footage of the plant. A titling program lets you add explanatory notes and credits right over the moving video. Finally, you add an original soundtrack you composed just by moving the Macintosh's mouse. Total production time: five hours, 20 minutes.

Thirty years have brought a mass revolution in video technology. It was just over a decade ago that video equipment aimed at consumers first appeared on the market. Now, nearly half of American households and businesses have VCRs, and a sizable proportion have camcorders, too. A parallel revolution has taken place in the computer industry. In 1978, nearly all computers were refrigerator-sized boxes in the inner sancta of corporations and governments; the personal computer was the way-out hobby of a few dedicated hackers. Today 20 million PCs are in use worldwide, including about 2½ million Macs, and big computers may be a dying breed.

Enter Desktop Video

Today the two revolutions are coming together in a new field called *desktop video* (DTV), the practice of linking low-cost video equipment and computers to generate sophisticated video programming for business, educational, and creative use. Current Macintosh DTV products let you mix live video and computer effects, add titles and text over video, turn video images into computer pictures, create computer slideshows, and even craft amazingly detailed three-dimensional animations. Desktop video is hot—many observers think it will have as big an impact on the world of the personal computer as desktop publishing did two years ago.

Like desktop publishing, desktop video brings a formerly difficult, exclusive, and expensive medium of communication within reach of anyone with a moderate amount of money and the will to learn. In fact, the rise of desktop video amounts to a democratization of video programming technology—Hollywood (or maybe just Burbank) on your desktop. Given the rapid evolution of industrial video and personal computers, it's likely the multimillion-dollar video production studio of today will be obsolete in five or ten years, replaced by flexible, creative individuals and small groups using DTV technology to create top-quality video on a shoestring. An investment of $3000 to $5000 will get you up and running on your Mac II with a system that boasts color graphics, three-dimensional animation, fancy titles, sound effects, and music. Don't feel left behind if you have a Mac Plus or SE, though; there are many DTV products that work well with these Macs for video applications that don't require color or fancy special effects.

Advantages of DTV

As a medium of mass communication, video has no peer. For good or ill, most Americans have grown up with TV; the majority of us watch it every day, sometimes for several hours a day. A slim two or three percent of American homes are without a TV. We look to TV for entertainment, information, relaxation, company, and can't imagine life without it. The primacy of television as the mass communications medium par excellence was demonstrated once again in the last presidential election. Both parties spent hundreds of thousands of dollars on print ads but tens of millions of dollars on TV commercials, with one side winning the election in part because of a few devastatingly effective ads.

In short, information communicated through video has a ready-made audience that often can't be reached in other ways. Given video's high density of transmitted information—music, sound, color, motion, text, photographic imagery, graphics, and narrative, available all at once—it's ideal for conveying any complex idea that can be shown or told. That's why businesses increasingly are using video for training, presentations, and corporate communications. Many schools play educational tapes every day. Video packs more punch and is more portable than any slideshow or overhead presentation. You can get the best of both worlds by simply taping your slideshow and distributing it on videotape for people to watch at their leisure.

Computer-enhanced video can be even more effective. For example, as part of a training course for hospital technicians on how to use the RXScan MRI scanner, ScanTech decides to provide a video as well as on-site instruction. An important part of the course is showing how to interpret the scanned data. Jane, who is producing the video as part of her overall job of presenting the new scanner, takes a sample printout from the RXScan and scans it into her Mac, which is connected to a VCR using a video board that outputs Mac graphics as ordinary TV video. Using a compatible paint program, she then points to different areas of the scan with the pointer, draws boxes around relevant images, and magnifies hard-to-see areas—and it all is recorded directly to tape for later editing into the final program. These are effects that would be difficult and costly to produce with traditional animation techniques, but are easy to do with a Mac and a VCR.

Creating with DTV

How does desktop video work? Conceptually, it's fairly simple (although the details can be quite complex, as you'll see in later chapters). A typical DTV system is, as you might expect, compact enough to sit on a desktop. It requires a camcorder or video camera, a Macintosh computer, a separate device for bringing video into and out of the computer, software for graphics, and a VCR. Footage shot on the video camera or camcorder is fed into the computer, where it's mixed with computer graphics, titles, animation, or whatever images you like. The mix is then output from the Macintosh and input into a VCR, which records it to tape. The tape may then be played back on any compatible VCR at any location.

There are any number of variations on this basic setup. You can dispense with the camcorder, for example, and just create programming in the Macintosh for recording on the VCR. Or you can capture video images as computer pictures and save them on disk for Mac-displayed presentations, bypassing tape altogether. A growing number of software packages and hardware devices provide a dazzling range of DTV capabilities, from the simple to the elaborate, the amateur to the thoroughly professional. Later in this chapter you'll find descriptions of each type of DTV peripheral, along with guidelines for setting up a basic DTV studio. Appendix A lists manufacturers and publishers for the major Macintosh DTV products.

Many DTV projects will be rather simple—the creation of a simple video logo or a set of titles, for example—calling for minimal effort in planning and production analysis. Other projects will be more elaborate but still primarily functional, with well-defined goals. You have to create a presentation for the production VP using such-and-such data for the big project, for example, and you've only got so many hours and so much money to accomplish the task. In such cases, creative issues tend to fall in line behind the imperatives of message, money, and time, making it easier to see what choices have to be made.

Then there are DTV projects that are purely creative in intent, such as art animations or "guerrilla videos." A creative DTV director needs to keep in mind all of the requirements listed above, plus the overarching imperative of being true to the vision of the piece. A talent for striking visual design; a sensitivity to narrative rhythm; a good sense of drama, comedy, or satire; an ear for sound and music; and the need to strive for perfection (or, at least, the ability to recognize these traits in others and get those people to work with you) are all traits that will help the creative DTV director.

Professional DTV. Anyone who turns on the TV is bombarded by sophisticated computer video graphics. Network spots are filled with flying text in every imaginable material, from bronze to glass to marble. Computer-generated footballs of simulated pigskin sail through computerized end zones before every NFL game. Elaborate animated maps accompany every local TV weatherperson. The 1988 Summer Olympics saw the greatest blitz of computer graphics offered to date on American TV; the dazzling effects, far more imaginative than the live coverage of events, were so ubiquitous that we took them for granted.

Yet, common as flashy computer graphics have become on TV, they're incredibly expensive and time-consuming to create, even well out of the financial reach of most professional producers. It's the rare industrial production or TV commercial that can budget several thousand dollars per *second* for broadcast computer graphics—and that's what the video special effects studios charge. That why video professionals are increasingly looking to DTV to provide video graphic pizzazz that would otherwise be unaffordable.

DTV isn't right for every professional situation; there will always be clients who need the ultimate in image quality, and have the money to pay for it. However, it can be a budget and schedule saver for the video pro who is short on time and money—conditions most producers must cope with on every project. Even quality-conscious clients are increasingly ready to accept the low-resolution "look" of desktop video as it shows up in more and more broadcast material, just as people consider laser-printed books and magazines as acceptable, even though they don't have the quality look of typeset publications.

Video Basics

NTSC. RS-170A. Subcarrier phase. Horizontal and vertical sync. The jargon of video is likely to make a Mac user's head swim. Video comes out of the world of analog electronics, where the nice, simple digital rules that make computers so easy to understand (aren't they?) just don't apply. By the same token, videographers aren't comfortable with the digital world of bytes and CLUTs, buses and DMA. Most people in the video world ignore the world of computers, and vice versa, which is easy to do, since they don't even talk the same language.

To be a successful DTV creator you'll have to give up some of the bliss of ignorance. A basic grounding in both video and computer concepts as they apply to DTV and the Macintosh is really a prerequisite for success, especially if you plan to enter DTV in any professional capacity. This knowledge will help you arrange hardware in any configuration you need, cope with strange setups when you have to use them, and recognize the sources of technical problems when they arise. Just as important, you'll be able to converse with the real videoheads and computer graphics nerds without feeling too embarrassed at your own ignorance.

What follows isn't by any means an exhaustive discussion of the technical side of video and the Mac—that would fill several volumes—but just enough to get you started. To help you get your bearings, here's a much-simplified explanation of how video works. Later we'll look at how video mixes with Mac graphics.

Video is a method of transmitting and displaying sound and visual images. A scene and ambient sound are converted by a video camera and microphone to an electrical signal that carries the video information. The signal is broadcast with a transmitter or carried along a cable to a television receiver, which recreates the scene and sound, or to a video tape recorder, which records the signal on magnetic tape for later replay.

Think of video as a little like plumbing: The signal flows like water from one component to another as long as electrical power is supplied to the system and the right "valves" are open (that is, the right components are attached in the right way). Figure 5-1 is a block diagram of the flow of video in a typical video system.

Figure 5-1. Video System

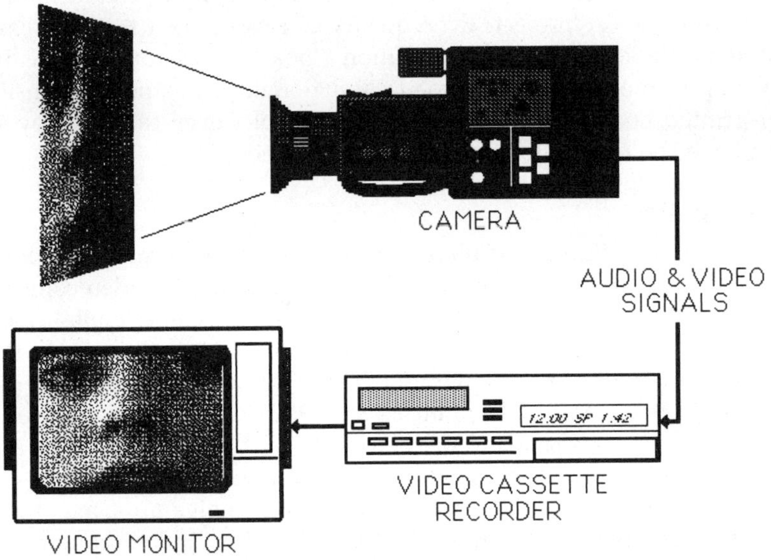

The signal won't flow and be useful without the proper components. The three main components are the video monitor, the video camera, and the VCR. Let's look at how each of these works, as well as examine the video signal in more detail. As an example, we'll use the typical camcorder, which combines all three basic video components (Figure 5-2).

Figure 5-2. Camcorder Components

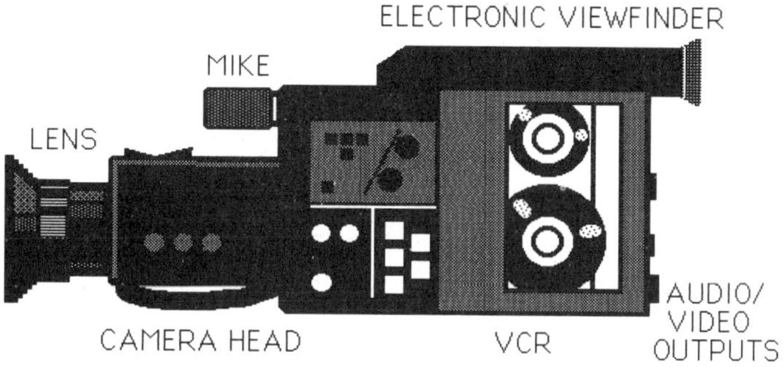

The Camera Head

The *camera* is the pickup device that first converts the image of a scene into a video signal. In most modern camcorders, a lens focuses light from the scene—for the purposes of this discussion, let's say the camera is focused on a red rose—onto a light-sensitive plate, called a *CCD* (Charged Coupled Device). The CCD is divided up into small elements called *pixels;* each pixel generates an electrical current based on the amount and color of the light falling on it. Circuitry in the camera combines the outputs of all the pixels into one analog video signal that contains all the information about the scene that the camera could resolve. With the CCD pickup system, the amount of scene detail the camera can "see" is limited by the number of pixels on the CCD plate; the more pixels, the more detail. At the same time, a microphone in the camera is picking up ambient sounds and converting them to an audio signal. The video signal from the camera is routed to the *viewfinder,* a small monitor on top of the camcorder, and audio plus video goes to the VCR part of the camcorder.

The Viewfinder

The camera image is displayed in the viewfinder. If the viewfinder is the electronic type possessed by most better camcorders, it's essentially a tiny black-and-white monitor, and it works the same way. Inside the viewfinder is a *CRT* (Cathode Ray Tube) containing a gun that scans a beam of electrons across a field of tiny phosphor dots on the back of the monitor screen. The dots glow when hit by the scanspot of the beam. The signal from the camera head contains the information necessary to vary the intensity of the electron beam so that it activates only those phosphor dots needed to create the image on the screen. The beam scans back and forth 15,750 times a second, creating the image out of individual lines of activated phosphors as it zips left to right while moving top to bottom. This happens so fast that, at a reasonable viewing distance, your eye reads the image as a solid picture. Up close to the screen, though, you can see the individual lines. Figure 5-3 illustrates this process. The video screen image, composed of the scanlines created by the electron beam, is called a *raster*.

Figure 5-3. Scanning

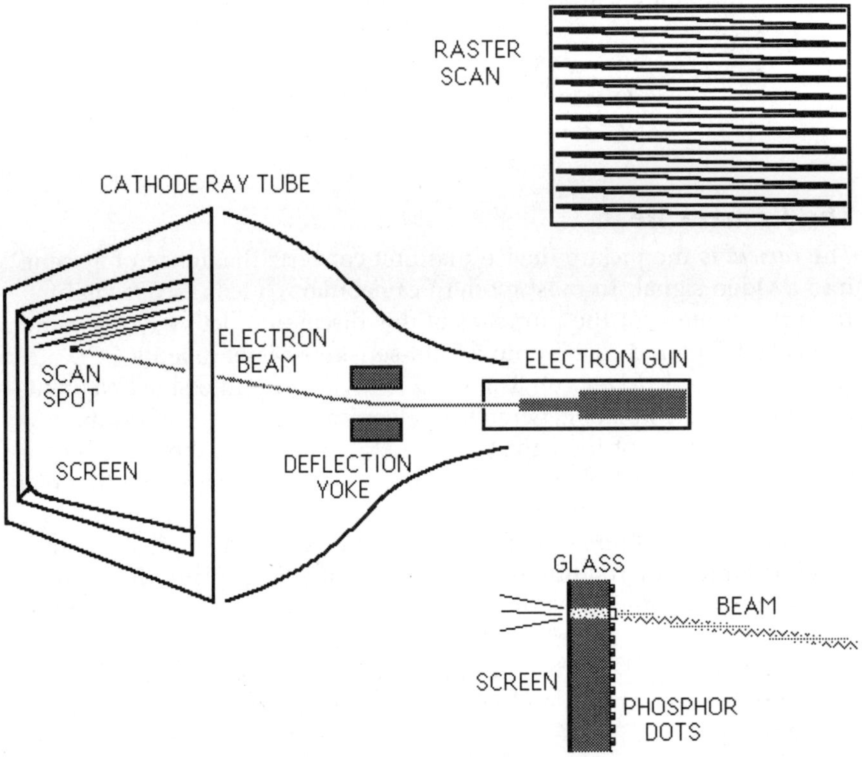

The complete raster has 525 horizontal lines (of which only about 490 are visible on the screen), but not all are written at once. Actually, two partial images called *video fields* are created, one every 1/60 of a second. The beam writes one set of lines for the first field, skipping every even line (that's $262\frac{1}{2}$ lines per field), then returns to the top of the raster to write the second field, which includes all the odd lines skipped in the field before. (See Figure 5-4 for an illustration.) The alternate writing of video lines is called *interlacing*. The complete video image created by two fields is a *video frame;* there are 30 frames every second.

Figure 5-4. Interlacing

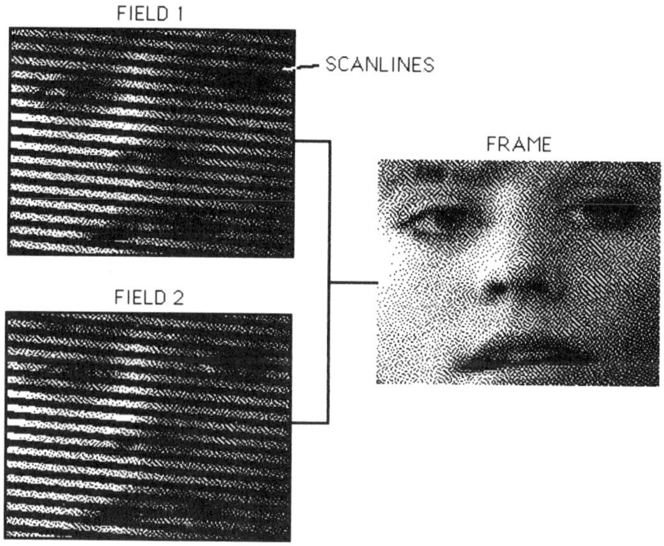

Color video is electronically similar as far as scanning goes, but mechanically more complex. The back of most color monitor screens is coated with three colors of phosphors—red, green, and blue, the primary colors of video. These colors are grouped in threes, with one of each color in every group. Many video monitors have three electron guns, with the beam of each gun targeted for phosphors of only one color; Sony Trinitrons, like the standard Apple RGB monitor, have only one gun and a split, three-part beam. A *shadow mask* located right behind the screen has thousands of tiny holes aligned with the phosphor groups; the beams shoot through the holes at slightly different angles, so the beam from the "blue" gun hits only the blue phosphors, the "red" gun hits the red phosphors, and the "green" gun hits the green phosphors. Figure 5-5 shows how this works. In the picture of the rose, for example, the beams will activate mostly red phosphors and a few green phosphors to re-create an image of the petals, but mostly green and a few red phosphors to re-create the leaves.

As you've probably noticed, all video displays, including the viewfinder, have the same *aspect ratio,* or proportion between width and height of the screen. This ratio is three units high by four units wide and applies to any size video screen. Uniform display proportions are necessary so a broadcast video signal, which contains instructions that rigidly control the scanning process and location of the scanspot, will send the scanspot to the right locations on any TV or monitor receiveing the signal. Measurements of screen size are usually given in inches

Figure 5-5. Color Picture Tube

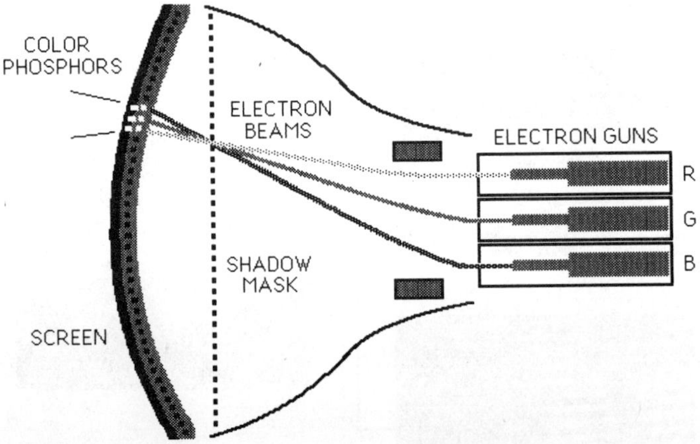

across the diagonal of the screen; a 20-inch monitor measures 20 inches from the upper left to the lower right of the screen.

An audio signal, either mono or stereo, is sent to the typical monitor along with, but separate from, the video signal. Sound is re-created with an audio amplifier and speaker or speakers in the monitor. The typical viewfinder has no speaker attached (although at least one model of camcorder does offer this); the audio signal is routed to a headphone jack instead for use with standard audio headphones.

The VCR

The video and audio signals are also routed to the video cassette recorder in the camcorder. The VCR records the signal onto recording tape in a cassette so it can be regenerated for display at any time. The tape is composed of a plastic substrate, coated with ferrous particles that are sensitive to the magnetic fields created by the VCR recording heads.

Inside the VCR are two or more rotating *video heads,* small electromagnets inside a head drum. When the tape is loaded it wraps around the head drum in one of several possible configurations, depending on the tape format and type of VCR (see below for more on tape formats). No matter which wrap format is used, all modern VCRs wrap the tape at a slight angle around the head drum. This angle is important because it enables the heads to record more video information on tape.

Tape and video heads move at the same time. In VHS camcorders running at the SP speed, the video heads spin at 2700 rpm, and the tape moves at 1.32 inches per second in the reverse direction from the spin of the heads. The faster the tape moves, the better the image quality of the recording. This might seem counterintuitive, but it's true; the slowest VHS speed (extended play, or EP, at .45 inches per second) yields the poorest picture, as any VHS user knows. That's also the reason for spinning the heads—to create the fastest possible relative speed of tape to recording head without having to move the tape so fast that it breaks. A slower tape speed does have the advantage of allowing longer recordings to be fit on a tape.

When recording, a portion of the incoming signal is send to each video head, which turns the voltage into a small magnetic field. Each video head in turn sends out a magnetic pulse to the passing tape that lays down a *track* slantwise across the tape, as in Figure 5-6. Each track contains the information for one video field. A separate head or heads lays down one or more audio tracks and a *control track,* a separate signal that controls tape motion in playback. The control track contains pulses that demarcate each frame to provide information about frame timing. An *erase head* blanks the tape. In some VCRs, the erase head spins inside the head drum and can erase individual tracks, a necessary feature for videotape editing (see below and the following chapter).

Figure 5-6. Tape Tracks

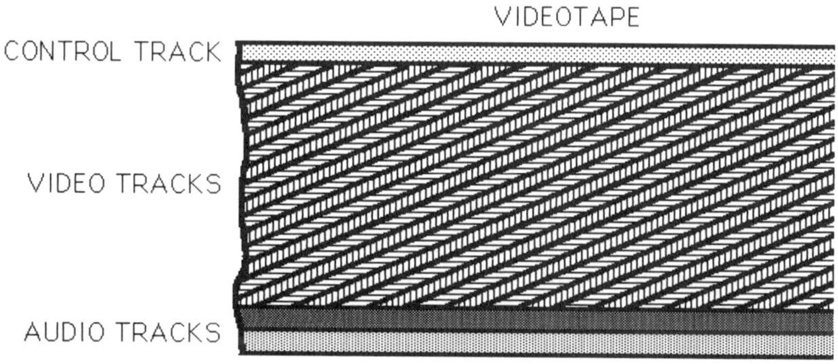

In playback, the video heads read rather than write information. The magnetic field in the tape induces a current in the heads that's amplified to output a standard video signal, which can then be displayed on a monitor or recorded to another VCR.

The Video Signal

What's in the color video signal that enables the monitor to re-create an image of the scene and the VCR to record it? The *signal* is a series of small voltages, expressed as pulses and sine waves, that encodes information about each line of the picture and tells the electron beam how and when to scan.

The part of the video signal that actually creates the picture includes the following information:

- *Luminance,* the brightness of the image; also called the Y part of the signal. It carries information about blacks, whites, and grays.
- *Hue,* the percentage of red, blue, or green in each part of the image.
- Color *saturation,* the intensity of the image colors. Together, hue and saturation are called *chrominance,* also called the C part of the signal. Color video components can display or record the chrominance part of the signal, while monochrome components (a black-and-white TV, for example) ignore it, displaying only the luminance part of the signal. Other parts of the signal contain reference waves that make sure each line is always set to the proper color and amplitude.

Also included in the video signal is synchronizing information to control the timing and location of the scanspot, making sure each element of the video signal occurs in lockstep with the others. All components in a video system must be *in sync* with the others; that is, they must abide by the synchronization commands of the video signal, or video won't travel from one component to the next.

Bandwidth. The amount of information a video signal can carry is in part determined by its *bandwidth.* The bandwidth is the maximum frequency range—from the peak white level, requiring the maximum voltage, to the blackest black, requiring the least—of the luminance part of the transmitted signal, measured in cycles per second, or *hertz.* Think of the bandwidth as the hole that sand pours through in an hourglass. A wide hole will let a lot of sand through. A small hole will only let a small amount of sand through. It's the same with the signal; a wide bandwidth can carry more luminance information than a narrow one. Video requires a wide bandwidth to carry all the luminance information—about five megahertz (MHz, millions of cycles), and six MHz when you include audio and sidebands. You can tell some useful information about video components, especially VCRs, if you know the bandwidth they can transmit or record, as you'll see later.

Composite Video. The mixed video signal, including all color and synchronizing information, is called *composite video,* and is the signal type used by all consumer and nearly all professional video equipment. (It isn't the type of video produced by Macs and most other computers, as you'll see below.) To yield acceptable quality, a composite video signal in the U.S. must meet a technical standard known as RS-170A set by the National Television Standards Committee (NTSC). Casual references by videoheads to "composite video," "NTSC video," or "RS-170A video" mean essentially the same thing—good quality, TV-type video. Discussions and diagrams in this book will deal with NTSC video. Other television standards include PAL, widely used in Europe and Latin America, and SECAM, used in France, the USSR, and many African countries, among other places. These TV standards use different scanning rates and a different number of lines in the raster.

Component Video. An increasingly popular alternative to composite video is *component video,* in which the color parts of the signal are kept separate to prevent them from partially interfering with one another, as happens in composite video. The Super-VHS tape format, for example, uses a component video scheme called *Y/C,* in which the luminance information is separated from the chrominance information, not combined into one signal, yielding a higher-quality picture. Computers and some professional video equipment use another component system in which the red, green, and blue elements of the picture are transmitted separately. Composite and component video schemes are electronically and mechanically incompatible, requiring some kind of converter device to translate component into composite video and vice versa.

Analog to Digital

Up to now we've been talking about analog electronics—waveforms and so on, where information is carried by the amplitude and frequency of a continuously varying small electrical current. You might think of the analog waveform as being an analogy of the scene—carrying a kind of representation of the scene in the shape of the wave itself—and in fact you can tell something about the appearance of the scene by looking at the video waveform on a waveform monitor. On the other hand, computers, at least in their internal operations, use *digital* electronics; digital information is carried as a string of discrete pulses that are in one of two possible states, on or off (1 or 0). In digital video, the scene is converted into a series of binary numbers that, if you were to look at them, would convey no visual information at all to the human eye. The computer understands the numbers, however, and can reconstitute the scene perfectly every time.

The two methods of encoding information are electronically incompatible—digital signals look like random noise to analog equipment, and analog signals are completely incomprehensible to computers. A device called an *Analog-to-Digital encoder* (an A/D device sometimes called a *scan converter)* is needed to convert video information to digital format; a Digital-to-Analog encoder (D/A) converts the signal from digital back to analog. Such encoders are at the heart of computer-video systems, and are what make DTV possible.

One thing you as a computer user might need to get used to is that analog information, including video, isn't forever, and can easily be degraded. Each time an analog signal is processed through a component, the quality of the signal is diminished. Signal strength is lost any time it's carried over a cable; that's why every piece of video equipment contains several amplifiers to boost and reconstitute the signal. It follows that analog video is also degraded when you copy it from tape to tape. A good analogy is the process of copying a picture on a photocopy machine. Take a picture and copy it. This is the first generation copy. Then take the copy and copy that to create a second generation copy. The first-generation copy has less detail than the original, and the second-generation copy has less detail than the first. The more you continue this process, the less information is in each succeeding generation, until you finally get a copy that's completely unrecognizable, with no useful information. The same thing happens in video, as anyone knows who has copied a tape down several generations. This is just a fact of life of the analog world. You might say that entropy is always trying to reduce the analog signal to random noise.

But in the digital world, as long as the numbers are transmitted correctly, you get the same picture every time, no matter how many times you copy, view, or transmit it. Mac artists can copy a picture file as many times as they like, down as many generations as they like, and have exactly the same information in each file.

Video users, who currently have to struggle to copy their first-generation videotapes down as few generations as possible to produce completed programming, can look forward to the eventual replacement of analog video with digital video. The invasion of the analog world by the digital world is proceeding rapidly. Almost all video special effects are now produced with computers and then output in analog form. Video editing systems use computers to control machines and record the list of editing decisions. On the professional level, the first practical digital VCRs are already in use. But for now, the analog and digital worlds have to be bridged with inelegant converters, digitizers, and other devices.

Mixing Mac Graphics and Video

With the video basics under your belt, you're probably ready to jump right in and start using your Mac to create great DTV presentations. Unfortunately, it's not that easy. The big hurdle you have to cross, as hinted above, is that Mac graphics and NTSC video are electronically incompatible.

To get a high-resolution screen for the original Macs, Apple opted early on for a display system that uses a different scan-rate and requires a higher bandwidth than standard NTSC, yielding a sharper, clearer picture but no video compatibility. The Mac video system uses a 60 Hz scan rate, noninterlaced, as opposed to 30 Hz, interlaced NTSC, so you can't record unaltered Mac video on a VCR, display it on a TV, or synchronize it out of the box with any NTSC video component. Apple's video card for the Mac II does a certain amount of conversion, taking the digital RGB system the Mac uses internally and outputting it as an analog RGB signal for Mac monitors, but this isn't compatible with NTSC, either. While the Mac display is wonderful for computer graphics, Apple probably wishes now that there were some easy way to make the two standards work together.

The only way to mix video and Mac graphics short of pointing a video camera at the Mac screen and taping it is with the help of additional hardware, some of it fairly expensive. For example, to record Mac graphics on a VCR you must purchase an *NTSC encoder,* a device that sits inside or beside the Mac and converts Mac video to NTSC video. Apple has taken a step in the right direction by offering a basic encoder for the Mac Portable called the *Mac Portable Video Adapter*. This little box, which plugs into the video jack on the Portable, can drive standard Mac monitors and NTSC video displays as well. It also works with the PAL and SECAM video standards used in Europe, Africa, and Latin America. Unfortunately, it only works in monochrome, and only with the Portable.

To get composite video into the Macintosh so you can mix video imagery and Mac graphics, you need third-party devices not offered by Apple. (No Macintosh, or any other computer for that matter, offers a video-in jack.) There are a number of devices that do this in different ways: *RGB encoders,* to convert composite video to analog RGB; a *genlock,* a device that synchronizes one video source with another so that Mac graphics may be superimposed on moving video; a *digitizer,* a device that captures video images from a camera and converts them to digital picture documents, usually PAINT, TIFF, or PICT2 files; and a *frame grabber,* to capture frames from tape. Two or more of these devices are likely to be combined in one video card or unit. Let's take a closer look at the operation of these components.

Encoders. These are the A/D and D/A devices that do all the conversion from NTSC video to Mac video, and back again. There are encoders that clip to the inside of a Mac Plus or SE and let you tape Mac graphics on a VCR, but most Mac encoders are incorporated into color video cards that slip into Mac II NuBus slots to provide direct composite video output. Differences among the various Mac NTSC video cards are a matter of video output quality—whether or not the video card provides true "broadcast-quality" NTSC RS-170A; the options it offers, such as genlocking and frame grabbing; and the price of a fully configured board. Simple encoders cost under $1000. Figure 5-7 shows a simple Mac video setup using a basic encoder card.

Figure 5-7. Basic Mac Video Setup

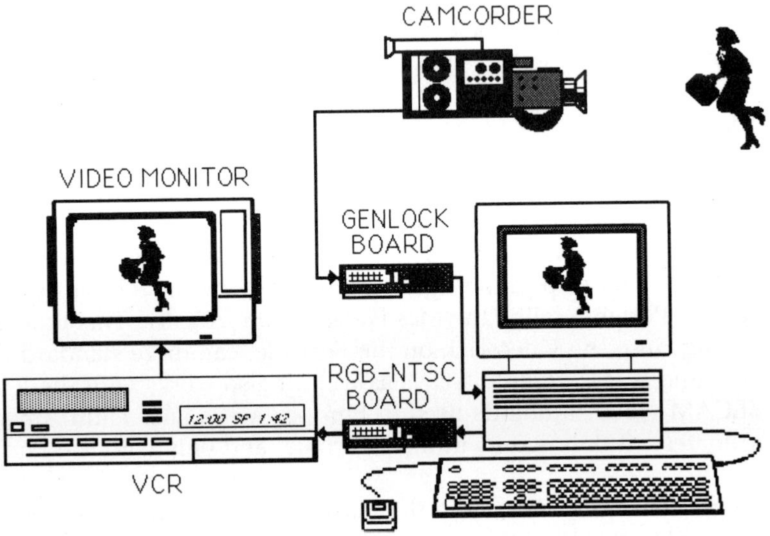

Genlocks. A *genlock* is a device that synchronizes one video source with another for recording to a VCR—in DTV, computer graphics with live video. For example, with a composite signal from one VCR routed through a genlock and into the computer, you can display a moving video picture in place of a selected color in an Macintosh computer graphic—usually the background color of the graphic, but some genlocks allow you to overlay video on any color or combination of colors you specify. (In other words, all Macintosh genlocks incorporate a *keyer* as well.) You can't modify the incoming video from your computer, but you can mix together the Macintosh graphics and composite video and output the mixture for recording on tape.

As an example of how a genlock may be used for presentation programming, say you want to lay a chart over taped footage shot at your organization's headquarters. First, set up your equipment as in Figure 5-8. Then create the chart on your Macintosh with a graphics program, with black as the background color. Pop the taped footage of the headquarters into the player VCR and route the VCR output to the Macintosh through the genlock. On the Macintosh monitor, the video footage appears only over the background black. The combined image is output back out of the Macintosh through the genlock card to the record VCR. When you play back the recording, you see the chart superimposed over the video. Figure 5-8 shows how this works. Other typical uses for genlocks are to superimpose Mac-generated titles or animations over video sequences.

Figure 5-8. Genlocking Business Graphics

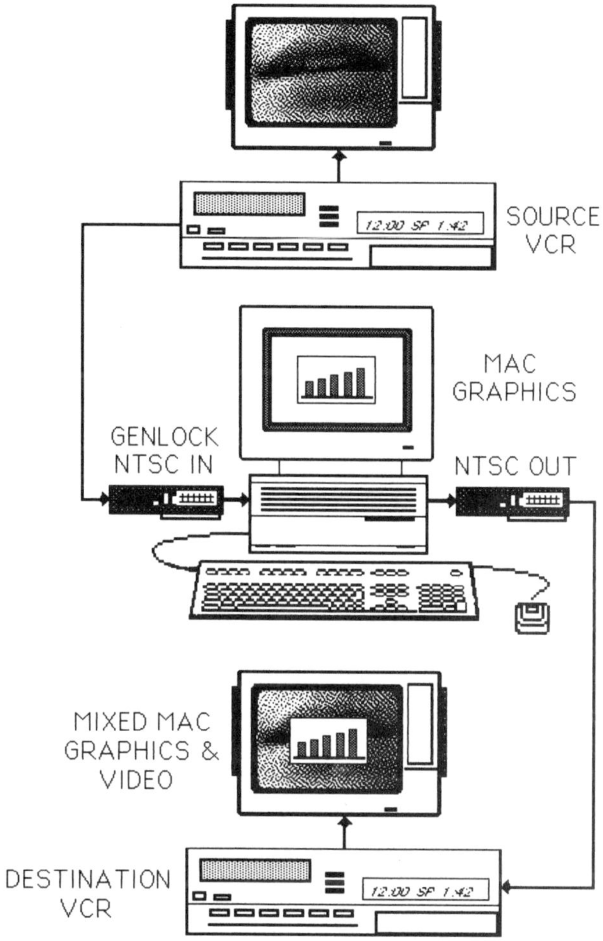

All genlocks come with software to adapt the Macintosh for genlock use, and to provide some software control over genlocking operations.

Digitizers and Frame Grabbers. Another method for getting images into your Mac is by using a device called a *digitizer,* hardware for taking a video camera signal and converting it to the RGB format and picture file types the Macintosh uses. Many digitizers, such as MacVision (see Appendix A), work best with black-and-white CCTV cameras. The camera feeds a signal to the digitizer itself, which is basically an NTSC encoder with software to reconstitute the incoming image information into a Macintosh picture format, usually a PAINT, TIFF, or PICT2 file. Figure 5-9 is a diagram of a standard digitizer setup. The main advantage of a digitizer over a scanner is that a digitizer can capture images of any three-dimensional scene. Scanners are better for flat art.

Figure 5-9. Digitizer

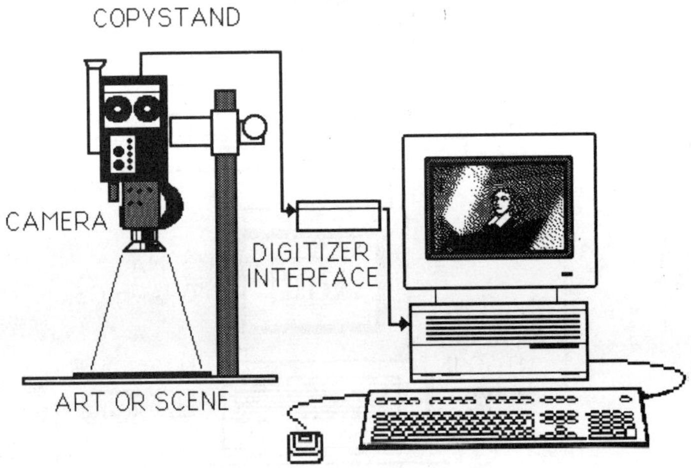

A *frame grabber,* also called a *frame buffer* or *stillstore,* can capture a single video frame from a live or taped source by storing the entire picture in RAM. An encoder in the frame grabber converts the image to Mac RGB; software then converts the stored image to a picture file format, usually 24-bit PICT2. Using a frame grabber, you can grab a still right off a tape playing on a VCR and feed it into your Macintosh for graphic embellishment. Or the frame grabber can be hooked to a camera and grab a still at specified intervals—one every second, for example—for time-lapse video, which can be very effective for showing speeded-up industrial processes. The concept of frame grabbing is illustrated in Figure 5-10.

Since the various Mac frame grabbers are quite different in capability, try each out before you purchase one. Be sure it can accept both live and taped video, that the machine co-resides well with other Macintosh hardware, and that the digitizer software handles the effects you want to find. Keep in mind that you'll not be able to grab long sequences of video in RAM. At 30 frames a second, and with each grabbed frame using more than one megabyte (and probably a lot more), you'll fill your memory in less than a second, and your hard disk in two or three.

Digital Video Effects Processors. Newest in the Mac video world are video processing boards that can create the amazing digital video trickery we've come to expect on broadcast TV—flipping, swirling, flying, and dancing frames of moving video. These components are

Figure 5-10. Frame Grabbing

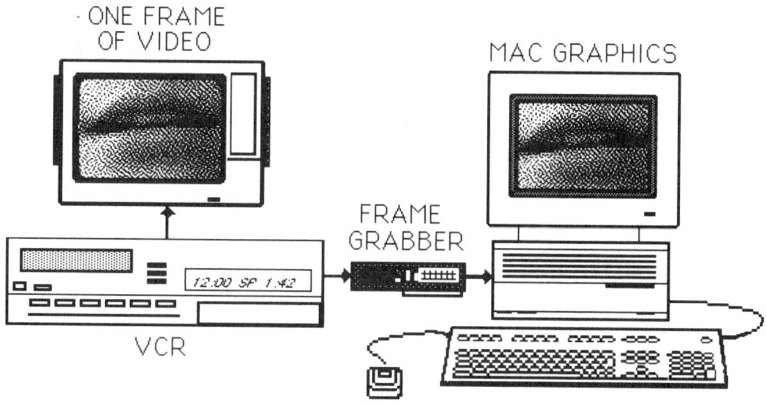

used in tandem with NTSC video boards and genlocks, with the fancy video effects controlled by software.

While digital video effects (DVE) are spectacular and fun, it's hard to say that they add enough to a presentation to balance the amount of work they require to plan and choreograph. Still, a well-planned DVE transition from one segment of a video to the next can wake up your audience and add professionalism to your program.

The Mac Video Studio

As you can see, Mac video presentations are far more hardware intensive than the typical slideshow. When you start exploring the idea of setting up your own desktop video studio, you'll find it's a jungle out there. Competing tape formats, incompatible software, computer peripherals galore—it's hard to find your way through the underbrush to the system you need. You should ask these questions:

- What do you want out of your DTV system?
- Will you be creating graphics for existing video programming or assembling original programs from footage you shoot on location?
- Will sound or animation be an important part of your programs?
- Does your system need to be compatible with any other system, either video or computer?
- What level of quality are you willing or able to buy?

The more questions you ask beforehand, the less likely you'll be stuck with a system that doesn't really meet your needs.

DTV Hardware

When evaluating video equipment, keep in mind that the industry classifies components into three levels:

- Broadcast, professional video equipment that yields top-notch imagery, with prices to match. For pros only.
- Industrial, ruggedly built units with good image quality, but not as good as broadcast. Prices are correspondingly lower. Good for serious individuals and small companies.
- Consumer, video equipment built with price rather than image-quality in mind. At the high-end of the consumer market, however, you may find components that match industrial quality.

VCRs

After the Macintosh in system importance comes the video cassette recorder. A VCR can store immense amounts of image and sound information, far more than is possible on optical disks, and lets you easily distribute your work for viewing wherever there's a compatible VCR. This is the component on which you'll probably be spending the bulk of your system budget.

Today there are many VCR formats, differentiated primarily by the width of the recording tape (1-inch, $\frac{3}{4}$-inch, and so on), the recording speed, and the quality of the recorded image. Each major format is electronically compatible with the others, but the formats are mechanically incompatible—you can't play a $\frac{1}{2}$-inch cassette in a $\frac{3}{4}$-inch VCR, for example, or vice versa. Within each format there's an increasing number of subdivisions and choices, some of which are also incompatible with the others. Here's a quick guide to the current formats.

1-inch

This is what the big boys and girls play with—the video tape recorder (VTR) format used by the networks and big production houses. 1-inch VTRs are strictly *broadcast-quality*—offering the best available image. With 1-inch decks costing several tens of thousands of dollars (not to mention all the support equipment and technicians needed to run them), it's unlikely you'll be buying one for your DTV productions. However, should you ever land a professional project with a budget to match, 1-inch is the currently the only way to go.

$\frac{3}{4}$-inch

The $\frac{3}{4}$-inch cassette format (or U-Matic, as its inventor, Sony, calls it), is the format of choice for field recording and lower-cost professional editing. Professional-end $\frac{3}{4}$-inch recorders offer true broadcast quality and can be operated by broadcast computer edit controllers. $\frac{3}{4}$-inch decks also come in an industrial grade, which may be within your budget for presentation recording.

The recently introduced U-Matic SP format offers improved resolution while remaining compatible with all older $\frac{3}{4}$-inch equipment. The letters *SP* appear in the name of SP tapes. Standard or SP, portable $\frac{3}{4}$-inch equipment is big and heavy, requiring a separate deck operator and carrier on location productions (see Chapter 6).

$\frac{1}{2}$-inch

The $\frac{1}{2}$-inch market is dominated by VHS, the standard for consumer recording. Although VHS VCRs and camcorders are relatively cheap and easily obtained, VHS picture quality is relatively poor, with low resolution, fuzzy color, and low-fi sound. Decks with *VHS-HQ* (high-quality) and Hi-Fi yield somewhat improved video, much better audio, and are worth the additional investment. Industrial-quality VHS systems are also available with heavy-duty tape transport systems and slightly better video specifications. Most VHS camcorders use a variant format called *VHS-C*. The VHS-C cassette is smaller and records only 20 minutes. It can be played in standard VHS decks with a cassette adapter.

Super-VHS (S-VHS). This is an enhanced version of VHS, with better color purity and higher resolution—not quite broadcast quality, but a lot closer than ordinary VHS. The higher resolution is achieved by splitting the chrominance part of the video signal from the luminance part so each can be processed optimally. This requires a split connector called a *Y/C connector* on any equipment used in an S-VHS system if the full resolution of the S-VHS picture is to be maintained. If you choose S-VHS, you'll need to purchase an S-VHS camcorder and/or an S-VHS VCR, an S-VHS–compatible monitor, and specially formulated S-VHS tapes. S-VHS is downward-compatible with ordinary VHS—that means you can play VHS tapes on an S-VHS machine, but not vice-versa. S-VHS is probably the best all-around format for creating presentations, because you can get good quality videos for a relatively modest investment.

ED (Extended Definition) Betamax. This is Sony's bid to recapture some of the consumer $\frac{1}{2}$-inch VCR market from VHS, which killed Sony's Betamax a few years ago. ED-Beta offers better resolution than S-VHS and sharper color. Like S-VHS, ED-Beta is a component format that requires compatible equipment with a special Y/C connector. It is downward-compatible with older Betamax equipment and tapes.

M-II and Betacam. These $\frac{1}{2}$-inch broadcast formats are smaller and more convenient than U-Matic SP or 1-inch while offering comparable quality. They may ultimately replace the big formats for professional field recording. At least one network has already adopted M-II as its preferred in-house format.

8mm. The newest tape format, 8mm, offers ½-inch video quality in a compact package. 8mm tape is about half the width of ½-inch, and 8mm cassettes are only a little larger than audio cassettes. This makes for small VCRs and camcorders, an important consideration for field production. 8mm sound quality is far better than that of most ½-inch decks; in fact, an 8mm VCR makes an excellent audio cassette recorder with audio quality near that of CDs or DAT (Digital Audio Tape). The latest wrinkle in industrial 8mm is a compact videotape editing system consisting of a single unit with two built-in VCRs, a monitor, a keyboard, and an onboard edit controller computer. Sony has introduced a handheld 8mm VCR-color monitor combo, the Video Walkman, that would be handy for location production.

8mm Hi-band. This new 8mm subformat, just becoming available in the U.S. at the time of writing, is roughly equivalent in quality to S-VHS and ED Beta. It features an expanded high-frequency band for the luminance part of the signal, offering resolution similar to S-VHS if recorded and viewed with the proper equipment. 8mm Hi-band is downward-compatible with earlier 8mm equipment.

Table 5-1 gives the tape types, lengths, recording speeds, and running times for the ¾-inch, ½-inch, and 8mm VCR formats. Table 5-2 compares selected technical specs of the more popular formats.

Table 5-1. Formats, Tape Speeds, and Recording Times

Format	**Tape Speed (in inches per second)**		
U-Matic	3.75		
Cassette	**Recording Times**		
KCS-5	:05		
KCS-10	:10		
KCS-20	:20		
KCA-30	:30		
KCA-60	:60		
Format	**Tape Speed (in inches per second)**		
VHS	SP 1.32	LP .66	EP .45
Cassette	**Recording Times**		
T-20	:20	:40	1:00
T-25	:25	1:00	1:25
T-40	:40	1:20	2:00
T-60	1:00	2:00	3:00
T-80	1:20	2:40	4:00
T-100	1:40	3:20	5:00
T-120	2:00	4:00	6:00
T-160	2:40	5:20	8:00

Format	**Tape Speed (in inches per second)**		
Betamax	Beta I 1.54	Beta II .79	Beta III .45
Cassette	**Recording Times**		
L-125	:15	:25	:45
L-250	:25	1:00	1:25
L-370	:45	1:25	2:15
L-500	1:00	2:00	3:00
L-750	1:25	3:20	4:25
L-830	1:40	3:20	5:00

Format	**Tape Speed (in inches per second)**		
8mm	SP .56	LP .28	(playback only)
Cassette	**Recording Time**		
Standard 8mm	2:00	3:00	

Table 5-2. Selected Format Technical Specifications

	¾″	VHS	S-VHS	ED-Beta	8mm
Signal Type	composite	composite	Y/C	Y/C	composite
Tracks	control, 2 linear audio	control, 2 linear audio, 2 hi-fi	control, 2 linear audio, 2 hi-fi	control, 1 linear, audio, 2 hi-fi	no control, 1 AFM, 2 PCM audio
Luminance S/N (db)	46	45	48	47	45
Luminance Bandwidth (MHz)	3.2	3	5.0	6.2	3.2
Horiz lines of resolution	260	240	400	500	250
Audio S/N (db)	48	45 linear, 72 hi-fi	44 linear, 95 hi-fi	70 hi-fi	70 PCM

Tips for Choosing a VCR

Choosing the right VCR is crucial for obtaining the level of video quality you need for your programming. If you're planning to purchase one especially for high-quality presentations, get the very best machine you can afford. Here are some things to consider:

- Choose the format appropriate to the task. If you're planning to do semi-professional work, S-VHS, ED-Beta, or ¾-inch are the formats to choose, with ¾-inch the semi-pro format of choice. Distribute your video presentation on VHS, the most popular format.

- Choose an editing VCR. These high-end machines have a wealth of additional features, including the ability to perform frame-accurate edits (see Chapter 8), edit marking, random-access searches, digital special effects, and more. Check that the VCR has *flying erase heads.* These are tape heads in a VCR that erase tape with frame accuracy, yielding perfectly clean edits.
- VCRs with high-fidelity stereo sound can record a far greater audio range. An *audio dub* feature allows you to record new audio over one audio track without disturbing the video tracks. This is convenient for quickly adding narration or music to a tape.
- The front panel should have easy-to-understand and logically arranged controls. A jog-shuttle wheel gives better control of tape viewing speed. Look for a digital counter that shows seconds and frames, not a mechanical counter that displays arbitrary numbers on little wheels. Also look for VU or LED meters for audio and video levels.
- Special effects, such as freeze-frame and slow-motion, should yield a noise-free image. You'll find these most often in decks that offer "digital" special effects.
- VCRs with direct drive motors, rather than belts and pulleys, are more reliable and offer smoother and more accurate tape transport.
- A good remote control will make it easier to operate your Macintosh and your VCR at the same time, or to run the VCR from the podium.

Cameras and Camcorders

A video camera or camcorder is another essential piece of DTV equipment. With a camera, you can grab scenes from your world and incorporate them into your DTV presentations.

Cameras come in two basic types: *standalone cameras* and cameras incorporated into *camcorders.* A standalone camera is a good choice when you need high-quality camera output—up to broadcast quality—and system flexibility. The higher-priced cameras yield better images than most camcorders do and can be teamed with any VCR, so you're not limited to one VCR format or level of quality as you are with camcorders. Low-end industrial black-and-white cameras can be used with any VCR for digitizing (see below) and cost far less than camcorders.

Camcorders, on the other hand, are small, convenient, and available. For field use, you can't beat a unit that weighs two pounds, can be held in one hand, and needs no setting up to roll tape. The better camcorders are laden with features, including all the usual camera and VCR functions plus titling, special effects, electronic camera stabilizers, high-speed shutters (see below to read about these), and more. Broadcast-quality camcorders are also available (in the Betacam and MII formats), but these are very expensive.

Tips for Choosing a Camera

If you're choosing a video camera or camcorder for presentation programming, ask these questions: Will you be using it in a studio? In field productions? Do you need a camera to scan flat art for digitizing? What level of quality do you need, and what can you afford? Does the camera have to interface with existing equipment?

Look for these features:

- CCD versus tubes. Many broadcast and industrial cameras still use camera tubes instead of charged coupled devices to pick up the image. Tubes yield better images, but they're fragile, need to be periodically aligned, and can be "burned" by too much light (for example, if you point the camera at the sun or a floodlight). A CCD camera is recommended—they're rugged, lighter, need less maintenance, can't be burnt, and make for smaller cameras. Look for a CCD pixel count of at least 250,000.
- High resolution. Broadcast cameras yield 525 lines of horizontal resolution or better; 400 lines is still good quality and suitable for DTV. A video camera that yields under 300 lines is probably not worth getting.
- Light sensitivity. Video cameras don't record well in poor light. The minimum illumination for a camera is usually given in *lux,* with some cameras claiming to provide decent images down to ten lux or under. This is very little light, and the images won't be very good even with a top-quality camera. You might be able to adjust the *gain,* or light sensitivity, of the camera, but the higher the gain, the noisier the image.
- A good lens. Zoom lenses are standard on video cameras. Look for a zoom ratio of 6:1 or better and a variable control that will zoom in faster when you want to and slower when you don't. A *macro* feature lets you focus up close to small objects to get magnified images—useful for digitizing.
- Auto-aperture. This feature automatically adjusts the iris of the lens to allow the optimum amount of light into the camera, saving you the trouble of setting the iris yourself.
- Auto-focusing. An auto-focus lens uses a sonic or infrared rangefinder to determine the distance to the subject, usually the object in the center of the viewfinder. A chip tells the lens motor how far to twist the lens so the subject will be in focus.
- Full color controls. These include a *white balance* adjustment to set the white level for each lighting condition you encounter; a lighting type

adjustment for setting the camera to work with tungsten (incandescent) light, fluorescent light, or daylight; and a color temperature control to set the amount of red or blue in the image. Newer cameras and most consumer camcorders take care of color adjustments automatically.

- An electronic viewfinder. This is the type that's actually a small video monitor, letting you see exactly what the camera sees (in black-and-white, anyway).
- A complete range of audio and video connections, including: composite video out, a camera cable connection (for remote control of the camera from a matching portable VCR), two microphone-in jacks, one or two audio-out jacks, a headphone jack, a battery connection, and AC power.
- A camera that's comfortable to handle, light in weight, and easy to operate, with conveniently placed controls.
- A full range of features in the VCR part of a camcorder, including flying erase heads for seamless transitions between scenes.

Video Displays

For DTV work, you'll need one or more video displays to supplement your Macintosh monitor. The ideal setup is to have a display for each piece of equipment—the camera, computer, and VCR(s)—so you can see what is happening with each. That doesn't mean you must purchase expensive color monitors for every DTV component you own; a cheap black-and-white monitor can be quite adequate when all you want to do is position an object in the field of view of your camera. You can use any TV to monitor your VCR, just as you play tapes on the TV now. But to see the output of a camcorder, camera, or pro VCR, you'll want a color monitor with a composite video input. When you present your video to an audience, you'll want the best, biggest display you can find.

Video displays come in several types:

- TVs. The traditional TV, still to be found at the low end of the video market, has a television tuner and amplifier but no provision for direct display of composite video. Video has to be converted (*modulated* is the technical term) to an RF signal for input through the TV's antenna terminals, then demodulated inside the TV for display on the screen.
- TV-monitors. These are basically TVs with provision for accepting a composite video signal. Most higher-priced consumer TVs fall into this category. Some TV-monitors have Y/C jacks for connection to the new super format equipment. The current picture tube size limit for TV-monitors (and any device using a CRT) is about 35 inches diagonal.

- Video monitors. These accept only composite input and are generally used by professionals. They're likely to provide the best picture and cost the most.
- Projection TVs. Instead of using a standard picture tube, projection TVs project the image through a lens or lenses onto a screen either in front or in back of the projector. The projected image can be quite large, up to 100 inches across or larger, and thus suitable for viewing by large audiences. But the picture is correspondingly dim, best seen from directly in front in a darkened auditorium.
- Monitor-VCRs. These combine a monitor and a VCR in one compact, portable package, useful when you need to make quick presentations. Sizes range from Sony's handheld model with an 8mm deck to portable projection units with a built-in full-sized VHS deck.

Tips for Choosing a Color Display

Picture, sound, connectivity, and controls are the most important aspects to evaluate when choosing a color video display.

Picture. Monitor picture quality depends on several factors. Among them are the type of display technology—CRT, projection, or color LCD; the number of lines of resolution produced by the display; the size and number of phosphor dots on the screen and the precision of the holes in the shadow mask behind them; the existence of picture-enhancing circuitry; the size of the display; and the flatness, squareness, and reflectivity of the screen. The best-looking displays have a high number of lines of resolution (400 or better), a small *dot pitch* (the distance between phosphor dots of the same color) of .34 mm or less, a comb filter or digital circuits to reduce color noise in the picture, a picture no bigger than 27-inches diagonal, and a flat, black, glare-free, square-cornered screen. These general principles apply to computer monitors as well.

Sound. Sets with hi-fidelity stereo speakers designed for proper operation within the magnetic fields generated by CRTs provide the best sound and are worth the extra expense. The extra punch of superior sound can make a big difference to a presentation.

Connectivity. Good connectivity means you can hook the set up to any other component you have. The display should include composite video (LINE) in and out, RF in (for use with VCRs and antennas), stereo audio in and out, and standard antenna screws.

Controls. A full set of display controls includes brightness, contrast, hue, vertical and horizontal hold, audio levels (for both channels if it's a stereo set), channel, power, and a knob to switch among video sources. A full-function remote control is worth having, so you can control the display from the podium or anywhere in the room. Controls should be easy to reach and unambiguous in function.

Other Video Components

There are other types of components you might want to know about, especially if you're planning to get into DTV presentations in a big way.

Edit Controllers. An *edit controller* is basically a type of remote that lets you precisely control the actions of two or more compatible VCRs for editing videotape—that is, assembling footage into a coherent narrative. The controller, which displays the current frame for each VCR and has buttons for searching tape, marking editing points, and automatically executing edits, makes the process fast and easy. Generally these must be used with compatible editing VCRs from the same manufacturer. Macintosh-controlled editing systems are just coming on the market. See the next chapter for more on editing.

Single-Frame Controllers. This is a box that takes over the transport functions of a high-end VCR—usually under software control from the Macintosh—so you can record images on one frame at a time. The sole use for transport controllers is to produce frame-by-frame computer graphics animations. (See Chapter 8 for more on animation.)

Special Effects Devices. Several different types of video equipment have been developed to create those video special effects we all know and love.

A *switcher* is a device for instantly cutting between several live or taped video sources. A switcher is what makes it possible to cut between the input from various video cameras in a live news show, for example.

A switcher is usually part of a *special effects generator*, or *SEG*. This is a device for creating and controlling transitions and other effects during video production and editing. It's the SEG that makes the fancy wipes and dissolves between scenes you see used regularly in sports and game shows.

A *keyer*, often included in the SEG unit as well, is hardware that makes it possible to replace part of the image from one video source with the image from a second video source. Keying can be over a specified gray level in the video *(luminance keying)* or over a specified color (*chrominance keying*, or *chromakeying*). An example of keying is the insertion of video of a weather map over the blue screen behind a TV weatherman.

Digital Video Effects (DVE). These machines are computers dedicated to creating flying, twisting, turning, and perspective effects. When you see the screen image turn on its side and fly away into the distance, you're seeing DVE in action. With your Macintosh and a NuBus effects board like Mass Microsystems' ColorSpace/FX (see Appendix A), you can create many of the same DVE effects.

Processing Amplifiers. A *processing amplifier*, or *proc amp*, takes a weak and/or substandard composite signal and boosts it to proper voltage levels, while tweaking all the little signal details to get them just right. Broadcast edit rooms and studios have proc amps costing several thousand dollars that are invaluable when you need to bump your Macintosh DTV efforts up to broadcast quality.

Basic Audio Equipment

So far in this chapter we've barely mentioned video sound. But sound is, in fact, a crucial element of any DTV production. Sound designers will tell you that most of the emotional impact of video is in what you hear, not in what you see. You can easily test this for yourself by turning on any TV action drama and then turning down the sound. You can still tell what's happening—you've seen every TV action plot a hundred times already, so no surprises—but it isn't nearly as engaging. Now switch to a comedy. Without the laugh track, music, and pratfall sound effects, Bill Cosby isn't that funny, even if you can read his lips. (Charlie Chaplin and Buster Keaton *are* funny without sound, though; we've just been conditioned to expect sound to help us connect with video).

Probably worse than no sound is bad sound—sound that's muddy, unpleasant, or unintelligible. A Mac DTV training tape won't have much effect if the audience can't hear what the instructors are saying. Unfortunately, audio is often neglected by the presenter in search of stunning visuals, and that's a shame, because getting effective sound on tape isn't that difficult.

But before you add those wonderful sounds to your tape, you've got to capture them. As with video, there are standard pieces of audio for the job.

Microphones. A microphone, as you know, is a device for turning sound into an electrical signal. There are various types, with different levels of directional sensitivity. Many amateur DTV directors take mikes for granted and use whatever one is handy, such as the small mike that comes built into every camcorder, but all microphones aren't created equal. Most camcorder microphones, for example, are the inexpensive *omnidirectional* kind, which means they pick up sound in every direction. That includes the sound of the camcorder's autofocus device, the zoom motor, your breathing, and jet planes flying overhead. If you don't really care about the quality of the sound in your DTV production, use the camcorder mike.

You'll get far better sound with a modest investment in a better mike. For field production, a *shotgun mike* works best. This is the long, aggressive-looking microphone you see on top of news cameras. A shotgun mike picks up sound in a narrow cone in front of the mike, and very little to the side or behind, so you only record the sounds coming from the subject where the camera is pointing. The shotgun can be mounted on the top or side of the camcorder, and plugged into the external mike jack.

For studio production, especially for talk shows and the like, *lavalier mikes* are a necessity. These tiny devices clip onto ties, behind lapels, and under collars. Lavaliers are relatively weak microphones, but this is an advantage—they pick up only their wearer's voice. A general-purpose mike useful for interviewing, on-camera work, and ambient sound recording is the *cardioid* (so-called because of its heart-shaped pickup pattern), which has good recording characteristics and is fairly directional. Variations in tone quality can be achieved by simply pointing a cardioid mike at a slight angle to the subject.

If you're going to plug an external mike directly into your camcorder, make sure it has a matching *impedance,* measured in ohms. Most mikes have a low impedance (under 600 ohms) and should match the impedance of most camcorders, but check both the mike and your camcorder manual before assuming just any microphone will work.

Audio Tape Recorders. Your VCR may or may not make a good Audio Tape Recorder (ATR). The typical inexpensive VHS VCR or camcorder isn't high-fidelity and doesn't record any more sound than the typical 3-inch television speaker can put out. Ask any audiophile, standard TV audio is about the worst there is. So if sound quality is important to you, you might want to invest in a good ATR. Marantz and Sony, among other manufacturers, make high-quality, moderately priced portable stereo cassette recorders that are expressly designed for field production. Expect to pay $150 to $400 for one of these. For studio use, consider an open-reel ATR, which costs more ($750 and up) but yields much higher fidelity recordings. Even an inexpensive stereo Walkman-type recorder will make better-sounding tapes than an inexpensive VCR.

However, hi-fi ½-inch and 8mm VCRs make excellent, cost-effective ATRs. This is one of the best-kept secrets in the audio industry. In fact, some DTV producers buy hi-fi VCRs to use solely as ATRs. (Forget digital audio tape, the much-heralded DAT, which is currently very expensive and might never catch on in this country.) The advantages of using a good VCR as an ATR are obvious: you get several hours of sound on each tape, and the sound is already in a format that's easy to edit with other video. Just plug microphones or other audio sources (including your Mac) into the mike or line inputs of the VCR, and roll tape. For the best audio, record at the fastest available speed—in VHS, the 2-hour SP speed, for example.

Audio tape recorders might be able to record one, two, or multiple *tracks* of sound. (A *track* is a separate strip of recorded sound on a tape.) For example, a stereo ATR can record two tracks, Left and Right; a mike plugged into the left track will record sound only onto that track if the right track recording level is set to 0. By plugging microphones into both mike inputs and adjusting the recording levels on each track, you can perform basic audio mixing (see below). More sophisticated ATRs provide four or more tracks, one track for each sound source. Generally, these are open-reel machines, although you can find four-track cassette recorders. Recording each sound on a separate track lets you do more with them in post-production.

Hi-fi VCRs offer two audio tracks, but lower-quality ones don't provide controls for setting audio levels. Something new in VCR audio is *Pulse Code Modulation* (PCM), a digital recording method that yields recording quality close to that of compact disks. You'll find PCM mainly on Sony 8mm decks and on some high-end 8mm camcorders offering two channels of PCM and one FM monaural channel.

Headphones. These are indispensable for any audio work and should be part of the kit on every location shoot. Wear headphones connected to your camcorder as your shoot, and you'll hear the action as the camcorder is hearing it. The rare earth-magnet types provide the greatest audio range and are lightweight as well.

The Macintosh itself can generate a wide variety of sounds, from bizarre computer sound effects and artificial voices to digitized sounds from the real world, or fully orchestrated scores for elaborate presentations. As more musicians turn on to the advantages of electronic music—versatility, speed of composition, and low cost—they are discovering the Macintosh. When audio must be synchronized to video or animation, the Macintosh is the obvious choice for a computer synthesizer, because you can output both video and audio from the computer at the same time. While a full discussion of Mac music is beyond the scope of this book, a number of hardware and software products in the field are listed in Appendix A to help you get started. See the next chapter for tips on recording sound for video productions. For more on audio for interactive presentations, see Chapter 9.

Setting Up the Studio

How do you put DTV components together to create a working DTV studio? It helps to draw up a plan and scout for the proper location.

- First, decide what tools you need to make your programming. Make a list of desired abilities and match them to the available components, keeping in mind the level of video quality your budget can support. Remember that you can always start small, with a Macintosh Plus, a camcorder, a lower-cost NTSC encoder, and a paint program, and build your system from there.
- Find the best site for the studio. You'll need a separate room or at least a secure, quiet area away from traffic. Even glare-free lighting is important, as is air conditioning in the summer—computers and video

equipment need a temperature-controlled climate to operate properly. You should also be sure of a steady, uninterruptable source of adequate, grounded electrical power. Don't place a studio near a freight elevator or heavy machinery that might cause dips and surges in power or unusual magnetic fields.

- For bigger productions and bigger budgets (a regular talk show with the president of the firm, for example), consider installing a real television studio with a control room, a sound stage, lights, backdrops, and so on. Advanced stage and studio design is really beyond the scope of this book, but several sources in Appendix A can give you more information.

Figure 5-11 diagrams a full-blown studio for producing presentations with Mac graphics, sound, and editing capabilities.

Figure 5-11. DTV Studio

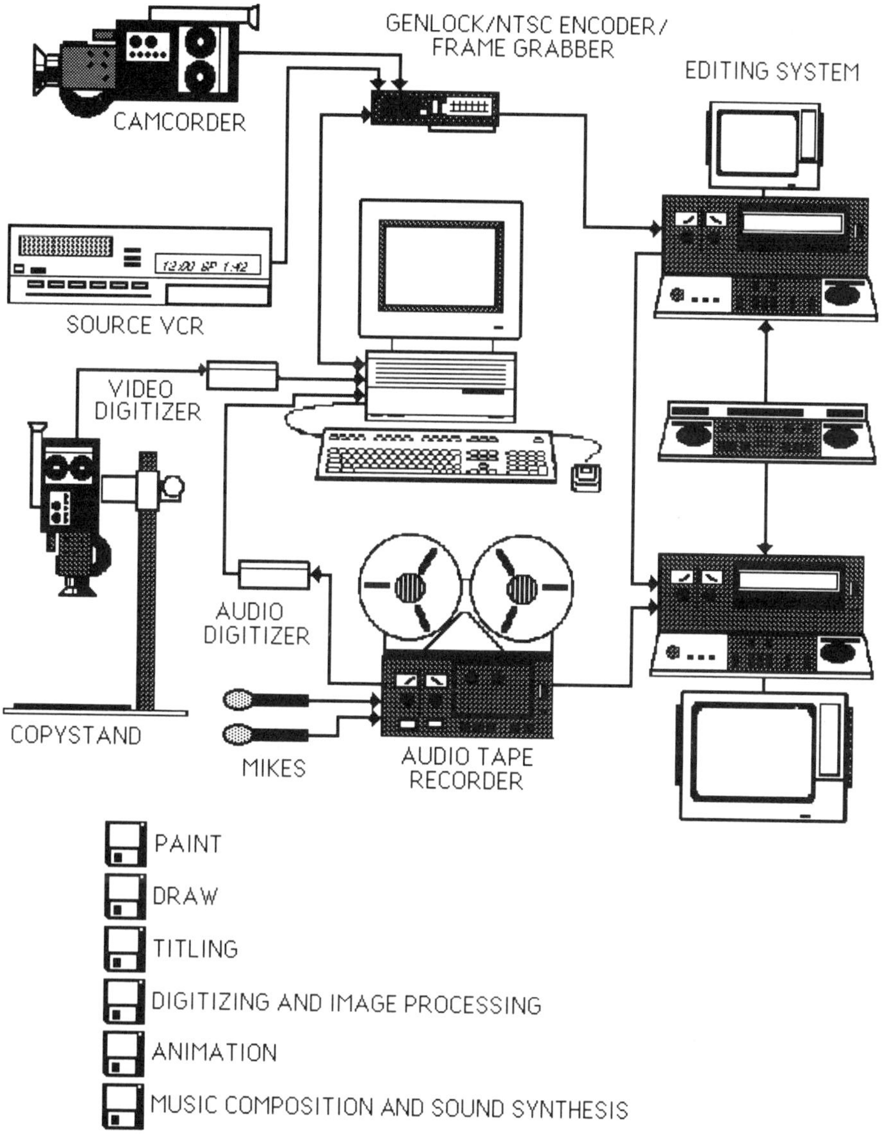

Tips for Maximizing Your Signal

Gremlins, in the form of external electronic noise and interference, are in every studio, waiting to ambush a defenseless video signal as it travels from one component to another. You can minimize interference and maximize your signal by taking these steps:

- Don't stack components one atop the next. Separate them by a foot or two on a table or rack. Put the Macintosh on another table at least four feet away; it can emit stray radio frequency signals that can interfere with the operation of other equipment.
- Make all connections carrying a video or audio signal with 75-ohm shielded coaxial cable. Gold-plated connectors work the best.
- Keep wires straight and untangled. Don't wrap one wire around another or bundle them all together with a wire tie. Keep power cables from crossing or twisting around signal cables.
- Run all equipment, especially the computer, from surge- and spike-protected outlets. Power protection boxes are available from computer supply stores.
- Don't start or stop electrical machinery, such as air conditioners or household appliances, while recording on tape or saving data to a disk.

With mastery of desktop video theory, equipment, and studio setup, you're ready to tackle a real production. The next chapter shows how to put your Mac video knowledge to good use in creating a video presentation.

CHAPTER 6

Mac DTV Production

Creating a desktop video for your presentation can be a spontaneous business. You get some equipment together, recruit a friend or two to help, and play around with the materials at hand until you've made something that works. In fact, that's a good way for beginners to learn the basics of operating hardware and software without feeling the pressure of a definite goal. But that's not how most video productions happen, especially not in the business world. Instead, everything is planned to a T, then everyone involved scrambles to make the real world conform to the plan (even though the world often refuses to do so). Why? Simply because video production is usually so expensive and difficult to pull off that careful planning is the only way to ensure results.

Desktop video presentations are less expensive to produce, and so more amenable to experimentation and spontaneity, but it's still good practice to plan ahead and know the right techniques for getting the job done. This chapter covers the basics of setting up a DTV production and getting good video down on tape.

As a framework for this chapter, we'll look at production techniques used in the creation of a promotional tape for the RxScan. The tape is called "Introducing RxScan," and it's being produced in-house by producer/videographer/director/jack-of-all-trades Jane and her Mac. The tape will provide basic information about ScanTech and its product, be shown at industry conventions, and be distributed to prospective clients.

The Stages of Production

Videographers recognize three major stages any video production must go through:

- *Pre-production,* the paper and planning stage in which the basic form of the video is worked out and materials and manpower are assembled.
- *Production,* the actual taping of the program material.
- *Post-production* (often just called *post),* in which the raw tape is edited to create a narrative, and sound and special effects may be added. Much of desktop video, such as titling and graphics overlays, falls into what most videographers consider post-production.

A simple DTV presentation, when you shoot a quick scene with your camcorder and use the Mac to lay some titles or animation over it, doesn't require a lot of definition between production stages. Productions become complex and call for a lot of preparation when there's extensive video footage to shoot, many resources to manage, and other people's money to spend. Jane's video presentation on the RXScan is quite complex and needs considerable planning. In pre-production, Jane writes a script and prepares an *animatic* (an animated storyboard of the whole production) for approval by her boss; then she draws up a budget and schedule, secures permissions and releases, hires additional personnel, and rents or purchases the necessary equipment. In the production stage, she gets her equipment and personnel to each location and makes sure all necessary scenes are captured on tape, while dealing diplomatically with any unexpected problems that crop up. In post-production, she logs each shot; adds graphics, special effects, and titles; creates a short animated sequence; works on the soundtrack; and edits the whole thing into a seamless whole.

Pre-Production

After getting the assignment to produce the tape, Jane sits down and outlines the main ideas her company wants to communicate—that the scanner is new, inexpensive for hospitals and doctors to purchase and operate, and able to provide more accurate information than other types of scanners. Jane takes this basic information and turns it into a concept, a storyboard, and a script, expressing her own vision of the product.

Concept or Premise. This is the unifying idea behind the presentation. The concept outlines the goals of the program, describes the audience, sets the tone the piece will take, and details the resources needed to complete it. For larger productions, the concept is usually worked up into a formal proposal of a page or so. Once the concept is approved by her boss, Jane sticks with it; nothing dooms a presentation faster than losing sight of the concept.

The main part of Jane's concept for "Introducing RxScan" looks like this:

"Introducing RxScan"
Proposal for a Promotional Video

The RxScan is a revolutionary magnetic resonance imaging system looking for a market. Because ScanTech is a small company with limited resources for advertising and marketing, it needs to bring the message about RxScan to doctors, hospital administrators, and institutional researchers in the most efficient manner. The best way to do this is by producing a promotional videotape that will show off the many strengths of RxScan to potential buyers at conferences, trade shows, and sales contacts.

The video will begin with a walk through the ScanTech plant with Dr. Beverly Gold, ScanTech's CEO, as she introduces the company and its newest product. Dr. Henry Damian, chief scientist, will describe the features of RxScan that make it superior to offerings from competitors. As Dr. Damian talks, videotaped and computer-animated segments will illustrate the technical concepts. Finally, location footage will show the RxScan in actual operation at the Valley Hospital installation. Dr. Palmer, head of radiology at Valley, has agreed to an interview. Beverly Gold will close the tape by inviting prospects to attend a technology demonstration.

The Script. Once the concept is approved, it's time to write a *script*. The script fleshes out the concept by

- creating a narrative about the subject of the program that engages the audience's imagination
- giving the audience all the important information about the subject
- defining the length of the program
- breaking the production into manageable parts, or scenes, based on location or time of day
- specifying the shots or camera setups for each scene
- providing general directions to the production staff
- providing words for the narrator and/or actors to say

Scriptwriting is an art, like any other creative endeavor, and a full discussion of that art is beyond the scope of this book. If you've never written or seen a script before, you might want to consult some of the books that teach scriptwriting form and that discuss methods for building narrative (see the bibliography in Appendix A).

In our example production, Jane has a much easier job than the writer of a movie-length drama. It's already clear what the program has to say, and the script is largely a practical matter of showing how to say it. She has to decide on the total length of the presentation (about ten minutes), the number of scenes, the location of each scene, approximately how many individual shots should be in each scene, and the action that will take place in each shot. She also has to draft words for the actors (called the *talent* in video and film parlance) to say, but here she can use the practiced pitches already developed by ScanTech's president and chief engineer, who know exactly what they want to communicate to the audience and can ad-lib if necessary. Jane has to make sure the progress of shots and scenes adds up to a coherent whole; that no shot or scene is out of place; and, above all, that the message about ScanTech and its product comes through loud and clear, without distraction. At the same time, Jane tries to keep the number of shots, scenes, and effects to an efficient minimum to save production time and money.

Part of Jane's finished script looks like this:

INTRODUCING RXSCAN
—SCRIPT—

SCENE 3—INTERIOR, SCANTECH RESEARCH LAB

We begin in Dr. Damian's office. He is looking at some scanned prints with an assistant, signs off on them, and looks up as the assistant exits. As Dr. Damian begins to talk, we precede him out of the office into the adjoining lab, where an RxScan unit can be seen in the background.

DR. DAMIAN

I'm Dr. Henry Damian, chief scientist at ScanTech, and this is our research lab. Let me take a few moments to show you what the RxScan can do and what makes it different from other MRI systems on the market.

Some of you may not be familiar with MRI imaging. In brief, magnetic resonance imaging is based on the principle that the atoms of certain substances resonate with a characteristic radio frequency, or RF, when immersed in a powerful magnetic field and bombarded with an external source of RF.

INSERT AN ANIMATION SHOWING THE BEHAVIOR OF ATOMS DURING MAGNETIC RESONANCE.

DR. DAMIAN

Atoms of hydrogen, potassium, and other elements in the patient's body emit a readable RF signal inside the RxScan's imaging module. A matrix of sensors in the module transmit the RF signal data to a computer, which converts it to a three-dimensional computer image of the location of each element in the scanned area. Not only does MRI provide a highly detailed picture of the patient's interior anatomy, it also creates an accurate, real-time portrait of patient physiology—without invasive measures of any kind.

Dr. Damian walks us through the various parts of the RxScan, pointing or gesturing to each part as he describes it.

DR. DAMIAN

Here is the RxScan main imaging unit, where scanning takes place. Those of you familiar with other MRI scanners will notice right away that RxScan is much less bulky than others. This is because RxScan uses permanent ceramic magnets, rather than superconducting magnets. This means no liquid helium to cool the superconducting coil, no refrigeration systems, and radically reduced capital and operating costs. But the magnetic field is still quite strong—10,000 gauss.

Dr. Damian places a monkey wrench in the "tunnel" of the imaging unit. The wrench jumps out of his hand and stays suspended in midair.

DR. DAMIAN

In addition, the extreme sensitivity of our RF sensing matrix makes it unnecessary to build an RF-shielded room for the imaging unit, one of the most expensive aspects of previous MRI installations. . . .

Stopwatch in hand, Jane reads aloud the draft of her script and jots down how long it takes to read each page. This lets her know approximately how long each scene will be, as well as the total length of the program. She reworks the script as necessary to bring it to the needed length of ten minutes.

Storyboard and Animatics. A script is a narrative in words, but video is a visual medium. Taking their cue from filmmakers, videomakers often use a *storyboard,* a visual outline of the narrative of a film or video production, to provide a boss or client with an idea of what the program will look like, as well as what it will say.

You might think of a storyboard as a comic-strip version of your program, with a cartoonlike picture or panel for each shot. The art in the panels should show the subject and camera angle of each shot, together with a brief text description of what's happening in the shot and any dialogue.

But let's face it—storyboards are passe, and they go against the philosophy of desktop presentations. The Mac way to do it is to create an *animatic*—a video storyboard that incorporates sound and motion. What an animatic can do that a storyboard cannot is give viewers an understanding of the length and pace of the piece, as well as a sense of how it really will look.

Jane tries to use materials already at hand to create an animatic for "Introducing RxScan." When she scouts the two locations for the production, she takes some camcorder footage and instant photos of the locations of each scene, trying to match her shots with the shots she'll use later in the actual production. (This material will also come in handy later as she and her production crew try to anticipate lighting needs and set up times.) She also uses existing 8 × 10s of the RxScan and Drs. Gold and Damian, as well as a promotional audio tape Dr. Gold has made about the product.

Back at her office, she uses a grayscale scanner to bring the photos into her Macintosh, and then adds text and graphics to the pictures with

Figure 6-1. Animatic Flowchart

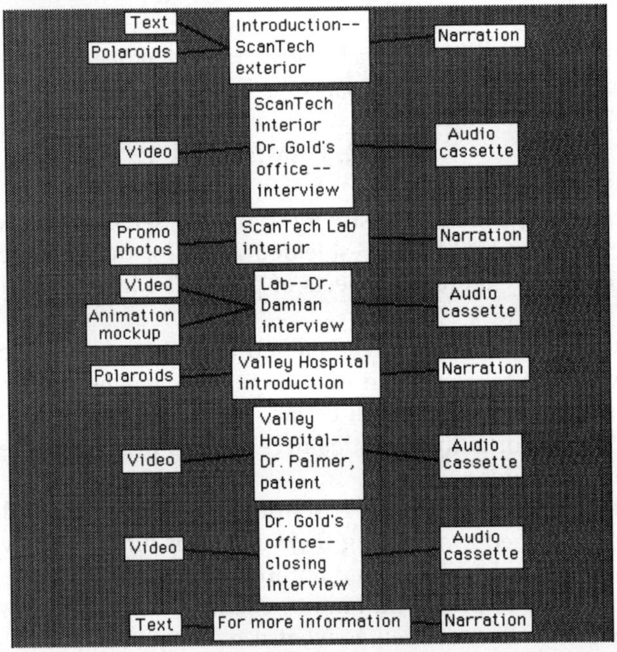

a paint program. Next she uses a slideshow program to create a presentation, complete with transitions. All the Macintosh material is then transferred to tape through an NTSC video card (see the previous chapter). Using her desktop editing system and following the events in her script, she cuts together the Macintosh tape with portions of the camcorder footage she shot on location, narration from Dr. Gold's audio tape, and a narration she records herself with a mike and cassette recorder to create the finished animatic. (See later in this chapter for more on video editing, and Chapter 9 for tips on audio.) Figure 6-1 is a flowchart of the animatic.

It might seem like a lot of work to create an animatic, and it can be. For a small production, the effort isn't justified. But for bigger jobs, an animatic can be a very useful aid to conceptualizing the actual production. Problems with concept, pacing, location, graphics, and animation will often show up at this stage, before any serious money or time has been spent. From ScanTech's point of view, the animatic, together with the script, provide real assurance that the company will get the production it wants, and that Jane understands how to get the job done.

Scheduling. Once the script and storyboard or animatic are complete, they become the basis for the *shooting schedule* and *post plan.* The schedule takes each scene in the script and assigns it a date and location. Also the schedule shows what talent, props, and effects are needed to accomplish each scene.

For example, this is how Jane's shooting schedule looks:

Table 6-1. "Introducing RxScan" Shooting Schedule

Date	Scene	Location	Talent	Props	Effects
9/10/89	1	ScanTech HQ—ext			
9/10	2	ST int.—	Dr. Gold		Wireless mike, window scrim
9/10	5	Dr. Gold's office ST int.—	Dr. Gold		Wireless mike, window scrim
9/10	3	Dr. Gold's office ST int.— Dr. Damian's office, lab	Dr. Damian	Scanprints, monkey wrench	Wireless mike, window scrim
9/17	4	Valley H. int.	Dr. Palmer	Patient, scan-prints	Wireless mike

Note that the shooting schedule groups scenes by location, rather than scene number. That's because Jane will shoot all scenes that take place in one location before she moves to the next one.

The post plan lists all post-production effects (often abbreviated "EFX" or "F/X", and "SFX" for sound effects or special effects) for each scene. These may include still graphics, animation, sound effects, and music. Jane needs the following post effects for "Introducing RxScan":

Table 6-2. "Introducing RxScan" Post Plan

Scene	Title and/or Graphics	Anim	SFX	Music
1	"Introducing Electronic RxScan—An MRI Scanner from Scan-Tech"	logo	ScanTech	theme
2	"Dr. Beverly Gold, Founder of ScanTech"			
3	"Dr. Henry Damian, Chief Scientist"	NMR effect, T1 and T2 charts	NMR sfx	
4	"Valley Hospital" "Dr. Paul Palmer"			
5	"Dr. Gold"			
Closing	"For a daylong technology demonstration, please contact your ScanTech representative, or call 1-800-333-3333"		Narration	Electronic theme

Budgeting. In part, all this preliminary work—scripting, storyboarding, timing, shooting schedules, and post planning—is simply preparation for making a *budget,* the anticipated total cost of producing the DTV program.

Realistic budget making requires a thorough understanding of what a production requires. Usually, this understanding comes with experience—you know how much it costs to create a certain video effect because you've done it before. Still, video production budgeting is one of the blackest of the black arts, and even experienced video producers sweat over budgets to make sure that every penny shows up on the small screen. If you lack experience, a read through one of the many books on video and film production budgeting is a must. Then call around to production, post-production, and rental houses to learn the going rates for various services. You can get various preprinted budget forms from video supply houses. The AICP (Association of Independent Commercial Producers) standard video production budget form is generally considered one of the most comprehensive; it budgets for estimated and actual expenses for every possible category of production expense. AICP forms are readily available—ask around.

Elaborate productions, such as "Introducing RxScan," involve both *fixed costs* (such as for tape stock and above-the-line personnel, like an outside director) and *variable costs* (such as rentals, payment to crew, and most post-production costs, all of which may increase if the production is delayed). There's no limit to the amount of detail your budget can include. All the little budget items are summarized on one page called the *top sheet*. Jane's budget for the production is relatively simple. Since she is producing and directing the tape as part of her job, there are no producer or director fees, but a budget prepared by an independent production company for a client would include fixed amounts to pay management, as well as built-in amounts for profit.

Once the budget is approved, Jane hires the crew, arranges equipment and transportation rentals, and launches any post-production activities (such as animations) that might take a while to finish. Jane plans to use a four-person crew—a camcorder operator, a lighting person, a sound person, and herself as director. She rents two S-VHS camcorders, two color monitors, two tripods and a dolly, a lighting kit, a high-quality audio cassette recorder with several microphones, miscellaneous cables, and a van. She also brings along her Mac, an NTSC video card/genlock, a printer, a word processor, and a program for creating video titles, in case she needs to create documents on the spot.

The pre-production stage *wraps* (ends, in film and video lingo) the night before the first day of shooting, when you sit around looking at all the stuff you've assembled and make sure it's all in working order.

Production

All the planning and preparation of pre-production begins to bear fruit in the production stage. Here's where the images and sound are recorded, later to be assembled into a finished presentation during the post stage.

Productions fall into two general categories:

- Field or location productions, shot wherever the subject is. You must bring all production equipment and personnel with you to the location.
- Studio productions, shot in a space specifically designed for video production. The studio is quiet and has a flat floor, high ceiling, built-in lighting system, and a control room for observing and directing the action.

In this section we'll look at basic techniques for both field and studio production. All of these can be applied in some form to DTV presentations you create in the office or classroom. For example, techniques for handling a camcorder in the field apply whether the location is a jungle in South America or your own backyard. Lighting in your garage follows much the same principles as lighting in a studio.

It can't be stressed enough that planning is everything when you begin field production. As mentioned, you should have already scouted your location and obtained any necessary permits and releases. If you'll be shooting a narrative, rather than just covering an event, your shooting schedule and shot list should be in final (or nearly final) form. Elaborate productions may use multiple VCRs, cameras, switchers and SEGs, tripods, a dolly or crane, mikes and sound equipment, lights, cables, generators, props, makeup and costumes, tools, transportation, talent, production personnel, food, and even portable toilets. Lay out the equipment the night before and test everything before you go. Carry backups for as many components as you can.

If you want to do studio productions, first you need a studio. If you're a teacher, you can probably use the TV studios run by most high schools and colleges. Increasingly, many businesses have their own small video studios as well. Local cable stations are required by law to maintain a public facility for video production; you might be able to book time in one of these also. Major cities usually have at least one place where basic production facilities can be rented at rock-bottom rates. Professional studios are also available, at premium prices.

Basic Camera

In video, the camera is the surrogate for the director's and the viewer's eyes. So it follows that the meaning and impact of any program is determined in large part by where the video camera looks and how it's moved. An ineptly handled camera is like a storyteller who constantly stumbles over wording; a well-handled camera is like a storyteller so adept that you don't just hear a voice, you enter into the tale and hear it in your own voice. Luckily, it's easy to learn the basics of film and video camera handling, since you see the work of professional camera operators in every movie or TV program you watch. You need only to step back from the program and watch it analytically. What is the camera doing now, and why? Whose point of view does the camera show? How does the camera move? Does that movement further the narrative?

Probably the most fundamental thing to learn when first handling a camera for DTV production is to keep it level, steady, in focus, and pointed straight at the subject. (In this discussion, *camera* stands for camcorder, too.) Everyone has seen home videos in which the camera wanders aimlessly about, sometimes on the subject, sometimes off it, sometimes in focus, sometimes out of focus. Hard to watch, aren't they? Lackadaisical camera is barely tolerable for home video, where people don't expect much, but it just won't do for business or classroom presentations. Always be sure the camera shows exactly what the viewer ought to see—and that means, as the DTV director, you have to take the viewer's part above all.

With today's lightweight camcorders, you can shoot a lot of the production from your shoulder. A handheld camera yields footage with spontaneity and immediacy, good for fast-moving events but not so well-suited to static setups or long scenes. A video *tripod* keeps the camera steady and adds a professional look to your footage. Use a tripod for scenes that run a long time, or when you'll be holding closeups (see below) for more than a moment or two. The best tripods have a *fluid head,* which means the moving parts of the tripod head are hydraulically damped to make camera motions very smooth. Fluid head tripods are expensive. Lower-cost *fluid-effect heads* that use friction plates rather than hydraulics don't work as well but are still preferable to an undamped tripod head. Some tripods come equipped with wheels, so you can move the camera smoothly through the scene.

Composition. The video screen is relatively small and square, and that affects how you'll set up a composition for the camera. Wide, movie-like panoramas are out; tight, intimate compositions are best. Keep video compositions down to one, two, or, at most, three main elements. Move your elements together so they fit in a small space, or move your camera to view them from a different angle—for example, when a group of people is talking, shoot over one person's shoulder.

It's tempting to make all compositions balanced and symmetrical. Too much symmetry, however, leads to visual boredom. Try unbalancing some shots. Leaving space to one side of an actor, for example, leads the viewer to expect that the actor will move in that direction. If the actor moves, you'll have created a dramatic expectation with composition that leads to a payoff in action.

Shots and Angles. The camera can show the subject or scene from various distances and angles. Each has its own significance to the program narrative. These are the basic shots, as illustrated in Figure 6-2.

Long Shot. This is a view taken far away from the subject. It places the subject within a larger environment. The long shot is more objective and neutral.

Medium Shot. The subject dominates the screen. If you're shooting a figure, you'd see from the head down to the waist.

Closeup. The subject fills the screen—there's no room for anything else. For a figure, the closeup shows the head and shoulders. This is the typical "talking head" shot. It's more intimate and personal.

Figure 6-2. Camera Shots

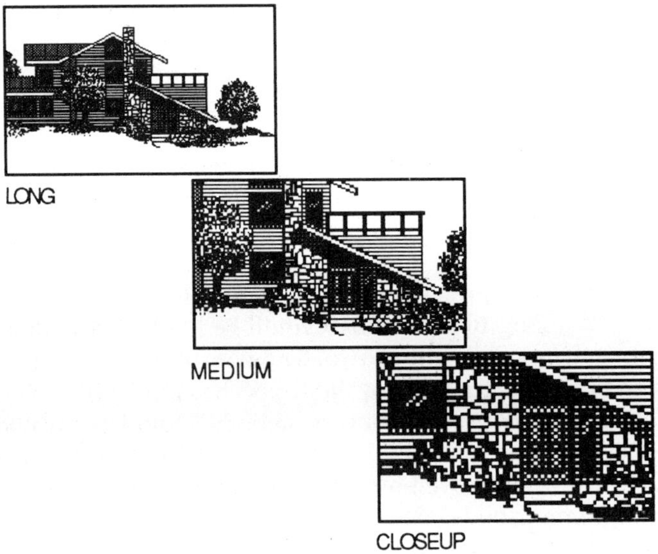

There are shades and degrees of in-between shots. *Extreme long shots* are popular in film but not too popular on video, as tiny details in a large panorama tend to get lost on the small screen. *Extreme closeups,* on the other hand, are very popular and very effective on video; the majority of TV shows contain many shots where someone's face completely fills the screen.

Almost all video camera come equipped with *zoom lenses,* giving you the capability of shooting both wide shots and telephoto shots. With the lens set wide, the camera sees more of the total scene, and more of the scene remains in focus. A *wide shot* is appropriate for panoramas and scenes in which both foreground and background elements must be in focus. In a *telephoto shot,* the camera sees a small part of the scene and shows that part up close; the rest of the scene isn't in focus. The area the lens sees looks compressed and flattened. A classic telephoto shot, often used in westerns, is of horsemen on a ridge framed by a huge setting sun that appears to be right behind them. The telephoto exaggerates the size of the sun relative to the figures, and flattens the space so all elements seem to be in the same plane.

The angle of the camera is of great psychological importance. A *low angle,* with the camera looking up at the subject, makes the subject appear bigger and more important. Political candidates in campaign spots are inevitably shot from a moderately low angle, to give them a aura of power and authority. You should probably shoot the CEO of your company the same way. A *straight* or *normal* angle, with the camera at the same level as the subject, is neutral in effect. This is the angle most often chosen for talk shows. A *high angle,* with the camera looking down at the subject, makes the subject appear smaller and less important, even puny. Don't shoot your CEO from a high angle. High angles also put the subject in the context of its environment. The classic example, which appears in innumerable action shows, is a shot from a helicopter looking down at a car chase through city streets.

Angles can also be subjective and objective. A *subjective angle* shows the scene from the viewpoint of one of the actors in the scene. Subjective angles are used constantly in thrillers, where the camera shows the view of the criminal stalking his victim. The *objective angle* is most popular, though; it shows the scenes as they would appear to a neutral observer who isn't involved in the action.

Camera Moves. Video would be a dull visual medium indeed if the camera always stayed in one place. Instead, the camera should be free to move whenever and wherever the action calls for it. The standard camera moves are shown in Figure 6-3.

Figure 6-3. Camera Moves

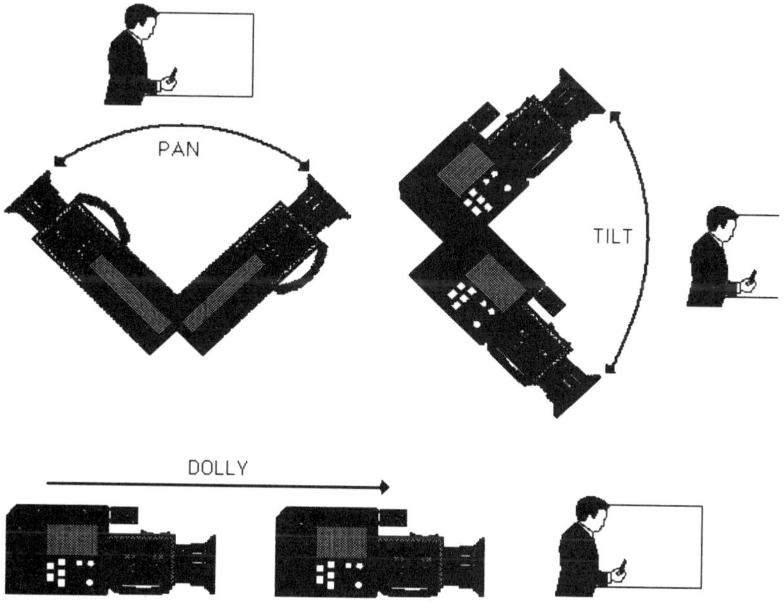

Pan. The *pan* is a rotation of the camera parallel to the ground. Typically, the pan is used to follow a moving subject, or to slowly reveal details in the environment. To execute a handheld pan successfully, you should pick the beginning and end points of the pan, set your feet facing the end point, then twist around to face the beginning point. This will give you maximum control at the end of the pan, where you'll need it most.

Tilt. The *tilt* is a camera rotation perpendicular to the horizon. It's used to reveal the height of the subject, or follow actions that move vertically.

Dolly. The *dolly shot* moves the camera laterally to follow along with a movement in the scene—an actor running, for example. The standard dolly is the *walking dolly,* so called because you simply walk along with camera following the subject, trying to keep the camera as level and steady as possible. (This isn't easy, because a dolly often requires that you walk backwards to precede the subject, who is walking forwards.)

Dolly shots taken with a wheeled tripod pose some special problems, because you may not have a smooth, even surface to roll over. Film production companies build tracks to roll on; you can get away with laying some plywood or Masonite along the dolly path and taping the edges together with gaffer's tape. An old trick is to use a wheelchair as the dollying vehicle; the chair's big wheels provide a smooth ride. For fast dolly shots where the camera is close to the ground, dispense with the wheelchair and tape the camera to a skateboard or tricycle. If the terrain is right, you can shoot the scene from a moving car driving at slow speed. This works well for lengthy dolly shots of actors walking down the street.

Zoom. The *zoom* shot uses the camera's zoom lens to get closer to or farther away from the subject in one smooth "movement." A zoom isn't really a camera move per se, but it does give the effect of a changing viewpoint.

The best thing about zooms is that they allow you to get close without moving the camera, but they're also intrusive and too "video-like." Zooms should be used sparingly, and the zooming action should move slowly, not fast. You can often hide a zoom by moving the camera in another way at the same time, such as panning while you zoom.

Jane combines a number of these camera effects in the first shot of Dr. Damian in Scene 3 of "Introducing RxScan." This is the most difficult shot in the production. She sets up the camcorder on a wheeled tripod in front of Dr. Damian's desk, with a dolly path laid out behind the camera, through the open door, and into the development lab. The camera is set at a slight low angle, so Dr. Damian looks imposing and also so the plywood boards along the dolly path won't appear in the shot. The shot begins with the camera stationary, pointed at Dr. Damian in a medium shot. As he moves around his desk and into the corridor, the camera gently zooms out a little to widen the shot, pans to follow him, and at the same time begins a backward dolly movement, always staying in front of Dr. Damian as he walks. In the shot, it appears that Dr. Damian is walking toward the viewer. Viewers can also see the bustle of activity through doors in the corridor.

The camera then moves into the lab, stops on a mark, and zooms out to widen the shot further while panning smoothly to follow Dr. Damian as he walks past the camera and stands next to the scanning unit. Now the camera sees the entire scanner in a wide shot, and the angle is nearly level. When Dr. Damian puts the monkey wrench into the magnetic field of the scanner, the camera zooms in to see the wrench more closely. The intent of this fairly elaborate shot, which Jane rehearses a few times with the crew, is to allow Dr. Damian to give his pitch without interruption, while also giving him freedom of movement through his domain, the lab. Figure 6-4 shows the entire sequence.

Figure 6-4. Shooting Dr. Damian

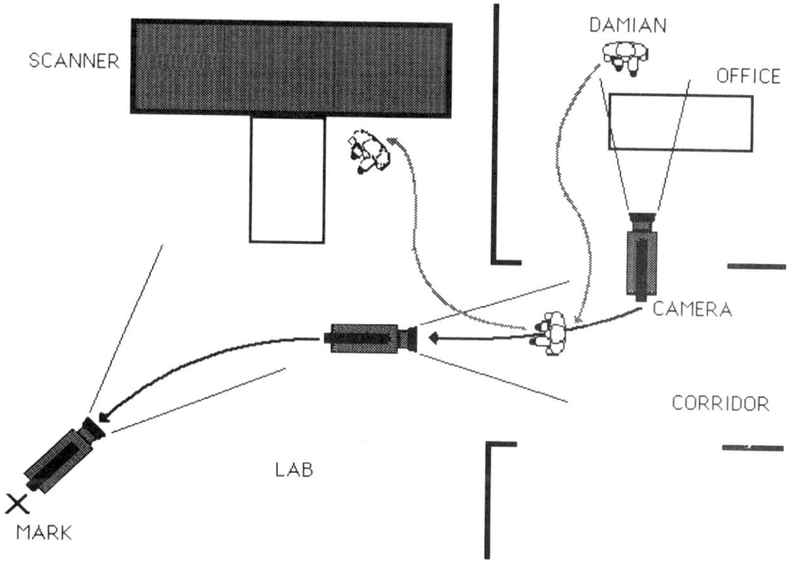

Multiple Cameras. The intricate choreography of multiple cameras in a big TV studio or on location is a subject beyond the scope of this book, but there are a few aspects of studio camera handling worth noting for DTV production. It makes sense to have several cameras covering once-in-a-lifetime events, so there will be backup footage from several angles for editing later, but the cameras or camcorders must be closely matched (that is, of the same make and model) so all the footage looks the same in terms of color, resolution, and so on. It won't do to have the talent appear to be wearing a red tie in one shot and a magenta one in the next.

The typical studio production uses three cameras, positioned as in Figure 6-5. One camera is stationed well back in a fixed position and gets the wide angle shot, so there will always be a wide shot to cut away to if something happens to the other cameras. Another camera is up close at an angle, and gets medium shots and closeups. The third camera might get medium shots and closeups from the opposite angle, or can be used handheld anywhere on the stage if the program calls for a cinema verité look. More outré productions might call for other camera angles, such as the up-from-the-floor angle, the flying-overhead angle, and the extreme closeup or "in-your-face" shot.

Figure 6-5. Studio Cameras

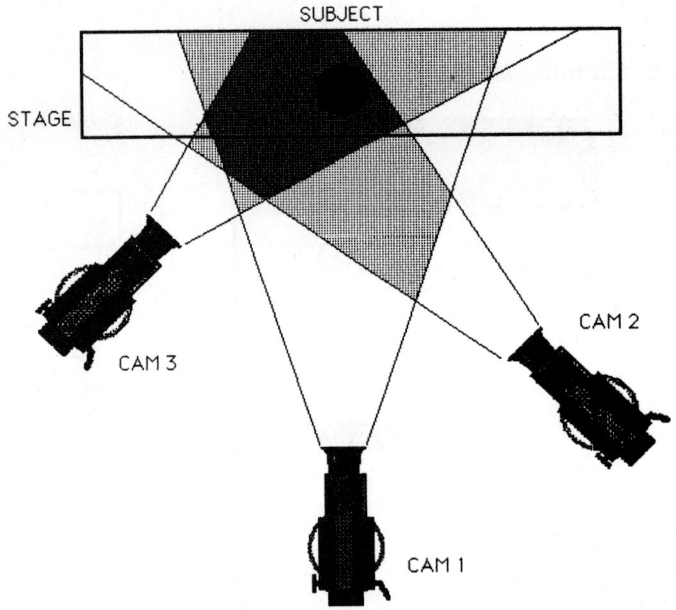

When you have multiple cameras to deal with, a *switcher* comes in handy. As noted in the previous chapter, this device accepts video from several sources (usually cameras, but they can be any synchronizable device). Expensive cameras also have the ability to be controlled from a remote, so you might not need an operator for each camera.

Shooting for Narrative

The cleanest and most economical way to shoot is to tape scenes and events as far as possible in the sequence determined by the script and to do as much editing as possible in the camera. A camcorder with flying erase heads makes it possible to achieve clean edits just by pausing the tape between setups. With practice, you'll learn to create short programs entirely within the camera without post-production editing, ready for graphic enhancement with your Macintosh. If editing is required, having the raw footage in its approximate final order makes post-production much easier. Old hands also believe that if you shoot expecting to edit out all the bad parts, you'll lose your edge and possibly miss that perfect shot. This is especially true when you shoot important one-time-only happenings, such as meetings or news events. No amount of editing can make up for crucial shots missed. Remember that your aim is to create a seamless narrative with your shots, so the story of your presentation is told without glaring disjunctions or missing information.

However, you can't edit every production in the camera. So when you can't, you must compensate by making sure you have all the footage you need for later editing. Besides taking all the shots called for in the script, you might find it necessary to get additional material, both to take advantage of opportunities not covered in the script and to provide alternative footage in case of mistakes.

It's especially important when shooting on location to get an *establishing shot,* a shot that sets the scene for the viewer. Have the camcorder running as soon as you get out of the car to capture the exterior of the building, the doorway, a sign, the landscape, a street corner. Hold each shot for a few seconds so there'll be enough to work with in the editing stage. Get one or more wide shots of the subject(s). When you're inside a building, shoot the corridor, the office, the machinery, whatever is necessary to fully tell the story on tape. You might not use most of these shots later, but tape is cheap, and you don't want to have to return to the location to get a missing shot.

When you're shooting from a script, consider shooting key scenes more than once, and from more than one angle. The additional versions supply *cutaways,* alternative views of a scene that can be intercut in post to provide visual interest. *Reaction shots*—the facial expressions of viewers to an event—are also ideal for cutaways. When taping a sports event, for example, make sure to get reaction shots from the crowd—but don't miss the main action while you're doing it.

Jane's program will be put together mainly in post, so she doesn't worry too much about editing in the camera. She does use her second camera to get establishing shots of the ScanTech and Valley Hospital exteriors, and she also tapes cutaways for each scene, just in case.

Lighting

The purpose of lighting your production is, first and foremost, to ensure that you have adequate illumination to capture the scene with good fidelity on tape. Most video cameras aren't very light sensitive, and need as much additional illumination as you can give them. So professional DTV producers always take lights with them in the field, where lighting conditions are rarely perfect for video.

For handheld taping of daytime exteriors, you can shoot without the benefit of additional lighting. While you have no control over the illumination, you'll get footage with a completely natural look. When you move indoors, though, lighting becomes much more important. A simple solution that involves minimal expense is to mount a single bright light on top of the camera or camcorder that points in the same direction as the lens. Camera lights give flat, rather harsh illumination, but that's expected in many cases, such as footage of news and sports events.

Light Types and Colors. Lights comes in several lamp types and light colors. In video and film, the two common lamp types are the *floodlight,* which gives a broad illumination, and the *spotlight,* which lights a small area with a high-intensity beam. Combinations of the two types, plus reflectors, masks, filters, and so on, modulate the light, generating all the different kinds of artificial illumination you see on tape.

The higher the wattage of a bulb, the more light it emits but also the whiter the light. So try to use higher wattage bulbs whenever possible. You'll most often use *tungsten* or incandescent lights (color temperature 3,200 degrees K), since that's how most video and film cameras are *balanced*—they are engineered to see the light as pure white. Make sure you've set the camera color adjustment to the "lightbulb" setting before rolling tape. Other light colors are created by daylight and fluorescent light.

Key, Fill, and Backlight. For more elaborate productions, taking the time to set up a basic lighting system can result in a much more professional product. That doesn't mean you need a lot of lights. The traditional setup to light a single subject is to use three lights: a *key light,* the primary source of illumination; a *fill light,* which fills and softens the shadow cast by the key light; and a *backlight,* which shines on the subject from behind, separating it from the background. The key light should be about twice as bright as the fill light, with the backlight softer still. Figure 6-6 shows how these lights should be arranged.

You might not have three lights, but you can get by with just a key light and a large *reflector*—a piece of white posterboard or foamcore works well—positioned as in Figure 6-7. Be sure the background is dimmer than the subject, and position the subject several feet from the background.

Figure 6-6. Three-Light System

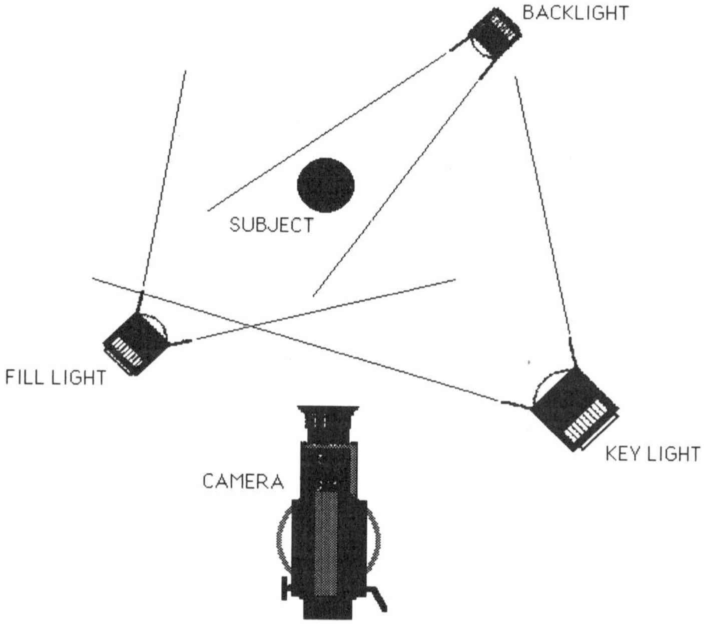

Figure 6-7. One Light and Reflector

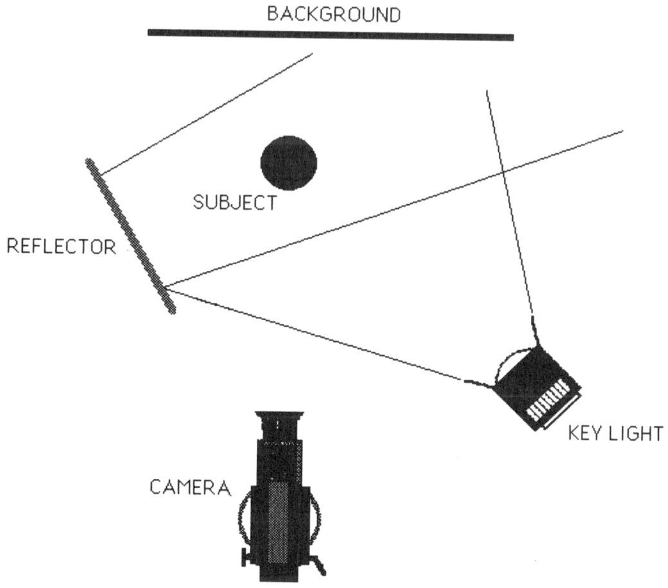

Things become more complicated if you're lighting two or more subjects, as when you're shooting an interview or talk show, but the same basic rules apply. Figure 6-8 shows one two-light method for illuminating two subjects sitting face to face. Make sure no shadows are cast on the other subject.

Figure 6-8. Lighting Two Subjects

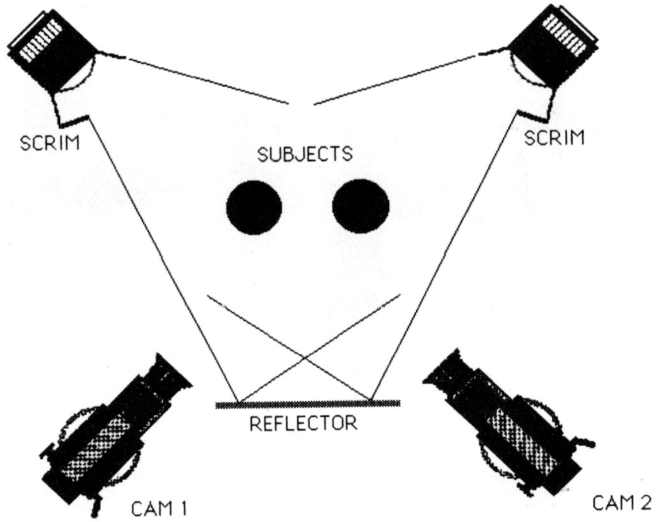

A *set light* directed at the background can help mask any shadows cast there. Colored gels can be fixed over lights to add color. Shining the set light through a patterned *scrim* (a paper, cloth, or plastic sheet) can add texture to a plain background. Experiment with each lighting element until you achieve the effect you want; check the camcorder viewfinder or run some test tape and play it back to check the results.

There are no hard and fast rules for lighting action, especially if the subject is moving through a complicated space. You might need many lights to illuminate a wide area. Often a dramatic effect can be achieved by creating zones of light and darkness the subject can move through, for instance, lighting a doorway but leaving the hall behind it dark, so the subject appears to be bursting into the room.

Every location offers its own mix of artificial and natural light. However, mixed light types will result in odd colors on tape, especially noticeable in flesh tones. In an interior, natural light is the hardest to control. For example, Jane has to tape Dr. Gold, the ScanTech CEO, in an office with a big picture window behind the desk. The window faces south, so the sunlight streams in, but there's also a good view of the

ScanTech building through the window. Jane brings along a plastic gel she bought at a local photo and film supply store. She cuts it to shape and applies to the windows; the gel changes the daylight color to match the color of the lights she is using, and also cuts down on troublesome reflections. She lights Dr. Gold with a soft key and fill, but uses the window illumination as a backlight.

To get good results, follow these lighting tips:

- With lighting, less can be more. Try lighting for a natural, cinematic effect, rather than the bright, harsh lights usually seen in video. This uses less equipment but more skill and imagination.
- If you do a lot of lighting, buy or rent a lighting kit. These include three or more lights with bulbs, clamps, and barn doors; reflectors, umbrellas, and scrims to filter and direct light; poles, tripods, and other mounting hardware; and a case to hold it all.
- Check the power supplies on location in advance. No one will thank you if you blow the fuses in someone's home and you have to make a ten-mile trip to the hardware store to get new ones. Bring plenty of long, heavy-duty (15-amp) extension cords and multiple outlet boxes with circuit breakers.
- Consider renting a small gas generator and use that to power two or three lights. Position the generator as far away from the shooting location as possible so the noise won't overwhelm the ambient sound—that's where those long extension cords come in handy.

Recording Sound in Production

Getting good sound on tape during the production stage is mainly a matter of proper mike selection, placement, testing—and common sense. For example, what kind of mike should you select to record the conversation of a group of people sitting around a table? An omnidirectional mike is the type to choose, placed in the center of the table. In fact, there are mikes designed especially for that situation, and practically any other you might imagine.

As mentioned in the previous chapter, even if you're out there shooting alone with an inexpensive camcorder, your DTV audio will really improve by replacing the camcorder mike with a good ($50–$100) cardioid or shotgun. For newsgathering, documentaries, special events, and such, a shotgun and a pair of headphones are all you'll need. More elaborate productions call for more variety in mikes. Interviews should be shot with a good cardioid mike held by the interviewer, or perhaps lavaliers on the interviewer and subject. A live music performance might call for a shotgun on the camera, cardioids placed near the instruments, and a wireless mike on the singer. This kind of multiple-microphone situation calls for audio mixing, discussed below.

The distance you position a mike from the sound source is a matter of judgment and experience. In general, the mike has to work in conjunction with the camera. A mike placed close to a speaker, for example, gives a tight, close sound presence (as well as possibly picking up any sibilance in the speaker's voice), which won't work with a long or wide shot. Miking the speaker from a distance cuts sibilance but adds more room noise, and won't match a closeup. The mike should point directly at the speaker, not at an angle (unless you're looking for an oblique sound effect), and the angle shouldn't change during the recording session. Try not to point mikes directly at nearby walls, so as not to record unpleasant sound reflections. And caution speakers not to fiddle with the mike, rub their fingers on the top, or put their mouths right up close to it.

Even harder is to mike a shot in which the subject is moving. The mike has to move in tandem with the camera and keep a constant distance and angle to the subject. This is tricky in the case of dolly shots. Moving shots will probably require putting the mike on top of the camera, or assigning one person the task of following the subject while maneuvering the mike, perhaps on the end of a long pole or *boom*. Audio stores sell a variety of booms for extending mikes over an actor or scene, but a broom handle and some gaffer's tape works just as well. In any case, test the miking to see if it matches the shot you've planned.

Audio Mixing. If you want to incorporate many layers of sound in your production, you need an *audio mixer*. Audio mixing can be done on location or in the studio using a *mike mixer*, a device for setting the levels and combining the input of several microphones or monaural audio sources. *Disco mixers* accept stereo inputs rather than monaural inputs but are essentially the same beast. Many mixers accept both mono and stereo inputs, as well as *mike level* (low-strength audio signal) and *line level* (high-strength audio signal) inputs. (If you plan to send the mixer output directly to a camcorder that only has a mike input, make sure your mixer can output a mike level signal.)

In a typical recording setup, you'll place microphones at each source of sound, for example, a lavalier on each actor and perhaps another mike to catch background sounds. Each mike is connected to the mike mixer, and the monaural mixer output is sent to the VCR's audio input. (Or, if you're planning to sample the sound, you might send the mike mixer output directly to an audio digitizer connected to your Macintosh.) The output of any stereo hi-fi device can also be send to the mixer, with each stereo channel requiring its own input; for example, the left and right channels of your receiver are plugged into separate inputs on the mixer. A typical moderately priced mixer might offer 8 inputs, which can be mixed down into four channels for a 4-track ATR or two channels for stereo recording. Better mixers can have 16 or 32 inputs and the ability to send partial mixes to a variety of special sound processing devices.

Most mixers provide *equalization* (tone control) for each input channel. Test and set each mike and audio component recording level with the *Volume Unit* (VU) meters on the mixer. The VU meters give you visual feedback on the strength of the incoming signal. Do a test recording on a monaural VCR or camcorder with the mixer output set to different levels; choose the strongest one that yields the least distortion. Hi-fi VCRs with VU meters make it much easier to adjust the levels. You might need to recalibrate the VU meters on your mixer so the 0 VU on the VCR and mixer are the same. Many mixers can generate a *0 VU test tone* that provides a standard level for recalibrating the VCR's VU level.

Understand that VU levels are somewhat arbitrary; do test recordings and trust your ears rather than a number on a meter. As you work, always monitor your audio mix on a standard TV. What you hear is what the viewers of your video will hear. What sounds tinny to you will sound tinny to them.

Figure 6-9 shows how Jane uses a mike mixer on location for "Introducing RxScan." She uses lavaliers on the patient, Dr. Palmer, and his assistant; a cardioid placed well away from the scanner but pointing at it to catch the scanner sounds and other room noises; and a shotgun on the camcorder to cover herself if the other audio goes wrong (for example, if the magnetic field of the scanner overpowers the lavaliers). The shotgun output goes to one track on the camcorder, the three lavaliers

Figure 6-9. Mixing on Location

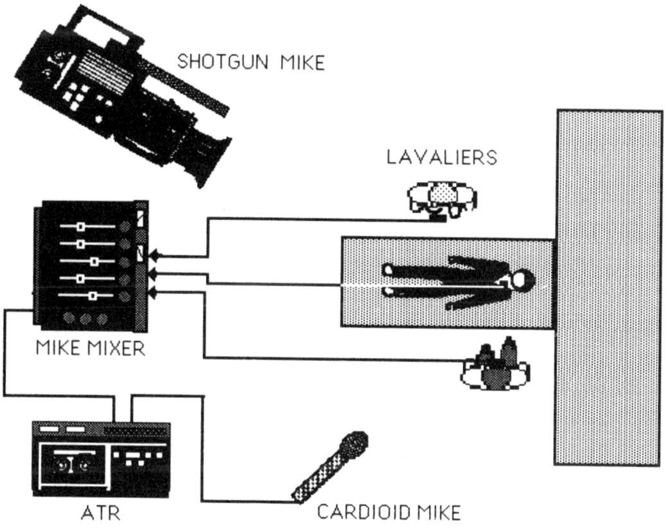

are mixed onto one track of an ATR with the mike mixer, and the cardioid output is recorded to the second ATR track. Later, she'll mix the sounds together in post.

Using a mike mixer during the production stage saves a lot of post-production audio mixing, but, since you might not be able to correct any mistakes you make on already mixed audio, it might be better in critical situations to record the output of each microphone with a separate ATR or on a separate track of a multitrack ATR. (This might not be practical for a music video, where there may be a dozen or more microphones and other audio sources onstage; you'll have to do some on-the-spot mixing.) You can then check each tape or track before you mix them all down to one or two tracks in post.

Working with Talent

Your DTV presentation is very likely to involve the onscreen actions of people—teaching lessons, pitching products, communicating in every way. As the DTV director, you should have some sense of how to get the best performance from the people in your video.

The management of professional actors is a subject of great subtlety, and not within the scope of this book. There are many books written by theater, film, and video directors that can give you more insight into professional directing than can be encapsulated here. It's worthwhile to use professionals when the material (and your budget) call for it (especially for narration, where a professional speaking voice is de rigeur), but more often you'll be using amateurs who have some connection with the project. Your task is to be sensitive to their needs and fears while coaxing from them their best possible performance.

For "Introducing RxScan," Jane is lucky that the main actors in the production, Drs. Gold, Damian, and Palmer, are all professionals speaking about their areas of expertise. They don't have to be coached on the basic information. As the chief representative of her company, Dr. Gold is fairly experienced with media in general and will be delivering a pitch she has given many times before.

Dr. Damian isn't so experienced, so Jane rehearses his scene with him several times until he feels comfortable with his movements and the pace of his speech. She advises him to speak slowly and clearly, to pause between sentences, and to look directly at the camera at all times. She tapes one of his rehearsals and analyzes it with him. She also talks to the other personnel in the area, who will be working while the scene is being shot. They're instructed to act completely normally, to avoid looking at the cameras and production people, to talk softly and not make loud noises, and to keep away from the immediate area of the shoot. In general, Jane's attitude is patient and reassuring, and it pays off—Dr. Damian gives a natural, confident performance that clearly conveys the necessary information.

Tips for Looking Good on Video. Video performances can be ruined by things that have nothing to do with the actor's behavior, such as the wrong suit. Here are some tips for getting your actors to look their best on tape:

Clothing. Avoid loud, contrasting patterns (especially herringbones and stripes); glossy white shirts and blouses; and white, navy, or black suits. For men, solid medium blue or gray suits; light blue, tan, or gray shirts; and dark red ties work well (all the politicians wear them). A conservative dress or business suit is good for women, with a minimum of shiny jewelry. (None of this applies if you're taping real actors or rock musicians, who can wear any bizarre thing they think will catch the audience's eye.) Check that little clothing details are in order before the tape rolls—your boss won't thank you if his fly happens to be open.

Body language. Audiences are extremely alert to body language and tend to judge what's said on the basis of what's seen. People on tape should remember to sit forward in their chairs and look alert. In a promotional or instructional video, the performer should always look directly at the camera when explaining important points. The eye contact brings home the information to the viewer. Keep hands relaxed and free to gesture.

Speech. Clear speech and a confident voice make words credible. Mumbling is completely incomprehensible on TV—remember those tinny little speakers that most sets have. Do a sound check before rolling tape to let the guest know how he or she will sound, and adjust the guest's mike level accordingly.

Broadcast DTV Production

The following section isn't meant as an exhaustive discussion of big-time video production; that would take several books to cover (some useful guides are listed in Appendix A). It will introduce you to some of the methods and equipment currently used in broadcast video, and give you some tips on how to proceed when you're ready to take the big step.

What Broadcast-Quality Really Means

What's meant by broadcast video? In Chapter 5, you learned about the NTSC standard for color video, RS-170A. The narrowest definition of broadcast video is that it meets every NTSC and RS-170A parameter. The only way you can really tell if a video signal meets RS-170A is by running the signal through a waveform monitor and a vectorscope while referring to the published specifications. That, of course, is what broadcast professionals do.

A more general definition of broadcast video has to include less technical, more visible criteria, such as:

- a stable, jitter-free picture
- sharp edged, clear colors without excessive noise or crawl
- a strong signal suitable for genlocking and editing (see Chapter 7)

Practically speaking, if you can run your video through broadcast equipment without the need for amplification or processing, and get something that looks just like regular broadcast TV, your signal is broadcast quality.

Beyond signal quality, the production values of broadcast video are also high. Scenes are properly framed and lit; colors are consistent throughout the program; edits are clean and noise-free; sound isn't just hearable but clear, strong, and perfectly in sync; narrative continuity is unbroken. To achieve this level of quality takes good equipment and the skills to use it.

When to Go Broadcast and When Not To. Why go broadcast at all? It's really a matter of professionalism. If you don't plan to ever show your work on TV or to video professionals, it would be a waste of time, money, and resources to attempt to meet broadcast standards. All the typical educator or business presenter needs is a few DTV programs and a decent genlock to get watchable video out of the Mac and onto a consumer VCR. The look and feel of broadcast only becomes important when your presentation will be on broadcast TV, when you want to impress video pros or others who demand professional-level quality, or when you absolutely need an effect, such as a dissolve between tapes played on two VCRs. This can't be obtained with current Mac desktop video technology. It's worth thinking twice before setting your cap for broadcast, because it can be difficult and expensive to satisfy real video snobs who can only accept the video coming out of the networks as being truly up to broadcast specs.

The Mac and Broadcast

It's a basic fact of life in the Mac DTV world: the video you can create with most DTV products doesn't measure up to the technical specs professional broadcast programming requires. This applies not only to inexpensive consumer video equipment, but to the output of the Mac itself.

As one observer of the DTV scene has put it, Apple has been rowing away from NTSC for several years, searching for the clear, clean land of RGB display. Now, looking back, Apple sees the island of video and realizes the Mac has to go there. That means a lot of painful reevaluation of what computer graphics should be like, and to what standards it should adhere. Meanwhile, the broadcast video community is intrigued by the power and cost-effectiveness of the Mac, but looks rather scornfully at the computer itself, waiting for Apple to come to them.

The funny thing is, NTSC composite video as a standard for the display of visual images is plainly inferior to the RGB method used in displaying computer graphics—try to use your TV as a monitor for word processing, and you'll immediately see the truth of that for yourself. NTSC (an acronym that insiders jokingly claim means "Never The Same Color") is a jerrybuilt system that suffers from overcomplexity and lack of stability. Nonetheless, it has the weight of history (and hundreds of millions of color TV sets and VCRs) behind it, so computer makers, including Apple, have to make accommodation. As for third-party developers, most of them still haven't grasped the possibility that a personal computer really can be used in a professional video setting, and so they aren't making products that measure up to professional requirements.

This doesn't mean it's impossible to use your Mac to create broadcast video, just that at this stage in the game it definitely requires a sizable investment in hardware, and being picky about the right software, to get truly broadcastable results. Let's take a look at what's involved.

Tips on Mac Graphics for Broadcast

There are a few important steps to take when designing Mac graphics to make sure they're the best they can be before you put them on tape.

- As mentioned in Chapter 2, don't use highly saturated colors that overstress NTSC's color handling method. Even the best processing amplifier can't completely eliminate color noise from a pure Mac red or purple. Some Mac presentation programs, such as MacroMind *Director* (see Chapter 8), provide color palettes specially adapted to the limitations of NTSC. You can even design such a palette yourself using *Studio/8* or one of the other color paint programs.
- Use antialiasing or smoothing, if available, to cut the apparent jaggedness of diagonals and curves in graphics created with paint programs. *Pixel Paint Professional* (SuperMac, see Appendix A) is one program that offers antialiasing.
- Use the best available genlock/encoder. Graphics recorded through an inexpensive genlock just won't look that good. If you can't afford one of the $2,000 genlocks, perhaps you can find someone who has one and borrow or rent it. User groups often have such equipment for rental or can put you in touch with someone who does. Or a local post-production facility might have a Mac already equipped with a top-notch genlock (see Chapter 7).
- Record your graphics directly to a quality tape format. That means S-VHS or ED-Beta at a minimum; even better, use one of the broadcast

$\frac{1}{2}$-inch formats (MII or Betacam) or $\frac{3}{4}$-inch, since many post-production facilities still don't have the capability to handle the $\frac{1}{2}$-inch superformats. A cost-effective practice is to use your own consumer VCR to work out the bugs in your desktop presentation, then use a $\frac{3}{4}$-inch VCR to record the final product. You can rent a $\frac{3}{4}$-inch machine for $150–$200 per diem (don't forget the proper cables and tape stock), or bring your Mac to a post-production facility. If you'll be genlocking Mac graphics over another video source, make sure the incoming video is high-quality—a broadcast camera or a good superformat or $\frac{3}{4}$-inch VCR.

Broadcast Production

If your DTV presentation isn't simply coming out of the Mac but will involve field or studio production, you'll need to dramatically increase your hardware requirements. Cameras and decks should be up to broadcast specs, and that means higher rental costs, and more money up front from your client or yourself. You'll want to establish a relationship with a video rental company, many of which offer stage and post-production facilities as well. For first-time renters, many companies require an equipment insurance policy and/or a deposit equal to the cost of the equipment (that might amount to tens of thousands of dollars). It helps to establish a record with the company by renting small items first.

A broadcast camera such as a high-end Sony or Ikegami is likely to be the most expensive single item on a shoot. A Betacam camcorder outfitted for ENG (Electronic News Gathering) can cost up to $30,000, with standalone ENG cameras running in the neighborhood of $10,000 to $20,000. Fully loaded studio cams can cost $50,000 or more—the ones used by the networks are worth in excess of $100,000, not counting the hydraulic pedestals! Rental costs are around $500–$750 per diem for an ENG camera, $750–$1000 for a camcorder.

Portable broadcast VCRs are less expensive, but hardly cheap. Sony's top-of-the-line portable $\frac{3}{4}$-inch machine, the BVU-150SP, costs about $7,000, and perhaps $250–$300 per diem rental. And of course, you can rent all kinds of other equipment, from color monitors, lights, and ATRs to mikes, switchers, and SEGs. In addition, since you'll be using a broadcast-level post-production facility, you'll want to record *time code* on all your raw footage (see the next chapter for a discussion of time code and broadcast post).

All this price-quoting is meant to suggest that you might be better off hiring someone to do the shooting for you. As mentioned, broadcast production values are exacting. Camera movement, lighting, and audio recording must be professional, and so should set design, makeup, and costuming. Whenever possible, professional talent should be behind and in front of the cameras. A DTV producer without previous broadcast experience should hand the actual taping over to a small production company while you kibbitz from the sidelines. Here are a few suggestions for working with a production company:

- Choose a production company carefully. Don't investigate just one, try several. Get recommendations from the company's other clients, and call at least one client. Look at the company's demo tape to see what they consider good work, and whether they've worked on projects similar to yours.
- Make sure the production company understands the level of quality you're seeking. Companies will take technical short cuts if you let them, so set up several review times during the production stage when you can monitor how things are being done. Get it in writing.
- You don't have to take the first budget the company submits to you—negotiation is everything—but don't expect high production values to come cheap.
- Draw up a detailed contract that defines exactly what the production company is and is not responsible for, and who will pay for what. Make sure the company is bonded and properly insured.
- Be prepared. Provide a script, storyboard, and prop/effects list well in advance of the production dates. Listen to the recommendations of the production director, but remember, it's your show.
- It's worthwhile to try to instill some of your own enthusiasm for the program into the people working with you. A "special" project will get a little more attention than "just another commercial."
- Finally, make sure the production director understands you'll be visiting the production site. You won't interfere with the director (unless you see something really bad going on), but you will be watching to see that the production is going as planned. Almost always, the director wants and needs you there, because you're the one with the contacts and vision that's driving the whole endeavor.

If you're willing to do more work yourself but still want help with your production, you can get more mileage from your budget by using a not-for-profit production facility. Often such facilities offer a sound stage with broadcast cameras and decks, audio and video rentals, and student interns to help you set up, all at much less than the cost of a professional production house. The equipment might not be brand new, but it's still likely to be better than anything you, your business, or your institution can afford on your own.

Once you've shot the video, whether on location and in a studio, you must weld it together into a seamless presentation. How to do that is the subject of the next chapter.

CHAPTER 7
Mac DTV Post-Production

Your Macintosh desktop video footage is "in the can," as they say in the film world. But all the raw footage in the world isn't worth much without organization. The post-production stage is when you turn that great footage into a meaningful, polished desktop video presentation.

Some DTV directors love post because that's when you get to play with the Macintosh itself, creating the fantastic effects only a computer can create. DTV directors with a bent for editing feel comfortable putting together a program from disparate parts in post, especially if they haven't been able to plan the pre-production and production stages in much detail; this happens in shooting documentaries, for example. Some desktop video programming, notably pure animation, might never go through a production stage at all; instead it moves directly from pre-production to post.

Other DTV directors hate post. Post is when you have to make up for the bad footage, shortsightedness, and other problems you introduced in the pre-production and production stages—if you can. (Of course, a botched editing job could make great raw footage look bad, as can second-rate animation or graphics.) But before you get to the editing stage, you usually have additional effects to create that can't be done in the production. In Macintosh DTV, these can involve adding graphics, titles, and animation. We'll look at graphics and titling below, and then tackle animation in the next chapter.

Mac Video Graphics

Even more than with graphics for slide presentations, the best graphics for video are *simple, direct,* and *bold*. Only simple designs will get your message across on a low-resolution television screen. Video imagery usually moves so fast that viewers simply won't be able to see complex designs well enough or long enough to make sense of them. Functional designs give all the necessary information to the viewer in compact fashion, so the most message gets through with the minimum of confusion. Dull, lifeless graphics won't even garner the attention paid to a soap commercial. Keep in mind that everyone in your audience is well practiced in tuning out dull TV.

There are a variety of means to accomplish these three desirable qualities. Simplicity is achieved by paring the number of elements in a graphic to the minimum; keep them large and obvious, unifying all with a central or master idea. Directness is inherent in graphics that possess only the elements necessary to tell the tale and no others, with each element chosen carefully and arranged in a straightforward fashion. Boldness is harder to achieve; it might require a mixture of bright, eyecatching colors and shapes; the juxtaposition of appropriate but unexpected images; and the expert choreography of movement. Beyond that, a truly penetrating graphic derives from the designer's thorough understanding of the subject's emotional impact on the intended audience.

Placing Graphics Onscreen. Probably the most basic part of composition for video graphics is making sure the titles are visible on the screen. Video producers talk of the *safe image area*, comprising the central 90 percent of the screen; no important imagery should extend outside this area, since it might not be visible on some sets. Text and other graphic symbols should be placed in the *safe title area*, the central 80 percent of the screen (see Figure 7-1).

Figure 7-1. Safe Image and Title Area

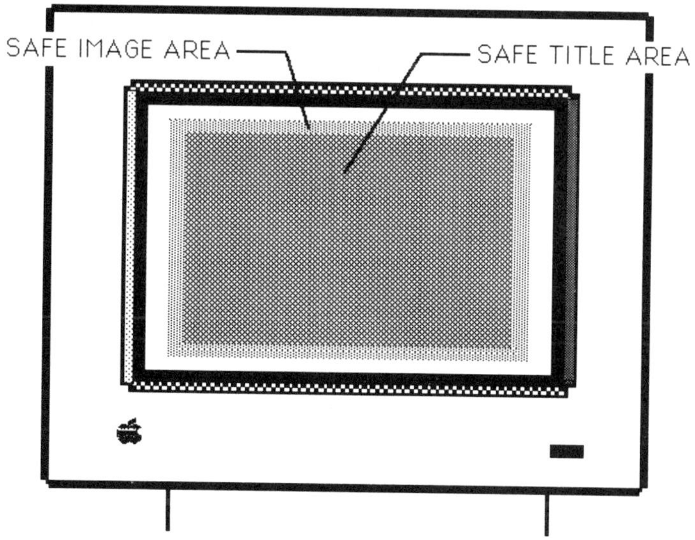

Overscan. One aspect of Mac video graphics you'll want to know about is *overscan.* Mac graphics, as you'll notice, leave a thick black border around the image area. For video applications, this border is undesirable; viewers want their desktop videos to fill the entire screen, just as broadcast does on ordinary TV. At present, most Mac DTV products haven't solved this problem, but as new generations of products are re-

Figures 7-2 and 7-3. DTV Graphics

leased, you'll see hardware and software extending the image out to the edges of the screen.

Figures 7-2 and 7-3 provide some examples of basic graphics for video: a corporate logo and a news graphic.

Tips for Better Video Graphics. The suggestions for designing Mac graphics discussed in Chapter 2 hold true for NTSC video as well. However, there are a few additional points to keep in mind.

- Don't use thin vertical lines that contrast against the background, such as black lines on white. Thin, contrasting lines jump very noticeably on video, which you can see if you look at a typical Mac dialog box displayed on NTSC. Thin lines tend to disappear when seen from typical TV viewing distances.
- Fine patterns of contrasting colors also flicker badly when seen on video. Patterns to avoid are checkerboards, herringbones, crosshatches, dot patterns, and fine stripes.
- Avoid heavy use of red, magenta, orange, hot pink, and brown. Video displays have the most difficulty rendering these colors with fidelity and clarity. Red and magenta are particularly unstable, and red areas almost always exhibit *crawling* (a shimmering border effect) along their edges. You can avoid this to some extent by always using colors that are less saturated. Black, white, blue, green, and gray are the most stable video colors—and, you'll notice, the most used in broadcast video graphics.
- Keep in mind that the colors you see on your Macintosh (analog RGB) monitor won't look quite the same when seen on a composite monitor. The better your encoder, the truer the colors will translate from Macintosh to video. Reds and blues seem to suffer the most in translation.

Adding Titles

Titling, the process of adding text to video, is probably the most common video "special effect." Use titles to:

- Identify and introduce the presentation.
- Label events and people.
- Mark transitions between scenes.
- Provide textual information.
- List the credits and end the presentation.

Video studios use dedicated *character generators* (also called *titlers*) to add titles with drop shadows, moving text, and more. With the right software, your Macintosh can do everything a character generator can do, with more colors and greater flexibility; in fact, the Macintosh, with its wealth of text styles, makes a truly superior titler.

DTV titles are generally added in post-production. You create the title with titling software, run video through the Macintosh with a genlock/NTSC card, and superimpose the title over the video at the proper point.

The standard use for titling programs is to produce subtitles and credits. The aim in subtitling is to position the text in just the right place, so it clearly labels the subject or action but doesn't obscure it. Subtitles also must be very legible; a strong sans-serif font in white or yellow with a dark blue or black border will show up well against most kinds of video backgrounds. Or the text might appear in a block of solid color. Most titling programs also offer you a number of ways to move text. You can dissolve from one page of text to the next, scroll text up from the bottom of the screen, move text sideways, and so on. Generally, you'll be able to use the same kinds of transitional effects available in slideshow/presentation programs, as discussed in Chapters 3 and 4.

Leave the subtitle or credit onscreen long enough for the viewer to read it; don't flash information faster than it can be absorbed. On the other hand, titles should disappear when they're no longer needed. An interesting exercise is to study the use of video text names under the guests on a Sunday news program. When do the names appear? What font and what color is the text? How long do the names stay? How many times are the names shown before the TV director decides viewers already know who the guests are? You can be sure the directors of these programs have the use of subtitles down to a fine art. Jane follows the same principles when she adds titles to identify the speakers in her video on the medical scanner. She superimposes the name of Dr. Damian on the screen when he first appears, as well as having the narrator speak his name—the double identification makes sure the audience remembers who he is.

One Mac software package designed expressly for video titling, rather than font manipulation for printing or desktop publishing, is *Showcase F/X* by Aegis Development (see Appendix A). With *Showcase F/X*, you can create text with any Mac screen font in a variety of video-type styles, including neon, block, embossed, and prism effects, with full control over the colors used in each part of the letterforms. In addition, *Showcase* comes with so-called *polygon fonts*, fonts created from vectors. Unlike the bitmapped fonts you normally see on your Mac, these can be slanted, resized, and rotated on the screen without the jagged edges letters normally assume when you distort them. That makes them perfect for video, although so far you're limited to the polygon fonts Aegis supplies with the program. Figure 7-4 shows a selection of *Showcase F/X* fonts and styles.

Figure 7-4. Showcase Fonts and Styles

Showcase F/X also has animation capabilities for creating moving titles. Animation is discussed in more detail in the next chapter.

Live Titling and Teleprompting. The Mac can be used as an impromptu titler during a live presentation, though it takes quick wits, accurate fingers, and a titling program that allows you to type without showing a cursor or menubar. The setup is similar: Send live video from a camera through a genlock to the Macintosh, which is running a titling program; type in the proper title at the right moment; and record the video on a VCR or send the video to a closed circuit system. A more practical approach, useful if you know in advance what titles you'll need, is to create the titles and save them in a slideshow/presentation program as separate slides in the order you'll need them; then summon each slide with a keystroke at the proper moment.

A Mac running a titling or slideshow/presentation program makes a serviceable *teleprompter*, a video device to display the text of a speech to an actor so it can be read on camera. Text in large letters is displayed on a video screen next to the camera for the actor to read, with new text scrolling up from the bottom or a new block of text appearing just as the actor finishes reading the previous block. A skilled actor or news anchor can create the illusion of speaking extemporaneously rather than reading a speech.

For teleprompting, a Mac, software, NTSC video board, and TV monitor are required. Before the shoot, type up the text of the actor's speech with the titling or presentation software, using large, easy-to-read letters and as many screen pages as necessary. At the shoot, set up the Macintosh RGB monitor so you can see it, with the composite monitor facing the actor (see Figure 7-5). Using the software's built-in scrolling or slideshow function, show the pages of text to the actor, putting up a new screen as he or she reads the old one. In a pinch, you can even use an ordinary Mac word processor, typing text in the biggest available font and using the cursor keys or mouse to scroll down the document as it's read.

Figure 7-5. Macintosh Teleprompter

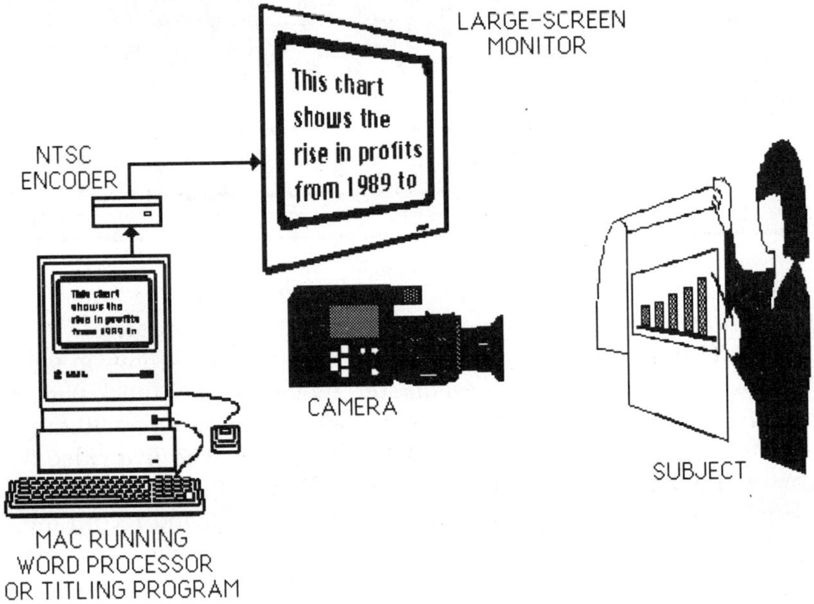

The esthetics of text—fonts, text colors, placing type, and special titling effects—are covered in Chapters 4 and 5.

Digitizing. Video digitizers offer a quick way of getting realistic color, grayscale, or black-and-white still images into your DTV graphics. While not as sharp as pictures from a flatbed scanner, a digitized image is more than adequate for most presentation uses, and digitizers are significantly less expensive than scanners. You do need a composite video source such as a camcorder or VCR to generate the images, but these are readily available.

Computereyes (Digital Vision, see Appendix A) is a typical low-cost grayscale digitizer that works with any Macintosh, including the Mac Plus. The hardware itself is a small plastic box with connections for power, video in (an RCA connector), and signal out to the Mac's serial or printer port.

As described in the previous chapter, the basic digitizing setup involves routing video through the digitizer to the Mac, where software controls the actual digitizing and image processing. *Computereyes'* software offers two capture modes, Fast (a 6-second capture time) and Slow (24-second capture), with Slow yielding better detail and grayscale fidelity, as well as a larger picture (up to 640 by 480 pixels). Neither capture mode is well suited to digitizing children, pets, or other moving objects; however, the software can capture still frames from a VCR that has a good, low-noise freeze-frame mode. *Computereyes* deals well with color video, the kind produced by any consumer camcorder, but you'll also

Figure 7-6. *Computereyes* Scan

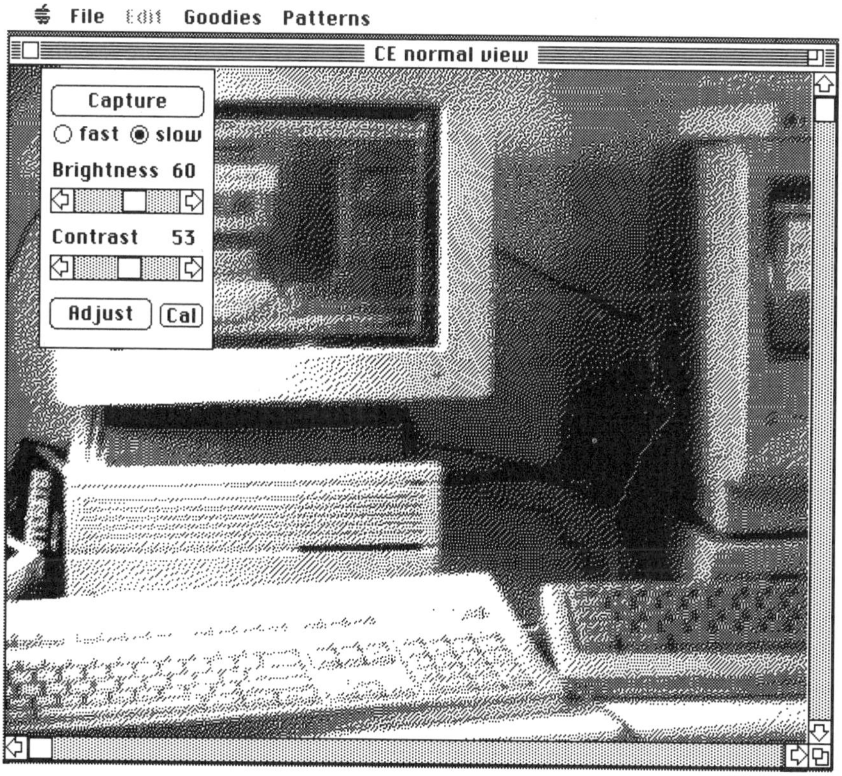

get good results with input from a black-and-white CCTV camera like Panasonic's WV-1410.

Two sliders let you adjust the brightness and contrast of the scan via software; other image-processing options include image flipping, mirroring, negative inversion, and choices of various dither patterns. (Figure 7-6 shows a *Computereyes* scan and adjustment window.) The digitized image can be saved in the most popular Mac graphics file formats, including *MacPaint*, TIFF, PICT2, and EPSF. That means you can work further changes with any *MacPaint* or image processing program; *ImageStudio* (see Chapter 2) is a good choice. *Computereyes* scans can also be colorized with a color paint program such as *Studio/8*.

Digitized video can be used in presentations in the same ways as other kinds of scans: as backgrounds for charts, substitutes for photographs, and documentation for complex processes. A sequence of digitized pictures grabbed off a video sequence can be plugged into an animation program (see Chapter 7) and inserted as moving images into any onscreen or video presentation. Jane at ScanTech uses *Computereyes* to grab frames at regular intervals from video sequences she shoots in ScanTech's service department. She copies them into a *SuperCard* stack and adds text, animation, and sound. The result is an interactive training tape for ScanTech's field service technicians (see Chapter 8).

Video Editing

It wasn't so long ago that video editing was done with a knife and tape, just like film editing. Things have gotten a little more advanced since then. Now video, whether it originates from a camera or your Mac, is always edited electronically by transferring selected material from raw footage on a playback VCR (or *source*) to a master tape in a recording VCR (the *slave* or *destination* VCR). Only a signal passes from the source to the destination.

It's the quality of that signal and how it's manipulated that determines the technical quality of the finished edits, or *cuts*. As you might guess, there's a right way and a wrong way to edit.

Punch and Crunch. Anyone with two VCRs can cut tape. Here's how:

- Hook up the output of the source VCR to the input of the destination VCR.
- Put your raw footage into the source VCR and a blank tape into the destination VCR.
- Search the raw footage for the beginning of the first shot in your program and put the source VCR in play-pause. Put the destination VCR into record-pause.
- Hit both pause buttons at the same time.

- When the first shot has finished, put both machines into pause again.
- Look through your raw footage for the next shot in your program, and repeat the process until you've completely edited the program.

This is called *assemble editing,* or *punch and crunch editing.* Why is it called punch and crunch? The "punch" part is from the necessity of punching the two pause buttons at exactly the same moment, but the "crunch" part isn't readily apparent until you play back the edited tape. With this method, you'll discover that edits aren't smooth but cause a jump in the video that interrupts both sound and picture.

There are a couple of reasons for this. For one thing, the destination VCR tape transport system can't get up to speed fast enough to record the first frame coming over from the source VCR, so you get broken-up video. The other reason is that assemble edits record over the destination tape's control track, erasing some of the track after each edit. That makes it hard for the destination to sync up with the signal from the source.

There are other shortcomings with assembly editing as well. The main one is, you can't easily go back and fix mistakes or add additional material. Suppose you've made a program with ten edits, and you want to go back and put in a graphic in shot 3 while leaving the audio part of shot 3 intact. If you were to try that by assembly editing, you'd record over the audio as well, plus ruin a few seconds of footage after the edit. All in all, you can see that assembly editing is the wrong way to go if you have any choice in the matter.

Insert Editing. The right way to edit is to *insert edit.* Insert editing doesn't disturb the control track of the master tape, so you can record new video over existing footage without ruining the video on either side. VCRs capable of insert editing have flying erase heads (see Chapter 6) that allow clean, glitch-free transitions.

Figure 7-7 illustrates a typical insert editing system. Among the many features a good insert editing system should offer are:

- Centralized control over the transport and recording functions of the VCRs with the edit controller
- Control of VCR preroll, so VCR transports are up to speed before the edit begins
- Digital readouts of the time of edit-in and edit-out points, and the total duration of your cuts so far
- Preview of an edit before anything is actually recorded
- Memory that can hold the edit-in and edit-out points of many edits and then execute them in a batch
- The ability to edit video and audio tracks separately

Figure 7-7. Insert Editing System

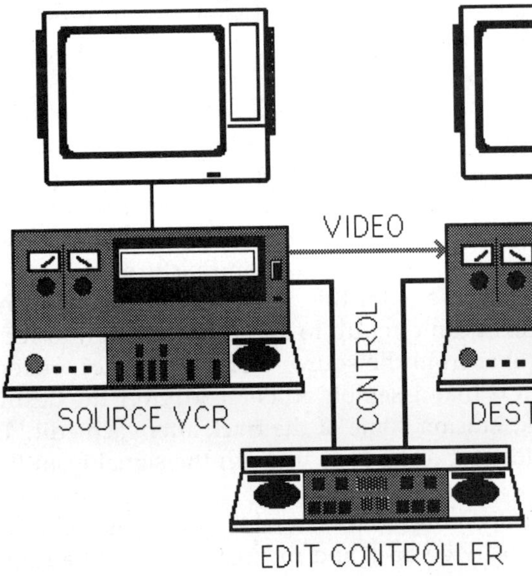

At ScanTech, Jane uses a compact 8mm insert editing system about the size of a Mac IIcx. The system has two 8mm decks and a monitor combined into one unit, along with an edit controller board. The unit takes up little room and is quick and easy to use.

Using an edit controller, the insert editing process for one edit typically works like this:

1. The raw footage is loaded into the source VCR and the master tape into the destination VCR. Both tapes are rewound to the beginning and the VCR counters are set to 0, as are the timer readouts on the controller. You choose whether you want to transfer just video, just audio, or audio and video.
2. Using the shuttle controls, you search the raw footage for the beginning of the first shot you want to use. Mark that point with the controller. The controller remembers the timer setting you've marked. You then roll forward to the end of the shot and mark that point also.
3. Next roll the master tape forward until you reach the first edit-in point. Now you've set up the basic situation for the edit.
4. To see a dry run of the edit, you hit the controller's Preview button. The controller rolls each VCR back a few frames before the edit-in point on both VCRs. (This is called *preroll.*) Both VCRs roll forward, and at the precise spot that you marked the edit-in point, you see the raw footage substituted for the master footage. Actually, no recording

has been done; the controller just sends the raw footage video to the monitor. At the end of the edit, the decks rewind back to the starting point.

5. If you're not satisfied with the way the edit looks, you can adjust the edit-in and edit-out any way you want. Once you've settled on the right edit, pressing the Edit button actually does the edit. The controller leaves the destination VCR paused at the last frame of the edit, ready for the next one.

Frankly, insert editing with an edit controller and compatible decks is so much faster and more flexible than assembly editing, and the results are technically so superior, that no one who has a choice should ever use "punch and crunch."

But do you have a choice? Until recently, insert editing equipment was restricted to the industrial and professional realms. For example, in 1989 a bare bones ¾-inch insert editing system consisting of two Sony VO-5850 VCRs ($8,350 each), a Sony RM-450 Editing Console ($2,300), and two Sony PVM 1271Q 12-inch Video Monitors ($1,095 each) would run you a cool $21,190. However, the DTV revolution has even invaded the editing suite. Now it's possible to find decks with insert editing capabilities at the consumer level. Sony, Panasonic, and JVC all offer complete systems, including compatible VCRs and edit controllers in either 8mm, standard VHS, S-VHS, or ED-Beta. You might be able to find a complete VHS insert-editing system for under $3,000.

Also keep in mind that it might be possible to edit your material with editing equipment at a school, local-access cable facility, or publicly funded video facility. You can even do the job at a professional editing house, many of which maintain a low-end (and relatively low-cost) edit room for insert editing only. There's more about working with editing professionals later in this chapter.

Something several manufacturers have been promising is hardware and software that makes it possible to use the Macintosh itself as an edit controller. There's nothing, in principle, that makes the Macintosh any less suited to the task than the dedicated computers used in professional editing suites. One of the most exciting (and most expensive) Mac-centered editing systems is being offered by Avid Technologies. Using a frame-grabber, the Avid system loads up to three hours of full audio and video onto eight 600 megabyte hard disks, so video can be edited without using VCRs and analog equipment at all. Avid's intuitive software allows you to drag pictures of every shot around on the Mac screen until they're in the proper order (in much the same way you might arrange slides in the presentation programs discussed in earlier chapters), add video transitions, and edit audio separate from video, all much faster than with VCR-based systems because all shots are randomly and instantly accessible. Infinite adjustments are possible, and you can play your edits at any time. This all-digital system, which is currently being tested by at least one major TV network, comes with a relatively high price tag—up to $80,000—so it's not something you'll be installing in your home office or high-school AV department. But this kind of technology usually filters down to more affordable levels within two to three years.

The Editing Process

The process of editing generally breaks down into several stages, or levels of approximation. The first and roughest stage is *logging;* here you record the beginning, ending, and duration of all your raw footage and start to make evaluations about what to keep and what to discard. In the *rough cut* stage, you take shots selected from the raw footage and piece them together into a smooth narrative. The final stage, or *fine cut,* is when you refine the rough cut, adjusting pacing and adding the final touches, including additional audio and graphics.

Logging. The logging stage is invaluable for seeing what you have, finding where the good shots are, culling the unusable shots, and deciding whether additional footage is needed before it's no longer possible to shoot any more.

Cautious editors log from exact copies of the raw footage called *workprints* (after their film counterparts), rather than the originals themselves. The less the raw footage is handled, the better. It's always possible to log footage by hand on legal pads, but you'll find it worthwhile to do your logging directly on the Macintosh using a word processor. This gives you the basic advantages of a readable log and the ability to search, replace, cut, and paste the text. Set up the Macintosh alongside the VCR and enter edit-in and edit-out points as you determine them.

Part of Jane's log list for "Introducing RxScan" looks like this:

Table 7-1. "Introducing RxScan"—Tape #6

Date: 10/1/90
Logged by: J

Shot #	Start Time	End Time	Duration	Notes
1	00:00:00:00	00:00:45:13	00:00:45:13	Good bldg ext.
2	00:00:45:14	00:01:20:30	00:00:35:16	Hallway; poor light
3	00:01:20:31	00:09:20:40	00:08:00:09	B Gold on goals of ScanTech

The numbers refer to hours, minutes, seconds, and frames.

You can also enter log information in a database manager or *HyperCard.* The advantages of using a database manager instead of a text editor is that the database manager can do a lot of the work for you, including calculating the duration of shots and sorting shots by any criteria you set up in advance, such as length, location, quality, and so on. All that's required is that you know enough about the functions of the database software to set up your own calculating and sorting criteria. Once you've entered the log information, you might find it useful to rearrange it with the database sorting and extracting functions to create a preliminary edit list.

The Rough Cut. This is the first real editing stage, when the rough outline of the program is blocked together into a continuous narrative. It's this stage where most important decisions are made about how the tape should be put together—the pacing, the order of shots within each scene, and so on. You sit back and look at the rough cut to finally get a sense of what the piece will really look like, and tinker with parts of the whole until it begins to look right. The decision-making becomes easier, of course, if you have written a solid script and held to it during the production stage.

At this point careful editors are still working closely with the log list, the storyboard or animatic, and the script, and are still using the workprint tapes, rather than the raw footage.

The Final Cut. This is the final edit stage, where the master tape is assembled from the original raw footage. During the final cut, the editor (and perhaps the director and producer, if they aren't the same person) hone the rough cut, substituting better shots for the ones chosen in the rough cut and making small adjustments in pacing. This is also when final effects are added, including special transitions and audio effects.

Of course, the stages of editing aren't always so cut and dried. DTV producers who are pressed for time might just do a rough cut right from the raw footage and call it final. Even when time is ample, the work of rough cutting inevitably shades over into final cutting.

Offline and Online Editing. When the final cut is to be done using a computer-controlled editing system, the editing process also breaks down into offline and online editing stages. The offline stage corresponds to the rough cut described above. Additionally, however, the editor prepares an *edit decision list* (or EDL) that specifies the in and out points of all the edits in the piece. Computer-controlled editing systems prepare and update such lists automatically.

In the online editing stage, corresponding to the final cut, the EDL is fed in electronic form to a computerized edit controller, which auto-assembles the master tape from the original raw footage. Should you plan to do your final edit at a professional editing facility (see below), you'll want to organize the editing process the same way—preparing an offline edit and an EDL yourself with whatever equipment you have handy before you go to the facility for editing online. (Even a paper edit decision list is better than nothing.)

Cutting for Continuity

The natural flow of events in a narrative is called *continuity*. Whether editing in camera or in post, you must have a vision of each shot and how it will match with the next. The action should flow smoothly, without a disturbing break that looks awkward or confusing to the viewer. For example, a typical continuity mistake is to shoot an actor walking toward the left of the screen and then cut to a shot of the actor moving in the same direction but seen from the other side, so it looks like the actor is walking in the opposite direction. Movements should seem to match throughout a sequence; each change in viewpoint and angle has to serve the narrative, not call attention to itself.

We'll discuss some specific aspects of cutting for continuity below, but there's one thing that has to be taken care of in the production stage. That is making sure certain small details are the same throughout a sequence. This can be hard when parts of a scene have to be shot at different times, even though the scene is supposedly taking place all at once. There's not much you can do in post-production to fix a scene in which the actor is wearing a green sweater in one shot, a blue suit in the next, and then the green sweater again.

Matching Action and Position. As with in-camera editing, you must maintain the proper screen position and movement for a subject throughout a sequence of shots. A person walking in one direction shouldn't suddenly seem to be walking in the opposite direction without some event to justify the change. When a motion across the screen does need to reverse, insert a neutral-angle shot between. Cutaways or reaction shots can be used for the same purpose. The key is to imagine yourself as the audience and make sure there's nothing to confuse or distract them.

There should be enough variety in the angle of consecutive shots that the audience doesn't get bored, but not so much that viewers become disoriented. Note that very small increments of change in the angle of consecutive shots can be just as disorienting as large changes. One thing that should never happen (except in avant-garde efforts) is to allow the point of view of the scene to shift from neutral to subjective, or from one actor to another, in adjacent shots. The audience is much more comfortable with a consistently neutral point of view, or the point of view of just one subject.

Many experienced editors feel the best time for cutting on action is just after the initiation of the act. Here's how Jane cuts a sequence from

"Introducing RxScan" that shows Dr. Palmer in Valley Hospital working with a patient.

1. Shot 1 is a medium closeup of Dr. Palmer looking at scanprints in the scanning lab. There's the sound of a door opening and Dr. Palmer begins to look up.
2. Shot 2 is medium wide, showing Dr. Palmer smiling and walking to greet the patient, who has just entered. They talk, and then Dr. Palmer gestures to the scanner. The patient begins to walk over to it.
3. Shot 3 is another medium shot from a slightly different angle on the same side of the room. The patient is still moving toward the scanner in approximately the same direction as in the previous shot. As the patient is getting onto the bed. . .
4. Shot 4 switches to a high overhead shot above the patient but still on the same side as the other shots, showing how Dr. Palmer operates the scanner's laser positioning device.

The aim in cutting this way is to create a smooth flow from one shot to the next, with the movements of the actors naturally motivating each transition. The last shot has a practical purpose, to show an action that can't be seen from another angle, but the center of attention is still the patient, and there isn't an abrupt change in viewer position.

Obviously, shooting and cutting have to work together here. If you don't keep action continuity in mind when you shoot, you won't have the proper footage to make smooth cuts. As stated before, no amount of editing can make up for crucial shots missed.

Audio. Another important way to create continuity is with sound. Music and ambient sound used across an entire sequence or scene can really help to coordinate material that otherwise might not hang together well. Narration and dialog can overlap from one shot to the next, smoothing transitions. Audio should be properly equalized and at a constant level across a scene; see Chapter 9 for more on Mac audio.

Matching by Shape and Sound. One trick editors use is to match a cut on a shape or a sound. For example, you could start with a picture of the earth spinning and cut to a closeup of a baby's face. Here, you're matching the round shapes of the world and the face (and making a comparison between the two, as well). To match by sound, find two sounds that are alike, and use them as the bridge between shots—a cut from a wide shot of a whistling train to a closeup of a whistling teakettle is a classic example.

Pacing

The proper pacing of sequences and scenes is one of the hardest things to learn; there are few rules for how long any particular action should take. When in doubt, though, you'll probably be kinder to your audience if you make your sequences shorter rather than longer, as long as all the necessary information is still there. Small adjustments in edit-in and edit-out points can make a big difference in the smoothness of a video presentation. Just remember that viewers have been conditioned to expect things to move fast on the small screen.

Study the work of other editors to get a feel for where and how to cut. Everything you'll need to know about cutting talk shows, interviews, and short presentations you can learn from watching Sunday-morning news shows. To go beyond basic, functional editing, look at the work of the great filmmakers instead—you can probably learn all you'll ever need to know by studying the films of Eisenstein, Hitchcock, and Kurosawa.

Transitions

In the chapter on creating a slide presentation, we took at look at basic visual *transitions,* the effects used to get from one slide to the next. Transitions are even more important in video presentations. Consistently using the right transition can further your narrative by providing important visual clues to the audience. Here are the major kinds of video transitions.

Cut. The *cut* is an instantaneous transition from one shot to the next. It's simple, direct, and honest. Whenever you're tempted to use a fancier transition, try the edit with a cut instead first.

A *jump cut* is created by cutting to create a discontinuity between shots—for example, cutting before the shot has quite ended, or cutting to an entirely unrelated shot. Jump cuts can add shock or excitement to a DTV presentation (music videos use them all the time), but in the typical business or educational presentation environment they irritate viewers and hamper your narrative.

Dissolve. A *dissolve* gradually replaces one image with another. A video dissolve substitutes one video source for another. This can be accomplished using a switcher or SEG between video from a VCR and a camera that accepts external sync, but not between two VCRs (at least without broadcast-level equipment beyond the scope of this book).

A dissolve between two Macintosh pictures (using a slideshow program, for example) just randomly substitutes the pixel information from the second picture for that of the previous picture. The dissolve can be fast or slow, fine-grained or "chunky." Using a genlock/keyer, you can always dissolve to and from Macintosh graphics and video.

Use dissolves for moving between shots that occur at different locations or at different times. An interesting effect can be achieved by maintaining a partial dissolve between shots—try it.

Fade. The *fade* dissolves the video or graphics from or to any solid color, usually black. Fades are a good way to start and end your program—they are gentle transitions—and to mark the beginning and ending of major scenes in the program. You can easily create fades in the camera while you're shooting (by opening or closing the iris or using the camera's fader option). In fact, it's a good practice to fade in and out of shots when you can.

Wipe. The *wipe* is a generic term for hundreds of different transitions in which one image replaces another along a border that moves across the screen. Like dissolves, wipes can't be accomplished between two VCRs without special equipment, but you can create wipes between Mac graphics and video.

Wipes are used much like dissolves, except they have a directional emphasis. A wipe left, for example, gives you the impression you're about to see something that's happening just to the right of the screen. (Wipes that seem to reveal a new image are called, logically enough, *reveals.*) Wipes can be slow or fast, simple or complex, hard-edged or soft-edged, borderless or with a colored border, and more. Figure 7-8 shows a selection of wipes, but these are by no means all of them. For most presentations, you should probably keep the kinds of wipes you use to the sober left, right, and checkerboard wipes.

Figure 7-8. Wipes

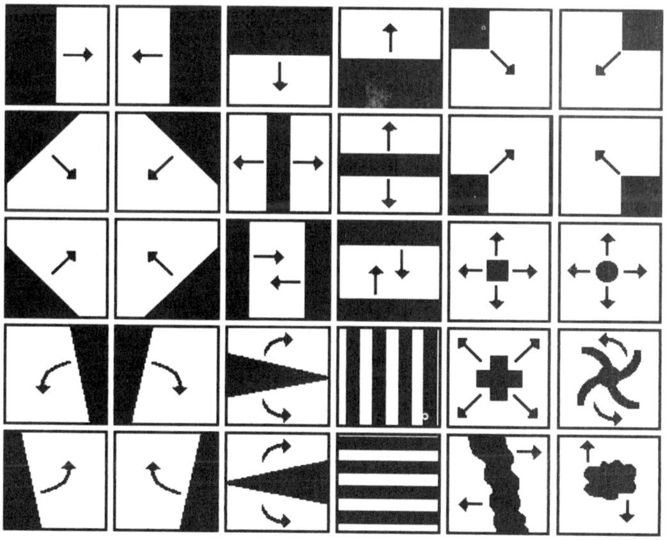

Digital Transitions. The most recent transition vocabulary comes from digital video. *Digital Video Effects* (DVE) computers like the Quantel, Mirage, and ADO have added new transition effects such as the following (several are illustrated in Figure 7-9):

- *cubing,* putting video or animation on the surface of a 3-D representation of a cube
- the *door swing,* rotating an image along the vertical axis
- the *mortice,* squeezing a video picture and surrounding it with a border
- *perspective rotation,* rotating the plane of the image along any axis in what appears to be 3-D space
- the *push, translation,* or *scroll,* moving the image smoothly around on the screen or off the screen altogether
- the *rubber band,* stretching or squashing the image
- the *section,* splitting the image into parts that can be put back together again, often used for exploding effects
- the *split or multiple screen,* combining images from two or more different video sources, each on one part of the screen
- *tiling,* repeating the image in a tile pattern on the screen
- the *twist,* warping one part of the image one way, the other part another way
- the *zoom,* moving the image into or out of apparent screen space

Usually, digital video effects are combined into one choreographed move. For example, a common DVE transition is to have the new shot, with perhaps a colored border, fly in from the corner of the screen as if from a distance. The shot, first seen at an angle, turns itself upright and expands to fill the entire screen, replacing the previous shot. An effect like this uses perspective rotation, translation, zooming, and morticing.

While you can create purely Macintosh-based DVE-style effects with animation programs (see Chapter 8 for an example), doing it with video currently requires a Mac II NuBus special effects video board such as Mass Microsystems' *Color Space II* and *ColorSpaceFX* (see Appendix A). The *ColorSpaceFX* board gives you the capability to do real-time zooms, squeezes, split-screens, tiles, flips, pushes, perspectives, and more with any incoming video source, with effects controlled entirely by Mac software, including *HyperCard.* The board also offers rock-steady, flicker-free 60-frames-per-second RGB output. The *ColorSpace* boards (you need both) list for about $5,000, which is quite inexpensive when measured against the $100,000 cost of a Mirage or Quantel. Nonetheless, you'll want to think very carefully about whether DVE special effects really will add a lot to your video presentation, or if all the fancy visual business will distract from your message.

Figure 7-9. Digital Video Effects

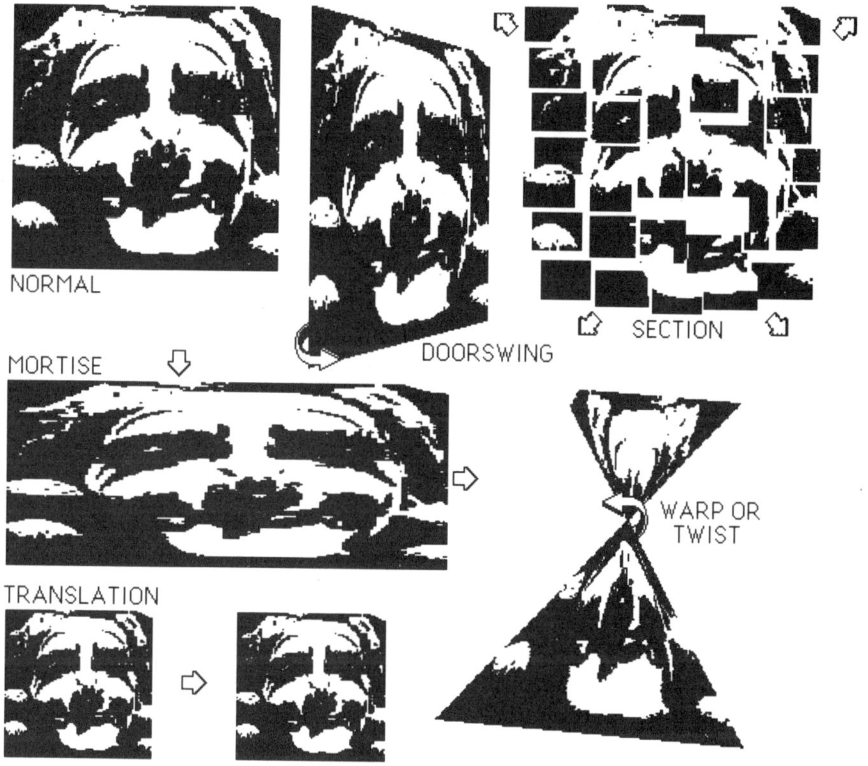

Audio in Post-Production

If you listen closely to the soundtrack of any television program or film, you'll hear not one but many layers of sound going on all at once. For example, in a party scene you might hear music, dialog, and several different sound effects at once—ice tinkling in glasses, champagne corks popping, the hum of background conversation, and so on. In nearly all cases, these sounds weren't recorded on videotape during the production but were added to the video during post-production. In fact, post is where most of the audio work on video gets done.

The handling of audio in post-production involves adding sounds that were not recorded on the videotape during production (these are called *wild sounds* because they aren't synched to any visual), and improving or *sweetening* sounds. You can tackle these tasks at various levels of complexity.

Audio Dub. The simplest way to add wild sound to your DTV program in post-production is by using the *audio dub* function on your VCR. This records new audio over the linear audio track on the tape without disturbing the video; the tradeoff is that you record over whatever audio was there before. On hi-fi or two-track VCRs, the audio dub may be recorded over one of the tracks (usually track 1). This way, you might be able to keep one track of original audio while dubbing new audio—say, narration or a musical score—over the second track.

To audio dub a sound effect onto your tape, all you have to do is plug a mike into the VCR or camcorder, cue up the tape, put the recorder into audio dub mode, and make the sound at the right moment. Punch-and crunch audio dubbing from an ATR to a VCR is only a little more complicated:

1. Set up your ATR and VCR with the ATR line output plugged into the VCR audio line input.
2. On the ATR, cue up a second or two before the beginning of the piece of audio you want to dub onto the videotape, and put the ATR in play-pause. (The second is to allow the ATR to get up to speed.) Cue up a second or two before the beginning of the piece of video you want dub over, and put the VCR in audio dub-pause.
3. Punch both pause buttons at the same time. If you've timed the cues just right, the ATR audio should start to dub over the VCR audio at the proper moment.
4. Punch the pause buttons again when the dub is finished. Play back the dub on the VCR to test the result. If the timing or sound level is off, you can try again.

If you're generating wild sound with your Macintosh, use the above method, treating the Mac as the ATR. One thing to note is that the Mac doesn't need preroll time—just hit the play key or click the mouse to start the sound at the right moment.

Insert Audio. As with punch and crunch video editing, a standard audio dub is simple to do, but haphazard in results. If you have access to an insert editing system, you have more flexibility and can produce a smoother program with more precisely timed audio. The insert edit controller may allow you to do inserts on one or both of the VCR audio tracks only. Even if the controller doesn't specifically control audio, you can probably do audio inserts anyway. Try this with a test tape: When you're ready to dub the audio in, manually press the audio dub button on the slave VCR (and release the record button, if necessary). Perform a standard insert edit. The audio should go on the test tape without disturbing the video.

The real skill in editing audio into video is matching the sound with the visuals. In punch and crunch, you depend on your own sense of timing—and the speed of your index fingers—to make sure audio and video are in sync. With insert editing, you can use the edit controller's frame counter to insert sound with near-frame accuracy, which is usually good enough for the ears of your viewers. The one time you must be right on the mark is when you have to sync wild dialog to video. Your viewers can inevitably tell if the dialog is even a frame or two out of sync with the lip movements of the speaker, so you might have to perform the audio insert several times to get it exact. If frame-precision is necessary for sound effects or dialog, consider organizing your audio effects using a detailed edit or cue sheet, just as you might for video effects. The sheet should contain the shot number, frame in and frame out, duration, and desired sound effects.

Audio can provide a useful way to pull together adjacent scenes. When you do an audio insert, let the audio from the previous scene bleed over into the next, past the cut in video. Or start the audio for the next scene a few moments early, before the cut. If your video is short, laying a single piece of music over the entire piece can bind it together effectively even if the video cuts are choppy. (Video and film directors depend on the score composer to do that for them all the time.) Use audio fades, which you can easily do with a mixer or the audio level controls on the ATR or VCR, to gently bring the viewer into or out of a scene. Try bringing up the audio at the beginning of the program before you show any video to create a feeling of expectation in your audience.

You can go the other way as well. Instead of audio dubbing sound over edited video, you can take a piece of prerecorded music and edit the video to fit. That's the way music videos are usually done—every edit is on a beat, and, in extreme cases, every beat has an edit. Most commercials are edited the same way. If the sound already has a structure, it only makes sense to use that structure. Just record the audio onto the master tape before you start to add video, and then do inserts as you normally would.

Mixing in Post. Conceptually, audio mixing in post-production isn't much different than mixing in production. The aim is the same—to combine many audio sources into one or two for recording onto videotape.

If you're willing to mix down two or more generations, you can layer dozens of sound sources together before adding them to the video. This is particularly useful when you have many sound effects to add to a tape but only a few inputs on your mixer. Audio doesn't lose as much signal quality as video does when it's recorded down a generation, so you don't need to be so concerned about rerecording the audio several times before laying it onto the edited master videotape.

Audio Sweetening. The term *sweetening* is often applied to any manipulation of audio done in post, but here we'll refer to it as the process of cleaning and improving inadequate audio. Probably the simplest form of sweetening is adjusting the volume of a sound to bring it up or down to the level of the rest of the audio, but you can do more than that. For example, you may have recorded the sound of a car door closing in the field, but when you get back home you find that you've also recorded the sound of a horn that partly masks the sound of the door.

To some extent, you can fix the overlapped sound problem with an audio mixer and an *equalizer,* or EQ, a device for adjusting the pitch or tone quality of a sound. The main use for an EQ is to clean up existing sounds or tailor them to suit a particular use. Using an EQ, you might be able to block the sound of the horn by filtering that portion of the recording with the pitch controls, which adjusts the level of set ranges in the audio spectrum (bass, midrange, and treble, measured in kilohertz). Equalizers may take several inputs, with separate controls to set the pitch of each input; they can be built into amplifiers and audio mixers or stand alone.

Another device called a *reverb* can add apparent depth to sounds. You can make a tinny recording of conversation sound deeper and more natural by rerecording the sound through a reverb, which is used in conjunction with the mixer. *Digital delays* and *echo boxes* change the timing of sound effects and make them sound as though they were recorded within a large space. Other devices can create and modify sounds in all kinds of unusual ways, but these are used mainly by professional audio technicians and aren't likely to find their way into a DTV studio.

Tips on Scoring

Music adds emotional impact to any production—if the music is appropriate and correctly handled. Whether you're creating your own score or getting music from somewhere else, make sure it fits the program material; the wrong musical ambience can cripple an otherwise effective program. It doesn't make much sense to use a delicate piano sonata to score a video about aliens attacking Miami (unless you're as sure of yourself as the film director Stanley Kubrick, who could put the Blue Danube Waltz in outer space and make it sound right). Appropriate music, on the other hand, can instantly establish the location, period, and mood of a scene or entire program. An alien-invaders video scored with electronic thriller music, or the soundtrack of a 1950s sci-fi film, or a parody of the "Miami Vice" score, would press the right buttons with certain segments of your audience, but perhaps not with others; be aware of what your prospective audience is likely to expect and how they'll respond. Even animation sparks viewer expectations when it comes to sound and music. Most of us have the entire musical library of the Warner Brothers' cartoons stashed somewhere in memory.

Knowing when to use music is as important as knowing what music to use. Traditionally, music is added to a video presentation at the beginning, end, and at important points in-between. Music can lead you into a situation, foreshadow an event, recall an event that happened earlier in the presentation, or shock you, as directors of thrillers often try to do. People and places in the video can have their own themes, which can be used to add layers of interpretation to dramatic events. One thing the music shouldn't do is overpower or contradict the video. In a training tape, a melodramatic theme played while the instructor is explaining the workings of an automated milling machine would work counter to the purpose of the scene, and invite laughter rather than learning. The same cautions apply to the use of sound effects, especially laugh and applause tracks. If you must use these, add them sparingly and consistently, with sensitivity to the context of each scene.

Matching Sound and Music. Things get complicated when you want to compose music and sound to match video events exactly—for example, if you want to place dramatic music and sound effects to match an animated data graphic. For sound effects, you can laboriously audio dub in the effects on your VCR, finding the right video frame in your edited version and inserting the matching audio. Musical scoring can't be done that way, because the music has to flow as a whole as well as hit a beat on the right events. Some composers just write an appropriate piece to the correct length without worrying about matching the beat with events on the screen. This approach is adequate for documentaries, instructional videos, and other programs where music with a strong beat isn't necessary or appropriate, but it results in lackluster scoring for more dramatic material. Others write music that's heavily percussive, so at least some events will hit on a beat. Low budget action dramas are often scored that way. A skillful musician can watch the video and play along with it on the keyboard, hitting beats as needed and adding more tracks and effects once the main framework of the score has been laid out.

Broadcast Post-Production

Broadcast post-production, like broadcast production, involves an entirely higher level of hardware and the operating skills to go with it. In almost all cases, you'll be doing post in a professional facility, with the aid of a videotape editor and sound engineer.

The thing that distinguishes broadcast post from "ordinary" post, besides the astronomically higher budgets involved, is the use of *SMPTE time code,* or TC. In essence, time code is a digital signal recorded on a tape that identifies every frame with its own unique number. The Society of Motion Picture and Television Engineers (SMPTE, pronounced "Semp-tee") has set the technical specifications for time code, so you'll often hear it referred to as "SMPTE time code," or even just "SMPTE."

How Time Code Works. The frames on a time-coded tape are numbered sequentially from the first to the last frame on the tape (to a limit of 12 or 24 hours) by hour, minute, second, and frame. The first frame is usually numbered 01:00:00:00, or one hour, zero minutes, zero seconds, and zero frames. *Drop frame* time code is a variant time coding method in which the occasional frame number is dropped to make the time code exactly match the real time as measured by an external clock. (To be precise, drop-frame TC skips two frames a minute except for every tenth minute.) Non–drop-frame time code gradually gets out of synch with an external clock because NTSC actually runs at 59.94 hertz, which means there are slightly more than 60 fields in a second, although the time code counts only 60 fields. (Why does NTSC run at 59.94 hertz, and not 60? Don't ask, but it's true.) A non–drop-frame program will end up being four seconds longer for each hour than is indicated by the time code. The upshot is, having the time code match external clock time is a big convenience, so choose drop-frame for computerized editing if you have a choice.

A *time code generator* is needed to impress the code onto a track on the tape. (The process of recording time code is called *striping*.) During the broadcast production stage, time code can and should be added to each tape with a portable time code generator attached to each VCR, with each time code generator in sync and sending the same number to each VCR. The time code can either be recorded onto the vertical blanking interval between fields (this is *Vertical Interval Time Code*, or *VITC*) or on a spare track, usually one of the audio tracks of the tape (this type is called *longitudinal time code*, or *LTC*). If BVU-type ¾-inch VCRs are used, time code is recorded on a special *address track*. Since VITC and LTC each have its drawbacks, many editors like to have both kinds on a tape.

Time code should also be striped onto the master editing tape as it's being blacked and onto any ATRs being used to record wild sound. Nagra ATRs, among others, are set up to record time code. You can always add time code to raw footage or wild audio in post, but it's more efficient and cheaper to do it in the production stage.

A *time code reader* makes it possible to see the time code, which otherwise is invisible. Usually, time code generators and readers are built into the same machine. It's also possible to "burn" the time code on a working copy of the raw footage so that it's always visible. Tapes with visible time code are called *window dupes*. Window dupes are very useful during the logging stage, making it possible to log by time code without having to use a time code reader.

Advantages of Time Code. The advantages of time code in post-production are many. It's possible to skip a control track pulse and make a sloppy edit with a control track editing system, but time code allows totally accurate insert editing, since the number on the frame never changes. You can always see just where you are in the tape by checking the time code number, which is very convenient for handling the raw footage during offline editing. Just use the time code number to identify the precise location of each shot in the edit log.

With computerized time-code editing systems, you can go directly to any frame on any tape by simply entering the right code. You can also go to the same frame, or perform the same edit, as many times as you like with perfect accuracy. The system logs scenes with just a few keystrokes and keeps track of the time code of all offline edits. An *Edit Decision List* (EDL) is prepared that specifies each edit by time code number; an online editing computer then auto-assembles the entire production from the EDL. A few developers offer software that can turn your Mac into an EDL computer; see Appendix A. Audio as well as video recorders can use time code, meaning you can easily sync an audio tape to video for precise audio mastering.

Until recently, the only place you'd find time code was on a pro shoot or in a professional facility. Now consumer video equipment manufacturers are starting to offer low-cost (under $500) time code generators and readers, so time code can be used in at-home DTV production as well. Striping time code onto work tapes with one of these units enables you to do much offline editing work at your convenience. This can save hundreds or thousands of dollars in edit room charges, and make the time you spend in the edit room more productive.

MTC. Professional film and video composers need to know just what video frames contain what action, so they can compose the soundtrack to match those frames. For that, you really need audio time code. A new time code standard called *MTC (MIDI Time Code)* combines features of SMPTE and *MIDI (Musical Instrument Digital Interface),* the music world's standard digital control interface for electronic instruments, into one coding system. An MTC reader reads SMPTE time code off your video, converts it to MTC, and sends it to the Mac via a MIDI interface. MTC-compatible applications can then direct MIDI devices to create music and sounds exactly in sync with video. For example, you could jot down the SMPTE numbers of frames you want to coincide with sound effects (the frames or events are called *hits,* and the list is a *hit list*). An MTC-compatible sequencer can watch for the frames in the hit list as the video plays and, when a hit comes up, command a synthesizer to play just the right sound. While a full discussion of MIDI and MTC is beyond the scope of this book, see Appendix A for other books that cover advanced sound and music in video post-production.

The Broadcast Edit Bay. The layout of a typical broadcast editing bay is shown in Figure 7-10.

Figure 7-10. Broadcast Editing Bay

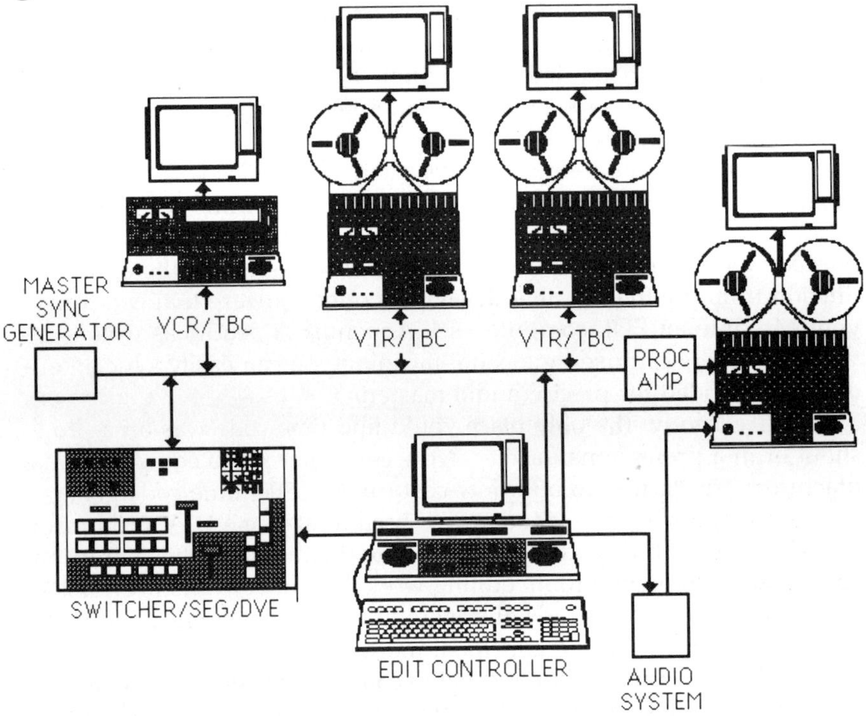

As you can see, several specialized pieces of video gear are used in broadcast-level editing. These include:

Master Sync Generator. This box just supplies a steady horizontal and vertical sync to all the video-processing components in the bay, so every component uses the same sync.

Switcher and DVE. All video in the system flows through the switcher, which is used to program wipes, keys, and other effects. Used in conjunction with the switcher is the DVE computer, which, unlike the Mac, can accept multiple channels of video.

Edit Controller. A computerized edit controller doesn't actually handle video and audio, but controls the components that do, the VTRs, VCRs, and ATRs, and often the switcher and DVE as well.

Proc Amp. A *proc amp* (processing amplifier) is the most valuable tool for reconditioning bad video. The proc amp allows precise adjustment of signal levels; brightness and color phase can be corrected at the same time. A good proc amp can help turn video recorded directly from a Mac with a less-than-broadcast genlock/encoder into video that can be handled by broadcast equipment.

Time Base Corrector. The *time base* of a video signal is the timing of each cyclical signal event—the horizontal and vertical sync pulses, for example. Unfortunately, all VCRs are imperfect mechanical devices that introduce *time base errors,* instabilities and irregularities in the tape's sync pulses, onto recorded material. The time base of one recorded tape is always slightly different than the time base of another recording, even a tape recorded with the same VCR. That makes it impossible to sync the signal from one VCR with the signal from another, something you need to do if you want to create an effect that involves two taped sources.

A *Time Base Corrector* (TBC) is a device that corrects time-base signal instabilities caused by VCRs during videotape playback, making it possible for two or more VCRs can be in sync. The TBC strips the old sync pulses from the recorded signal and inserts nice, clean, stable sync pulses instead. Most TBCs also include proc amps for sprucing up other parts of the signal, such as the black, video, and chrominance levels. Each VCR in a multideck editing system needs its own TBC; most broadcast VCRs or VTRs have TBCs built in. Most transition effects, such as an *A/B roll* that involves a superimposition between VTR A and VTR B, require two VTRs with TBCs.

The signal from a Mac, if it's part of the system, has no time base error and only needs to be sent through a TBC if the TBC incorporates a proc amp. Otherwise, the Mac output should go through a separate proc amp.

Multitrack Mixer/ATR. A multitrack audio mixer and ATR, time-code compatible, are always part of the editing bay arsenal.

Tips for Working with a Post-Production Facility. Complex DTV presentations will probably require that you hire an outside post-production facility, rather than editing the program yourself. As you might guess, preparation is all-important. Lack of foresight will invariably result in unpleasant problems and bad feelings, not to mention a more expensive product. These suggestions will help you get the most out of what is often a difficult experience:

- First, you should know how much you can spend. Fully equipped edit rooms are very expensive, running several hundred dollars an hour for the room plus the services of an editor and a technician. Budget for 30 percent more time than you actually think it will take to edit your presentation.
- Shop around. Edit room charges can vary greatly. In larger cities, you may find cut-rate, publicly funded facilities that will do the job.
- Make sure the facility has the equipment to handle your production needs: online computerized editing, the right tape formats, the right digital effects machines, the capacity to handle film-to-tape transfers and copy stand work, a 24-track audio mixer, a Macintosh, whatever. Draw up a complete post-production outline; then visit the facility be-

fore you commit yourself and talk to the facility manager. The better you know your own needs, the more likely you'll find a facility that meets them. Post facilities that use Macs in-house (the number is growing) should be first on your list, since they'll have already encountered and solved the signal problems inherent in Mac-to-video graphics. You may be able to just bring in a disk and let the facility transfer your graphics directly to broadcast tape through an high-quality genlock/encoder. At least, they can give you suggestions for revising your video to bring it closer to broadcast specifications.

- Find an editor you can work with comfortably. Remember, you're going to be cooped up with this person in a dark room for many hours at a time. In the edit bay, at least, most editors are easy going and professional; those are the only personality types who can survive daily contact with anxious, abrasive video producers. A good editor can really improve your project with suggestions based on his or her previous experience. If you don't trust the editor, you probably won't get the benefit of that experience. On the other hand, the final form of the production is ultimately your responsibility, so evaluate your editor's suggestions carefully, especially if they seem to go against your original vision of the piece.
- Do as much as you can before you enter the facility. Log the footage thoroughly. Know your material backwards and forwards. Consider using or renting an offline editing system and putting together a rough cut yourself—a control-track editing setup can be rented for $750–$1000 a week, against the $300 to $500 an hour for online editing. Bring an edit decision list and your entire supply of raw footage and sound on audiotape (neatly labeled) to the edit session. Let the facility know in advance what you'll need in terms of tape stock, audiotape, and so on, in what format(s) you want the master tape, and whether you need a separate audio master (for distribution as a sound recording, for example).
- Work out digital special effects in advance. The Mac can do a lot of magical things, but DTV effects still can't quite match those possible with dedicated DVE machines like the Quantel, ADO, and Mirage, notably manipulating multiple channels of video in real time. If you decide you need an advanced effect, go over your plan with your editor before the start of editing. You might be able to do a dry run to see how the effect will look. Because digital effects are expensive, review your needs to see if you can't use the Mac instead—that's the whole point of the desktop revolution, after all. Even if the Mac can't handle it, perhaps you can use Mac software to create an outline or simpler version of the effect that will give the editor a clear idea of what you're shooting for.
- Bring one or more associates to the edit session. Your partner will no-

tice continuity or other problems that escape you, and you can spell each other when the edit room gets claustrophobic.

Using Video in Your Presentation

Once you've created a Mac DTV program, how can you use it? One of the obvious advantages of video programming is that it can easily and cheaply be duplicated, distributed, and played on the more than 100 million VCRs in this country. Make as many copies as you need, either with two VCRs or by sending the tape out to a duplication facility (where you can have tapes created in different formats, such as VHS, 8mm, and $\frac{3}{4}$-inch). Then distribute the tape to your sales reps; play it at conventions, conferences, and meetings; include it with training materials and product instructions; show it on business television networks and to employees on in-house closed-circuit systems; play it in classrooms and at lectures; even recut the material as a commercial and buy airtime on local TV channels.

Tapes are easier to transport than Macs, but you need to give some thought to what system you'll need to show your video. Most businesses and schools have basic video equipment you might be able to borrow, but often you'll need to provide for yourself. For small presentations, consider one of the combined VCR-monitor units. These combine a 10- or 13-inch screen with a built-in video player; just pop in the tape and sit back. Meeting-room–size audiences will respond well to a larger screen; the 35-inch Mitsubishi monitor seems to be a favorite among Mac presenters. An auditorium or lecture hall calls for a large-screen projection TV. Definitely set this up in advance, as projection systems are less reliable and trickier to use than standard TVs.

There's no reason not to combine a video with other forms of presentations such as a slideshow. Since the video is the canned part of the presentation, needing little input from you and turning your audience temporarily into TV-watchers, you might want to show the video before launching into a slideshow, giving a lecture, or taking questions. If, on the other hand, the video is so powerful it overshadows the other material you have to present, save it for the end, so your audience goes out with a strong last impression. Include a copy of the video along with the other leave-behinds.

Some kinds of information can be shown only with animation, the art of moving graphics. Animation software for the Mac presentations, long a field without much innovation, is taking off in a big way. The theory and practice of Mac presentation animation is discussed in the next chapter.

CHAPTER 8
Presentation Animation

The dark screen lights up with colorful flying letters, turning in space as they spell out the name of your company. The letters transform into geometric shapes, which link together to form a working, moving model of your proposed new product. A cartoon character walks onto the screen and begins to tell your audience why it should approve your proposal. Eyes are riveted to the screen.

Your students are having trouble visualizing the difference between the Ptolemaic and Copernican representations of the solar system from the descriptions in the text. After class, you sit down with your Mac and create moving simulations showing both theories. When you show the animations in class the next day, faces light up, and you know everybody understands.

Those are just two examples of the power of presentation animation. With the techniques discussed in this chapter, you can make your own animated presentations, devise instructional tapes that engage your students while explaining hard-to-visualize concepts, and design sophisticated moving graphics for logos, commercials, promotional tapes, and animatics.

What Animation Can Do

When we think of animation the first images that pop into our heads are either from the great Disney animated films or the Warner Brothers cartoons we watched on television as kids. These animations were intended to entertain, as are most animations today. But animation has immensely practical uses for desktop presentations as well. Animation can show actions, events, and processes that cannot be seen directly, such as the movement of electrons in the atomic interstices of a new superconductor, or the docking of a Martian probe in outer space. Mac animation software makes it easy to create scientific and engineering visualizations like these. Similarly, network newscasts increasingly use computer animation as a stand-in when live action footage isn't available—for example, to diagram action in a war zone where no reporters are allowed. Such animation was used effectively to diagram the U.S.-Iran-Iraq skirmishes in the Persian Gulf. Animation can be superimposed over still graphics or taped action to emphasize any idea that will stick in the mind better when shown visually. Your audience might not remember that "tyrosine breaks the covalent bonds between oleaginous compounds and cellulose fibrin," but they'll notice animated detergent enzymes gobbling up the grime while scurrying over footage of dirty clothes in a washing machine.

Animation in presentations has entertainment value, too. There's no doubt that snappily moving text and images will keep your audience awake and interested. Used with sense and restraint, animations add force to major points in your presentation; the trick is to use animation to enhance presentation content, not upstage or obscure it. Done right, animation is one of the most effective forms of communication—something the classic animators always knew.

Traditionally, quality animation has been a craft that required a long apprenticeship to master and deep pockets to fund. The Macintosh, capable software, and low-cost video equipment make the technical parts of animation easier to learn. Even if you've never tried your hand at animation before, you'll be able to create useful animations with any of the programs discussed below. As you progress, you can concentrate on learning the really hard parts: rendering objects and environments, choreographing movement, even developing rounded, believable characters and structuring complete animated narratives.

If you're an experienced film animator who has hesitated to enter the highly technical world of video and computer animation, you'll find an Macintosh animation system the right place to begin. A suitably equipped Macintosh and VCR can substitute directly for the animation stand, allowing you to produce animations without the expense and drudgery of traditional techniques. While you might not be able to match the realism of drawing, smoothness of movement, and richness of characterization in the classic Disney cartoons of the later 1930s to mid-1950s, the high quality of Macintosh-produced animations may surprise you. Keep in mind, though, that even the power of the most advanced computer can't replace the accumulated knowledge and experience of an entire animation studio, and you shouldn't expect it to.

Animation Basics

Whatever you can set in motion in your mind's eye can be expressed through animation, the process of stringing together individual pictures to create the illusion of movement. The images themselves don't really move; instead, a sequence of related but incrementally changing images called *cels* or *frames* are displayed in succession so rapidly that, to the human eye, they give the appearance of smooth motion. All animation—and for that matter, all video and film imagery—takes advantage of this physiological effect, called *persistence of vision*.

For animation to appear smooth and fluid, the animation frames must be shown at a *frame rate* of at least 12 frames per second (fps). For film, the frame rate is 24 fps, often with each frame shown twice; for video, it's 30 fps, the same as the video frame rate. Frame rates slower than 12 fps result in animation that appears to hesitate or jerk between movements, which is usually not the effect you want to achieve. The more frames per second, the smoother the movement, but the more work is required to create an animation. Thirty frames per second means a lot of pictures—1,800 per minute, 162,000 for a 90-minute, feature-length program, assuming you make only the art you end up using. Walt Disney's *Snow White* required more than a *million* test and finished drawings, the work of scores of designers, artists, backgrounders, in-betweeners, inkers, and film technicians.

Luckily, your Macintosh can take over much of the tedium for you. Standard Mac editing techniques allow you to cut, copy and paste pictures, maintain a consistent palette, string together multiple sequences of movements, and instantly play back the results, all of which is surprisingly hard with traditional animation techniques. Most animation software goes further, doing much of the actual animation rendering from general instructions you set up in advance. For example, you can take a clip art picture of a rubber ball, load it into an animation program, draw a path for the ball to bounce along, tell the program how long to make the animation, and then sit back as the software does the rest of the work. You'll find that most presentation animations don't require much more than this.

Macintosh animation software can combine several of these features:

Page-flipping. *Page-flipping* is analogous to cel animation as practiced by filmmakers. A series of pages or frames is created by the animator with a paint or draw program. Each picture is incrementally different from the previous one; for example, a square could move from the left of the screen to the right in equal increments spread across 30 frames. When the sequence is finished, it's stored in memory or on disk. To run the animation, the pages are loaded into memory and displayed at the chosen frame rate. When you look at the animation, the square looks like it's sailing across the screen. If you've ever buzzed through the pages of an animation flip book, you'll understand the concept behind page-flipping. Figure 8-1 shows how it works.

Figure 8-1. Page-Flipping

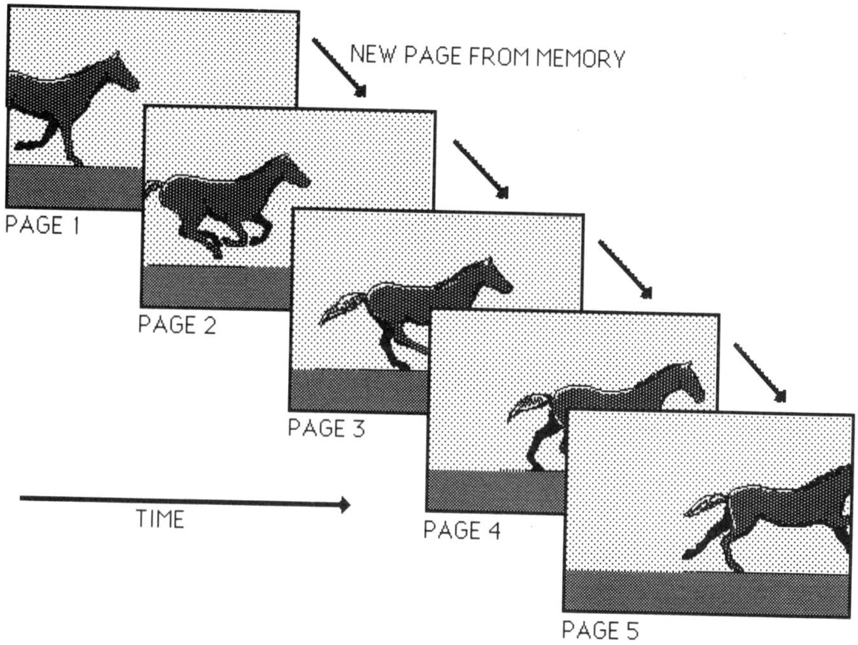

Key Frame Animation. Other Macintosh animation programs take a different approach. Rather than page-flipping, these programs work with animation objects called *polygons* that are manipulated as vectors rather than as bitmaps. Polygons aren't as detailed as bitmappped images, but they require less memory to store, and the computer can do more things with them.

For example, you can draw an object on one frame, define a path for it to move around on the screen, and then drag the vertexes of the object to create a new shape on a second frame. The program will then animate the entire sequence, including figuring out the intermediate shape the object should take to transform from its original shape to the new shape. This process is called *key frame animation:* The program figures out the shapes of the images you draw, which are called *key frames.* The in-between images are called *tweens,* so key frame animation is sometimes referred to as *tweening.* See Figure 8-2 for a graphic depiction of how key frame animation works. Obviously, having the program accomplish the movement for you saves a lot of work. Most Mac animation programs offer some combination of page-flipping and key-frame animation techniques.

Figure 8-2. Key Frame Animation

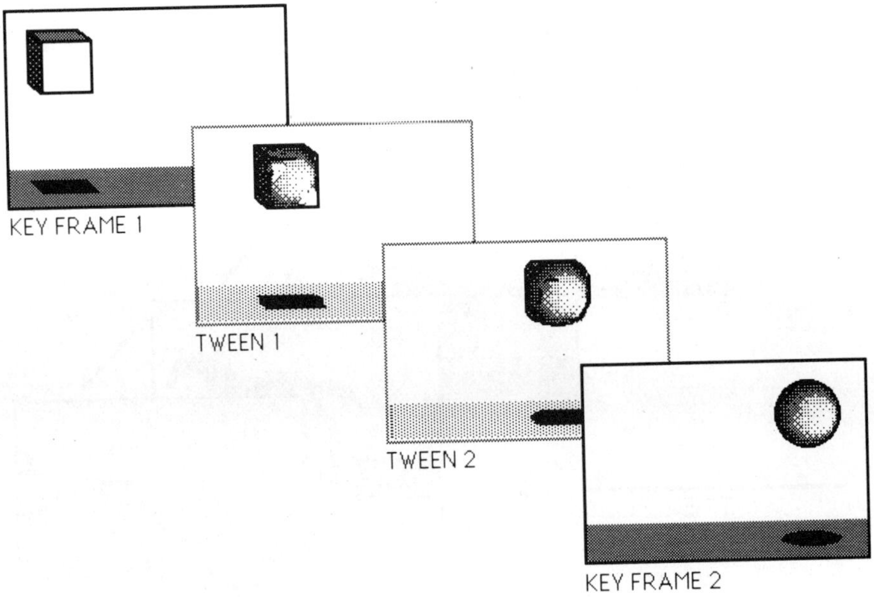

Two- and Three-Dimensional. Another distinction between animation programs on the Macintosh is whether they handle two-dimensional or three-dimensional images. What's the difference? Two-dimensional animation deals with images that are resolutely flat, while three-dimensional animation moves objects that appear to have full height, width, depth, texture, reflectivity, and shadows in an imaginary three-dimensional computer "space" or "world." These objects are created with three-dimensional object editing software, which is usually integrated into the animation software.

Three-dimensional animation is more difficult to learn than two-dimensional, partly because working in three dimensions requires an extra dimension to your thinking as well as demanding more from your Mac. Two dimensions is sufficient for nearly all presentation animation tasks. But with three dimensions you can create incredible (and impressive) animations not possible with two-dimensional programs. Engineering and scientific presentations often profit from the use of three-dimensional imagery, especially when you need to show the actual workings of a manufactured object. Even the use of three-dimensional letters and effects in a standard business or educational slideshow adds a slick, high-tech look. Also, three-dimensional animation is a fascinating subject in its own right, at the cutting edge of computer and animation technology. We'll look at three-dimensional animation in more detail later in this chapter.

Tips for Page-Flipping Animation

The following suggestions can save you time and effort in creating page-flipping animations on the Mac:

- Storyboard your work. Sketch out the plot and work out details of the background and character motions before you begin making the actual art for animation. Fine-tuning your concept before you start will save you frustration later. The more planning you do, the less likely you'll need to make changes in each frame of the animation after you've created 30 or 40 frames.
- Memory is usually the biggest constraint on the length and resolution of animations you can create, since many programs require that the animation be stored completely in RAM as you work on it. So it pays to design animations that use the least memory. One efficient method is to use *looping animations* that play the same few frames repeatedly. This approach can be satisfactory for animated business graphics, moving text, simple cartoon characters, and any animation in which a quick movement is all that's required.
- You can reduce the amount of work needed to create an animation by redrawing only the parts of an object or background that move. If you think about it, most cyclical processes, such as a figure walking, need only a few states for each movement—the swinging back and forth of each arm and leg, for example. You can draw the arm and leg positions as separate pictures and tack them onto a picture of the body. After you've created the various stages of the walking figure, some animation programs allow you to can pick up the entire animated figure and save it for compositing onto another animation.
- Save the art you create for animations in Scrapbook files. That way, they'll be immediately available for use with most animation programs. Build files of frequently used clip art for animation.
- Some programs allow backgrounds to be larger than the screen. An oversize background can be scrolled in its window to reveal new areas. With careful attention to the position of your objects you can even move the background while the foreground appears to be stationary.
- You may also be able to change color palettes in an animation sequence as often as you like—even for every frame. This frees you to use more than 256 onscreen colors (in the 8-bit color system) in the complete animation, although you'll still be limited to 256 colors in any one frame. Generally, however, a simple presentation animation should use the fewest colors necessary to get the message across.
- If you're taping your animation, remember to switch off the menubar, window frame, cursor, and any tear-off menus or tool palettes, or they'll record, too. Many programs take care of this automatically.

Using *Studio/1*

One way to get started with Mac animation is with *Studio/1* from Electronic Arts (see Appendix A). *Studio/1*, the one-bit, black-and-white version of *Studio/8* (see Chapter 2), offers most of the painting functionality of its bigger cousin, with the addition of sophisticated page-flipping and basic key-frame animation capabilities. Among the effects possible with *Studio/1* are automated moves in the plane of the screen; metamorphoses over a set number of frames; and the ability to pick up an animation as a brush and paste the entire clip animation, called an *animbrush*, onto another animation. Figure 8-3 shows the *Studio/1* screen playing a canned cartoon.

Figure 8-3. *Studio/1*

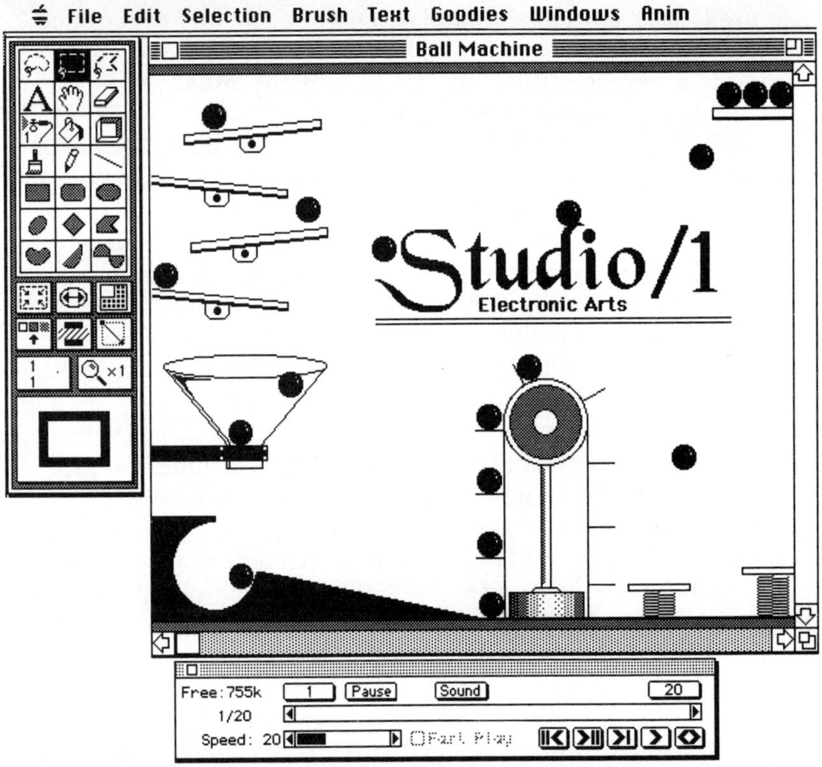

Animating an Atom. Jane's "Introducing RxScan" videotape discussed in the last two chapters also includes an animation of a vibrating, rotating atom, demonstrating the basic concept behind nuclear magnetic resonance. Here is the general procedure she uses to create this brief black-and-white animation with *Studio/1:*

1. Jane enters *Studio/1* and draws four views of a rotating atom. She draws position 1, picks it up as a custom brush, and flips it to create position 3. She then draws position 2, and then flips it to make position 4 (see Figure 8-4). When the four are put together in the animation, the atom will appear to spin.

Figure 8-4. Atoms 1

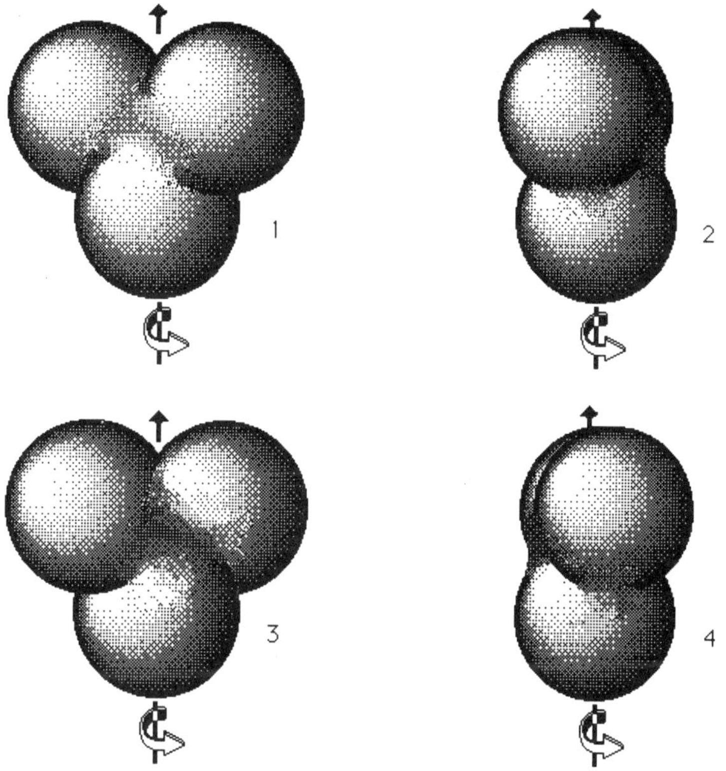

2. Now Jane makes four animation frames with an option in the Anim menu. Jane picks up each position of the atom as a brush and pastes it on its own frame, but in the same location on the screen. She plays the frames to check the positioning and effect. Minor adjustments can be made easily by working onto any individual frame with any paint tool.
3. Using the Pickup Selection option in the Anim menu, she picks up the entire animated sequence as an Animbrush. She saves it in case she needs it again later.
4. Jane clears the current animation frames and starts a new animation, this time with 60 frames (two seconds long at 30 fpi). She also turns

on the grid, a tool that allows the artist to paste brushes at precise intervals. Then she paints an atom animbrush at every grid intersection. Checking the result, she now has a two-second animation of rotating atoms filling the screen (Figure 8-5). Total time to create the animation: 45 minutes.

Figure 8-5. Atoms 2

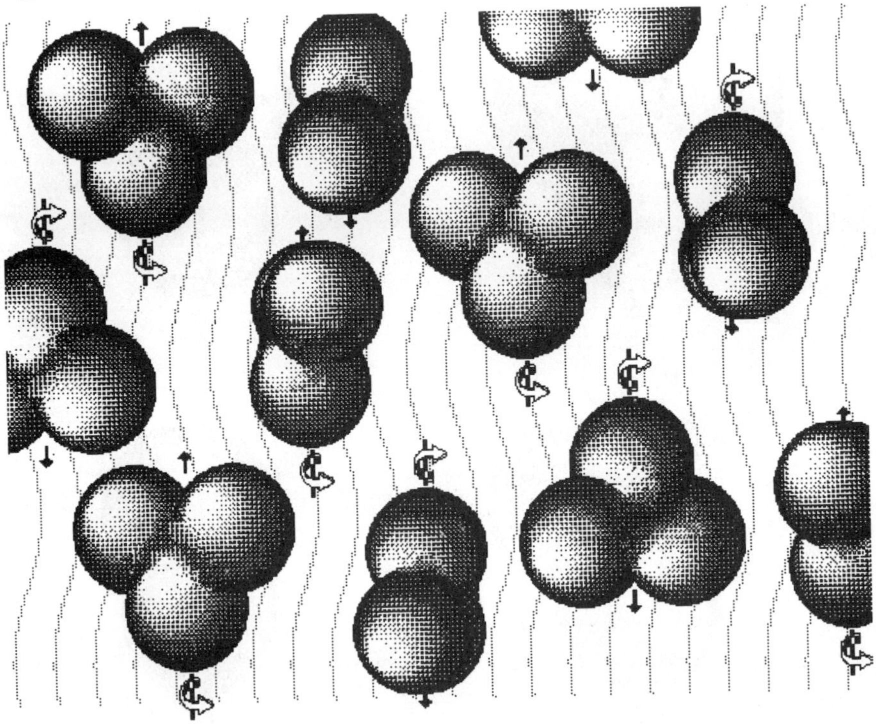

Anim 3D. One of the most useful features of any animation program is the ability to accomplish many difficult moves for you automatically. *Studio/1* can move a brush smoothly across the background in the plane of the screen; zoom it in and out; and do complicated turns, swoops, spins, and orbits. The key to these tricks is the integration of *Studio/1*'s perspective and animation tools through the Anim 3D dialog in the Anim menu (see Figure 8-6).

Here's how Jane uses the Anim 3D dialog to make a moving title:

1. She creates 30 animation frames, and then makes sure she's at the first frame.
2. Next, she types a line of text with *Studio/1*'s text tool, draws a selec-

Figure 8-6. *Studio/1* Anim 3D Dialog

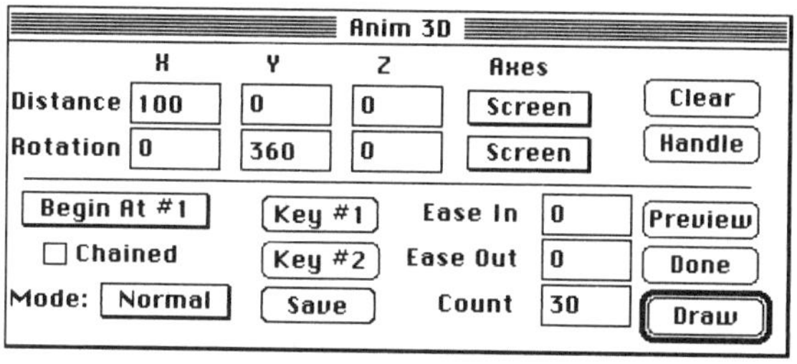

tion box around it, and positions it at the top of the screen, where she wants the text to be at the end of the animation.

3. Now Jane calls up the Anim 3D dialog. The settings in the upper part of the dialog refer to the direction and angle of motion of the text. Jane can enter an amount in pixels in the Distance row to make the brush move horizontally (x-axis) , vertically (y-axis), or into and out from the screen (z-axis). She wants the brush to zoom in along the z-axis, so she enters 1000 in the Z Distance box. Jane also enters -500 in the Y column to make the brush move up from the bottom part of the screen. Brushes can also be rotated along the axis of the brush handle by entering degree values in the Rotation column. In this case, Jane enters 360 (a complete turn) in the Z box. The other settings are left at their default values.
4. Jane clicks on Preview to see a *wireframe* (outline only) rendition of the move she's programmed. This lets her check the motion path and make changes before the animation is actually rendered. To do the animation, she clicks on Draw, and the sequence is automatically painted showing the position of the brush on each frame. On playback, the text swoops smoothly up toward the top of the screen while making a full turn, as shown in Figure 8-7.

The animation resembles the kind of flying text that costs thousands of dollars to produce at video special effects studios. This feature alone makes *Studio/1* an excellent tool for desktop video titles. The program also includes a number of animation templates, well-crafted movements and effects that can be applied to any drawing. You can make your own templates as well.

Figure 8-7. Moving Text

Animation with *MacroMind Director*

Currently the most sophisticated animation program for the Mac is *MacroMind Director* (see Appendix A), an advanced version of the company's popular *VideoWorks II. Director* provides the basic page-flipping features of *Studio/1,* as well as key-frame animation, animation templates, and text animation—and in color. *Director* can also integrate three-dimensional object animations, drawn and bitmapped graphics, and sounds, all within a multilevel working environment that provides several different approaches to animation creation. At *Director*'s Overview level (Figure 8-8), you simply piece together presentation animations from ready-made elements by arranging icons in a window, in much the same way most slideshow programs allow you to arrange slides. At the nuts-and-bolts Studio level, you can fine-tune existing animations or create entirely new sequences.

Director is a complex program, but using it to make many kinds of basic presentation animations isn't hard. The program includes canned animation sequences you can quickly adapt to your own presentation needs. For example, you don't have to reinvent the wheel every time you want to make an animated bar chart—there's an animated bar chart template already in *Director*. Here's how it works:

Figure 8-8. *Director* Overview

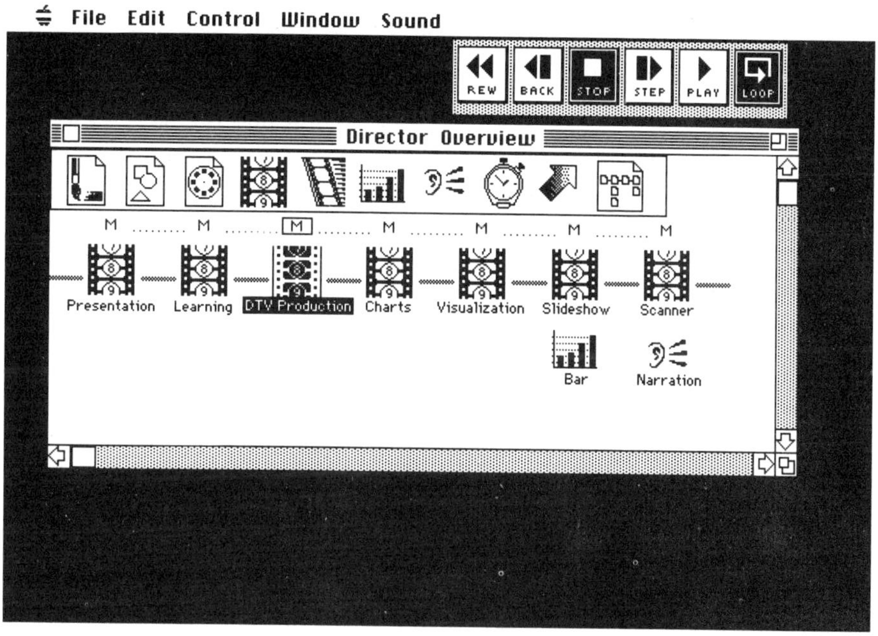

1. Choose Auto Animate from the Edit menu. This opens a dialog (Figure 8-9) with a list of ready-made templates, including bullet charts, bar charts, and animated text.

Figure 8-9. Auto-Animate Dialog

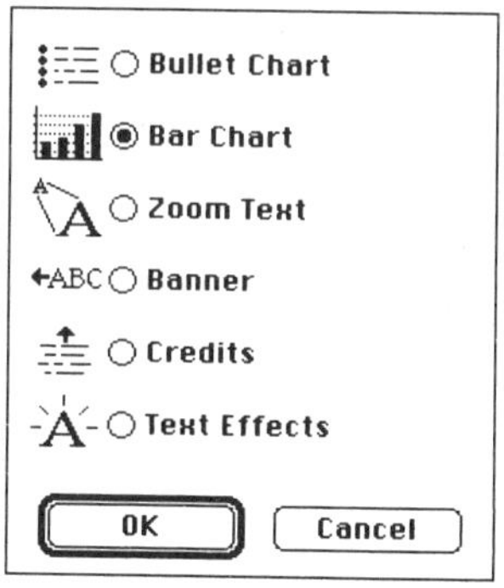

2. Choose the bar chart icon. A second dialog (Figure 8-10) opens, with fields for entering the bar data, as well as options for setting the text size and color, the speed of the animation, and the type of bar graphic. Set the required values.

Figure 8-10. Bar Chart Dialog

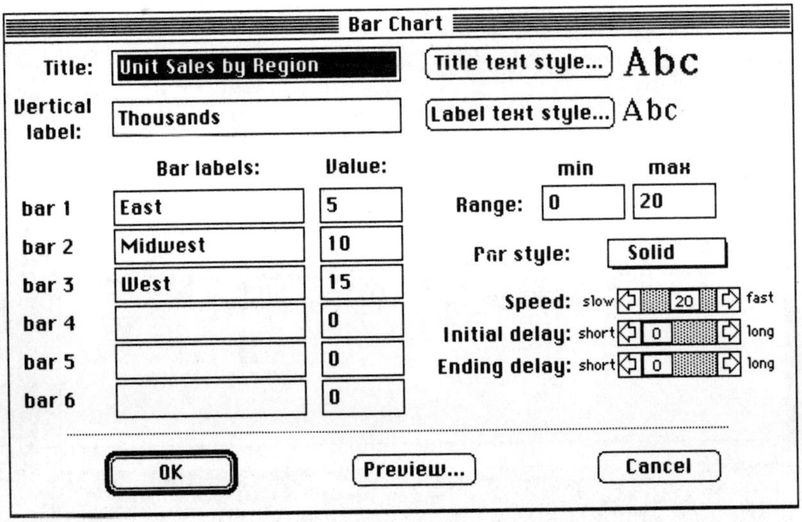

3. Click on Preview to see the animation. The chart appears, with the bars rising from the base *x*-axis value in sequence from left to right. Not flashy, but it does the job with minimal effort. You can go back to the bar chart dialog to tweak the animation, making it move faster or slower, changing the typeface, and so on. Save the chart when you've got it the way you want it, for later videotaping or incorporation into an entire Director presentation.

Animating a Scan

Animations created this way are simple and effective, but not very flexible. If your data or concept doesn't fit the templates and clip animations provided, you'll need to go to *Director*'s Studio level for the custom effects you want. That's what Jane at ScanTech does for a simple animation that shows how the RxScan scans a patient. In an overhead view, the animation will show the patient sliding into the scanner on the scan table while being scanned with radio waves. The computer-processed scan then appears on the control console's video screen.

First, Jane needs to create the art. She can do this within *Director,* which includes complete color paint and object-oriented drawing utilities. Opening the Paint window, she draws the elements of the animation—a patient lying on the scan table, the scanner itself, a console with video screen, a scan, and some color effects to show radio waves. Each of these is saved as a castmember, available from the Cast window (Figure 8-11).

Figure 8-11. Castmembers

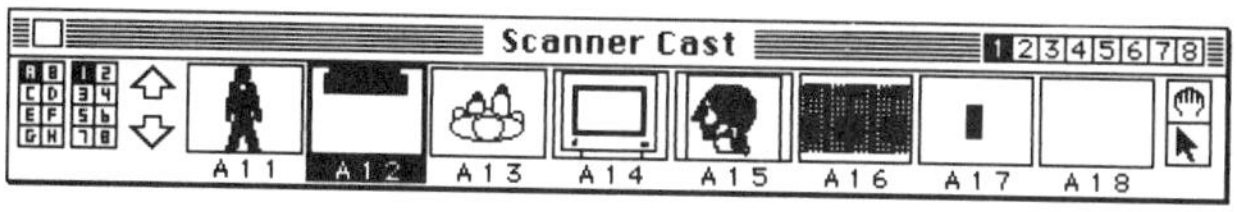

The key to organizing animations in *Director* is the Score window (Figure 8-12), essentially an animation spreadsheet. Each column in the Score corresponds to an animation frame, and each row to an animation *channel* (the action of one castmember, as well as channels for sound, colors, tempo, and transitions). By selecting rows and columns in the Score, you indicate how many frames an animation will take, which castmembers are involved, and which actions will be tweened between what frames.

Figure 8-12. Score Window

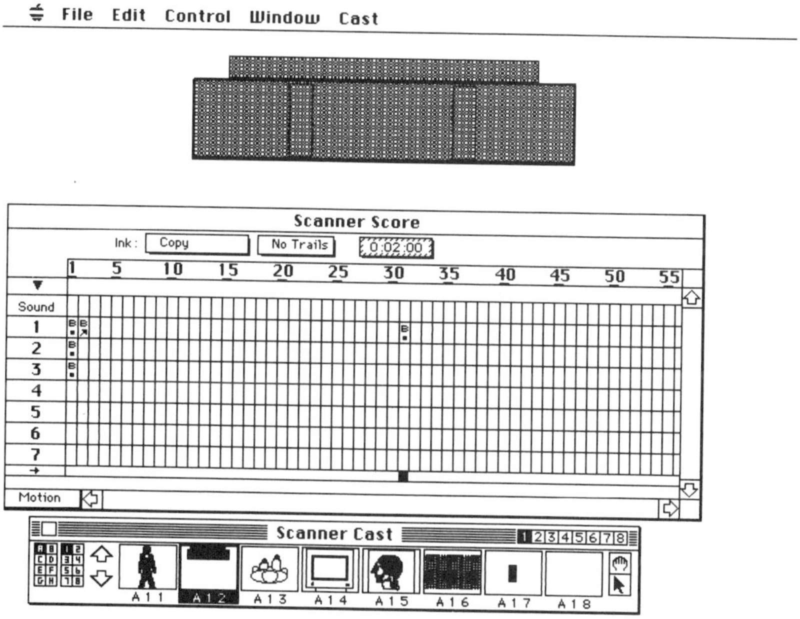

Jane wants to move the patient lying on the scan table vertically up the screen into the scanner.

1. She positions the patient castmember on the Stage for the first frame by dragging it from the Cast window.
2. She then selects the number of frames she wants the animation to

last in the Score. Sixty frames yields a slow, smooth movement. The first castmember automatically is assigned the first channel (row) in the Score, but Jane can cut and paste it to any other channel.

3. By choosing In-Between from the Score menu, Jane tells Director to tween the movement of the patient from the first frame to the last.
4. Starting at frame 1, Jane presses Option-Command and drags the patient castmember on the stage in the direction she wants it to go. Pressing the Shift key at the same time keeps the movement in a straight vertical path. On playback, the patient moves smoothly upward for the chosen number of frames.
5. Now Jane returns to frame 1 and chooses the second castmember, the scanner. It occupies channel 2 in the Score. She positions the scanner on the Stage so the patient will appear to move into it during the animation, and then repeats the tweening process for the scanner (but leaving it in place).
6. When she plays back the sequence, the patient moves into the scanner. (Actually, the patient castmember moves "under" the scanner castmember—higher-numbered castmembers always paint over lower-numbered ones—but visually, the effect looks the same.) Now Jane can continue with the other segments of the animation (flashing radio waves on the patient, and making a scan appear on the console), using essentially the same techniques. Figure 8-13 shows a frame of the completed animation.

Figure 8-13. *Director* Animation

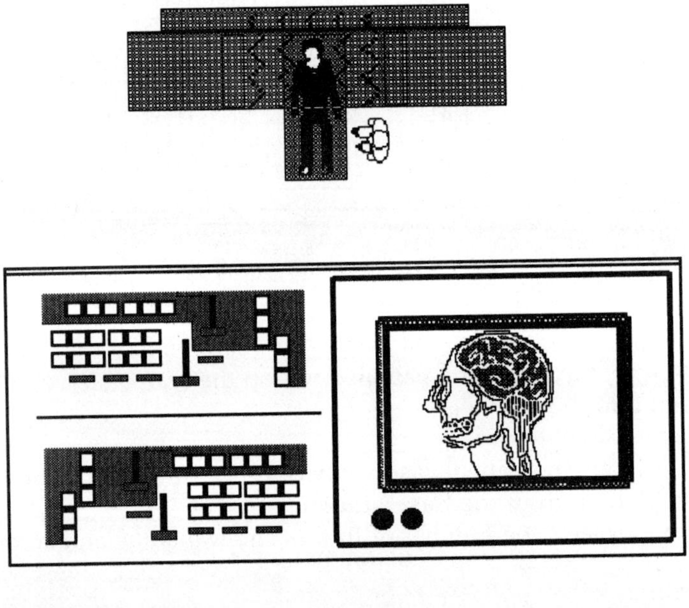

You can take a variety of approaches to creating an animation such as the one above, depending on how you feel most comfortable using the Score tools. All manner of fine-tuning is also possible: adjusting pace and tempo, changing colors, adding moving text, and so on.

3-D Animation

One type of animation you can't create within *Director* is 3-D animation. Animation in three dimensions really requires two separate processes: (1) designing and editing three-dimensional objects with a 3-D object editor, and (2) moving them in space, usually with a key-frame animation utility within the program. We'll look at editing and movement in the context of a full-featured 3-D package, *Swivel 3D* (see Appendix A). Other Mac programs such as *Super3D* (Silicon Beach) offer similar tools and techniques.

Object Building

The first step in creating three-dimensional animation is to build the objects you want to animate. As you might imagine, this is a more complicated business than simply painting them on the screen. You must specify all the surfaces and details of the object in all dimensions, as well as its color, shininess, and other physical characteristics. Since you can't actually see three dimensions on your computer screen, most three-dimensional programs show you three views of the object (the top, front, and right side, or a cross-section of each) and let you manipulate each of these more or less as you would in a standard two-dimensional drawing program. In *Swivel,* a fourth window contains a perspective view of the object (Figure 8-14). Changes made in one view automatically affect the other views. Any readers who took metal shop back in high school will recognize the *Swivel 3D* "four-view" as a variation on the orthographic projections used in mechanical drawings.

Swivel 3D objects are made of *polygons,* flat planes that form the object's surfaces. The Design Object Window contains several tools to create the vertexes (corners) of each polygon. You can simply draw a closed outline in the side view, for example, and have it duplicated in the top view. By dragging the vertexes around in the windows, you can create any kind of symmetrical or asymetrical shape, simple or complex, simply by modifying an existing shape. In addition, there are some special operations you can perform to rapidly create certain classes of objects.

- Lathing. Another method of creating objects in *Swivel 3D* is to draw an outline, then rotate it around a central axis. This is somewhat like drawing a template for a table leg, and then turning a piece of wood

Figure 8-14. ***Swivel*** **Object Design Window**

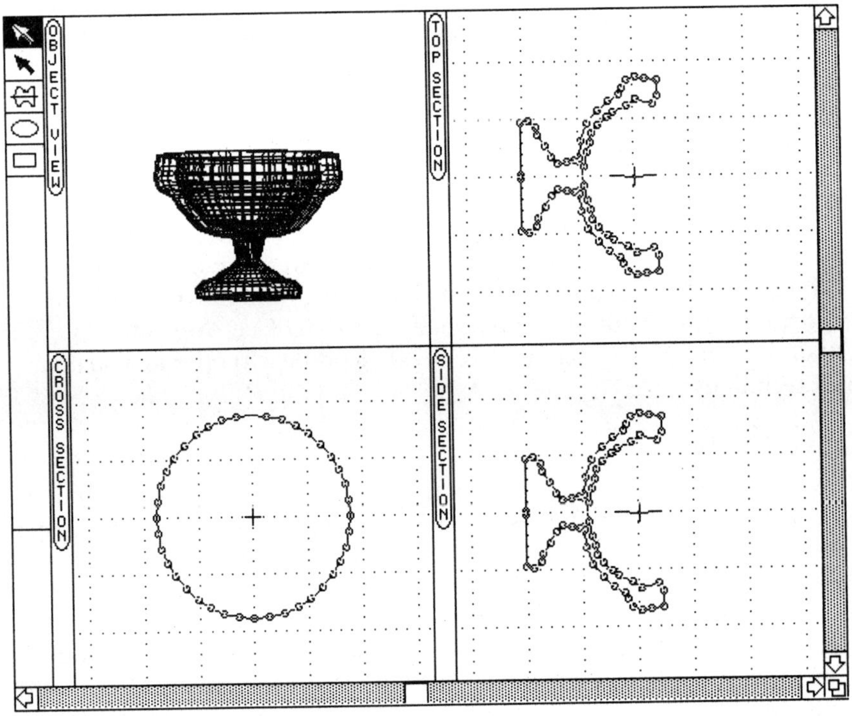

on a wood lathe until it has the same profile as the template. To take a simple example, a sphere can be created by revolving a circle around its diameter. A lathed object is also called a *surface of revolution.*

- Extrusion. *Extrusion* builds three-dimensional objects by stretching a two-dimensional outline along a third axis. This is like squeezing a plastic block through a shaped nozzle. If you've used a pasta-making machine or watched kids squeeze modeling clay through their fingers, you know how extrusion works. Extrusion is particularly useful in creating three-dimensional fonts; you draw the letters in outline, and then extrude them to create the sides.

Since the object exists in 3-D space, called the World in *Swivel 3D,* you can rotate it to see any part of it. Tools in *Swivel*'s World window (Figure 8-15) let you rotate an object in any dimension. In addition, you can change your own viewpoint on the World, looking up or down on it, at either side, and from the top or bottom.

Object Surfaces. 3-D computer objects can have a variety of surface characteristics, just like objects in real life. These include:

Figure 8-15. *Swivel* World View Window

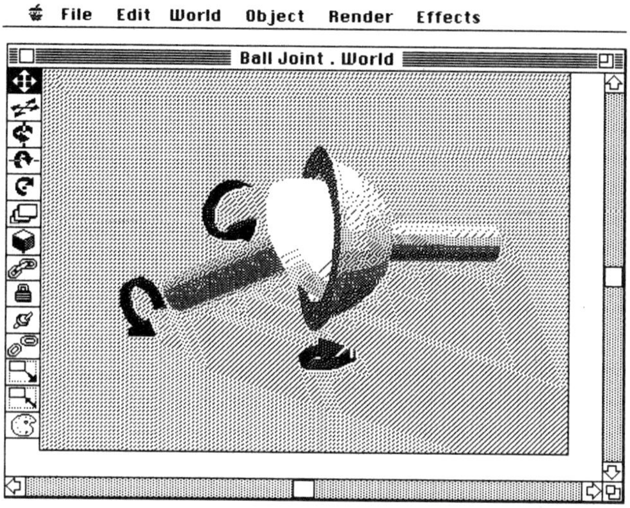

- *Shading* or color.
- *Transparency,* the amount of light that can pass through the object. Some 3-D programs (not *Swivel 3D)* can create objects with the transparency of air, water, glass, and so on.
- *Luster,* or the reflectivity (sometimes called *albedo*) of the surface. Objects can be dull, glossy, or mirrorlike, or imitate the luster of metals or plastic.
- *Luminescence,* the amount of light the object surface emits. In some packages, objects can give off their own light in any color.
- *Texture,* a pattern wrapped onto the object surface to give it the characteristic appearance of a familiar material, such as an orange rind. Usually this is accomplished by projecting or mapping a two-dimensional picture created with a paint program onto the object. This is also called *surface mapping*.

Not all 3-D programs offer every object surface option; in fact, Mac programs tend to be a bit weak when it comes to realistic 3-D representation, as compared to programs on other computer platforms. But this will change as the power of 3-D realism for presentations and graphics is more clearly understood by Mac developers.

The Scene

Objects can exist in a featureless 3-D computer void, but you can also give your object a detailed environment. Scenes can have the following characteristics:

- A sky and ground plane. Some 3-D programs allow you to define an infinite ground plane and sky, while other programs allow the use of a picture as sky or ground plane. You can also create additional objects to put in the background—for example, flat planes to act as the walls of buildings, a sphere far away to pose as a moon. That's how you create scenes in *Swivel 3D,* which has no tools for creating world environments per se.
- Upcoming Mac 3-D software will include options for creating irregular, lifelike 3-D landscapes with simple mathematical entities called *fractals.* Fractals are forms that are similar in structure at any level of magnification. A typical example of a fractal in nature is a coastline, which has much the same kind of ragged, seemingly random edge whether seen from space, from an airplane, or from six feet above the ground. Landscape generators that use fractals are responsible for the moonlike scenes IBM used in a series of recent TV commercials, and they can be used to advantage in your 3-D presentations as well.
- Light sources, or lamps. Think of these as the lighting kit of your scene. You can position one or more lights in any color, at any distance—even inside objects—and with any intensity. The position and intensity of the light source determines how the object is modeled; by moving the light, you can throw the object into sharp relief or make it look flat and featureless. More sophisticated packages even create cast shadows on other objects. Just as with real lights, you'll need to experiment to achieve the effects for which you're looking.

Rendering

Once you've defined all the properties of your objects and the scene they inhabit, it's time to *render* them—that is, create a fully detailed picture out of them. Generally, 3-D packages offer several levels of rendering realism, including:

- *Wire-Frame,* a representation of the scene as a hollow structure of wires showing shapes but no interiors or shading. It provides a sense of the scene with minimal computation. Wire-frame can be an appropriate rendering strategy when your presentation should look like it was done on a computer.
- *Surface model,* where the object is rendered with realistic shading and hidden areas removed, but without shadows, reflections, transparency, and texture. This is an intermediate rendering strategy that does the job for most animations where you require some realism but don't want to spend the time computing surface details. Solid model scenes generally render in a few seconds. Most Mac software offers more than one variation of surface modeling, from just showing contours

with hidden lines removed to full-color, shaded models with surface mapping.

- *Ray-traced,* a highly realistic method of rendering that traces the path of a ray of light from the observer's point of view to every element in the scene. With ray-tracing, you get accurately rendered shadows, reflections, and textures, but at a cost—it may take hours or even days to fully render an object or scene because of the many calculations needed to compute the color of each pixel. Ray-traced animations take a very long time to render, even on a 68030 machine (multiply the number of frames in your animation by the number of hours each takes to render, and you'll see why), so they're not practical for most presentation uses. But the breathtaking realism of a ray-traced scene has to be seen to be believed, and it can be very impressive for short animations, like a rotating view of a new car body prototype.

Object Movement

How do you move a 3-D object in a 3-D space when you can only see a flat representation of it on the computer screen? Luckily, there's already an accepted framework for describing location and movement in space—the three-axis Cartesian coordinate system diagrammed in Figure 8-16 (and mentioned above in the discussion of *Studio/1*'s 3-D Anim dialog box). As you can see from the figure, movement of an object along the *x*-axis is movement from side to side on the computer screen. An object rotated along the *x*-axis flips head over heels; this motion is sometimes called *pitch*. Movement on the *y*-axis is along the vertical dimension of the screen. An object rotating on its *y*-axis spins like a top; this rotation is called *yaw*. Movement in depth—from close to the viewer to far away—is measured along the *z*-axis. Rotation on the *z*-axis rotation, known as *roll,* is like that of a windmill seen from the front. Linear coordinates along the *x*-, *y*-, and *z*-axes define the object's position; degree coordinates of pitch, yaw, and roll define the object's orientation or *attitude*.

One way to position any object in a scene is by specifying its *x, y, z,* roll, pitch, and yaw coordinates. Generally, such coordinates are measured from the *zero point* in the world (where the spatial axes intersect) to the center of the object or a chosen corner. Traditionally, positive numbers refer to the front and right half of the coordinate system, negative numbers to the left and back half. Each coordinate number along the *x*-, *y*-, and *z*-axes corresponds to an arbitrary unit of length such as a meter or inch. Roll, pitch, and yaw are measured as degrees of circles, with zero degrees at the top of the circle. For example, a full description of the position of the center of an object might read: x = 10 units, y = −20 units, z = 15 units, roll = 30 degrees, pitch = 10 degrees, yaw = 0 degrees. To animate the movement of an object, you set the coordinates

Figure 8-16. Spatial Axes and Rotations

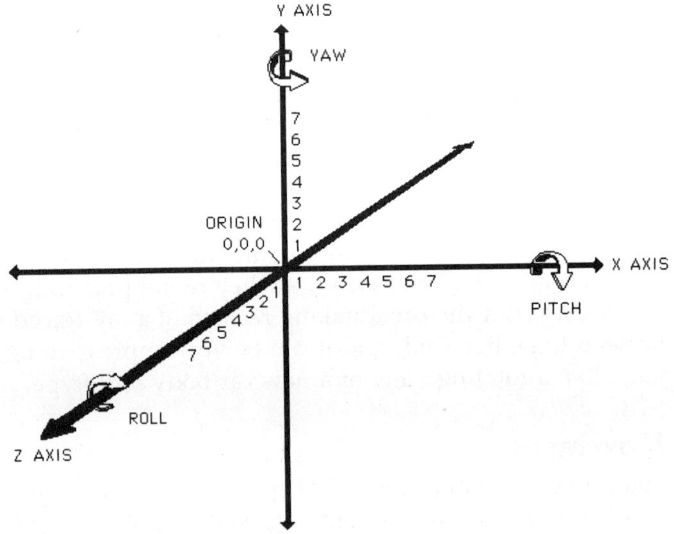

of the beginning position and the end position, and the program moves it from beginning to end over a number of frames; this is the basic key-frame animation process.

Positioning an object by specifying its coordinates is precise, but not quick or easy. You have to know the true dimensions of your object (to find its center) and the exact coordinates where you want to move it, all of which takes some math. A more intuitive method, and the one *Swivel 3D* and most other 3-D programs recommend, is to simply position the object in the first key frame, drag it to a new location and orientation in the second key frame, and then have the program create the tweens for you and save them, usually to the Scrapbook. In *Swivel,* a simple dialog (Figure 8-17) takes care of basic animation features.

Figure 8-17. *Swivel* Tweening Dialog

Object Metamorphosis

Motion isn't restricted to moving on the planes of the screen. Objects can change size and shape as well, split into multiple objects, or combine into one. As with other key-frame operations, object metamorphosis requires you to create the object for the first key frame, then change its shape and other properties for the second key frame. The program then takes care of the in-between transformations through the number of frames you've specified. In this way, for example, you can make an alligator turn smoothly into a polo player. Generally, object metamorphosis works best if many key frames are used, with relatively few tweens between them; this gives you the best control over the intermediate stages of the metamorphosis. One common use for 3-D metamorphosis is to turn a line of 3-D text into the object it names; for example, Jane could use *Swivel*'s 3-D letters to spell out "RxScan" in key frame 1, then use the object building tools to turn the letters into a model of the scanner itself for key frame 2. Animating between the two frames results in a fanciful transformation.

Light sources and world views can move as well. Moving the world view gives the effect of dollying or flying through the scene. Architects love this effect—you can fly your client through your design from room to room. Or you can simulate the view of a jet pilot zooming over a landscape. Moving a light source can also be a useful effect in special cases. For example, you can create the illusion of a swinging lamp by having a light source travel back and forth along a short arc directly over the object. Moving the light source in a long arc high over the object gives the impression of passing time, like the sun casting highlights and shadows as it moves across the sky.

Object Links and Hierarchies. Perhaps the most powerful aspect of *Swivel 3D* and other 3-D animators is their ability to link objects and movements together. *Swivel,* for example, uses a unique system that lets you create objects with ball joints, sliding joints, and free-moving joints. This makes it easy to prototype simple machines and control panels, since you can simulate the actions of wheels, gears, levers, sliders, switches, buttons, joysticks, and so on.

Linked objects are organized into *hierarchies,* or families of parent and offspring objects. The motion of objects in an object hierarchy is linked to the motion of other objects according to levels of influence; for example, an arm may be made up of a hand object, a forearm object, and an upper arm object, with the upper arm motions determining the forearm motions, and the forearm determining the hand motion, but not vice versa. Figure 8-18 diagrams a simple hierarchy of an entire human body.

To set up a hierarchy, you first create and name the various objects—"leftthumb," "lefthand," "leftforearm," and so on—and then link each one with its parent and offspring objects. The naming and linking is accomplished with a *Swivel 3D* dialog. When the whole object is created out of all the various levels of subobjects, you can then define joints for each part. Assuming all parts have been named, linked, and

Figure 8-18. Object Hierarchy

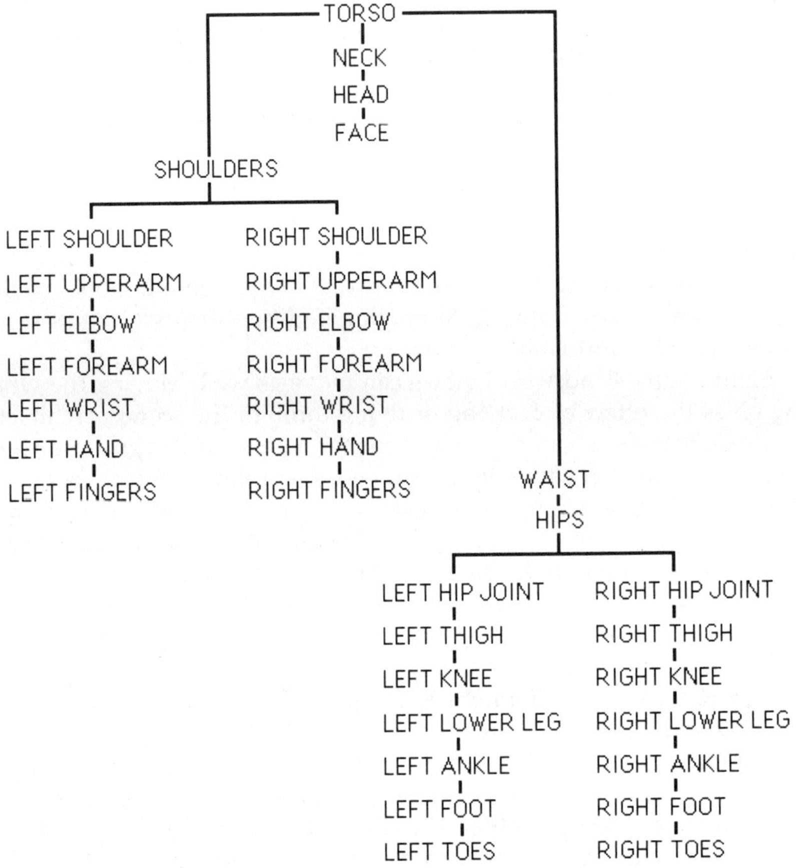

jointed correctly, the object can exhibit extremely complex movements, such as those your own body is capable of performing. But if you look at your body objectively, you can see that it's no trivial task to design and move a 3-D human body simulation. In fact, it's hard to image a desktop presentation that would require a complete human simulation, tempting as it might be to try and build one. Before you tackle such a project yourself, you should be aware that there are clip object disks that contain complete, if generic, 3-D human bodies, already linked and ready for you to customize and animate. If that sounds like science fiction, well, doing 3-D animation on a personal computer was science fiction just a couple of years ago.

Perhaps more useful to the presentation maker are clip object disks of 3-D fonts that make the generation of slick animated logos a snap. *Swivel* and most other 3-D programs offer at least one 3-D font with the program. Letters can be linked and jointed like any other objects, so lines of text can be manipulated as one object.

A complete tutorial on 3-D animation would require a book all to itself. If you're really interested in the world of 3-D, the best and only way to learn is to get a package and plunge in. Simple applications, such as creating titles of 3-D text from ready-made fonts, can be mastered in a few hours of study. However, the learning curve for true mastery of 3-D computer graphics is steep and long, so expect to devote a lot of time to it. Be sure you need 3-D for your presentations before you begin.

Sharing Objects and Animations Among Programs

One problem with Macintosh 3-D animation software is that each program creates its own type of object file format. *Swivel 3D* objects can't be loaded directly into *Super3D*, and vice versa. This is frustrating to animators who, for example, like *Swivel 3D*'s jointing capabilities but prefer *Super3D*'s object-building tools, and would like to be able to move objects between the two programs to take advantage of the best features of both. What's needed is a utility to translate 3-D object files from one program to another.

In the future, this problem may be solved by the wider acceptance of the *Renderman* rendering and 3-D object file format. Originally developed at Pixar, the Renderman standard, a flexible object description language that can handle nearly any nuance of surface color, shading, transparency, texture, and luminance, is gaining converts among Mac 3-D developers. Byte by Byte, developer of *Sculpt 4D*, a ray-tracing object editor, promises Renderman support, and other programs are likely to follow.

Mac animation files—the files containing all the rendered animation frames, whether two- or three-dimensional—don't have a standard format either, although this situation might be changing as well. Some animation programs simply save animations as collections of Scrapbook pictures, which are played back in sequence when you want to view the animation. This method is slow, inefficient, and wasteful of disk and RAM space, but it works. More practical are *compressed file formats*, which squeeze many animation frames into a single, relatively small file, so lengthy animations can fit into the one meg of RAM available on most Macs. Currently, the PICS compressed animation file format supported by MacroMind and Silicon Beach products appears to be emerging as a standard for most Macintosh animation programs. Any animation created in the PICS format can be loaded and saved in a PICS compatible program. For example, you can use PICS files in *SuperCard* (see Chapter 8), *Super3D*, and *MacroMind Director*. Another animation file format, the Aegis/Sparta ANIM format, is supported by Aegis Development products; this is the file format most popular on the Commodore Amiga, and it might gain in popularity for the Mac as well. *Studio/1* uses a third proprietary animation format, S1AN, but it can also load and save PICS files.

Animations on Disk and Tape

Animations, in both two and three dimensions, can take up a lot of memory and disk space. Fairly lengthy animations are possible with *Director* or *Studio/1* even on a Mac Plus, but a second of three-dimensional animation saved as pictures in the Scrapbook can easily exceed the machine's memory and floppy disk capacity. And forget three-dimensional color animation on a Mac II unless you've got several megabytes available on your hard disk. Actually, you can create an animation of any length with any animation program as long as you have the disk space to store it. But playing that animation back in one piece might be impossible, since animation programs usually require the entire animation to be loaded into memory before playing.

Computer animators try to get around this limitation with various techniques. *Looping* is creating a short animation and playing it over and over again to give the impression of a longer work. Or you can make several short animations that are separated by still sequences, which gives the computer enough time to load the next animated part from disk. That's a technique that works well when you're integrating animation into a presentation created with *HyperCard* or one of the *HyperCard* extension programs, like *SuperCard*—see Chapter 9. *SuperCard*, by the way, offers some powerful animation capabilities of its own, which we'll look at in that chapter.

However, your presentation might require a long, uninterrupted animation sequence. The most practical way of storing and displaying a big animation is on videotape. As it happens, tape has a far greater storage capacity than memory or disks, and at far less cost. Normally, you'd record a Macintosh animation to tape in the same way you'd record any other Macintosh graphics, through a genlock to a VCR; then, if desired, you would edit it into a larger work in post-production (see Chapters 5 and 6). That works in most cases.

But suppose your animation is so large you can't play it on your Mac all in one piece, or even in a few big chunks? The trick in that case is to get each frame of animation onto a single frame of video, which requires specialized equipment, including a *single-frame recording VCR* that can accurately record one frame at a time. With the current state of the art, that's neither easy nor inexpensive. Consumer and industrial VCRs just aren't accurate enough to let you record on a single frame. A broadcast VCR can do it; certain VCRs such as the Sony ¾-inch U-Matics have attracted third-party hardware that takes over control of the VCR transport, also making frame-accurate recording possible. The minimum required system is diagrammed in Figure 8-19.

Figure 8-19. Frame-Accurate Animation System

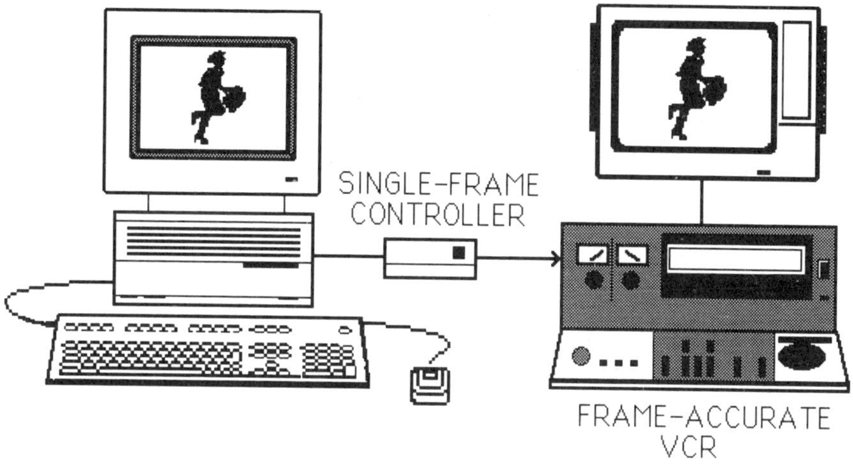

If this is the route you want to go, expect to lay out money for a VCR with frame-accurate capability, a transport controller box, a high-quality genlock, transport controller interface software, and animation software. In other words, you should already be a video professional, have access to professional equipment, or be willing to pay for professional services before you consider it. This level of animation is something that should definitely be jobbed out, at least at the current level of desktop technology, and that's now becoming possible. As more and more animators get into the Macintosh, service bureaus are appearing that will render animations and record them on tape, just as service bureaus have sprung up to develop slides and print DTP documents. You can drop off your disks with the animation all programmed and come back later (perhaps much later) for the finished product.

Scoring Animation

Traditionally, synching sound with animation has been one of the animator's biggest headaches, especially for animated characters who speak on screen. The main problem is figuring out what the character's mouth should be doing in any frame to give a believable impression of speech. The way it's usually done is for the speech to be recorded first, then broken down by phonemes into frame-length segments 1/30 or 1/15 of a second long. The animator draws the mouth, making the proper shape for the phoneme associated with each frame. You can tell this is hard work, because many cheap Saturday morning cartoons hardly bother to make speech look realistic; mouth movements of the characters are generic and could be saying almost anything. Also note that Saturday-morning characters rarely talk and move at the same time; it's even harder to get speech and realistic body movement to work together.

With the Mac, you can do better. Some animation programs make it easy to sync sound. *Studio/1*, for example, comes with a few built-in sounds you can add frame by frame to animations. Sounds, specifically, *SND resources* (see Chapter 9), can be attached easily to any frame; when the animation plays back, the sound begins at the frame you've chosen and plays through until the sound ends. *Director* uses a somewhat similar system to attach sounds to its animations, but with finer control.

You can create an animation sound effects library of computer noises, laser blasts, bangs, crashes, and directional sounds—"up," "down," "squash," "zoom," and so on—using a sound digitizer such as *MacRecorder* (Farallon, see Appendix A and Chapter 9). With *MacRecorder*'s software, you can customize any captured sound with the help of mouse-alterable controls for volume, balance, echo, frequency, duration, and looping. Digitized speech can be chopped up into phonemes for attachment to individual frames to match the mouth movement of animated characters. Then the trick is simply to tag the right frame with the right sound. For complex animated sound, keep a log of each sound with its associated frame on an *exposure sheet* (a small representation of each frame arranged in storyboard form), which you can create with the paint parts of either *Studio/1* or *Director*.

Animation in Presentations

Usually, an animation isn't the sum total of a presentation but merely a segment that needs to be integrated into a longer show, which might include slides, overheads, a lecture, and so on. If you're using a presentation program such as *Persuasion* or *PowerPoint* to show slides directly on a Mac monitor, an overhead projector adapter, or a large-screen TV, you won't be able to smoothly move from animation to slides, since these programs won't automatically load any current type of Mac animation as part of the presentation. If you only have one computer, you'll have to pause the presentation, load your animation program, play the animation, and then return to the slide program. Plan your presentation so interruptions like this don't come near the climax of the show.

The show will go more smoothly if you use one Mac to show your slides and a second one for the animation. Cue up the animation so it's ready to play, and then quickly switch to the second Mac at the right moment. A variation on this is to record your animation to video, and have a VCR loaded with the tape and connected to a video monitor. Run the slide part of the presentation on the Mac, turn on the VCR, and play the animation from the VCR. Or record the whole presentation on video (see Chapters 5, 6, and 7).

There are ways to combine animation with slide-type presentations into one seamless program that can run entirely on one Mac. For that, you'll want to turn to multimedia programs like *HyperCard* or *SuperCard*. We'll cover these in the next chapter, as well as the creation of interactive programming that runs under audience control.

CHAPTER 9

Hypermedia Presentations

Lee is a shy student who has problems following class lessons because he is not a native English speaker. Although he needs extra attention, he is afraid to ask for it, and in the press of the day his teacher often can't give him the help he needs. One evening she goes home and creates a special reading lesson for Lee on her Macintosh, using *HyperCard*. It covers just two dozen words he has been having difficulty with. The lesson includes the digitized voice of the teacher saying the words while the computer spells them out on the screen. There is a place for Lee to type in the words as he hears them spoken; the lesson can tell him whether he has spelled them right or not, and offer him as many chances to do it again as he needs. Each right answer is rewarded with a little melody and an animated cartoon. He can also try pronouncing the words himself and listen to the lesson play them back. Behind the scenes, the lesson also keeps tabs on Lee's progress, and can prepare a report for the teacher.

The next day, Lee's teacher takes him aside and shows how to use the lesson, and then she leaves him alone. Later that morning she finds that he has learned all the words and is trying harder to make friends with others in the class.

Sometimes presenting information to a passive audience is not enough. In many situations, like the one described above, you must reach out and include the audience in the presentation, using every tool and communication medium available. Such a "reach out and touch" presentation falls under the general category of *interactive multimedia*, or *hypermedia*. This chapter will help get you started in this brave new world by providing a potpourri of suggestions for creating your own hypermedia presentations, with an emphasis on interactivity. Keep in mind, though, that designing such complex presentations is an art, not a science. There are no absolute rules to follow, and very few models to emulate. Also included in this chapter is information on Mac sound, music, and speech, all integral parts of any hypermedia presentation.

About Hypermedia

Chapter 1 gives a general introduction to the concepts of multimedia, hypertext, hypermedia, and interactivity. Because the terms are used in various ways, it's worth defining them again.

- Multimedia. A multimedia presentation incorporates several information types, such as words, music, and pictures. *MacroMind Director* is an example of a multimedia application: It can integrate and display graphics, animation, sound, music, and text.
- Hypertext. Hypertext can be thought of as a standard text document taken to a higher dimension. Significant words and phrases in hypertext are cross-referenced instantly to related information by references, links, and trails. The hypertext reader can jump at will from any text available to the system to any other, following a trail of associations rather than a linear narrative. Hypertext documents can only exist on computer, since only a computer can create the necessary links and provide fast, random access to a wide range of materials.
- Interactivity. A presentation is interactive when it gives the audience some control over the course of the presentation, usually within a framework and limits established by the presenter. Interactive presentations may allow users to make choices about what information to view and how it is presented; they may also solicit information from viewers, ask questions, and store information for future use.
- Hypermedia. Hypermedia blends multimedia and hypertext. Like multimedia, hypermedia presentations can mix words, pictures, sound, and motion; like hypertext, hypermedia has a linked structure that allows the user to explore the presentation along many paths. Hypermedia is invariably interactive, since users must make decisions about what trails to take, and the presentation must be able to accept instructions about how to take them there.

In this chapter we'll use the term "hypermedia" to describe interactive multimedia with a hypertext structure.

Using Hypermedia. Hypermedia presentations can be an effective adjunct to rather than a substitute for slideshows, overhead presentations, and video programming. Since hypermedia has to be run on the computer, it's tied to the Mac screen and is not suited for group presentations; slideshows or large-screen video presentations are still the best bet there. The interactive nature of hypermedia also means that such presentations are geared to the single viewer, or perhaps two or three viewers. On the other hand, hypermedia can be applied to the communication of many kinds of information that the standard slideshow or overhead presentation can't handle, and even animation and video can't address. When your presentation mixes text, numbers, graphics, animation, and sound, describes complex, nonlinear information, or needs to interact with the audience, either by following audience directions or by obtaining information from viewers, you should consider a hypermedia approach. Hypermedia presentations can be used effectively for:

- Public information systems
- Point-of-sale demonstrations
- Training
- Simulations
- Tutorials
- Product catalogs
- Tours
- Corporate annual reports

Education and training is one area where hypermedia is already making significant inroads. Students can progress through a hypermedia lesson at their own pace, absorbing information in screen-size packets. Hypermedia training can be interactive—the program itself can monitor student responses and tailor the lesson to suit student strengths and weaknesses. For example, you can program the lesson so a student who enters a wrong answer is immediately shown a new screen that discusses the problem in more depth. Mac hypermedia in the form of *HyperCard* stacks should be especially attractive to educators because *HyperCard* offers all of the Mac's sophisticated features but is very easy to program. Later in this chapter you'll find an extensive discussion of *HyperCard*'s capabilities as a presentation vehicle.

Sound and the Mac

So far, this book has not said much about how the Mac handles sound, but since sound is an important element of hypermedia, in the form of music, sound effects, and speech, the following section covers the use of sound in more detail.

It's always possible to record audio onto a tape cassette (using the techniques discussed in Chapters 6 and 7) and play the cassette next to your Mac, or to accompany your slideshow. But that won't work with hypermedia, where sound needs to be responsive to what the program, presenter, or viewer is doing. For hypermedia, you need to make use of the Mac's own sound capabilities.

The built-in sound of older Mac models, such as the Plus and SE, are relatively limited. These Macs can only generate mono, not stereo sound, and the quality of the sound that comes out of the Mac's small speaker is not exactly high-fidelity. Since the Mac Plus and SE don't offer standard RCA or XLR audio output jacks, you can't directly play Mac sound through a stereo system or record it on an audio tape recorder, either. (Special cables and adapters are needed to do that.) Newer-model Macs, like the IIcx, have a dedicated sound generator that can drive stereo headphones or stereo equipment via the audio port, which accepts a stereo mini phone plug. With an amplifier and the right cables, you can play IIcx audio through a presentation stereo setup or public-address system, as shown in Figure 9-1.

Figure 9-1. Setup for IIcx Audio

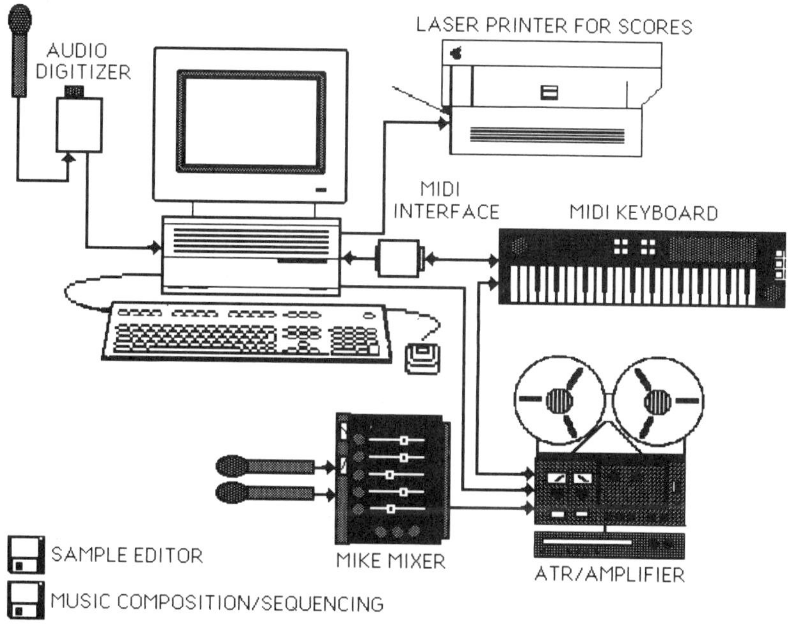

Sampling Sounds. The sounds supplied with the Mac System—the boing, beep, monkey squeak, and so on—aren't very useful for presentations. You'll want a way to get all kinds of realistic sounds, including music, voices, and sound effects, into your Macintosh. Unfortunately, standard audio, like standard video, is an analog waveform, and thus incomprehensible to your computer, which can only process digital information, so an analog-digital converter is required. A *sampler*, or sound digitizer, is a device for converting live or recorded analog audio to a digital form that the Macintosh can understand. Samplers are really just audio versions of the video digitizers discussed in Chapters 5 and 7. When an analog audio signal is fed into the sampler (from a microphone or other audio source), the sampler divides the continuous analog signal into equal, discrete parts—called *samples*—and assigns each part a digital value based on such factors as the amplitude (volume), frequency (pitch), and phase of the sound waveform. (The series of samples that together make up an entire sound is also called a sample). The digital values can be processed by the Mac and reconstituted as sound through the Mac's speaker.

The more samples per unit of time, the more accurate the digital version of the sound. For example, suppose you were to sample Beethoven's Fifth Symphony for 1/60 of a second, once every second. The sample wouldn't sound much like the Fifth Symphony on playback—59/60 of the music would be lost. Sampling the music at a much higher rate—say for 1/250 of a second, 128 times a second—would give you a much better approximation of the real symphony, although you'd still be missing about half of it. So the higher the sampling rate, the more lifelike the sample. On the other hand, the higher the sampling rate, the more memory and disk storage the sample requires. The software that comes with most samplers allows you to choose an appropriate sampling rate: high for sounds, such as music and singing voices, that call for good-quality playback, and lower for sounds, such as the spoken voice, that don't call for high sound fidelity. Sampling software can also compress the sample file into a smaller size by a file compression process similar to the one used in many animation programs (see Chapter 8).

Sampler software also lets you play with the sound after it has been sampled—adjusting duration, frequency, amplitude, and harmonics (timbre)—by using the mouse to modify a waveform of the sound. Here's where you can turn a sample into a sound that seems to have come from outer space. In fact, the possibilities for tailoring sound effects are limitless. One of the simple tricks you can accomplish with a sampler is to sample your own voice saying a word—"Macintosh," for instance. When you play back the sound in the Mac at different pitches, you'll hear your voice saying "Macintosh" going up and down the scale.

MacRecorder. MacRecorder (Farallon, see Appendix A) is a useful, low-cost sound digitizer that is more than adequate for Mac presentation audio. MacRecorder consists of the digitizer, a box that plugs into a serial port on the Mac, and contains a microphone and jacks for an external mike and input from an audio device like a CD player or audio cassette recorder. Sound converted to digital format by the digitizer is processed by one of two MacRecorder programs—*HyperSound,* which installs sounds as resources in any *HyperCard* stack, and *SoundEdit,* a utility for modifying and customizing sounds (the *SoundEdit* screen is shown in Figure 9-2).

To record a sound, you hook up the MacRecorder and click on the

Figure 9-2. *SoundEdit* Screen

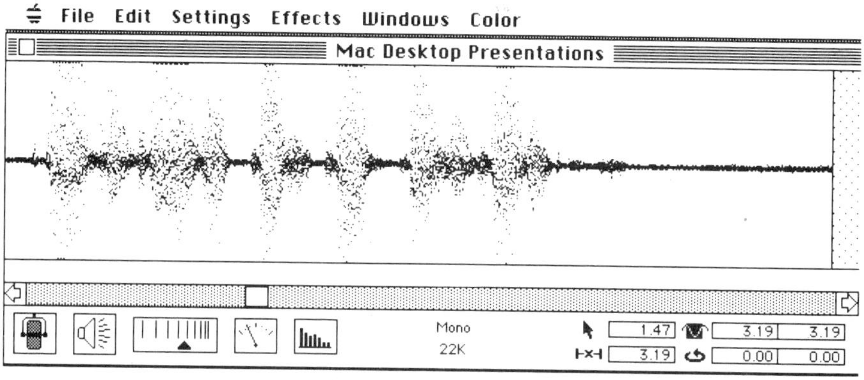

microphone button. You can record in stereo by using two MacRecorders, each hooked to a serial port (the modem and printer ports), or record sounds separately on one channel and mix them in *SoundEdit*'s four-channel mixer. (See Chapters 6 and 7 for more on mixers and sound mixing.) When you stop recording (by clicking again on the record button) or your recording time is up (as determined by the amount of memory in your Mac, the sample rate, and the amount of file compression you've chosen), a waveform of the sound appears onscreen. The waveform for the spoken words "Macintosh Desktop Presentations" appears in Figure 9-2. *SoundEdit* tools allow you to change the pitch (tone) and amplitude (loudness) of any sample; draw lines around the waveform to change its *envelope* (the outline of the waveform) and thus its sound; add echoes and bends; filter it through the Mac equivalent of a graphic equalizer; and even run the sound backwards. Modified sounds can be saved in the most popular sound file formats (see below).

Using Sound in Presentations. The more exotic tools in *SoundEdit* can be used to create some incredible sound effects, which, for example, can be added to presentation animations created with *Studio/1* or *Director*. These programs can read MacRecorder samples directly. A clever sound-effect can really make an animated chart or diagram memorable; hitting the sound at just the right frame helps focus your audience's attention on the point of the graphic. "Logo sounds" are also becoming popular; these are the highly tailored sound effects that high-tech companies such as AT&T and GE play when the corporate logo appears in their commercials. You may be able to devise an appropriate sound to go with your company logo as well.

More likely, you'll be using a digitizer to record voice for use in your presentations. Voice grabs the attention far more effectively than text; people are more likely to follow instructions that are heard as well as read. (The designers of the typical point-of-sale or convention-floor presentation try to amplify this effect by using narration in a throaty female voice; with the rapid increase of women in middle and top management, there's no guarantee that this approach is valid any longer, if it ever was.) Use voice to narrate the presentation, issue instructions, read long blocks of text, and give your presentation a unique personality. That personality can be enhanced by using a celebrity voice. Many well-known actors maintain a profitable second career as narrators for presentations, documentaries, and so on; such services are not inexpensive, though. You may do just as well with a less–well-known professional actor who charges much less.

MacRecorder does an excellent job of digitizing speech, even at relatively low sampling rates and high compression. You may be able to digitize a single speech sample of up to two or three minutes long, long enough for most presentation uses. Record each speech segment as a separate file (clearly labeled by the first words in the sample, by animation frame number, or some other method), and play them at the right moment in the presentation. Use the same method for sound effects and music.

If your presentation may be used for commercial purposes or broadcast, be cautious when you use sampled music. Music, like books, art, film, and photographs, can be and usually is copyrighted. Recent music is very likely to be copyrighted in the name of the composer or performer. Even if it's too old to be copyrighted outright (classical music, for example), music may be copyrighted in the form of a particular performance. Since using a copyrighted piece of music in your presentation without permission is illegal, and more and more likely to be noticed and made the subject of a lawsuit, you are safer sampling music placed expressly in the public domain by the performer and/or composer, hiring a composer to write music for you, or creating your own.

A full discussion of Mac music-making deserves a book of its own, so we'll just touch on the subject briefly here. If you plan to try your hand at composition, there are many Mac music programs available. These range from programs that graft your own melodies onto ready-made musical backgrounds, to full-fledged composition tools for professional composers. An "instant music" program such as *Music Mouse* (OpCode Software, see Appendix A), which creates original, listenable music in a selection of styles (jazz, rock, and so on) just by moving the mouse, is probably the best bet for nonmusicians wanting to score their own presentations. Presenters with more musical experience should look into *Deluxe Music Construction Set* (Electronic Arts, see Appendix A), a music creation and editing program that's easy to use and has many public-domain musical scores available. In fact, there's such a wide variety of scores and instruments available for the Mac in the public domain that, with a little searching, you will probably find the music, instrument, or sound you want without having to create it yourself.

Tips on Sound File Formats

Like graphics and animation, Mac sounds can be handled in a variety of file formats.

- In *HyperCard* and related applications, sounds are saved as SND resources.
- The *Audio IFF (Interchange File Format)* is the format approved by Apple for sound files. An increasing number of sound and music programs can read and write this format.
- The *SoundEdit/SoundCap/SoundWave* format is a file type tailored to sample editing that is compatible with those applications.
- The *Instrument* format can be read by music programs such as *Jam Session* and *Studio Session.*

Unfortunately, many music programs are still incompatible with one another, making it necessary to use a file conversion utility. *SoundEdit* does a good job of converting samples from one format to another; a number of other music and sound programs can also handle more than one format, and some do conversions as well. Still, when you set out to assemble a Mac sound system, make sure all the software works together.

Working with *HyperCard*

Apple's *HyperCard* dominates the world of hypermedia for two good reasons. The first reason is that *HyperCard* is everywhere; Apple gives it away with every new Mac and makes it available to everybody else at low cost, so *HyperCard* applications are a logical vehicle for presentations. The other reason is the high quality of the program itself; it's easy to use, easy to customize, and surprisingly sophisticated. Even if you end up using other hypermedia programs to create your applications, most of these borrow the *HyperCard* look and feel to some extent, so a thorough discussion of *HyperCard* will help orient you to the general techniques of hypermedia and interactivity presentation design.

The next section covers *HyperCard* in some depth, discussing it's elements, structure, and presentation design and development. The discussion that follows also applies to the workings of *SuperCard* and other *HyperCard* extension programs—a *SuperCard* tutorial follows the discussion of *HyperCard*—and has a bearing on hypermedia presentations in general. For a complete description of *HyperCard* and how to use it, it is strongly recommended that you consult one of the many books on the program.

HyperCard Elements. Bill Atkinson, *HyperCard*'s creator, calls *HyperCard* "a software erector set." Like an erector set, the program is made up of several kinds of elements, each with a different function, that can be combined in limitless ways. Figure 9-3 shows the types of objects—a card, a stack, a background, a field, a button, tools, graphics, and the message box—and diagrams the relationships between them.

Figure 9-3. *HyperCard* Elements

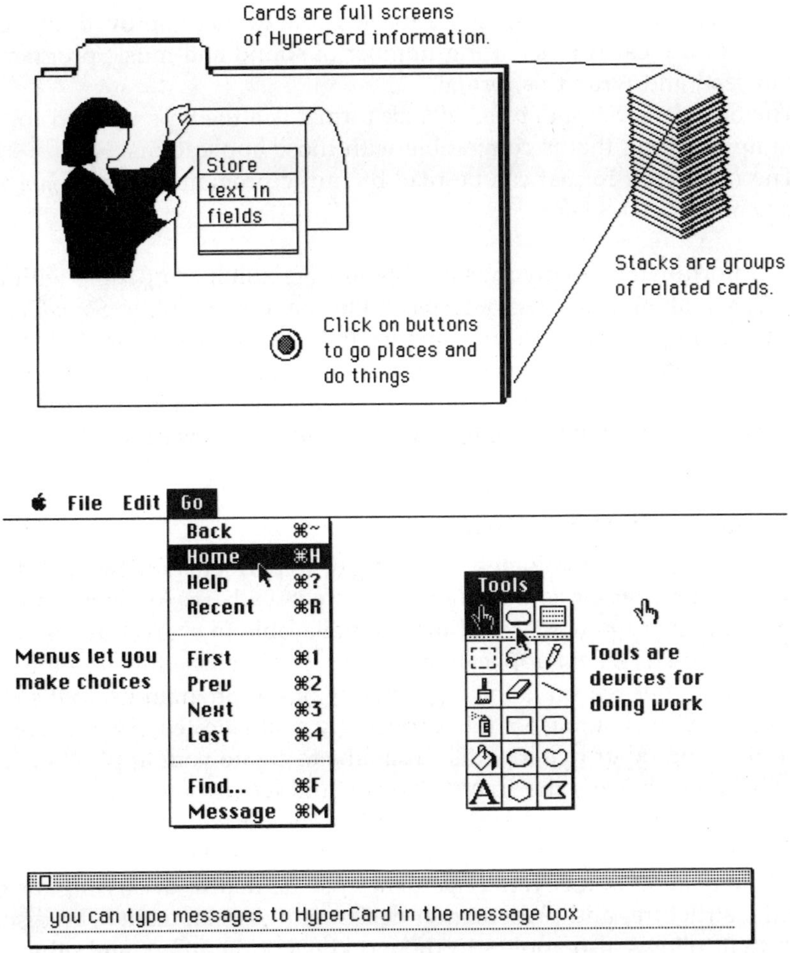

Cards. At its most basic, *HyperCard* is like a simple card file. All *HyperCard* information is stored on *cards,* similar in concept to 3 × 5-inch index cards. You can write, draw, and paste clippings on index cards; you can do the same (or their electronic analogs) with *HyperCard* cards. *HyperCard*'s cards can contain not only words and pictures, but also sounds, music, and animation, and can be linked together in just about any way you can imagine. The program can display one card at a time.

Stacks. Related cards are grouped together into *stacks,* a group of related cards kept together in a single *HyperCard* file. You can think of a stack as the *HyperCard* equivalent of a document or file in another application. The cards in a *HyperCard* stack can be organized alphabetically, or by subject, or by any criteria that you find useful, including links by association that let you jump from one idea to a related one with just a mouse click. Only one stack can be open at a time.

Backgrounds. The cards in a stack may share one or more *backgrounds;* that is, they may share the same general appearance and built-in functions. A background is like a layer behind all related cards. A stack can have more than one background, but not more backgrounds than there are cards in the stack.

Home. A special stack required for proper operation of the program is the Home stack. It is the place to begin and end your travels in *HyperCard;* it also contains sets of instructions that affect the workings of every stack. The Home stack must be somewhere on your hard disk for *HyperCard* to run.

Buttons. *Buttons* are rectangular objects that you click on to initiate an action, such as going to another card. Buttons link cards and stacks together, but they can also do just about any other kind of work that *HyperCard* is capable of. Buttons have a variety of properties, including position, size, style, icon, a name, the ability to highlight when clicked on, and so on.

Fields. Cards and backgrounds also have areas where you can enter text. These are called *fields.* You can type in them just as you can in a word processor. Field properties include size, position, style, text size, style, and alignment.

Tools. *HyperCard* includes a specialized menu, the tool menu, that contains tools for changing working modes—browsing, or using the program; button creation; and field creation.

Graphics. Also in the tool menu are *HyperCard*'s full set of *MacPaint*-style black-and-white paint tools, indispensable for creating *HyperCard* presentation graphics. You can paint right on cards and backgrounds; put buttons and fields over graphics, and put graphics over buttons and fields. *HyperCard* can import any PAINT file that isn't bigger than 512 × 342 pixels, since all *HyperCard* cards are limited to that size, but it cannot handle draw, TIFF, or EPS graphics. Nor can *HyperCard* display color images, although *SuperCard* and other *HyperCard* extension programs can.

Message Box. This is a window that lets you type instructions directly to *HyperCard* using the program's command language, HyperTalk. If you're serious about *HyperCard* presentations, you'll have to learn HyperTalk. Luckily, HyperTalk is very similar to English, and you can master the basics in a few hours of study.

Scripts. *Scripts* are sets of instructions that can be attached to any object in *HyperCard*. Scripts are written in HyperTalk and typed into a script window, shown in Figure 9-4. It's through scripts that you can create sophisticated hypermedia links, animations, songs, computer speech, and more.

Figure 9-4. *HyperCard* Script Window

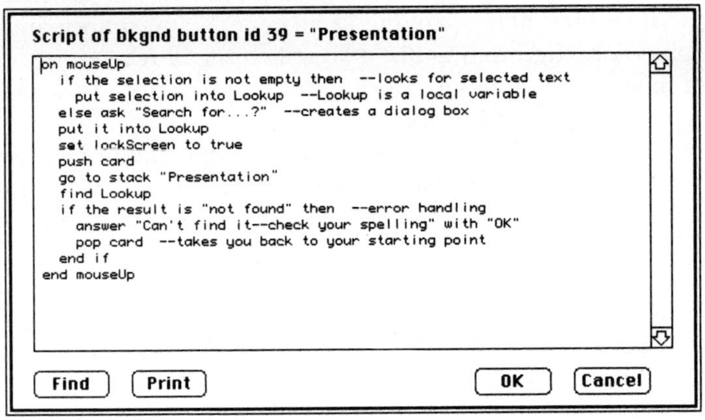

HyperCard Structure. How do all the elements fit together? Each type of *HyperCard* object does not exist in a vacuum—it has a definite relationship with the others, and that relationship is hierarchical. This hierarchy is like a ladder of *HyperCard* objects, as shown in Figure 9-5. The hierarchy begins at the bottom rung, with buttons and fields, and progresses to the card, the background, the stack, the Home stack, and finally, at the top rung, to *HyperCard* itself.

As you can see, each rung includes the one below—cards contain fields and buttons, stacks contain fields, buttons, cards, and backgrounds, and everything is contained within *HyperCard* itself. Cards can't contain stacks, however, or fields other fields. Changes you make at higher levels—to the stack or Home stack—encompass every object below. Good stack designers generally start at the top rung—the stack level, or perhaps the Home stack level—and design down to the field/button rung.

HyperCard screens are composed of two domains—the card domain and the background domain. The background domain contains the ob-

Figure 9-5. The Object Hierarchy

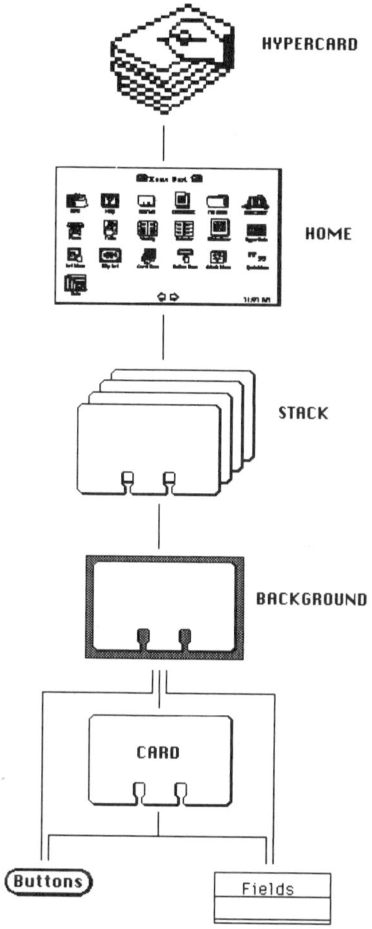

jects and graphics common to all cards that share the same background. For example, the arrow buttons that move you around a stack usually reside in the background domain; all cards in the stack need those buttons, so the stack designer naturally assigns them to the background. The card domain contains objects and graphics belonging only to one card. A button that takes an action pertaining only to the current card will be in the card domain.

Figure 9-6 shows a finer-grain "exploded view" of a typical *HyperCard* screen. As you can see, when you look at a *HyperCard* screen you are actually looking at a sandwich of layers. Think of each button, field, card, and background as being on its own sheet of transparent plastic. The sheets of plastic are laid one on top of the next in a very definite order to create the screen. The structure of layers is invisible when you look at the screen, but the layers must be carefully arranged to produce the right effect.

Figure 9-6. Layers

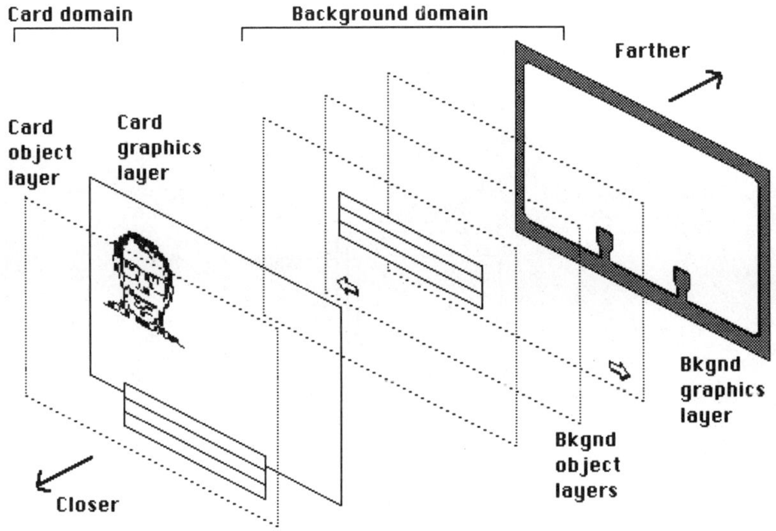

Graphics have their own layers, just like objects. A graphic can be in the background or card domain, but will always be behind fields and buttons in its domain. Graphics can never be moved in front of objects in the same domain.

Modes. Another fundamental fact of life for *HyperCard* presentation designers is that the program operates in *modes*. A mode is a restricted state of the program; it is, for example, a state in which you can only work with buttons. There are seven *HyperCard* modes—background mode, card mode, browse mode, field mode, button mode, painting mode, and script editing mode. In browse mode (activated by choosing the browse tool in the Tools menu), you can operate buttons, enter text into fields, and move about at will, but you can't modify any object or use any other tool. *HyperCard* presentations are normally restricted to browse mode, though you can use scripts to activate other modes, if desired. Most modes are mutually exclusive; for example, you can't manipulate buttons, fields, and graphics at the same time.

Object Properties. Every class of *HyperCard* objects has well-defined *properties*. A property is any characteristic of an object, such as its name, location, or style; for example, there are seven possible button styles, and more than 100 possible button icons (plus any you create and install yourself). Much *HyperCard* authoring work involves setting the properties of objects you've created.

Getting Object Information. You can find out anything you want to know about any *HyperCard* object from its Info dialog box, available from the Objects menu. These Info boxes not only provide basic information on objects, but also let you modify their properties and gain access to their scripts, the HyperTalk programs that tell the objects what to do. The Button Info and Field Info boxes are available only when the button or field tools are selected, but the other boxes are always available. Figure 9-7 shows the Button Info box; changing the settings in this box changes the properties of the button.

Figure 9-7. Button Info Dialog Box

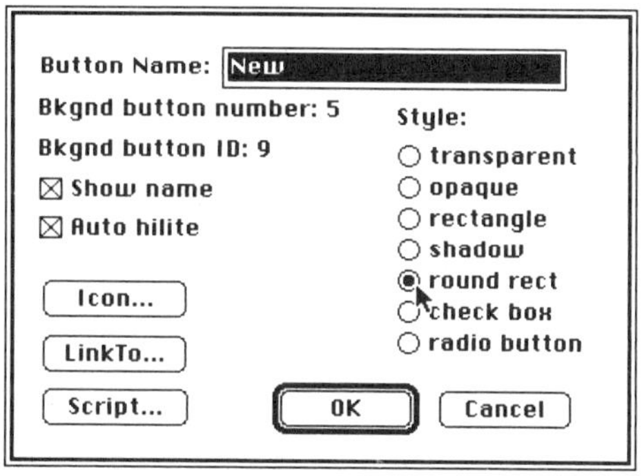

Creating Objects. *HyperCard*'s Edit and Objects menus give you the tools to create any of the five common *HyperCard* objects: stacks, backgrounds, cards, fields, and buttons. For instance, to create a new button:

- Choose the button tool.
- Decide if you want a card or background button. If you want a background button, enter background mode by choosing Background from the Edit menu.
- Choose New Button from the Objects menu. A new round rectangle-style button named "New Button" will appear in the center of the screen. It will already be selected, ready for modification.
- Double-click on the new button to make style and format choices via the Button Info and Icon dialog boxes.
- Size and position the button by dragging it by the corner and the center.
- Cut, copy, paste, or delete the button with the standard Macintosh editing techniques. Hint: Since you can only work on one *HyperCard*

object at a time, set all the properties of the original object *before* you make any copies, or you'll have to reset the properties of each copy separately later.

Linking. *Links* are one of the keys to hypermedia's power. A link is a direct path or shortcut between one area of a presentation and another—for example, between an information card and a map card. In *HyperCard,* buttons are the main linking devices. In a stack on Dutch art, clicking on a button next to a self-portrait by Rembrandt on one card might take you to another card containing a short article on the history of self-portraiture in Northern painting, even though that card might be in a very different place in the stack. The Button Info dialog box (Figure 9-7, above) has a tool for creating navigation buttons that link any two cards. More elaborate links are possible by writing special linking scripts for a button (or other objects, for that matter). It's the web of links that ties together a *HyperCard* presentation and gives the information it contains both form and meaning.

HyperCard Presentation Design

Designing a presentation on *HyperCard* or any other hypermedia application follows the same pattern as designing a slideshow—you must plan, do audience research, organize your information, settle on a presentation design, do the actual work of creation, and then test the results before going public. Since hypermedia presentations tend to be more complex than the standard linear presentation, the design, creation, and testing stages become more complex. Let's take a look at some of the issues affecting the design of a *HyperCard* presentation stack, and then take a look at how Jane at ScanTech creates a self-running presentation incorporating animation, music, speech, and interactivity.

Before you set out to design your presentation stack, sit down and outline your goals. As with any presentation, you have to answer these basic questions:

- What do I have to say?
- Who is my audience?
- What's the best way to arrange my information?

The design of your stack flows logically from the answers.

Organizing Your Information. The obvious first step toward any stack design is to gather your information and distill from it the message your presentation will convey. Some suggestions for doing this are in Chapter 4. You'll find immediately that most information already appears to possess a natural organization. For example, addresses are logically grouped in an alphabetical list, maps in an atlas by geographic region, electronic parts in a product catalog by function or features, and events in a narrative by scenes or chapters. That organization in turn imposes an order on the stack—in other words, form follows function. A play-only trade-show guide will be linear in form, running from one card to the next and looping back to the beginning. On the other hand, an interactive stack that lets you branch from one part of the stack to another (or to other stacks entirely) based on responses you give to prompts, must be organized much more tightly, probably in a tree-like structure.

When it's not immediately obvious how to organize your information, it helps to divide your data up into small pieces. Keep in mind that *HyperCard* allows you to display only a screenful of information at once, so information that can't be broken up into modest-sized bites is not well suited to *HyperCard*. For example, don't try to display a large engineering drawing that doesn't fit on a 512 × 342 screen; use a smaller overview on one card and exploded details on others. *SuperCard* and other *HyperCard* extenders partly address this problem by offering scrollable windows and full use of a Mac II screen.

Identifying Your Audience. Now that you know what you want to say, ask yourself who your audience is. Are they experienced *HyperCard* users? Specialists in a particular field? Mac neophytes or people who may never have worked with a computer at all? Or possibly any and all of these?

It's easy to design a presentation for advanced *HyperCard* users, because they'll know all the *HyperCard* conventions already and be experienced in figuring out how stacks work. Likewise, if you are presenting data to a group of specialists, you can at least depend that your audience will be able to put the information into context and understand your terminology. But the more kinds of viewers that will encounter the stack, the more basic your design must be, until, at the most basic level, you can't even assume the person knows how to use the mouse. Actually, *HyperCard* is ideal for a general audience because it's so easy to create a stack that runs by itself with minimal input from the viewer. Typical examples of these kinds of stacks are point-of-sale displays and public-access information systems, where a wide range of people will encounter the stack and use it in a public setting. Educational stacks for young children also fall into the same category—they must assume the minimum level of skill possessed by children in the age range you're addressing. You shouldn't, for example, design a stack for four to six-year-olds that requires them to read instructions. Use speech synthesis or pictures instead.

Designing a User Interface. The next step is designing a *user interface*. A user interface is, basically, the way an interactive presentation looks and the way it asks you to work with it. User interfaces can be friendly, helpful, and intuitive, or unhelpful and nonintuitive; a bad interface design is guaranteed to get in the way of your presentation's message. When in doubt, stick close to the Mac interface, and always keep in mind the characteristics of the audience you are addressing.

Tips on Creating a *HyperCard* User Interface

In general, the interface of a well-designed informational stack is functional, clean, easy-to-use, and bug-free. This means, first, that you'll be best off adhering to some general conventions of *HyperCard* software design.

- Consistency is important. Make sure familiar objects work the same way all the time. For example, buttons with house icons should always take you Home. And if the objects are standard items in the Mac interface, use them in the expected way—don't use checkboxes the same way as radio buttons.
- Don't assume that the user is experienced, or understands what you are trying to do. Provide online help, explanations, keymaps, stack diagrams, tables of contents, and/or indexes. These guides are *de rigeur* for complex stacks, just as tables of contents and indexes are standard equipment for books.
- Give users all the information they need. Don't, for example, hide the menu bar without providing other ways to navigate through the stack, or include important information in hidden fields without showing how to get at those fields.
- Redundancy is helpful. Provide more than one way to organize or gain access to information.
- Keep it simple. Use only the buttons, fields, and graphics the stack needs; never throw in extraneous decorations and functions just because you can—extras are just static interfering with the information you want to convey.
- Make it look good. Use screen space efficiently, but don't clutter things up with too many objects. If necessary, rethink your stack design or separate objects by function onto different cards or backgrounds. Symmetrical arrangements of objects are easiest for users to understand. Group related objects together.
- Weed out the bugs. Mistakes are not only wrong, they're confusing. No one is perfect, but try to be. Check carefully for minor errors.

Visual Design Issues.

HyperCard's powerful graphic tools can be used to clarify and enhance your information. When designing the look of your stacks, here are some issues to keep in mind.

Settle on a visual metaphor for the presentation as a whole, just as you would for a slideshow—this will help to orient the viewer. The information you'll be putting into the stack should give you a clue about what metaphor to use. A hypermedia annual report calls for a slick corporate look. An education stack could have the appearance of a high-quality textbook or workbook. A point-of-sale presentation might resemble an animated catalog. Don't, however, devote a lot of time to creating an elaborate visual environment at the expense of organizing and clearly presenting your information. Avoid fancy backgrounds that add no information to your cards and use up precious screen space.

Decide what sort of visual transition from card to card is appropriate for the information. You can script a variety of video-style transitions with HyperTalk scripts. Wipes (right, left, up, and down) are good for slideshow-type stacks. Several styles of dissolves are available for smooth transitions to different parts of a stack, to indicate the passage of time or a distance traveled, or for animation effects. Use zoom-ins to go to a card that zeroes in on a selected item to give more detail, and zoom-outs to get back to the big picture. Barn-door transitions should open up and close down new areas of the stack. It's even possible to use blackouts and whiteouts for emphasis, appropriate for stacks that run by themselves or possess a narrative. Each transition can be slow or fast as well.

Use a minimum number of fonts in field and graphic text. Many different letter sizes and styles make for a confusing, ugly, and hard-to-read stack. Try not to mix serif and sans-serif fonts on one card, and use only capital letters for titles or emphasis.

Sound Design Issues. Like graphics, sounds can add to the impact of your stack presentation. Here are a few general items to consider.

HyperCard comes with four built-in sounds (boing, dialing tones, harpsichord, and silence), stored as SND resources, and you can add others with MacRecorder's *HyperSound* or sound moving utilities. The familiar Macintosh beep can be invoked with HyperTalk's beep command; all other sound resources can be played with the *play* command (see below). Use the beep to alert the user to something important—usually, an error, a limit reached, or an action that must be taken. The boing sound can be used in somewhat the same way—when a student gives a wrong answer to a question posed in an educational presentation, for example. A right action can be rewarded with an upbeat little tune, perhaps synchronized with a visual effect.

Tips on Making *HyperCard* Music

HyperCard contains a built-in synthesizer that allows you to write simple or complex monophonic (one note at a time) melodies. All *HyperCard* composing involves the *play* command, which acts on any digitized sound resources in the stack or *HyperCard* itself. The basic form of play is:

play "<sound name>"

If you put the statement

play "boing"

into a script, you hear the boing sound when the statement executes. Play also has a number of parameters that let you take any sound and turn it into a series of notes. Here's the complete parameter format for play:

play "<sound name>" [tempo <speed>] [<notes>] [# (sharp) | b (flat)] [octave] [duration]

- The sound name is the name of the instrument or sound you are manipulating. Any sound resource available to your stack can be used here.
- Tempo, the general speed at which the music plays, is always a number, with the default value set at 200 (neither fast nor slow). 400 is faster than 200.
- Notes are specified by *a, b, c, d, e, f,* and *g,* as in the musical scale, and can be designated sharp or flat with the # symbol for sharp and *b* for flat—for example, c# is C sharp, and fb is F flat. Rests are designated by *r.*
- The first note in the melody should have an octave number attached. An octave is a musical interval that spans all the notes from one note to its next occurrence—for example, on a piano keyboard, the 12 notes from middle C to the next C up the scale. *HyperCard* octaves 3, 4, and 5 correspond to the middle octaves on a piano. The melody stays in the set octave until you change it by inserting a new octave number after a later note.
- Note and rest durations can be a whole to a thirty-second. Whole notes and rests are designated by *w,* half notes and rests by *h,* quarters by *q,* eighths by *e,* sixteenths by *s,* thirty-seconds by *t,* and sixty-fourths by *x.*

The play command differs from other HyperTalk commands in that it can continue to execute even while other scripts are running, or the user is working with buttons, fields, and tools. You can also divide songs into two or more lines if they're too long to fit on one line in the script window. Try this sample song in a *HyperCard* button script:

play "boing" tempo 300 cq3 cq dh ch fq ew cq cq dh ch gh fw
play "boing" tempo 300 cq3 c4h ah fh3 eh dw bbq bbq ah fh gh fh

Speech Synthesis. Your Mac can synthesize speech as well as music, providing you've got the right resources. While the state of the art in Mac speech synthesis doesn't allow for very attractive voices as yet, synthesized speech does humanize your presentations, and it uses far less memory and disk space than digitized speech, the kind you record with MacRecorder. More importantly, with speech synthesis your presentation can say anything the user may type in—for example, the user's name. Having the presentation greet the user by name makes interacting with it a more engaging and friendly experience, and this can be very important in educational presentations and situations where the audience may not be comfortable or familiar with computers.

To make your Mac speak, you need two programs. One is the speech synthesis utility MacinTalk, which is supplied with the Mac system software. The other program you need is a stack called HyperMacinTalk by Dennis C. DeMars; it is highly recommended as a good introduction to all aspects of Mac speech synthesis. HyperMacinTalk contains the external commands and functions (XCMDs and XFCNs) that let you access MacinTalk from *HyperCard,* and it will automatically install them in any stack. With some modifications to the stack script that are clearly explained in HyperMacinTalk, you can have *HyperCard* utter any string of English words using the *say* command. Here's the format:

say the English words
The text to be spoken must be in quotes. For example:
say "The only thing we have to fear is fear itself."

What you hear will sound rather robotic and uninflected (that's not too surprising), but it should be understandable. You can modify inflection by using the standard punctuation marks, such as periods, commas, and question marks; adding extra spaces between words and letters can aid in understandability, too. Macintalk's pronunciation isn't perfect though, so you may find that some creative misspelling will make Mac speech more understandable. For example, the Mac can't cope too well with the word *mouse;* it makes it sound like *muss.* Simply respelling it *mouwse* really improves the pronunciation. Try alternative ways to spell problem words until you find one that works well; you can even set up a pronunciation table of your own for future reference.

If MacinTalk doesn't give you the speech quality you want, you can always digitize real speech and include it in your stacks as a sound (SND) resource. Unlike music, speech can be recorded at lower sampling rates and higher compression without serious loss of intelligibility. You might be able to fit up to several minutes of compressed speech into your stack presentation, depending on the available space on your disk. Invoke each spoken sound with the play command, like any other sound.

Design for Interactivity. An interactive presentation can do more than simply wait for the user to click the mouse on a button to take him or her to the next card. Presentations can show pictures and animations and speak words on demand; repeat any segment of the presentation when asked; solicit information from the user and present only the level of information appropriate to the user's level of understanding; watch the pattern of movement that a user makes through a presentation and make suggestions about future paths; ask questions and correct wrong answers; and even "remember" information about the user for a future presentation. In short, your presentation can establish a kind of dialog with the viewer that makes the presentation that much more effective.

A fully interactive presentation is best organized in a tree-like, branching structure, as in Figure 9-8. The user begins at the trunk, and can proceed along any branch; at each branching the user has to decide which route to follow. Or the program can decide which branches to offer, depending on responses the user makes to prompts and queries. (Scripts can grab information typed in by the user and use the text to determine what options should be available, or a script can look to see what cards have been viewed recently and decide what route the user should take from the current point.) Users should always be able to go forward, to backtrack and review, or to return to the trunk and take another main branch via a map or index card. Special links should also make it possible to jump directly to related subjects. For example, in an annual report presentation, a button on a data graphic showing current sales might be linked directly to a card showing a list of top sales personnel, even though that card belongs to another branch discussing personnel management.

Organizing the presentation into a branching structure involves dividing up your information into small units and creating a flow chart of paths through them. (A Mac project planning program can help here.) You'll be surprised at the amount of information that's required to cover all the necessary paths, one reason that hypermedia products tend to take up a lot of disk space. Remember, it's the pattern of connections that count, not the actual number or location of the cards in the presentation stack. There might be many potential routes to a particular piece of information, and several approaches to the presentation of informa-

Figure 9-8. Branching Structure

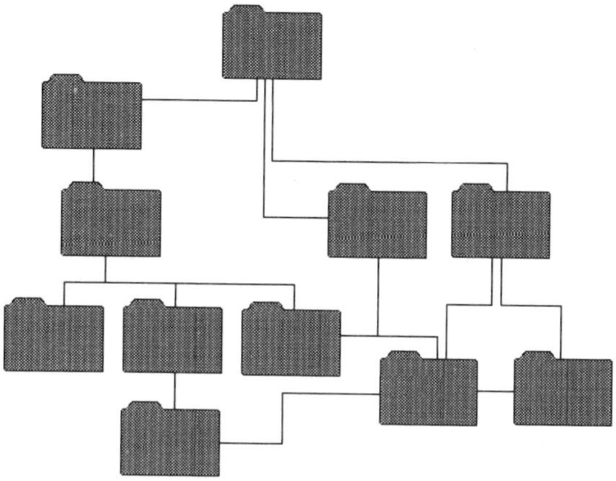

tion in the stack, some more and some less complex. For example, your presentation might have two levels of complexity and depth of information. The first card in the stack asks users to click on a "No Experience" or an "Expert" button depending on their knowledge of the subject. Clicking the "No Experience" button leads to those parts of the stack that cover the subject at its most basic level, with options to obtain more information. Clicking the "Expert" button presents a summary of the latest and most advanced information. A similar approach can be taken in presentations for children, which ask for the child's age and then present information tailored for that age level.

Queries to users usually should be presented in multiple choice form. A series of radio buttons or checkboxes can be offered, each with a different assigned value, or you can use *HyperCard*'s answer box (see below). The point is to limit the possible replies to those you can anticipate when designing the presentation. Don't ask open-ended questions and expect to be able to deal with any answers. Exceptions to the multiple-choice rule are when you're looking for the user's name, address, age, or other specific words; these can be asked for in an ask box or a field.

By the way, you can look for and use the contents of fields in any script, and use scripts to put query replies into fields. That's how you program *HyperCard* to remember user information for future recall. For example, earlier your presentation might have asked a viewer named Jim for his name, age, experience level, business title, and some other information. The answers were all saved to a hidden field. When Jim opens the presentation again, he types in his name. The presentation looks in the hidden field for "Jim," finds it, and retrieves the rest of the information associated with it. Jim doesn't have to answer any other questions about himself before viewing the presentation. At the same time, the stack can automatically keep tabs on just who is using it, including age, career, income level, and any other information you can convince the audience to provide. This kind of information is invaluable for demographic and market research, compiling lists of follow-up contacts, and so on.

Interactivity isn't limited to text manipulation. A stack can say anything a user types or selects in a field, for example. *HyperCard* graphics can be made to change under user control, also. Simple scripting techniques can activate any of *HyperCard*'s painting tools, so users can add their own visual ideas and notes to the stack. (Clearly designate an area for doodling so users don't alter any graphics you put into the stack.) Animation on demand is easy, as long as you've set up the necessary graphics and scripts in advance. For example, page-flipping *HyperCard* animation can be achieved by rapidly showing a sequence of cards (see Chapter 8). By clicking on an "animate" button, the user of a presentation stack could animate the expansion of the corporate international sales effort across a world map, or zoom in on a human cell to show the actions of various organelles. (Easier than creating animation in *HyperCard* itself is to import animations from dedicated animation programs. *Studio/1* and *VideoWorks II* [see Chapter 8 and Appendix A] offer animation drivers for just this purpose. Or, you can turn to a *HyperCard* extension program such as *SuperCard,* which has enhanced animation capabilities built in.)

Finally, you have to decide how much interactivity is enough. It's possible to make a stack so complex, with so many fascinating turns, twists, and diversions, that the main point of the presentation is lost while the user explores all the interesting nooks and alleys and tries out all the fascinating gadgets. (In fact, one of the main criticisms of most hypermedia is that it gives the viewer too much choice and not enough guidance.) An overinteractive stack is like a stereo with dozens of knobs and buttons; you can control every little function of the deck, but the welter of controls is also confusing and distracting, and you probably don't use most of them anyway. Make the presentation responsive only in ways that enhance your message, or that benefit the user.

Stack Structures

With some basic design issues settled, you're now in a position to block out the presentation stack design. Several aspects are covered below.

Backgrounds. The basic unit of stack design is the background; for most stacks, that's where the major fields, buttons, and graphics are, and where you'll be spending most of your design time.

You can have as many backgrounds in a stack as you have cards. Generally, the information will tell you how many the stack needs. If it is all of one type, such as a simple slideshow with a series of data graphics and text slides, then a single background will do. If there are several different kinds of information in the stack, such as maps, text articles, artists' renderings, and indexes, then you'll need several backgrounds, one for each type of information. Even if your stack has many backgrounds, you should try to give each background a similar look, using the same fonts, button icons, and so on, to give coherence to the design of the stack as a whole.

Card Order. In most cases, cards can be in any order as long as they are linked correctly. A stack, background, or button script can sort the cards by whatever criteria you specify. Cards introducing the stack should obviously be at the beginning of the stack, even if the rest of the cards are in no particular order. Map and index cards should be well linked to every other card, so the user can always step back for an overview of the stack at any point.

Objects and Domains. Once you've decided how many backgrounds you need and the order cards should be in, it's time to figure out in which domain, card or background, to put graphics, fields, and buttons. Objects and graphics common to all the cards in a stack should be placed in the background domain. Navigation buttons that take the viewer from card to card should be in the background domain, for example. One-time-only objects and graphics belong in the card domain. Buttons linking one specific card to another should be in the card domain.

Field Design. As stated, fields are the main information holders in your stacks. To maintain the clarity of text in your fields, settle on similarly styled fields per card. A mixture of fields with and without outlines, lines, and scroll bars is not advised, as is mixing more than one or two fonts on the card. Try using a gray tint in the background to make opaque fields stand out more clearly.

Button Design. Set button properties in a manner consistent with their function. For maximum clarity, give the button an icon and a name and show the name, so there is no question about what the button is supposed to do. You can write the button script so it's highlighted when clicked or touched, or so a sound effect, like a beep or boing, sounds when the button is clicked. (This will slow down the button's response, though.) Transparent buttons can be placed over graphics or text in a nonscrolling field without interfering with the look of the underlying item. Use radio buttons to offer a choice among various options, and checkboxes to turn on or off one or more properties or functions at a time.

Always provide arrow buttons for navigating the stack. These can use icons only, and even be rather small and tucked away along the bottom border of the card. If you are offering the presentation on a touchscreen, though, make buttons large enough to be hit consistently with a finger.

Prompts. *HyperCard* offers several ways to prompt the user for information or a reply to a question. You have at your disposal two custom dialog boxes, the *ask* box, shown in Figure 9-9, and the *answer* box, in Figure 9-10. These can be called up from a script with the *ask* or *answer* HyperTalk commands. The ask box contains an area where the user can type in a short reply to a question, such as a name. You can then use the typed in reply in a script. The answer box offers up to three alternatives that the user can choose among by clicking on the relevant button.

Figure 9-9. Ask Box

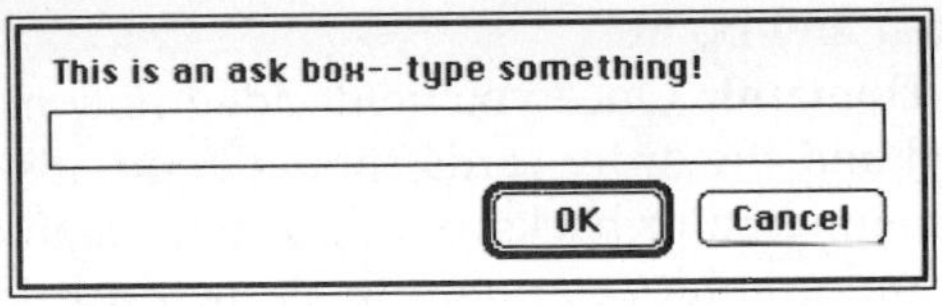

Figure 9-10. Answer Box

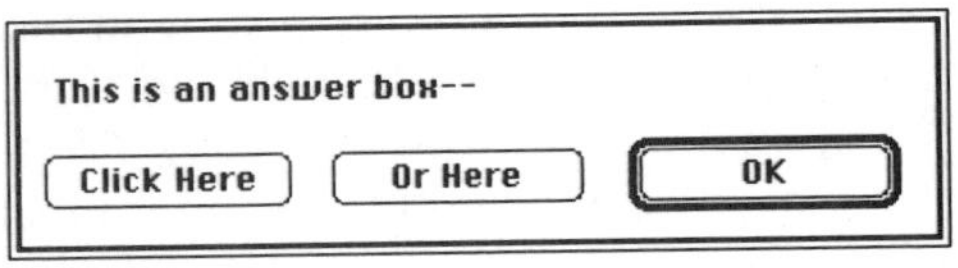

Testing and Quality Control. Presentation stacks are complicated things, with plenty of opportunity for errors. Consider your first try at the stack a first draft, too. Don't try to finish every detail all at once, but test out the stack at an early stage—you may decide to make major changes. When you do feel that you've gotten close to a final design, check and double-check everything. Test every button, put text into every field, go to every card, look at every background, follow every path. If you need approval from higher management, you can print out the stack as cards and submit that as a progress report. At the same time, check each card for consistency and graphics errors. Check for typos in field text and graphic text, too; this is something many stack authors seem to neglect. Make sure that indexes, maps, and tables of contents are linked to their proper sections, and that cards are in proper order, if card order is important in the stack.

Even so, you won't find all the problems or think of all the things your stack should have. You've got to field test it before releasing it. Get at least one and preferably a group of potential users to try out the stack at both the first draft and the final stage, and watch how they use it. The feedback you'll get will be invaluable. Observe whether your testers quickly grasp the point of your stack and learn to use it without trouble. Ask them to suggest additional features that would give your presentation stack more impact.

A Self-Running Presentation with *SuperCard*

For all its versatility, *HyperCard* does have some limitations as a presentation environment, such as no color, small card size, and paint graphics only. *SuperCard* (Silicon Beach, see Appendix A) emulates *HyperCard*'s rich presentation environment, complete with cards, buttons, fields, scripts, and graphics, but takes it several steps further. Among the improvements and enhancements are:

- Full 8-bit color, with different palettes possible on every card
- Draw as well as paint graphics
- Ability to create and display two- and three-dimensional animations in PICS format
- Multiple documents onscreen
- Cards of any size, including 640 × 480 pixels
- Custom menus
- Access to all seven Macintosh window types
- Buttons of any shape

While *SuperCard* follows most *HyperCard* conventions, there are a few other differences. *SuperCard* presentations are called *projects;* stacks are called *windows* (each window can show one card at a time); *SuperCard*'s superset of HyperTalk is called SuperTalk. Presentations are actually created in a separate program called SuperEdit; *SuperCard* runs the projects you've created in SuperEdit. It's possible to create presentations in SuperEdit that can only be played, not modified. This is one big advantage over *HyperCard,* where stacks can almost always be tinkered with by a savvy user familiar with the program. You can import *HyperCard* stacks into *SuperCard,* but *SuperCard* projects or windows can't be imported into *HyperCard.*

Jane at ScanTech plans to create a self-running presentation about the RxScan for the company booth at medical equipment trade shows and conventions. Because she wants access to color, animation, and a larger screen size, but wants the easy programmability and the interactivity of *HyperCard,* she chooses *SuperCard.* The major element of the presentation system is a Mac IIcx with a hard disk and four megabytes of RAM housed in a kiosk (both to protect the equipment and shield the users from the technology). The kiosk also includes a protected power supply and a small stereo system. The computer, keyboard, and mouse are hidden; only the monitor and the speakers can be seen by the audience. The monitor is outfitted with a touch-sensitive screen so viewers can direct the presentation by simply pointing a finger, without having to type information or use the mouse. This makes for a presentation that's easy to approach and use, while reducing the risk of computer damage or malfunction.

Jane's *SuperCard* project has several interlinked areas, as shown in the diagram in Figure 9-11. These give a basic introduction to ScanTech and the RxScan; discuss the science behind magnetic resonance imaging; give an engineer's tour of the workings of the scanner; present two case histories of patients helped by the scanner; list institutions that have the scanner installed, with comments from administrators and doctors; and describe current prices and contacts. The science and engineering areas make extensive use of color animation and sound effects, while the case histories and institutional endorsements use digitized voices and scans for a documentary effect. Any area of the project can be reached at any time by putting a finger on the right button, or by going to an index/map card (Figure 9-12).

Figure 9-11. *SuperCard* RxScan Project Structure

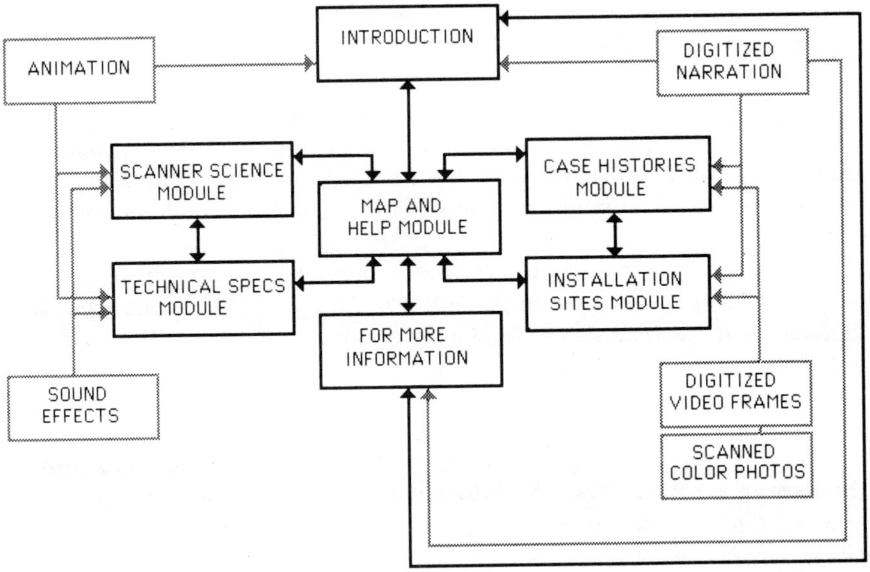

Figure 9-12. RxScan Project Map Card

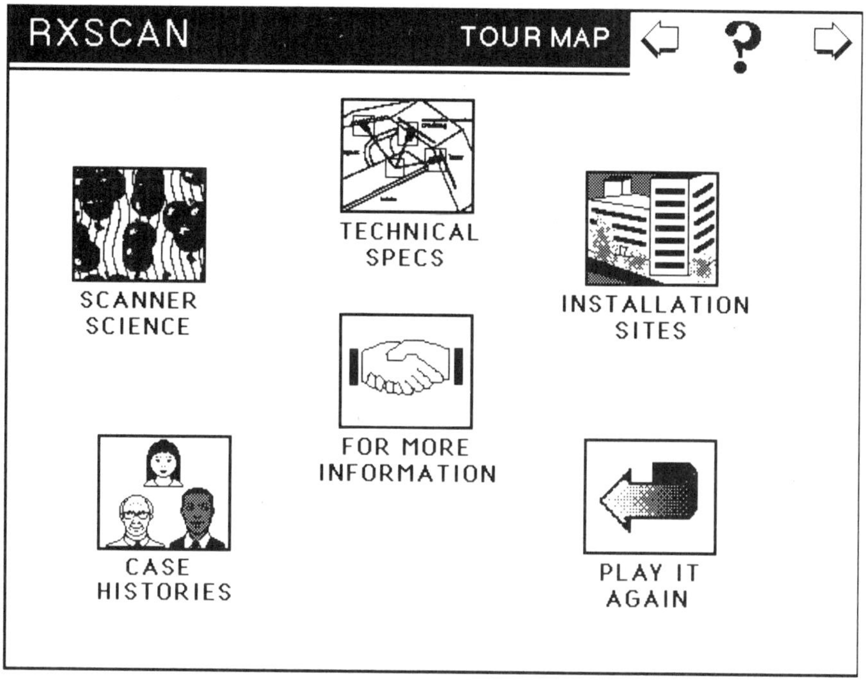

An introduction card simply gives the presentation title, and has a button that starts the action. This is the card that the presentation always returns to at the end, so things are set up for the next viewer. Next is a short sequence that gives a brief slideshow-style description of the scanner and the company, with digitized voice-over, ending at the map card. At this point a series of ask and answer boxes puts some multiple-choice questions to the viewer—type of business, management position, level of interest in the product—and asks the viewer to drop his or her business card into a slot in the kiosk. Questions are asked here and not later because some viewers won't proceed further into the presentation than this. Also, it would be useful to have viewers type their names, phone numbers, and so on directly into the presentation with the keyboard, but Jane decided to sacrifice this in favor of a more secure and approachable display. If no answers are given or buttons touched in a specified period (a minute or so), the presentation returns to the title card.

Viewers can go to any of the branches from the map card by touching the proper button. A card from the technical specifications branch of the presentation is shown in Figure 9-13. Every card follows the general design established for the presentation as a whole, and also includes navigation buttons for going backward, forward, to the map card, and to the first card of that branch. Invisible buttons cover most of the picture; the viewer can touch the part of the scanner that he or she wants more information about, and the invisible button shows a card with an expanded view, or reveals a hidden field with a text discussion. The Help button takes the viewer to a card that describes how to use buttons and move from card to card.

Figure 9-13. RxScan Technical Specs

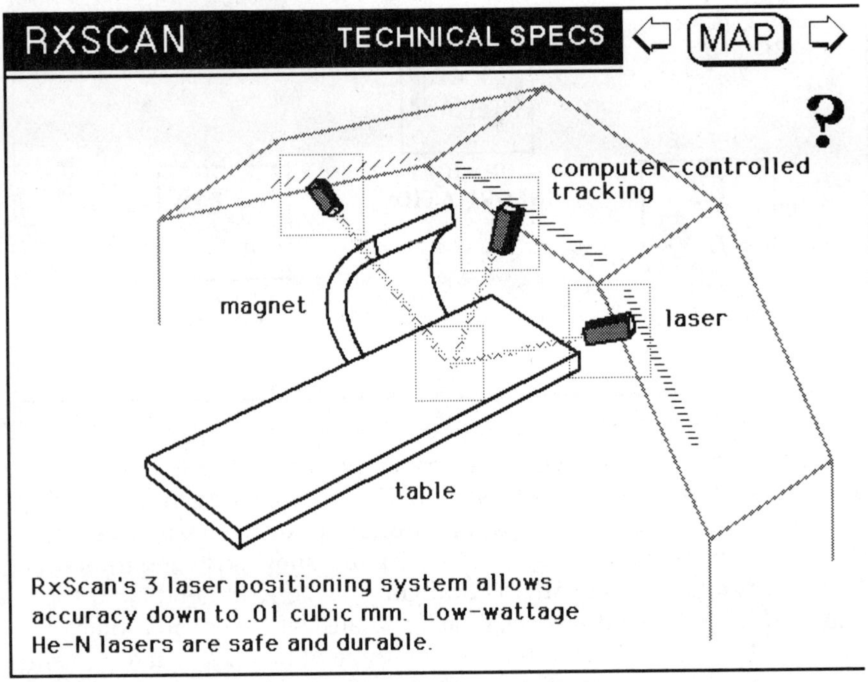

The animations in the science of scanning branch have been imported from *Studio/1* and *MacroMind Director.* (Jane decides against 3-D animation, since it takes too long to create and uses a lot of memory to display.) In fact, she can use the same clips she created for the video in Chapter 8. All the voices in the case histories were recorded from the original participants with an ordinary tape recorder, and then digitized and edited with MacRecorder.

The entire presentation takes Jane about two weeks to develop and program, with much of the work devoted to creating graphics and capturing sounds. On the convention floor, the presentation attracts potential buyers and investors to the ScanTech booth; Jane knows people will approach an interactive computer display when they might be unwilling to talk to a salesperson. The presentation also answers many questions that salespeople would otherwise have to answer, and provides information, such as the exploded technical drawings and animations, that could not be provided any other way. Brochures coordinated with the presentation are available at the booth, so visitors can take away information.

CD-ROM and Videodisks

One medium that Jane does not use in her self-running presentation is video. As mentioned in the video chapters, the Mac itself isn't capable of storing and playing video off a typical hard disk. But video can be stored on CD-ROMs (for "compact disk, read-only memory"), polycarbonate disks shot full of little pits by a laser. The pits encode binary information with incredible density—in a package 12 millimeters wide and less than 1 millimeter thick, a CD-ROM stores 656 or 748 megabytes, depending on the storage scheme used. Seven hundred forty-eight megabytes is about 374,000 pages of double-spaced text, or the equivalent of 600 300-page books, or several minutes of full-motion video and sound, with random, computer-controlled access to any information on the disk. The big siblings of CD-ROMs, videodisks, can store two hours of video, with the same random-access capabilities. (VCRs, which do not offer random access, can't compete in the multimedia arena.) The additional advantage of CDs as an information distribution medium is that they are read-only; that is, the user can't make changes in the information on the disk, only look at it (and/or listen to it).

To integrate video into an interactive presentation, you need a CD or videodisk player that can be controlled with the Mac; an interface box and cable; a genlock or video effects board; software to control the disk; software to display the video image on the Mac screen; and a disk with your video recorded on it. Figure 9-14 diagrams how it all fits together. Turnkey CD and videodisk systems are already available (Apple makes a CD-ROM player, for example), and *HyperCard* drivers for many models of videodisk players can be had from Apple or on computer bulletin boards. Programs are appearing that can display video in a window in a *HyperCard* stack or *SuperCard* project (see Appendix A). Videodisk mastering (recording video onto a master disk) can cost under $1,000, and CD mastering under $500. The hardest part, as you might expect, is actually shooting the video and organizing it into your presentation. Some resources for CD and videodisk presentations are listed in Appendix A.

Figure 9-14. Videodisk System

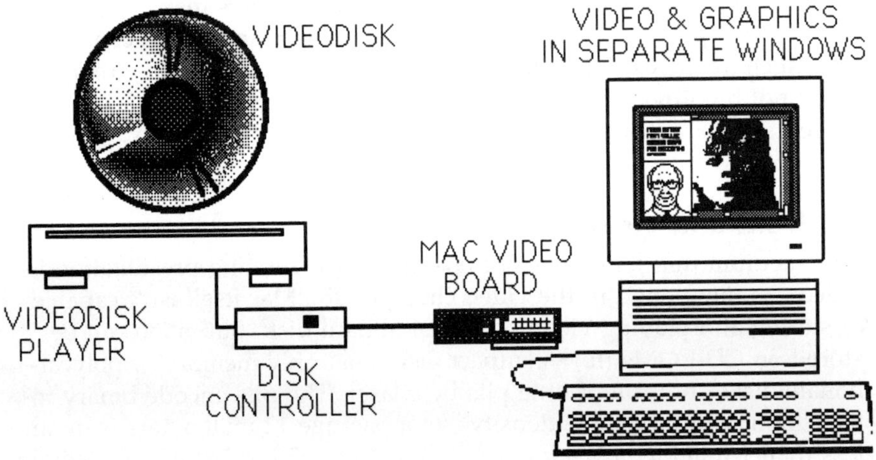

Multimedia File Formats

Apple has announced tentative plans for developing and supporting a standard file format for multimedia/hypermedia presentations. The Media Control Architecture (MCA), announced in mid-1989, is a set of protocols and device drivers that compatible applications and peripherals can access to run multimedia programming. The MCA will comprise a basic file format with "hooks" for running scripts and accessing graphics, scans, animation, sound, music, and text files; and a core interface code for accessing peripherals such as CD-ROMs and videodisks.

The advantages of a common architecture for multimedia are many: All programs and devices that support the MCA standard could be used together; the development of multimedia programs would be speeded up and streamlined, since all the parts would work seamlessly together; and hypermedia presentations could be shown without requiring the application programs used to create each part of the presentation. Right now, only programs such as *HyperCard*, *SuperCard*, and *MacroMind Director*, which can handle both graphics and sound, offer a simple way to put together at least some of the sensory elements that make up complex presentation.

Final Tips for Outside Production

After all this, you may still want to go to an outside production service to create the materials for your presentation, especially if it involves elaborate animation, video production, or interactive design. Here's an idea of what this might cost:

- A simple presentation, with slides, overheads, and leave-behinds, may run you $35–$50 an hour of development time from a small production service. Total charges depend on the length of the presentation and the number of slides or overheads, but could cost in the range of $3,000–$6,000 for a 20-minute presentation. A small, new production company—a description that characterizes most in the field of Mac presentation production—may be the best bet for getting a good price and enthusiastic service.
- Video is likely to cost $1,000 per minute of finished tape. Some production houses charge up to $3,000 per minute for top-quality broadcast video with digital special effects. If you are being charged by the hour, figure that each minute of completed tape can take at least ten hours of production time.
- Traditional cel animation on film costs up to $3,000 per *second*. Mac-generated animation (created with one of the packages discussed in Chapter 8, for example) will costs far less, under $500 per second. Obviously, it pays to plan very carefully before contracting for animation, since you'll be charged for the design and preparation time as well.
- For fully interactive presentations and training materials, double the cost of a typical production. Remember, interactive programming requires additional material for all the various branches of the interactive structure. You can spend up to $100,000 for an original interactive videodisk. If you can create the material yourself, however, mastering a CD costs under $500, with copies off the master varying in price according to quantity pressed.
- You'll save time and money if you streamline your own approval procedures. Know what you want; watch for problems and nip them in the bud, promptly sign off on satisfactory work, and resist the urge to make last-minute changes in the concept of your production.

Conclusion

This book hardly begins to touch on the possibilities inherent in Macintosh desktop presentations. Presentations technology, especially on the video and interactive fronts, is moving so fast that it's hard to keep up with the latest developments. In the future there will be new products and new techniques that will change the direction of the field, exceeding the capabilities of the tools discussed here. Nor have all the possible applications for desktop presentations been thought of, let alone explored. You and your Macintosh can make a major contribution, if you so choose. Good luck!

APPENDIX A

Desktop Presentation Resources

Collected here are some of the more important resources for Macintosh desktop presentations. This is not a comprehensive list of all organizations, products, vendors, services, and publications, but merely a selection of useful materials to get you started in your own explorations. Every effort has been made to include the latest information on products, prices, addresses, and phone numbers, but these things change daily, so there may be some discrepancies between the information here and what you find out in the real world.

Associations

Association for Computing Machinery-ACM Siggraph
11 West 42 St.
New York, NY 10036

Association of Independent Video and Filmmakers
625 Broadway, 9th Floor
New York, NY 10012
Dues: $35.00 per year

Berkeley Macintosh Users Group (BMUG)
415-549-2684

Boston Computer Society (BCS)
617-367-8080

Interactive Video Association
POB 1491
Evanston, IL 60204
312-364-5888

Interactive Video Industry Association
202-872-8845

International Interactive Communications Society
202-462-8888

International Television Association
214-869-1112

National Computer Graphics Association (NCGA)
8401 Arlington Blvd.
Fairfax, VA 22031

New York Macintosh Users Group (NYMUG)
212-691-0496

Professional Photographers of America
Electronic Creative Imagery Group
1090 Executive Way
Des Plaines, IL 60018

Society for Applied Learning Techniques
707-347-0055

Society of Motion Picture and Television Engineers (SMPTE)
862 Scarsdale Ave.
Scarsdale, NY 10583

Books and Periodicals

Books

Alton, Stanley R. *Audio in Media, 2d ed.* Belmont, CA: Wadsworth Publishing, 1986.

Ambron, Sueann and Kristina Hooper, eds. *Interactive Multimedia.* Redmond, WA: Microsoft Press, 1988.

Anderson, Gary H. *Video Editing and Post-Production: A Professional Guide, 2d ed.* White Plains, NY: Knowledge Industry Publications, 1988.

Anzovin, Steven. *Exploring HyperCard.* Radnor, PA: COMPUTE!, 1988.

Apple Computer. *Human Interface Guidelines: The Apple Desktop Interface.* Reading, MA: Addison-Wesley Publishing Co., 1987.

Berryman, Gregg. *Notes on Graphic Design and Visual Communications.* Los Altos, CA: William Kaufmann, 1984.

Blank, Ben, and Mario R. Garcia. *Professional Video Graphic Design.* New York: Knowledge Industry/Prentice-Hall, 1986.

Born, Robert, ed. *Designing for Television: The New Tools.* Tequesta, FL: Broadcast Designers' Association, 1983.

Dreyfuss, Henry. *Symbol Sourcebook.* New York: Van Nostrand Reinhold, 1984.

Fenton, Erfert. *The Macintosh Font Book.* Peachpit Press, 1988.

Field, Syd. *Screenplay: The Foundations of Screenwriting.* New York: Dell, 1979.

Fox, David and Michael Waite. *Computer Animation Primer.* New York: McGraw-Hill, 1983.

Gaskill, Arthur L., and David A. Englande. *How to Shoot a Movie and Video Story: The Technique of Pictorial Continuity, rev. ed.* New York: Morgan and Morgan, 1985.

Galluzzo, Tony. *Home Video Movies: How to Get the Most from Your Camcorder and VCR.* Radnor, PA: COMPUTE!, 1987.

Hubatka, Milton, Fredrick Hull, and Richard W. Sanders. *Audio Sweetening for Film and TV.* Blue Ridge Summit, PA: TAB Books, 1985.

Huff, Darrell. *How to Lie with Statistics.* New York: W.W. Norton, 1954.

Kerlow, Isaac V. and Judson Rosebush. *Computer Graphics for Designers and Artists.* New York: Van Nostrand Reinhold, 1986.

LeTourneau, Tom. *Lighting Techniques for Video Production: The Art of Casting Shadows.* White Plains, NY: Knowledge Industry Publications.

Naiman, Arthur. *The Macintosh Bible.* New York: Goldstein & Blair, 1988.

Nelson, Theodore. *Literary Machines.* Swarthmore, PA: Ted Nelson.

Robinson, Richard. *The Video Primer, 3d ed.* New York: Putnam, 1983.

Sculley, John. *Odyssey: From Pepsi to Apple.* New York: Harper & Row, 1967.

Tufte, Edward R. *The Visual Display of Quantitative Information.* Cheshire, CT: Graphics Press, 1983.

Zelazny, Gene. *Say It With Charts.* Homewood, IL: Dow Jones-Irwin, 1985.

Periodicals

Audio-Visual Communications
50 West 23rd St.
New York, NY 10010

AV Video
25550 Hawthorne Blvd.
Suite 314
Torrance, CA 90505

COMPUTE! Magazine
324 West Wendover Ave.
Suite 200
Greensboro, NC 27408

Computer Graphics World
119 Russell St.
POB 1112
Littleton, MA 01460

Computer Pictures
2 Village Square West
Clifton, NJ 07011

Desktop Presentations Yearbook
Desktop Presentations, Inc.
253 Martens Ave., Suite 10
Mountain View, CA 94040
415-968-4105

Electronic Musician
2608 Ninth St.
Berkeley, CA 94710

HyperLink Magazine
Publishers Guild, Inc.
POB 7723
Eugene, OR 97401
503-484-5157

MacUser Magazine
POB 56986
Boulder, CO 80321
800-627-2247

MacWeek
301 Howard St.
San Francisco, CA 94105
415-243-3500

MacWorld
MacWorld Communications
501 Second St.
San Francisco, CA 94107

Presentation Products
513 Wilshire Blvd
Suite 344
Santa Minca, CA 90401
213-455-1414

Videography
50 West 23rd St.
New York, NY 10010

Videomaker
381 East 4th St.
Chico, CA 95928

Presentation Hardware

Audio Hardware

Apple MIDI Interface $99
Apple Computer
20525 Mariani Ave.
Cupertino, CA 95014
408-996-1010
A basic MIDI interface

JamBox $269
JamBox $459
SouthWorth Music Systems
Harvard, MA 01451
508-772-9471
MIDI interfaces, SMPTE synchronizers for sync to videotape, MIDI filtering, more.

MacRecorder 2.0 $199
Farallon Computing
2201 Dwight Way
Berkeley, CA 94704
415-849-2331
Low-cost sound digitizer with *HyperCard* front end; turn samples into *HyperCard* or *SuperCard* sound resources. Good for digitizing voices.

CD-ROMs and WORMS

AppleCD SC $1199
Apple Computer
20525 Mariani Ave.
Cupertino, CA 95014
408-996-1010
Basic CD-ROM with *HyperCard* front end; plays music CDs, too.
CD ROM Development System $10,750 with hard drive, optical drive, and CD-ROM drive

Laser Optical Technology (LOT)
1803 Mission
Suite 403
Santa Cruz, CA 95060
408-426-7171
Relatively low-cost CD-ROM development system.

Teac Recordable Videodisk Division
Teac America
7733 Telegraph Rd.
Montebello, CA 90640
213-727-7675
Equipment for CD mastering.

Large-Screen Displays

E-Machines, Inc.
9305 SW Gemini Dr.
Beaverton, OR 97005
503-646-6699

Electrohome Limited
POB 628
Buffalo, NY 14225
800-265-2171

General Electric Company
Projection Display Products Operation
Electronic Park 6-205
POB 4840
Syracuse, NY 13221
315-456-2152

Mitsubishi Electronics America, Inc.
Computer Peripherals Division
991 Knox St.
Torrance, CA 90502
800-556-1234, x209, in CA 800-441-2345, x209

Moniterm Corp.
5740 Green Circle Dr.
Minnetonka, MN 55343
612-935-4151

NEC Professional Systems Division
800-562-5200 xNEC

Personal Computer Peripherals Corp.
4710 Eisenhower Blvd.
Building A4
Tampa, FL 33634
813-884-3092
800-622-2888

Radius Inc.
404 E. Plumeria Dr.
San Jose, CA 95134
800-227-2795

RasterOps Corp.
10161 Bubb Rd.
Cupertino, CA 95014
408-446-4090

Sony Presentation Products
1600 Queen Anne Rd.
Teaneck, NJ 07666
800-523-SONY

SuperMac Technology
485 Potrero Ave.
Sunnyvale, CA 94086
408-245-2202

Presentation equipment and supplies (projectors, cables, paper and plastic stock, and so on).

Avery
800-535-3232
Printing supplies, laser printer labels, acetates.

Comprehensive Video Supply Corp.
148 Veterans Dr.
Northvale, NJ 07647
201-797-7990
Production supplies, cables, and so on.

Eastman Kodak Company
343 State St.
Rochester, NY 14650
800-242-2424
Photographic equipment and supplies; projectors.

Visualon
3044 Payne Ave.
Cleveland, OH 44114
216-566-0506
Computer peripherals; presentation hardware and supplies.

Wolsten, Inc.
99 Washington St. and Park Ave.
East Orange, NJ 07017
800-338-3054
201-678-0008
Audio, video, and computer presentation products and supplies.

Printers

Apple ImageWriter II	$625
Apple ImageWriter LQ	$1,429
Apple LaserWriter IISC	$2,799
Apple LaserWriter IINT	$4,995
Apple LaserWriter IINTX	$6,995

Apple Computer
20525 Mariani Ave.
Cupertino, CA 95014
408-996-1010
Apple's line of printers: ImageWriter is a dependable 9-pin dot-matrix; ImageWriter LQ is a 24-pin dot-matrix; IISC is a QuickDraw printer only; IINT and IINTX are 300 dpi PostScript printers. Upgrade modules available for IISC and IINT.

Dataproducts LZR 1260 — $7,995
Dataproducts Corp.
6200 Canoga Ave.
Woodland Hills, CA 91365
818-887-8000
Top-rated, heavy-duty 300 dpi laser; better than the Apple IINTX, but pricier.

DeskWriter — $1,195
Hewlett-Packard
19310 Pruneridge Ave.
Cupertino, CA 95014
800-752-0900 x688E
Inkjet with close-to-laser print quality.

GCC Business LaserPrinter — $4,189
GCC Technologies. Inc.
580 Winter St.
Waltham, MA 02154
617-890-0880
Good value in a 300 dpi, Adobe-licensed laser.

Kroy Color Plus — $875
Kroy Inc.
14555 N. Hayden Rd.
Scottsdale, AZ 85260
800-521-4997
Not a color printer, but a method of embossing color and metallic foils onto LaserWriter printouts for slick report covers, and so on.

LaCie Panther PDX $3,495
LaCie Ltd.
16285 SW 85th St.
Suite 306
Tigard, OR 97224
503-684-0143
300 dpi, LCD PostScript printer; excellent image quality and mechanical reliability; not Adobe font-compatible; other fonts supplied. Identical model available from other manufacturers.

PaintJet $1,395
PaintJet Interface $125
Hewlett-Packard
19310 Pruneridge Ave.
Cupertino, CA 95014
800-752-0900, x688C
Popular, low-cost color inkjet printer with acceptable quality for presentations; requires interface.

Mitsubishi G330-70 $5,900
Mitsubishi Electronics
800-556-1234, x54R, in CA 800-441-2345, x54R
150 dpi color thermal printer

QMS Colorscript 100 Model 10 $9,995
QMS Colorscript 100 Model 20 $15,995
QMS Colorscript 100 Model 30 $19,995
QMS
1 Magnum Pass
Mobile, AL 36618
205-633-4300
800-631-2692, x222
PostScript four-color thermal color printers with vivid, sharp colors and good text; certified Pantone compatible.

Tektronix 4693D Color Printer $11,490
Tektronix
POB 500
Beaverton, OR 97077
or
POB 1000
Wilsonville, OR 97070
503-627-3472
Bit-mapped color printer; excellent color, text is jagged. Best with 8-megabyte Mac II.

Projection Panels

Apollo PC-9600 $1,850
Apollo Audio Visual
60 Trade Zone Ct.
Roankonkoma, NY 11779
516-467-8033
LCD panel; remote and cable for Plus or SE extra.

Datashow H/RM $1,595
Eastman Kodak Company
343 State St.
Rochester, NY 14650
800-242-2424
Versatile LCD panel at good price.

Network Specialties Flat Top $1,795
Network Specialties
296 Elizabeth St.
New York, NY 10012
212-995-2224
Panel with larger display area (640 × 400) than others.

Nutmeg LCD Interface/Kodak DataShow HR/M Projection Pad, Mac II version $2,095
Nutmeg Systems
25 South Ave.
New Canaan, CT 06840
800-777-8439
NuBus video board to link Mac II with Kodak Datashow HR/M LCD panel.

Mac Data Display $1,499
Computer Accessories Corporation
6610 Nancy Ridge Dr.
San Diego, CA 92121
800-582-2580
LCD panel for Mac Plus and SE; not well-suited to high-frame-rate animation.

MacViewFrame II+2 $1,850
nVIEW Corporation
11835 Canon Blvd.
Newport News, VA 23606
804-873-1354
Responsive LCD panel.

MagniView 342 $1,395
Dukane Corporation
Audio-Visual Division
2900 Dukane Dr.
St. Charles, IL 60174
800-356-6540, 800-634-2800
Mac version of PC panel; 16-color option.

PC Viewer $1,895
with memory and remote $2,795
In Focus Systems, Inc.
7649 Southwest Mohawk St.
Tualatin, OR 97062
800-327-7231
Panel with onboard display memory; dowload pictures to unit and leave your Mac on the desk.

Sharp QA-50 $1,395
Sharp Electronics Corp.
Professional Products Division
Sharp Plaza
Mahwah, NJ 07430
201-529-8731
Good price, responsive LCD panel.

Remote Controllers

DataShow Presentation Remote $245
Kodak
Rochester, NY
800-445-6325
ADB device that works with selected presentation programs.

SilentPartner $345
Presentation Electronics
Sacramento, CA
916-646-3402
Remote keyboard and mouse emulator; macro facility; works with any Mac.

Scanners

Abaton 300 S	$1795

Abaton
48431 Milmont Dr.
Fremont, CA 94538
415-683-2226
16-level, 300 dpi grayscale scanner.

Apple Scanner	$1799

Apple Computer
20525 Mariani Ave.
Cupertino, CA 95014
408-996-1010
Entry-level grayscale scanner with good *HyperCard* software.

AST TurboScan	$1,899

AST Research
2121 Alton Ave.
Irvine, CA 92714
300 dpi grayscale scanner with versatile scanning software.

Datacopy JetReader	$1,995
Datacopy 730, 730GS, 830, 840	$1,995–$7,495

Xerox Imaging Systems
1215 Terra Bella Ave.
Mountain View, CA 94043
800-821-2898, 415-965-7900
Scanner family with 300 dpi, up to 256 grayscale levels.

DEST PC Scan 2000	$1,495

DEST Corp.
1201 Cadillac Ct.
Milpitas, CA 95035
256-grayscale scanner; software additional.

Howtek Scanmaster	$8,195 complete

Howtek, Inc.
21 Park Ave.
Hudson, NJ 03051
603-882-5200
High-quality 24-bit color scanner with good software.

Microtek MSF-300 series	$1,595–$3,995
Microtek MSF-300Z	$3,995

Microtek
680 Torrance St.
Torrance, CA 90502
800-654-4160; in CA 213-321-2121
Scanners with up to 256-level grayscale, 300dpi; software offers contrast and brightness controls, halftone screen patterns. The MSF-300Z is a low-cost, 300 dpi, 24-bit color scanner.

New Image MacScanColor — $7,590
New Image Technology
9701 Philadelphia Ct.
Lanham, MD 20706
301-731-2000
Color scanner.

Nikon LS-3500 — $N/A
Nikon Electronic Imaging
Dept. E1-B
101 Cleveland Ave.
Bayshore, NY 11706
Film scanner with superior resolution; with color sep software for DTP.

ScanJet — $2,090
ScanJet Plus — $2,190
Hewlett-Packard
19310 Pruneridge Ave.
Cupertino, CA 95014
800-752-0900
Popular 300 dpi grayscale scanners.

ScanMan — $499
Logitech, Inc.
6505 Kaiser Dr.
Fremont, CA 94555
800-231-7717; in CA 800-552-8885
Handheld grayscale scanner.

Texnai TX-200 — $3,995
Forefront Graphics Corp.
500 Sheppard Ave. East, Suite 309
Willowdale, Ontario
CANADA M2N 6H7
416-226-4434
24-bit color, 200–300 dpi scanner with software.

ThunderScan $249
LightningScan $549
Thunderware
21 Orinda Way
Orinda, CA 94563
Thunderscan replaces the Imagewriter ribbon with a scan module; best low-priced 300 dpi scanner available; LightningScan is a handheld version.

Truvel TZ-3BWC $9,495
Truvel Zebra Image Processing Board $995
Truvel
8943 Fullbright Ave.
Chatsworth, CA 91311
818-407-1031
Overhead BW/24-bit color scanner that can scan 3-D objects as well as flat art; also, image processing board for superior line art scanning.

Visionscan VS200 Scanner $597
Visionscan VS300 Scanner $797
Mirror Technologies
2644 Patton Rd.
Roseville, MN 55113
612-633-4450
200 and 300 dpi scanners with innovative overhead design.

Slidemakers and Film Printers

Array Slide Scanner $20,000 (preliminary)
Array Technologies
7730 Pardee Lane
Oakland, CA 94621
415-633-3000
Super-high resolution scanner with advanced image processing.

BarneyScan Version 3 $9,495
BarneyScan
1198 10th St.
Berkeley, CA 94710
415-524-6648
Complete system with good color fidelity.

Eiconix 1435 Slide Scanner — $10,000 (preliminary)
Eiconix
23 Crosby Dr.
Bedford, MA 01730
617-276-5077
Kodak-built slide scanner; requires interface board and software.

Howtek Scanmaster 35 — $8,195 (complete system)
Howtek
21 Park Ave.
Hudson, NH 03051
603-882-4200

Image Maker — $4,995
Montage FR1 — $5,995
Presentation Technologies
743 N. Pastoria Ave.
Sunnyvale, CA 94086
800-345-3050
Imagemaker works with Mac PICT files, no bitmaps; not ideal for color or the Mac II; the Montage yields better graphics.

Lasergraphics Mac/LFR — $9,750
17671 Cowan Ave.
Irvine, CA 92714
714-660-9497
Fast, but only fair-quality images.

Matrix Procolor — $6,495
Matrix Slidewriter — $11,795
Postscript RIP — $17,900
MacHarmony — $1,995
Agfa Matrix Instruments, Inc.
1 Ramland Rd.
Orangeburg, NY 10962
800-852-8533, 914-365-0190
Procolor is a good midpriced slidemaker; the Slidewriter is a top Mac slidemaker, with price to match. The RIP (Raster Image Processor) processes color PostScript images and works with any Matrix slidemaker. MacHarmony is an interface for hooking Macs to IBM Matrix slidemakers.

Mirus FilmPrinter $5,895
4301 Great America Parkway
Santa Clara, CA 95054
800-654-0808
Slides in full color; reliable operation, Chooser driver.

Nikon LS-3500 $9,995
Nikon, Inc.
623 Stewart Ave.
Garden City, NY 11530
516-220-0200
High-resolution scanner; requires interface board and software.

Slide Service Bureaus

Autographix
100 Fifth Ave.
Waltham, MA 02154
617-890-8558

MAGICorp
800-FOR-MAGI

Genigraphics
4806 W. Taft Rd.
Liverpool, NY 13088
315-451-6600

Video Peripherals and Systems

Avid/1 Media Composer $20,000–$80,000 depending on configuration
Avid Technology Inc.
175 Bedford St.
Burlington, MA 01803
617-272-1680
Professional digital video editing system with real-time video access and CD-quality sound.

Canon USA Inc.
Video Division
One Canon Plaza
Lake Success, NY 11042
516-488-6700
Camcorders, cameras, and so on.

ColorBoard 64 $2,595
ColorBoard 100N $1,795
ColorBoard 104 $3,195
ColorBoard 108+ $1,495
ColorBoard 224 $N/A
ColorBoard 232 $N/A
RasterOps
10161 Bubb Rd.
Cupertino, CA 95014
408-446-4090
Line of NuBus 32-bit, 24-bit, and 8-bit cards; hardware pan and zoom; genlock daughter board available with overlay and chromakey.

ColorCapture $2,995
Data Translation
100 Locke Dr.
Marlboro, MA 01752
508-481-3700
NuBus frame grabber, RGB encoder, NTSC output.

ColorFreeze24 $1,999
with video card $2,600
Computer Friends
14250 NW Science Park Dr.
Portland, OR 97229
24-bit digitizer board for Mac II.

ColorSpace II $1,995
ColorSpaceFX $2,995
MASS Microsystems
550 Del Rey Ave.
Sunnyvale, CA 94086
800-522-7979
408-522-1200
ColorSpace II is a NuBus NTSC-encoder-genlocker board; the ColorSpaceFX board adds real-time DVE effects and flicker-free 60 frames per second RGB output (requires ColorSpace II).

Composite Video Adapters 2402, 2406, 2702, 2703 $129
Power R.
1606 Dexter Ave. North
Seattle, WA 98109
206-547-8000
Internal video adapter series for Plus and SE. Drive multiple external monitors or projectors.

Computereyes 1.2.1 $249.95
Digital Visions
66 Eastern Ave.
Dedham, MA 02026
617-329-5400
Lowest cost black-and-white digitizer for any Mac.

Genlock Converter $999
NTSC Converter $599
Julian Systems
2280 Bates Ave., #1
Concord, CA 94520
415-686-4400
Mac II genlock and NTSC boards; genlock requires separate video card.

GigaPix Price depends on configuration
Illusion Software Systems
1526 Cloverfield Blvd.
Santa Monica, CA 90404
213-829-5409
Mac to transport controller to two-gigabyte tape drive to video post-production equipment system for video/animation.

Hitachi Sales Corporation of America
Industrial Division
401 West Artesia Blvd.
Compton, CA 90220
Video and audio equipment.

JVC
41 Slater Dr.
Elmwood Park, NJ 07407
Video and audio equipment.

Kodak LC500 Video Projector $3,495
Eastman Kodak Company
343 State St.
Rochester, NY 14650
800-242-2424
716-724-3169
Portable color video projector for Mac II.

Mac II/TV Video Interface $595
with genlock $1,495

MacFX Studio Converter $1,495
Mac II version $2,995 (includes Mac II/TV)
Comtrex International
POB 1450
El Toro, CA 92630
714-855-6600
Composite encoder and software for RS-170A output; MacFX handles special effects.

MacLarger $449
Power R.
1606 Dexter Ave. North
Seattle, WA 98109
206-547-8000
Video monitor for Plus and SE; drive up to six monitors for class and presentation use.

MacVision 2.0 $399.95
Koala Technologies/Pentron Corp.
2560 Montague Expressway
San Jose, CA 95131
408-432-7500
Easy-to-use black and white video digitizer for all Macs.

Magic Digitizer $399.95
300 dpi software driver $49.95
New Image Technology
10300 Greenbelt Rd.
Seabrook, MD 20706
Black-and-white video digitizer for any Mac.

Microtouch Touchscreen $395–$995, depending on configuration
Microtouch
10 State St.
Woburn, MA 01801
617-935-0080
Low-cost, user-installable touchscreen system for interactive presentations.

NuVista 1M $3,395
VIDI/O Box $995
Truevision
7351 Shadeland Station
Indianapolis, IN 46256

800-858-TRUE
NuBus NTSC encoder, genlocker, frame capture, and RGB video card; optional VIDI/O box allows recording to videotape.

Panasonic
One Panasonic Way
Secaucus, NJ 07094
201-348-7183
Video and audio equipment; computer peripherals.

Personal Vision $N/A
Orange Micro
1400 N. Lakeview Ave.
Anaheim, CA 92807
800-223-8029
Color NuBus frame grabber.

ProViz GrayScale $1,095
ProViz Color $1,695
Pixelogic
800 West Cummings Park
Suite 2900
Woburn, MA 01801
800-678-1242
Stand-alone video digitizers; color version for the Mac II.

QuickCapture $1,595
Data Translation
100 Locke Dr.
Marlboro, MA 01752
617-481-3700
Grayscale frame grabber board for Mac II.

Redmond Cable
East Coast: 615-478-5760
West Coast: 206-882-2009
Custom Macintosh cables of all kinds.

Scuzzygraph $N/A
Aura Systems
619-438-7730
Add Quickdraw color capabilites to any SCSI-equipped Mac.

Sony Video Communications
Sony Dr.
Park Ridge, NJ 07656
201-930-1000
Sony Presentation Products
1600 Queen Anne Rd.
Teaneck, NJ 07666
800-523-SONY
Video and audio equipment and supplies; large screen monitors.

Sanyo Corporation
1200 W. Artesia Blvd.
Compton, CA 90220
213-605-6526
Video and audio equipment.

TV Producer $599
Computer Friends
14250 NW Science Park Dr.
Portland, OR 97229
NTSC genlock NuBus board for Mac II; requires Apple Video Card.

Video Image 1000 $1,195
Scion Corporation
3 North Main St.
Walkersville, MD 21793
301-845-4045
NuBus color video capture card and software that grabs video frames in real time and saves TIFF files.

VideoShow Companion $1,795
VideoShow Executive $2,695 (640K), $3,995 (1 MB)
StarTime Presentation Software $199
General Parametrics Corporation
1250 9th St.
Berkeley, CA 94710
800-556-1234, x234; in CA, 800-441-2345, x234
Hardware/software system with remote control; pop in your presentation disk and project onto a video monitor or screen. Additional peripherals and software allow slide and transparency making.

Presentation Software

Animation

Studio 1 — $149.95 (tentative)
Electronic Arts
1820 Gateway Dr.
San Mateo, CA 94404
415-571-7171
Black-and white paint program and page-flipping animator.

VideoWorks II	$195.00
Videoworks II Accelerator	$195.00
Videoworks II *HyperCard* driver	$99.95
Videoworks II Clip Animation Disks	$49.95–59.95
Videoworks II Clip Sounds Disks	$59.95
Videoworks II Clip Charts Disks	$59.95
Videoworks II Color Movies Disks	$25.00 each
MacroMind Director	$695.00

MacroMind
1028 W. Wolfram St.
Chicago, IL 60657
312-871-0987
Animation, storyboarding, and slideshow program for all Macs; color on the Mac II. Also, utilities for speeding up animations and inserting animations into *HyperCard,* plus clip animation collections. High-end professional version has many additional tools for desktop video.

Custom Fonts and Character Generation

Fluent Fonts — $49.95
Casady-Ware
POB 223779
Carmel, CA 93922
49-font, two-disk collection for system installation.

FONTastic Plus
Altsys Corp.
720 Ave. F
Suite 1090
Plano, TX 75074
Modify bitmapped fonts or roll your own, with nice effects.

Fontagrapher $395
Altsys Corp.
720 Ave. F
Suite 1090
Plano, TX 75074
Make your own PostScript fonts at 300 dpi.

Letrastudio $495
Letraset USA
40 Eisenhower Dr.
Paramus, NJ 07653
201-845-6100
Create custom typestyles; requires Letrafonts, $75 each from the company.

Showcase F/X $295
Aegis Development
2115 Pico Blvd.
Santa Monica, CA 90405
213-392-9972
Create color text for video titling.

TypeStyler $199.95
Broderbund Software
17 Paul Dr.
San Rafael, CA 94903
415-492-3200
Customize PostScript type and add special effects in color.

Draw and Paint Programs

Canvas 2.0 $299
Deneba Software
3305 NW 74th Ave.
Miami, FL 33122
800-6-CANVAS; in FL, 305-594-6965
Versatile color draw program.

Capture $79.95
Mainstay
5311-B Derry Ave.
Agoura Hills, CA 91301
818-991-6540
Not a graphics program, but an invaluable utility for capturing screens and converting images to the popular PICT file format.

Cricket Draw $295
Cricket Software
40 Valley Stream Pkwy.
Malvern, PA 19355
215-251-9890
Drawing program with PostScript output.

Cricket Paint $99
Cricket Color Paint $199 (tentative)
Cricket Software
40 Valley Stream Pkwy.
Malvern, PA 19355
215-251-9890
Black-and-white paint program for all Macs; low-cost color paint program.

Curator $139.95
Solutions Intl.
30 Commerce St.
Williston, VT 05495
Art cataloging program; indispensable for large clip art collections.

DeskPaint 2.0 $129.95
Zedcor
4500 E. Speedway, #22
Tucson, AZ 85712
800-482-4567, 602-881-8101
Black-and-white paint program and TIFF editor; useful DA version.

FreeHand 2.0 $495
Aldus
411 First Ave. South
Seattle, WA 98104
206-628-2320
Professional PostScript drawing program.

Illustrator 88 $495
Adobe Systems
1585 Charleston Rd.
Mountain View, CA 94039
Professional PostScript drawing program.

MacDraw II $395
Claris
440 Clyde Ave.
Mountain View, CA 94043
408-987-7000
New version of the popular draw program with updated tools, color, patterns.

MacPaint 2.0 $125
Claris
440 Clyde Ave.
Mountain View, CA 94043
408-987-7000
The original black and white paint program, with new features; for all Macs.

Modern Artist 2.0 $495
Computer Friends
14250 NW Science Park Dr.
Portland, OR 97229
Color paint program.

Photon Paint $299.95
Microillusions
17408 Chatsworth St.
Granada Hills, CA 93144
Color paint program; simulated 3-D surface mapping of paint images.

Pixel Paint 2.0 $395
Pixel Paint Professional $N/A
SuperMac Technology
485 Potrero Ave.
Sunnyvale, CA 94086
408-245-2202
Excellent color paint program with color separation capabilities; professional version is 32-bit compatible.

SmartScrap and the *Clipper* $59.95
Solutions Intl.
30 Commerce St.
Williston, VT 05495
Scrapbook enhancement DAs; good for general graphics and handling clip art collections.

Studio/8 $495
Studio/32 $N/A
Electronic Arts
1820 Gateway Dr.
San Mateo, CA 94404
415-571-7171
Top color paint program with all the bells and whistles; *Studio/32* is 32-bit compatible.

SuperPaint 2.0 $149.95
Silicon Beach Software
9770 Carroll Center Rd.
Suite J
San Diego, CA 92126
619-695-6956
Unique program combining draw and paint features; 300 dpi resolution.

HyperCard

HyperAnimator $99
Bright Star Technology
14450 NE 29th St.
Suite 220
Bellevue, WA 98007
Sync digitized voice to an animated face; requires *HyperCard*.

HyperAtlas
MicroMaps Software
POB 757
Lambertville, NJ 08530
U.S. and world maps with stacks of demographic and economic data.

HyperCard $49.95; free with Macintosh purchase
Apple Computer
20525 Mariani Ave.
Cupertino, CA 95014
408-996-1010
Apple's software toolkit; has basic animation capabilities.

HyperVision $195
Pixelogic
800 West Cummings Park
Suite 2900
Woburn, MA 01801
617-938-7711
Import black-and-white digitized video into your stacks; editing tools included; requires ProViz digitizer.

Plus $199
Olduvai Corp.
7520 Red Rd.
Suite A
South Miami, FL 33143
305-665-4665
HyperCard clone with color, full-screen cards, HyperTalk extensions, more.

SuperCard $199
Silicon Beach Software
9770 Carroll Center Rd.
Suite J
San Diego, CA 92126
619-695-6956
Enhanced version of HyperCard with color, multiple windows, more powerful tools.

Image Processing and Special Effects

ChromaScan $N/A
Imagenesis, Inc.
901 NE Loop 410, #630
San Antonio, TX 78209
512-824-1746
Color scanner image processing; especially useful with Sharp scanner.

Digital Darkroom $295
Silicon Beach Software
9770 Carroll Center Rd.
Suite J
San Diego, CA 92126
619-695-6956
Manipulate grayscale scans.

ImageStudio $495
Letraset USA
40 Eisenhower Dr.
Paramus, NJ 07653
201-845-6100
Retouch digitized graphics in grayscale

LaserPaint Color II $N/A
LaserWare, Inc.
POB 668
San Rafael, CA 94915
415-453-9500
Billed as a paint program, but more useful for color image processing and separations; PostScript capabilities.

PhotoLab $495
Orange Solutions, Inc.,
5743 Corsa Ave.
Suite 212
Westlake Village, CA 91362
818-707-9330
Color and grayscale scanned image editor, with contrast adjustment, rotation, and color remapping features.

PhotoMac $795
Data Translation
100 Locke Dr.
Marlboro, MA 01752
508-481-3700
Retouch, color correct, and color separate color scans and pictures.

Interactive Applications (see also *HyperCard*)

Carbon Copy Mac $299 for two stations
Microcom Software
55 Federal Rd.
Danbury, CT 06810
203-798-3800
Observe and control a second Mac in a window on your screen; works via LocalTalk and modem.

CourseBuilder (various configurations)
TeleRobotics International, Inc.
8410 Oak Ridge Highway
Knoxville, TN 37931
615-690-5600
Software and hardware for developing interactive training materials and courseware.

Course of Action $N/A
Authorware
8400 Normandale Lake Blvd.
Suite 430
Minneapolis, MN 55437
612-921-8555
Multimedia courseware and training authoring program.

Guide $135
Owl International
14218 NE 21st St.
Bellevue, WA 98007
Text-oriented hypermedia; better linking capabilities than *HyperCard*.

ScreenRecorder $195
Farallon Computing
2201 Dwight Way
Berkeley, CA 94704
415-849-2331
"Tape" any sequence of actions on a Mac screen for replay in a *HyperCard* stack.

Timbuktu $149 per station
Timbuktu/Remote $295 per station
Farallon Computing
2201 Dwight Way
Berkeley, CA 94704
415-849-2331
Programs for remote control and observation, of any Mac; *Timbuktu/Remote* works via modem; good for training.

Presentation Software

Cricket Presents $695
Cricket Software
40 Valley Stream Pkwy.
Malvern, PA 19355
215-251-9890
Presentation program with good graphics and master template function.

FastTrack Schedule $195
AEC Management Systems, Inc.
20524 Amethyst Lane
Germantown, MD 20874
800-346-9413
Create and update presentation schedules with graphics, charts, and text, plus outliner and import/export capabilities.

MORE II $395
Symantec
Living Videotext Division
10201 Torre Ave.
Cupertino, CA 95014
408-253-9600
Outliner and presentation program; great for text slides and charts, less capable for graphics.

Persuasion $495
Aldus
411 First Ave. South
Seattle, WA 98104
206-628-2320
Presentation program with many tools, color schemes, powerful master slide and template features.

PowerPoint $395
Microsoft
16011 NE 36th Way
POB 97017
Redmond, WA 98073
Presentation program with easy-to-use tools and features; slides to Genigraphics service bureaus.

PresentationPro $295
Strade Corporation
12600 W. Colfax, #B100
Lakewood, CO 80215
303-232-8282
Create slide presentations with many global modification features; send files directly to Crosfield/Dicomed Design Systems with included telecom functions.

StandOut! $395
Letraset USA
40 Eisenhower Dr.
Paramus, NJ 07653
201-845-6100
Primarily text-based presentation program; page-layout–type interface.

Visual Business No. 5 $395
Visual Business Systems
700 Lake St., #H
Ramsey, NJ 07446
201-327-2526
Charts and graphs for presentations; output manager for film recorder and color printer output.

Presentation Spreadsheets and Number Crunchers

Cricket Graph $195
Cricket Software
40 Valley Stream Pkwy.
Malvern, PA 19355
215-251-9890
Twelve graph types, in color and multiple windows.

DeltaGraph $195
Access Technology
555 Heritage Harbor
Monterey, CA 93940
408-648-4000
Charter with 40 functions, 30 chart types, and 3-D, export EPSF or PICT.

Excel 2.2 $395
Microsoft
16011 NE 36th Way
POB 97017
Redmond, WA 98073-9717
206-882-8080
The classic Mac spreadsheet with new charting and graphics features.

Fastat $195
Systat, Inc.
1800 Sherman Ave.
Evanston, IL 60201
312-864-5670
Statistical analyzer with presentation graphics, draw capabilities.

Full Impact $N/A
Ashton-Tate
20101 Hamilton Ave.
Torrance, CA 90502
800-437-4329
Presentation spreadsheet with page layout.

KaleidaGraph $249
Synergy Software
2457 Perkiomen Ave.
Reading, PA 19606
215-779-0522
General purpose graphing and data analysis; 14 data graphic types.

MacSpin $199.95
D2 Software
POB 9456
Austin, TX 78766
Chart multivariate data; spin your data to see it from all angles.

MapMaker $349
Select Micro Systems
40 Triangle Center
Yorktown Heights, NY 10598
Cartographic tool for demographers and marketeers; many map types.

StatView II $495
Abacus Concepts
1984 Bonita Ave.
Berkeley, CA 94704
Data analysis and charting; in color on the Mac II.

Trapeze 2.0 $395
Access Technology
555 Heritage Harbor
Monterey, CA 93940
408-648-4000
Presentation spreadsheet.

Wingz $399
University Edition $99
Informix Software, Inc.
16011 College Blvd.
Lenexa, KS 66219
800-331-1763, x3800
Spreadsheet with excellent graphing capabilities, including 3-D.

Sound and Music Software

Alchemy $495
Blank Software
1477 Folsom St.
San Francisco, CA 94103
Versatile sample editor; requires MIDI interface and sampler.

Cue $595
Timecode Machine $300
OpCode Systems
444 Ramona St.
Palo Alto, CA 94301
Sync sound to visuals using SMPTE timecode.

Deluxe Music Construction Set 2.0 $99.95
Electronic Arts
1820 Gateway Dr.
San Mateo, CA 94404
415-571-7171
Low-cost but capable note editor.

Jam Session $49.95
Broderbund Software
17 Paul Dr.
San Rafael, CA 94903
415-492-3200
Instant music for amateur musicians; good for fast, impromptu scoring in several musical styles.

M $250
Jam Factory $200
UpBeat $150
Intelligent Music
116 North Lake Ave.
POB 8748
Albany, NY 12208
518-434-4110
Line of sequencing and composition software; *UpBeat* is the best Mac drum machine; MIDI compatible.

Master Tracks Pro $395
Passport Designs
625 Miramontes St., #103
Half Moon Bay, CA 94019
Pro-level MIDI sequencer with excellent, intuitive interface.

Music Mouse $59.95
OpCode Systems
444 Ramona St.
Palo Alto, CA 94301
Move the mouse to create instant music.

Performer $395
Mark of the Unicorn
222 Third St.
Cambridge, MA 02142
617-576-2760
Versatile, powerful MIDI sequencer.

Q-Sheet $495
Q-Sheet AV $995
Sound Accelerator $995
Digidesign
1360 Willow Rd.
Suite 101
Menlo Park, CA 94025
415-327-8811
Sync your music with film or video.

Sound Designer $495 some versions; others $395
Turbosynth $349
Digidesign
1360 Willow Rd.
Suite 101
Menlo Park, CA 94025
415-327-8811
Flexible sample editor and synthesizer programs; both require MIDI setup.

Three-Dimensional Design and Animation

Dimensions Presenter $495
Ray Tracer Dimensions $995
Render Dimension $995
Visual Information Development
16309 Doublegrove
La Puente, CA 91744
818-918-8834
Object modeling, rendering, and animation modules, with ray tracing; interfaces with various Mac file formats.

enVision 3D $495
Strata Inc.
249 East Tabernacle
Suite 201
St. George, UT 84770
801-628-5218
Object creation and ray-traced rendering; many surface effects.

Mac3D 2.0 $249
Challenger Software
18350 Kedzie Ave.
Homewood, IL 60430
Black-and-white 3-D editor with light-source shading, PostScript resolution.

ModelShop $N/A
Paracomp
123 Townsend St.
Suite 310
San Francisco, CA 94107
415-543-3848
CAD surface modeler for architects, planners, designers.

Pro3D $495
PhotoFinish $1,995
Enabling Technologies
600 S. Dearborn St., #1304
Chicago, IL 60605
312-427-0386
Object creation and high-quality rendering packages.

Sculpt-Animate 4D $1,500 (tentative)
Byte-by-Byte Corp.
Arboretum Plaza II
Suite 150
9442 Capital of Texas Highway N.
Austin, TX 78759
512-343-4357
Full-featured 3-D ray-tracing object editor; animation and rendering modules available.

Super 3D 2.0 $395
Silicon Beach Software
9770 Carroll Center Rd.
Suite J
San Diego, CA 92126
619-695-6956
Color object modeler with animation, superior interface, editable animation text files.

Swivel 3D $395
Paracomp
123 Townsend St.
Suite 310
San Francisco, CA 94107
415-543-3848
Color object modeler with unique hierarchical animation features; create linked objects with several types of joints.

Video Production

EdgeWriter Price varies with configuration
EdgeWriter
30 Berry St.
San Francisco, CA 94107
415-957-1744
Match film with tape with auto frame numbering; lists shots in a HyperCard stack; requires Excel and included hardware.

Edit Lister $900
Comprehensive Video Supply Corp.
148 Veterans Dr.
Northvale, NJ 07647
201-797-7990
Create an edit list for offline video editing.

VideoMaker $N/A
Ed Hollander
408-429-8332
Offline video editing program for Mac Plus or SE; requires interface box.

APPENDIX B

Desktop Presentation Glossary

This glossary gives short definitions for most of the terms used in *Macintosh Dekstop Presentations,* as well as some words, commonly used in the video and computer graphics industries, that are not mentioned in this book. This is by no means a complete dictionary of all desktop presentation terminology; like all technical dialects, the language of computer graphics is constantly expanding to include new terms as new technologies and effects are incorporated into the field. With some exceptions, general computer language and terms specific to the Macintosh operating system are not covered here; see your Macintosh operating manual for more information.

A/B Roll—Switching between two synchronized and time-base–corrected VCRs for special effects like dissolves, wipes, and other transitions.

ADO (Ampex Digital Optics)—A popular broadcast device, manufactured by Ampex, for creating digital video effects in real-time—squashes, flips, twists, and so on. Some DTV programs offer ADO-like effects.

Aliasing—The jagged, stairstepped effect along the edges of computer graphics; also called "the jaggies." Also, the reduction in frequency of a digitized sound, resulting in distortion. See *antialiasing.*

Amplitude—The height of a waveform from trough to peak; corresponds to volume in audio and luminance in video.

Analog Video—Video information carried on a continously varying electric signal.

Anim—A compressed animation file format supported by some Mac programs.

Animatic—The visual outline of a video program presented in videotape form or on the computer screen; see also *Storyboard.*

Animation—A series of pictures shown quickly in sequence to create the illusion of movement.

Antialiasing—Image processing technique that reduces the appearance of aliasing, or jaggies, in a computer picture. Makes edges appear smooth and more natural, if less sharp.

Area Graph—Graph that expresses quantity in terms of the area of a bar or other element.

ASCII—American Standard Code for Information Interchange, a widely used file format for computer text.

Aspect Ratio—The ratio of screen height to screen width; in video, the ratio is 3 to 4.

Assembly Editing—Piecing together sequences of video directly from a playback VCR to a record VCR without benefit of an edit controller, pre-roll, or other features to ensure smooth edits; also called "punch-and-crunch" editing.

Audio—The audible part of a presentation; may be sounds, music, dialog, narration, or all of these.

Audio Dub—Recording new audio on a tape after the video has been shot using the "audio dub" feature on most VCRs. The dubbed audio records directly over one track of the original audio.

Audio Mixing—Creating a custom audio track from several different sources using a mic mixer or other sound mixing device.

A/V—Short for Audio-Video or AudioVisual

Available Light—Ambient or natural light; shooting in available light means not using artificial light in a location production.

Axis—One of the Cartesian screen directions; the x-axis is along the screen horizontal; the y-axis is along the screen vertical; the z-axis goes "into" the screen picture space. 3-D objects can have their own axes.

Backlight—Light placed behind the subject in a scene to create a separation between the subject and the scene background.

Backspacing—See pre-roll.

Bandwidth—The maximum frequency range of a transmitted signal, measured in hertz. Or, how fast video electronics can modulate the electron beams. High-resolution computer graphics require higher bandwidths used in standard video.

Bar Chart—Popular chart type that compares a data set at a single point in time by the height or length of bars

Betacam—Broadcast version of Sony's $\frac{1}{2}$-inch Betamax tape format.

Bezier—A type of mathematical curve defined by the placement of external anchors and magnets acting on the curve line; used in some PostScript drawing programs.

Bit-depth—The number of bits a computer uses to define a color "word" for each pixel; the greater the bit-depth, the more colors available.

Bitmapped Graphics—Computer pictures manipulated as a matrix of pixel values.

Bivariate Data—A data set defined by two values, such as time and distance.

Black—A video signal without picture information; also called *color black.*

Body Copy—Block of text in a presentation document that carries the main body of information.

Boot—Switching on a computer and loading the operating system; from "bootstrap."

Broadcast Video—Video that meets RS-170A signal standards with at least 525 lines of resolution; a video signal good enough to be broadcast, sent over cable, and so on.

Buffer—Area in computer memory reserved for a computer graphic or other information.

Build—A sequence of related slides that reveals additional information with each slide.

Bullet Chart—Simple chart type in which a few short lines of text are marked by bullets.

Business TV—Video produced in an inhouse studio by a corporation for creating records of meetings, orientation, training, product evangelism, demonstrations, and presentations; usually distributed live or on tape to other branches of the company.

Button—Mac screen object that initiates an action when you click on it.

Camcorder—Consumer device that combines a video camera and a VCR in one lightweight unit.

Card—A full screen of *HyperCard* or *SuperCard* information; stacks are made of cards, while cards can contain buttons, fields, and graphics. See *Stack, Button, Field.*

Cardioid—A type of microphone sensitive to sound in a heart-shaped pickup pattern in front of the mike.

CCD—Charged Coupled Device, a light-sensitive photoelectric plate used in scanners and replacing video tubes in most camcorders.

CDEV—Control Panel Device, any Mac peripheral that can be controlled through the Control Panel desk accessory.

CD-ROM (Compact Disk-Read-Only Memory)—Small-format laser disk for storing larges amounts of information; cannot be recorded on by user.

Cel—A single drawing or frame in an animation.

C-Format, One-inch VTR—The preferred tape format for broadcast video post-production.

CGI—Computer-Generated Imagery.

Character Generator, Titler—Hardware device, or similarly capable software for a computer, for creating video text and titles.

Chartjunk—As coined by Edward R. Tufte, extraneous and sometimes deceptive visual material added to data graphics.
Chooser—Apple-supplied desk accessory for picking an output device, such as a printer or slidemaker.
Chroma—Color in video.
Chromakey—Inserting video imagery over a chosen color in a second video source using a special effects generator or computer. Used every day in TV news for putting weathermaps behind the weather-person.
Chrominance—The color portion of the composite video signal; hue and saturation information.
Clipboard—Area of the Mac's memory reserved for storing cut or copied selections to be pasted elsewhere. See *Selection.*
Clipping—Distortion of an analog signal when processing equipment "clips" off the top and bottom of the wave if they exceed certain amplitude values.
Coax—Coaxial cable, the standard type of shielded cable for carrying video signals.
Color Bars—Standard color chart for adjusting the color balance in any NTSC video device.
Color Burst—Reference wave of the video signal for measuring hue and saturation.
Color Cycling—Repeatedly flashing a series of colors on the screen; can be used to create simple animations.
Color LookUp Table (CLUT)—Standard Mac resource containing a table or palette of all the colors—up to 256 for the current Apple color standard—in a Color QuickDraw picture.
Color Picker—The standard Apple color palette control dialog.
Color Registers—Areas in computer memory where color information is kept.
Colorization—Adding color to a black-and-white image, or changing the colors in a color image.
Column Chart—Chart with vertical bars.
Component Video—A video signal with picture information broken down into red, blue, and green compoenents; see *RGB.*
Composite Encoder—A device that converts RGB video to composite video.
Composite Video—Standard TV video with a signal containing sync and picture information.
Contrast—The level of luminosity, or balance of gray tones, in a video or printed image.
Control Panel—Apple-supplied desk accessory for setting parameters of the Mac system, such as the date, number of colors, or level of sound.

Control Track—Recorded signal on a tape that controls tape motion in playback. The control track contains frame pulses that provide information about frame timing to control-track edit controllers. Tapes without a solid control track are unstable in playback and often can't be edited.

Copy Stand—Device for holding and adjusting a video camera used to shoot flat art or small items.

Crawl—Annoying shimmer on the borders of bright colors in a poorly recorded videotape; more generally, the movement of titles or graphics across the video image.

CRT—Cathode Ray Tube; the standard TV or computer display device.

CUT—An abrupt, instantaneous transition between two scenes in a production; also, a video edit.

Cycle—A section of a waveform that is one period long. Cycles are measured in hertz, or cycles per second.

Data Density—As coined by Edward Tufte, the total amount of data per area of the data graphic.

Data Fork—Part of a Mac program or document in which data are stored. See also *Resource Fork.*

Data Graphic—A pictorial display of numeric information.

Data-Ink—As coined by Edward Tufte, the amount of ink (or the number of pixels, in computer displays) devoted to actually carrying information in a data graphic.

Data Point—Any numeric value shown in a data graphic.

Data Series—A set of related data points.

Decibel—A measure of loudness, corresponding to the smallest difference in sound that the human ear can discern.

Desk Accessory (DA)—Memory-resident ultilty program; listed under the Apple menu.

Desktop Media—Apple's term for multimedia programming on the Mac.

Desktop Presentation—Using a computer to prepare and present graphic information to business, educational, and technical audiences.

DeskTop Video (DTV)—Video production using low-cost video equipment and desktop computers.

Device Driver—A program that controls the operations of a computer peripheral, such as a scanner or printer.

Digital Video—Video information contained in a sequence of discrete binary numbers.

Digitizer—Device for converting an analog video image into a digital computer graphic.

Display Font—Large, fancy typestyle to grab viewer attention.

Dissolve—Scene transition that gradually replaces one image for another.

Dithering—Blurring the transition from one color to another in a computer picture.

Document—Any Macintosh data file—a picture, a letter, a presentation file.

Dolly—Rolling the camera along a path to follow the action in a scene; often used for chase sequences.

Door Swing—Rotation of a video image along any axis with a digital effects generator.

Dot Chart—Chart displaying the relationship between values on the *x*- and *y*-axes; also called a *scatter* or *x-y chart.*

Dot Pitch—On a color display, the distance in millimeters between phosphor dots of the same color. A measure of display resolution.

Dots Per Inch (DPI)—Number of screen pixels or printed blots per inch in an image. The standard Mac screen is 72 dpi, while the typical laser printer prints 300 dpi. Often used as a measure of display or print resolution.

Dot-to-Pixel Ratio—The number of phosphor dots on a monitor, or the number of inkblots on a printout, that correspond to a screen pixel.

Double Buffering—In computer animation, displaying an image in a sequence while keeping the next to be displayed in memory (employing two memory buffers for image information).

Draw Program—Application that creates object-oriented graphics, usually in PICT files, rather than bitmapped graphics. See *Object, Bitmapped Graphics.*

Dropout—Loss of a recording's playback quality due to wear and tear on the tape.

Dub—To copy a tape; also called *dupe.*

DVE—Digital Video Effects, the use of computers to create unique video special effects.

Dynamic Range—The range between the softest and the loudest sound that can be recorded by an ATR or other recording device; measured in decibels (dB).

8mm—A diminutive consumer tape format invented by Sony; offers superior sound recording.

Editing—Arranging video or slideshow sequences to create a finished presentation.

Edit Controller—Device that controls two or more VCRs to accomplish smooth, accurate video editing.

Edit Decision List (EDL)—A list of edit points in a production; fed to a computerized edit controller, the EDL allows the system to auto-assemble the master tape from original raw footage.

EFP—Electronic Field Production; basic one-camera location shooting.

Encoder—Signal-processing hardware to convert analog to digital or digital to analog.
ENG—Electronic News Gathering; EFP with easily portable equipment.
Envelope—A shape that shows the perimeter of a waveform, corresponding to its amplitude at each cycle.
EPS—Encapsulated PostScript File, the standard PostScript file format created by PostScript drawing programs.
Exposure Sheet—a printed representation of the sequence of frames in an animation, arranged in storyboard form.
Extrusion—In computer graphics, the process of creating a three-dimensional shape by stretching a two-dimensional shape along a third axis; like squeezing clay through a shaped nozzle.
Fade—A dissolve from video to black or any color; also, decreasing audio from full volume to zero volume.
Feedback—Endless looping signal of audio or video; a standard method of creating infinite regress images in video.
Field—In video, half a video frame; 262.5 horizontal lines written in 1/60 of a second.
Field—In *HyperCard, SuperCard,* and most databases, an object for holding text.
Fill Light—Light positioned to illuminate the shadows cast by the key or main light in a scene.
Film Printer—Device for creating slides or film prints of video or computer graphics images. Also called *slidemaker* or *slide recorder.*
Finder—The Mac desktop, where you work with disks, files, and folders, and launch applications.
FKEY—A utility program that issues a command or series of commands when you press a designated key, usually a function key, on the Mac keyboard.
Flatbed—Type of scanner with a flat pane of glass on which the original is placed for scanning by a moving light source.
Flip Chart—Printed charts on cardboard that can be flipped over a easel to reveal the next chart in the series; used as a supplement to a computer presentation.
Flow Chart—Data graphic that delineates the stages and structure of a system, such as the flow of information through a computer.
Flying Erase Heads—Tape erasing heads in a VCR that erase tape with frame accuracy, making perfect insert editing possible.
Foil—Another term for an overhead transparency.
Font—Typeface for titles or computer graphics.
Footcandle—A measurement of light emission: lumens per square foot.
Fractals—In computer graphics, method for producing irregular, lifelike landscapes and branching forms with simple mathematical formulas. Often used to simulate landscapes.

Frame—A complete still video image containing two interlaced video fields; 525 horizontal lines written in 1/30 of a second.

Frame Buffer—Device for temporarily storing one video frame.

Frame Grabber—Device for capturing and storing a video frame from an external video source, such as a VCR, for display in a computer.

Frame Rate—The number of frames displayed by a video device or an animation over a measure of time, usually a second (frames per second, or FPS). The standard video frame rate is 30 fps.

Frequency—The number of cycles per second in a waveform; measured in Hertz.

Gain—Amplitude or strength of an analog signal.

Generation—Number of times a videotape or other analog material has been copied. The original tape is first generation, a copy of it is second generation, a copy of the copy is third generation, and so on. Information stored in analog form is degraded with each generation.

Genlock—Device that synchronizes one video source with another (for example, computer graphics with live video) for mixing and recording.

Graphic Equalizer—Audio device for adjusting sound quality within set frequency ranges.

Grayscale—Even range of gray tones between black and white; easily created with paint and draw programs.

Halftone—A method for printing continuous-tone images by printing a grid of different-sized black dots that resolve into gray tones.

Hertz (Hz)—Electronic measure of cycles per second; the number of times an electrical event is repeated in a second.

Hierarchical File System (HFS)—Mac file handling system that allows multiple levels of nested files and folders.

Hierarchical Objects—In 3-D imaging, objects with motion linked to the motion of other objects according to levels of influence; for example, an arm may be made up of a hand object, a forearm object, and an upper arm object, with the upper arm motions determining the forearm motions, and the forearm determining the hand motion, but not vice versa.

HDTV—High-Definition TeleVision, any of several proposed standards for higher-resolution color television approaching 35mm film image quality.

High-Low Chart—A variation of the bar chart that shows high and low values of a variable over time. High-low charts are most often used in stock market analysis to show the high and low selling prices of a single stock.

Hue—Color, such as red or blue.

HyperCard—Apple's extensible software toolbox application.

Hypermedia—A form of information organization in which all areas of an information base are cross-referenced to each other and are instantly accessible from any part of the base; applies to text, graphics, sound, video, and other media.

Hypertalk—*HyperCard*'s programming language.

Hypertext—Multidimensional text; text cross-referenced by links to other related text.

Icon—In the Mac OS, a pictograph that can represent a disk, folder, file, tool, or function. Clicking on an icon initiates some action.

Image Processing—Using software to manipulate a scanned computer graphics image; for example, to add false colors, increase the contrast of shape boundaries, eliminate moire patterns, and so on.

In-Betweening—Drawing intermediate positions of an animated object between the key frames. Also called *tweening;* the in-between frames are called *tweens.* See *Key Frame.*

INIT—A resident utility program that loads into the Mac's memory on startup.

Insert Edit—Video editing technique in which audio or video is slipped seamlessly into already recorded material. Requires a control track or time code on both source and master videotape.

Interactivity—The process of establishing a dialog between computer or presentation and the persons viewing the material; viewers can steer the presentation in the desired direction.

Interlace—The alternate writing of video lines for two intertwined fields of video.

Interface—The appearance, toolset, and working methods presented by an application to the user.

Iris—A spiral wipe that imitates the opening and closing action of a camera iris.

Jaggies—The ragged edges of shapes in computer graphics. See *Aliasing.*

Jiffy—One sixtieth of a second.

Jitter—Instability due to video sync or tracking problems.

Jump Cut—Jarring edit that creates a visual non sequitur.

Kern—Adjusting the spacing between letters in text.

Key—Method of replacing part of the image from one video source with the image from a second video source. Keying can be over a specified gray level in the video (luminance keying) or over a specified color (chromakeying). For example, keying video of a weather map over the blue screen behind a TV weatherperson.

Key Light—The main light source for a scene.

Key Frame—In cel or tweening animation, pictures defining the beginning and end of a motion or sequence.

Lavalier—A small microphone worn on the lapel; also called a *lapel mike.*

Leading—The spacing between lines of text, measured in points.

Leave-Behind—Print or other materials that accompany a desktop presentation and are left behind for the audience.

Legend—Notes explaining the symbols used in a chart or map.

Light-Source Shading—In computer graphics, simulating the effects of one or more lights shining on a 3-D object.

Line Chart—Chart that shows the progress of a dependent variable over an independent variable, usually time, with the data points connected by a line or lines.

Link—In hypermedia, a software connection between two pieces of related information that allows you to jump directly from one to the other.

Logo—Distinctive design for a corporate name and/or symbol.

Loopback—Playing a section of a digitized sound over and over again.

Lumen—A measurement of light emitted by a lightsource at the point of emission.

Luminance—Strength of the grayscale portion of the video signal.

Lux—A measurement of light reflection: .1076 footcandles.

Mac OS—The Macintosh's disk operating system, used for accessing and managing files and some other operations.

Macro—A magnifying camera lens that can focus down to a few inches.

Macro—A command or series of commands issued when you hit a designated key or keys; many programs allow you to create your own macros.

Matte—Method of creating composite pictures by placing a multicolored image from one video source over a background from a second source; a form of keying. Also, a dull surface texture on a shaded object.

Mike Mixer—Device for combining and manipulating input from several microphones or other audio sources for recording in mono or stereo.

MIDI—Musical Instrument Digital Interface, the standard method of controlling musical instruments by computers.

Moire—A vibrating pattern of intersecting lines; vibration caused by video signal distortion.

Monitor—In video, a television with composite video inputs. A computer monitor usually accepts RGB rather than composite input.

Mortice—Technique of squeezing a video picture and surrounding it with a black or other border.

MultiFinder—Apple's FInder variation that allows instant switching from one program to another without returning to the Finder in-between.

Multimedia—Programs that integrate text, graphics, sound, and video/film to create new ways to access and understand information. See also *hypermedia, hypertext.*

Multimedia Control Architecture (MCA)—Apple's specifications for device drivers and file formats to be used in Mac multimedia applications.

Multivariate Data—A data set defined by more than two variables, such as time, distance, and mass.

Neon—Popular font style that imitates the look of neon signs.

Note Editor—Software for writing, editing, and playing music notation.

NTSC—National Television Standards Committee, professional body of the Federal Communications Commission that sets standards for video hardware and broadcasting.

Nubus—The Mac II bus architecture; also, the Mac II standard plug-in card format.

Object—A two- or three-dimensional entity defined as a database of mathematical formulas, not as a bitmap.

Object—In *HyperCard* or *SuperCard*, one of the main elements of the program, such as fields, buttons, cards, and stacks.

Object Editor—Software for creating and editing two- or three-dimensional computer objects.

Offline Editing—First video editing stage, where tape is reviewed from workprints, rough edits prepared, and an edit decision list compiled.

Online Editing—Final video edit stage, where the master tape is assembled from the original production footage. The edit decision list also may be fed to a computer editing system that auto-assembles the master tape.

Outliner—Software for creating outlines of text documents.

Overhead Projector Adapter—LCD device that allows computer graphics to be projected by a standard overhead projector.

Overscan—Area of the video field that extends beyond the limits of the visible TV screen.

Page—The computer graphics workspace; may be bigger than the visible part of the screen.

Page Flipping—Holding two or more pages in buffers and showing them in a defined sequence; used for cel-type computer animation.

Paint File—A standard bitmapped graphics file format, originally developed for *MacPaint*. Can't handle color information or large screen sizes.

Paint Program—Software for creating bitmapped computer graphics.

PAL—Phase Alternating Line, a video standard used in Europe, Latin America, and elsewhere; not compatible with NTSC.

Palette—The selection of colors available in a computer graphics system.

Pan—Camera move swinging along the horizontal *(x-)* axis.

Patch—Connecting video and audio equipment with cables or through a central Patch Panel.

Path—The trail along which a computer-graphics object travels.
Period—Distance between two adjacent peaks in a waveform. See *Cycle*.
Phase—The timing of an electronic signal; two signals in which the peaks and valleys of the signal occur simultaneously are in phase; if they occur at different times, they are out of phase.
Pica—A linear measure used by typesetters. There are six picas per inch.
PICT—The standard Mac graphics file format; comes in bitmapped and object-oriented versions. Also called *PICT1*.
PICT2—Standard Mac color graphics file format; comes in bitmapped and object versions.
Pictograph—A data graphic that uses pictures to convey quantities or trends.
Pictogram—A visual symbol that identifies a theme or idea in a graphic—for example, a glowing lightbulb to represent a bright idea; used in pictographs.
Pics—An animation file format supported by Macromind and Silicon Beach products, among others.
Pie Chart—Chart showing sections of a whole as slices of a circle.
Pitch—The low to high frequency of a sound; the higher the frequency (as measured in cycles per second, or Hertz), the higher the pitch.
Pixel—The basic picture element of a computer screen or graphics sensing array, such as a CCD; the smallest dot that a computer can create.
Pixellization—Using image processing software to break up a continuous image into rectangular blocks to give it a "digitized" look.
Point—A measure of type size. There are 72 points per inch.
Polygon—A flat geometric shape; one of the components of the surfaces of objects in 3-D modeling programs.
Polyhedron—A many-faceted solid object.
Post—Short for post-production, all elements of TV or film production occurring after the original stock is shot. Most DTV work would be considered as post by TV and film professionals.
Posterization—Using image processing software to divide a continuous image into flat areas of heightened color.
Postscript—Standard page-description language supported by desktop publishing programs, laser printers, and some graphics programs.
POV—Point Of View; the viewing angle and apparent position of the camera.
Preroll—Rewinding tape in an editing VCR to a cue point; so the tape is up to speed when rolled forward to the editing point.
PROC Amp—Processing amplifier, electronic device that massages a video signal to produce stable sync and good-quality signal levels.
Processor Direct Slot—Plug-in card format for the Mac SE/30

Quantel—Broadcast digital video effects system manufactured by MCI/Quantel.

Quantization—Distortion of a digitized sound sample caused by rounding off the amplitude of the original sound to the nearest whole value. Yields background hiss in the sample.

QuickDraw—The Macintosh OS's built-in graphics toolset.

Raster—The scanned area of the video screen; where the video image is displayed.

Ray Tracing—Highly realistic method of 3-D computer graphics rendering that traces the path of a ray of light from the camera point of view to every element in the scene; can accurately render shadows, reflections, and translucent substances.

Real-Time—The actual time it takes events to occur; action on the computer screen that corresponds in a one-to-one ratio to real clock time.

Render—Creation of a realistic two-dimensional object or scene from three-dimensional object information.

Resolution—The clarity or graininess of a video or computer image as measured by lines or pixels; the smallest resolvable detail in the image.

Resource—Building blocks of a Mac program or document. Resources can include ICNs (icons), CURS (cursors), SNDs (sounds), CLUTs (color lookup tables), and many other types.

Resource Fork—Part of a Mac program or document in which resources are stored.

RF—Radio frequency; used for transimitting video signals.

RGB—Red, Green, Blue, the primary colors of computer graphics; the video display system used by most computers and some broadcast video equipment.

RGB ENCODER—Device for converting composite video to RGB video; also called *scan converter.*

RS-170A—Set of technical specifications for "legal" video as defined by the National Television Standards Committee.

Safe Title Area—Area of the video screen, about 80 percent as measured from the center, that is always visible and available for placing credits, even in a poorly adjusted monitor.

Sample—Digitized version of a sound as processed by a sampler.

Sampler—Audio device that converts sound into digital information that can be manipulated by a computer.

Sans-Serif Font—Typestyle without little tails and bars on the letters; cleaner but less easy to read.

Scalable Font—Object font that can be resized or rotated without distortion; also called *outline font.* See also *Screen Font.*

Scanner—Hardware device for converting flat art into computer graphics.

Scatter Graph—Data graphic showing the relationship of two or more dependent variables as measured by dots plotted on the *x*- and *y*-axes. Also called *scatter plot, dot chart,* and *x-y graph.*

Screen Font—Bitmapped font used for display on the Mac screen.

Screen Shot—A photograph of the screen of a computer or video monitor.

Script—Written story of a presentation or production.

Script—In *HyperCard* or *SuperCard,* a series of written instructions that defines the characteristics, purpose, and action of an object.

Scroll—Moving pages of video text up or down on the screen; see *Crawl.*

Scroll Bar—Gadgets on the bottom and right edges of a window that let you see different parts of the document.

SECAM—Sequential Colour a Memoire, a video standard developed and used mainly in France, also in the USSR and several African countries; not compatible with NTSC video.

SEG—Special Effects Generator, video device for creating and controlling transitions and other effects during video production and editing.

Selection—Part of the document that you plan to perform an operation on; the object you specify by dragging over it or clicking on it with the mouse.

Sequencer—Software for controlling other musical devices via MIDI.

Serif Font—Typestyle with little tails and caps; more readable, but less efficient than sans-serif.

Shape—Waveform characteristic that determines the tonal qualities of a sound—a rounded waveform sounds sweet, an angular wave sounds jagged, a complex wave sounds rich and lifelike.

Shotgun—A type of cardioid microphone that picks up sound only in a narrow cone in front of the mike; usually camera mounted, it is good for recording sounds only in the direction the camera is pointing

S1AN—Animation file type used by *Studio/1* and other Electronic Arts products.

Single-Frame Recorder—A VCR capable of recording a single video frame at a time; used for animation.

Slidemaker—Desktop camera-and-display-in-a-box for shooting slides of computer pictures. Also called *film printer* or *slide recorder.*

Small Multiple—A series of small, related data graphics that, taken together, describe a larger event or trend.

SMPTE—Society of Motion Picture and Television Engineers, a professional organization that sets technical standards for film and video.

Snd Resource—One type of Mac digital sound format; used by *HyperCard* and *SuperCard.*

Solid Model—A computer-generated 3-D object with volume, realistic shading, and hidden areas removed.

Speech Synthesis—Simulation of the human voice by computer; MacinTalk is an example of a voice synthesis program.

Spin—In three-dimensional computer graphics, rotating a two-dimensional outline around a central axis to create a three-dimensional surface or volume; see also *Surface of Revolution.*

Spline—A curve defined by a mathematical formula; used to specify smooth paths for two- or three-dimensional object motion.

Split Screen—Video effect that shows images from two different video sources, each on one half of the screen. Multiple split screens shows images from several sources or different actions taking place in several windows in the screen area.

Stack—In *HyperCard,* a group of related cards that make up a unified *HyperCard* document.

Stencil—Paint program feature that allows the artist to create a mask that prevents painting over selected areas or colors.

Still-Store—See *frame grabber.*

Storyboard—A visual outline of the narrative of a film or video production.

Subcarrier—Frequency carrying NTSC video color information.

Super—Superimposition, laying titles or graphics over a background image.

Surface Graph—Data graphic type that presents multivariate data in a topographical, 3-D format.

Surface Model—A 3-D computer graphics object composed of surface polygons only, with no dimension of volume.

Surface of Revolution—A three-dimensional computer graphics object created by revolving a two-dimensional object around a central axis; for example, a sphere can be created by revolving a circle around its diameter.

Sweetening—Audio post production, with an emphasis on adjusting audio for the best quality.

Switcher—Electronic device for instantly cutting between several live or taped video sources.

Sync—Short for *synchronization;* the horizontal and vertical timing pulses that control the operation of video equipment.

Sync Generator—Device that generates stable sync pulses for use by all the video components in a video system.

Synthesizer, Synth—An electronic device for creating artificial sounds and sound effects. Also, software for creating similar effects through a computer.

System—The Mac's collection of operating system programs.

Talking Head—Video slang for the typical head and shoulders shot of guests seen on talk shows and newscasts.

Tape Format—Any of several videotape widths and recording methods, such as ½-inch VHS and ¾-inch U-Matic, used in video recording systems.

Texture or Surface Mapping—In computer graphics, wrapping a two-dimensional picture around a three-dimesional object to give that object a simulated surface texture or pattern.

Tick Mark—Small mark on a graph that indicates the division of a grid or the position of a data point or value

TIFF—A graphics file format often used for scanned images.

Tile—A rectangular computer image that is repeated in a pattern all over the screen, like tiles on a floor.

Tilt—A camera move swinging up and down along the vertical *(y)* axis.

Time Base—The timing of a portion of the video signal, particularly the horizontal and vertical sync pulses.

Time Base Corrector (TBC)—Device that corrects time-base signal instabilities caused by VCRs during videotape playback; makes it possible for two or more VCRs can be in sync.

Time Code—An electronic counter or index of videotape duration (the hours, minutes, seconds, and frames that a tape lasts) that is usually visible only with a special time code reader. Usually "burned-in" on the tape as the tape is logged during offline editing.

Time Series—A data graphic showing the change in a data set over time.

Tool—Software gadget for performing work; a brush in a paint program is a tool, for example.

Transition—The type of visual effect used to get from one image to another in a presentation; can include wipes, dissolves, fades, and so on.

Transparency—Graphic printed on transparent plastic (acetate or Mylar) for display with an overhead projector.

Transport Controller—A computer device that controls the operations of a VCR with single-frame accuracy.

Tree Chart—Data graphic that diagrams a branching hierarchy, such as the power structure of an organization. Also called *organization chart.*

Trend Line—The extension of a line in a graph beyond the known data to indicate a trend or anticipated performance.

U-MATIC—Trade name for the ¾-inch tape format invented by Sony.

Variable—An item of data with a value that can change.

VCR—Video cassette recorder. A video recorder using open reels (such as a 1-inch machine) is referred to as a VTR, or video tape recorder.
Vector Graphics—Another name for object graphics; draw and CAD programs create and manipulate vectors.
Vectorization—Converting line art or paint images to vector graphics.
Vectorscope—Video test equipment that displays information about the color part of the video signal.
VHS—Video Home System, most popular ½-inch consumer tape format, invented by JVC. An enhanced version is Super-VHS.
Video Signal—An analog waveform carrying video information.
Visual Effect—In *HyperCard* or *SuperCard,* the type of visual transition from card to card, including wipes, dissolves, and so on.
VTR—Video Tape Recorder, including reel-to-reel types.
Waveform—The shape of an analog signal.
Waveform Monitor—Video test equipment that measures and displays the parameters of an analog signal.
Window—A Macintosh screen object that defines an area of activity; it can contain pictures, documents, and other objects and be opened, moved, resized, stacked, and closed.
Wipe—Slideshow or video transition in which one image replaces another along a border that moves across the screen.
Wire-Frame—Representation of a computer-generated 3-D object as a hollow structure of wires with the shape of the object but no interior or shading; provides a sense of the object while cutting down on the computation needed to represent it.
Workprint—A copy of the raw footage of a video production; used in offline editing.
Zoom—Using a camera's zoom lens to get closer to or farther away from the subject without moving the camera; in computer animation, changing the focal length of the "camera lens" or "observer viewpoint" along the screen's *z*-axis.

Index